Does Higher Education Teach Students to Think Critically?

Edited by
Dirk Van Damme and Doris Zahner

This work is published under the responsibility of the Secretary-General of the OECD. The opinions expressed and arguments employed herein do not necessarily reflect the official views of the Member countries of the OECD.

This document, as well as any data and map included herein, are without prejudice to the status of or sovereignty over any territory, to the delimitation of international frontiers and boundaries and to the name of any territory, city or area.

The statistical data for Israel are supplied by and under the responsibility of the relevant Israeli authorities. The use of such data by the OECD is without prejudice to the status of the Golan Heights, East Jerusalem and Israeli settlements in the West Bank under the terms of international law.

Please cite this publication as:
Van Damme, D. and D. Zahner (eds.) (2022), *Does Higher Education Teach Students to Think Critically?*, OECD Publishing, Paris, https://doi.org/10.1787/cc9fa6aa-en.

ISBN 978-92-64-86297-5 (print)
ISBN 978-92-64-95496-0 (pdf)
ISBN 978-92-64-82985-5 (HTML)
ISBN 978-92-64-84829-0 (epub)

Foreword

In 2006, higher education ministers gathered in Athens for a ministerial conference organised by the OECD. I has just been appointed as the new Director for Education of the OECD. Angel Gurría, who had assumed his mandate as Secretary-General of the Organisation, chaired the meeting and succeeded in convincing the excellencies to embark on an ambitious new project of assessing higher education's learning outcomes. With the success of the OECD's Programme for International Student Assessment (PISA), the time seemed ripe to initiate a comparable initiative in higher education. After two years of preparatory work, the Assessment of Higher Education Learning Outcomes (AHELO) Feasibility Study started in 2008. It was one of the OECD Education Directorate's projects I was most personally committed to.

In those early years, the political support for AHELO was impressive. Despite 20 years of developing quality assurance in higher education, very little was actually known about its "quality". Global rankings of universities relied on bibliometric data and research indicators but could not provide any transparency on the quality of educational output. In turn, this led to a hugely distorted picture of the global distribution of academic excellence. Governments were unable to demonstrate how rapidly increasing funding for higher education institutions resulted in human capital growth. Qualifications, diplomas, and degrees matter, but the actual skills that graduates bring to labour markets and societies matter more. Qualifications are meaningless if they are not trustworthy guarantees of relevant learning outcomes. Early believers in the AHELO project felt that more transparency about graduates' learning outcomes would strengthen the hand of universities in any political debate.

The AHELO Feasibility Study was successfully concluded in 2013. After having demonstrated the proof of concept, we believed that countries would be willing to embark on the Main Study. Yet the project became quite controversial in some university associations. Capital cities were hesitant to push forward a project on universities against their support. After discussing a couple of proposals, the OECD's Education Policy Committee found itself hugely divided on the topic. It finally decided not to pursue the Main Study.

Nonetheless, a group of countries still supported the idea and decided to continue the work. They gathered informally and with the support of the Council for Aid to Education, which had developed the Collegiate Learning Assessment (CLA) instrument, they launched the CLA+ International Project in 2016. The group considered the CLA+ International assessment to be an excellent tool for measuring the critical-thinking skills of university students. Assessments would be a response to employers and others who criticised higher education institutions for failing to deliver skills that matter for the 21st-century economy and society.

As a result of past years' work in this informal group, this report brings together the assessment results in six countries. Some assessments were small-scale, covering only a few institutions; others were implemented nationwide. The data analysed and discussed in this report lead to important insights. Hopefully, they will lead to even more.

I am personally thrilled to see this work finally leading to relevant data and analyses, and am very grateful that the AHELO project was pursued under the professional leadership of Dirk Van Damme (OECD) and

Doris Zahner (CAE). I sincerely hope that higher education institutions and governments will see the value of these instruments in helping students develop the appropriate skills for their future life.

Barbara Ischinger

Former Director for Education and Skills, OECD (2006-2014)

Acknowledgements

This report was edited by Dirk Van Damme, former Senior Counsellor and Head of the Innovation and Measuring Progress division at the Directorate for Education and Skills at the OECD (Paris, France), and Doris Zahner, Chief Academic Officer at the Council for Aid to Education (CAE) (New York, U.S.).

Chapter authors include, besides the editors, Tess Dawber, Kelly Rotholz, Katri Kleemola, Heidi Hyytinen, Jani Ursin, Olivia Cortellini, Jessalynn James, Jonathan Lehrfeld, Alberto Ciolfi, Morena Sabella, J.G. Morris, Stuart C. Brand, Patricia Rosas, Carlos I. Moreno, Rubén Sánchez, J. Enrique Froemel, and Mark Keough.

The report benefitted from the guidance and support of Roger Benjamin, former President of CAE, who co-supervised the project with Dirk Van Damme between 2015 and 2019; Bob Yayac, President of CAE; Stephan Vincent-Lancrin, Senior Analyst at the OECD; and Andreas Schleicher, Director for Education and Skills at the OECD.

Clara Young, Alison Burke, Stephen Flynn, Della Shin and Cassandra Davis provided editorial and production assistance during the preparation and publication of the report.

Table of contents

3 CLA+ International 61

4 Ensuring cross-cultural reliability and validity 71

Part II CLA+ International Database 87

5 General CLA+ International results 88

17 Conclusions and prospects 257

FIGURES

TABLES

Follow OECD Publications on:

https://twitter.com/OECD

https://www.facebook.com/theOECD

https://www.linkedin.com/company/organisation-eco-cooperation-development-organisation-cooperation-developpement-eco/

https://www.youtube.com/user/OECDiLibrary

https://www.oecd.org/newsletters/

Executive summary

Higher education contributes immensely to economic growth, social progress, and overall quality of life through the skills students and graduates acquire. Qualifications awarded by higher education institutions are valued because they are perceived to signal the skills required by labour markets and broader society. Employers use these qualifications as ways to identify and select job candidates who master essential and requisite skills. Higher education is trusted by employers and society to the extent that there is an equilibrium between skills supply and demand.

However, there are signs that the skills supply of graduates no longer matches skills demand in the labour market. Quantitative qualifications mismatch is turning into a severe issue in many countries, compromising productivity, growth and the continued increase in prosperity. Even more significant is the qualitative mismatch between the skills demand generated by the economic and social reality in labour markets and societies, and the supply of skills by higher education institutions. Employers and economic organisations express with increasingly louder voices that they are no longer confident that graduates have acquired the skills needed for the 21st-century workplace, in particular, generic skills such as problem solving, communication, creativity, and critical thinking.

Whether perceived or real, skills mismatch poses a serious risk to the trustworthiness of higher education. What is needed is more transparency about the skills students acquire. Unfortunately, this has not been a strength of most higher education systems. Transparency tools such as international rankings are quite good at capturing research-related measures or input measures in education quality but do not provide any insights into students' actual learning outcomes. The few available measures, for example, provided by the OECD Survey of Adult Skills (PIAAC), are far from sufficient and invigorate the demand for more and better metrics.

Between 2008 and 2013, the OECD led the Assessing Higher Education Learning Outcomes (AHELO) feasibility study. Despite a positive conclusion on the feasibility of the initiative, the proposal tabled by the OECD in 2015 to start the main study did not attract sufficient support and the project was abandoned. However, a small number of countries that supported the project decided to continue the endeavour at a smaller scale. The collaborative work concentrated on what was perceived to be the most interesting and urgent issue, i.e. the assessment of the generic skills of higher education students and graduates. The initiative found a partner in the Council for Aid to Education, Inc., a non-profit organisation in the United States with a long history of assessing generic skills in post-secondary education with its proprietary Collegiate Learning Assessment (CLA+) instrument. This volume reports on the work pursued between 2016 and 2021 to assess critical thinking and written communication, and associated skills in higher education institutions in six countries (the United States, the United Kingdom, Italy, Mexico, Finland, and Chile).

Part I explores the conceptual and methodological dimensions of assessing students' generic learning outcomes. Chapter 1 outlines the issues regarding changing skills demand, skills mismatch, transparency, and trust in higher education.

Chapter 2 provides an extensive discussion of the methodological qualities of the CLA+ international instrument, which was used in the participating institutions and countries.

Chapter 3 provides a detailed insight into the development of the CLA+ International project, including the practicalities of translation and adaptation, test administration, scoring and reporting.

Part II of this report includes a statistical analysis of the integrated international database. The database has been constructed by aggregating the datasets from the assessments implemented between 2015 and 2021 in the six countries.

Chapter 5 includes the descriptive statistics of the database and the general distribution of mastery levels of scores and subscores.

Chapter 6 explores the relationships between demographic background variables and performance on the assessment, focusing on students' primary language, gender and parental educational attainment.

Chapter 7 discusses the relationship between test scores and post-higher education career outcomes.

Chapter 8 examines differences in performance by instructional format and field of study.

Chapter 9 addresses performance differences between countries for entering and exiting students (excluding Italy).

Part III of this report discusses the assessment in each of the six participating countries. Each chapter reviews policy context, test administration, mastery levels, score distribution and data regarding effort and engagement.

Chapter 10 discusses the assessment in the United States. The CLA+ assessment has a long history in the United States and the test has acquired strong status and recognition. As discussed in Chapter 11, Italy was the first country outside the United States to implement the CLA+ assessment as part of its nation-wide TECO project and its decision to move towards a different assessment approach.

Chapter 12 offers insight into the assessment in Finland, which implemented a system-wide administration in 2019-20.

Chapter 13 discusses the implementation of the CLA+ in a small set of institutions as part of a pilot study to assess learning gain in the United Kingdom. This case study shows the capacity of the assessment to serve as a diagnostic tool. The chapter also discusses the challenges associated with student recruitment and motivation.

Chapter 14 discusses the assessment in Mexico, more specifically the University of Guadalajara system, which has been one of the more enthusiastic early adopters of the CLA+ assessment outside the United States.

Chapter 15 deals with the test implementation and results in four private universities in Chile as part of an outreach attempt into Latin America. A similar situation is discussed in Chapter 16, which deals with the outlooks for implementing the assessment in professional and vocational colleges across Australia and New Zealand.

Finally, Chapter 17 summarises the main conclusions of the report and lessons learnt from the country experiences presented in the individual country chapters.

This report is a follow-up to the AHELO feasibility study and is one of the first international studies of generic skills proficiency in higher education institutions. It does not provide definitive answers but shows the power of assessing critical-thinking skills and how such assessments can feed into the policy agenda in higher education at national and international levels.

Part I Assessing students' generic learning outcomes

1 Do higher education students acquire the skills that matter?

Dirk Van Damme, OECD (France)

In today's world, higher education has acquired an economic and social status that is unprecedented in modern history. Technological changes and associated developments in the economy and labour markets have pushed the demand for high-skilled workers and professionals to ever-higher levels. Higher education has become the most important route for a country's human capital development and an individual's upward social mobility. It is where young people acquire advanced generic and specific skills to prosper in the knowledge economy and flourish in society. Though enrolment and graduation rates have increased massively in most countries, a higher education qualification still offers young people the prospect of significant benefits in employability and earnings. The higher education system also helps them develop the social and emotional skills to become effective citizens. Higher education attainment rates thus correlate strongly with indicators of social capital and social cohesion such as interpersonal trust, political participation and volunteering.

Introduction

On average across the OECD's 38 member countries, 45% of the 25-34 year-old age cohort obtained a tertiary education qualification in 2020 compared with 37% in 2010 (OECD, 2021[1]). By 2030, there will be over 300 million 25-34 year-olds with a tertiary qualification in OECD and G20 countries compared to 137 million in 2013 (OECD, 2015[2]). Many OECD countries have seen steep increases in their tertiary education enrolment and graduation figures. And emerging economies such as China, India and Brazil see investments in the expansion of higher education as an important route towards economic growth and social progress.

However, in several countries questions are being raised by policy makers about the sustainability of continued growth rates. Should knowledge-intensive economies aim for 60, 70, 80% of tertiary-qualified workers in 25-34 year-old cohorts? Or does continued growth of higher education lead to over-qualification, polarisation of labour markets and substitution of jobs previously held by mid-educated workers? What are the risks associated with over-education (Barone and Ortiz, 2011[3])? Added to such questions are concerns about higher education attainment exacerbating social inequality and the marginalisation of low- and mid-educated populations.

Central to these concerns is the question about the value of higher education qualifications. Does a university degree still signal a high level of advanced cognitive skills? Or did the massification of higher education cause erosion of the skills equivalent of a tertiary degree? Is massification leading to degree inflation and, hence, the decreasing intrinsic value of qualifications? The difficult answer to these questions is: We don't know. While the OECD's Programme for International Student Assessment (PISA) has become the global benchmark of the learning outcomes of 15-year-old students and hence of the quality of school systems, there is no valid and reliable measure of the learning outcomes of higher education students and graduates. Indirect measures of the value of a higher education qualification such as the employment rates or earnings of graduates are distorted by labour market polarisation and substitution effects. They are increasingly seen as unsatisfactory.

According to some economists, the increase in highly qualified influx into the labour market necessarily leads to over-education and an erosion of the higher education wage premium. In 2016 *The Economist* argued that the relative wage advantage for the highly qualified is severely over-rated and that there are massive displacement and substitution effects (The Economist, 2016[4]). In 1970 about 51% of the highly skilled in the United States worked in jobs classified as highly skilled; in 2015 this dropped to 35%. Many highly qualified workers now work in jobs for which, strictly speaking, no higher education qualification is required. Also, according to *The Economist*, real wages for highly skilled workers have fallen.

There are signs that global employers have started to distrust university qualifications and are developing their own assessment tools and procedures to test students for the skills they think are important. Governments are also concerned not just about overall cost but rising per-student cost. They are confronting universities with concerns about efficiency and "value-for-money". And, they are shifting the balance in the funding mix of higher education from public to private sources, thereby increasing the cost for students and families. When students are asked to pay more for the degree they hope to earn, they also become powerful stakeholders in the value-for-money debate. The impact of COVID-19 has accelerated the value-for-money debate: closures, poor teaching and learning experiences and disruptions in the examination and graduation procedures while maintaining high tuition fees have caused dissatisfaction among students, some of whom are reclaiming financial compensation from universities.

The traditional mechanisms of trust in higher education qualifications are under severe stress. This chapter explores these issues in more detail. In doing so, it builds a case for an assessment of the learning outcomes of higher education students and graduates. In the world of tomorrow in which skills are the new currency, qualifications – the sole monopoly of higher education systems – may lose their value if doubts about learning outcomes remain unanswered. These doubts can only be addressed by better empirical metrics of what students learn in higher education and the skills with which graduates enter the labour market. This chapter will discuss the signalling role of qualifications; transparency and trust in higher education qualifications; changing skill demand; and initiatives taken toward the assessment of students' and graduates' learning outcomes to rebalance information asymmetry and restore trust.

Qualifications versus skills

The value of higher education for the economy and society is mediated through the qualifications that students earn and build on in the labour market. As the sole remaining monopoly of higher education, qualifications are of critical importance to the existence of the sector. Globalisation and internationalisation have given almost universal validity to a shared qualification system based on the bachelor's/master's/PhD ladder. In turn, qualification frameworks are one of the most powerful drivers of skills convergence in global higher education (Van Damme, 2019[5]).

Traditional human capital theory centres on the substantive contribution the teaching and learning process makes to knowledge, skills and other attributes of students. But this traditional view is increasingly challenged by the 'signalling' or 'screening' hypothesis, which emphasises the selective functions of university programmes in providing employers with workers fit for jobs. This mechanism saves employers from expensive recruitment, selection and testing to identify the workers they need. In this approach, what students actually learn at university plays a less important role in the attribution of graduates to jobs, earnings and other status goods than selection itself.

Analysis of the OECD Survey of Adult Skills (PIAAC) has shown that across participating countries, earnings are more driven by formal education than actual skill levels (Paccagnella, 2015[6]). The institutional regulation of labour markets and professions, and symbolic power of university degrees ensure that degrees, not skills, determine access to high-level jobs and earnings. However, the meaning and value of tertiary qualifications levels is not purely symbolic. Employers value qualifications because they signal qualities the individual is perceived to possess.

For signalling to function well, there needs to be some convergence of skills around a tertiary qualification level. However, the evidence is almost completely missing on whether the learning outcomes and skills of graduates actually warrant the view that higher education qualifications represent converging levels of equivalence. In terms of learning outcomes and skills development, differentiation seems to be more important than convergence. Data from the OECD's Adult Skills Survey (PIAAC) of the skill levels of tertiary-educated adults point to between-country differences that remain pronounced even in areas with proclaimed convergence policies such as the European Higher Education Area. Figure 1.1 shows the percentage of higher education graduates younger than 35 who, in the Survey of Adult Skills, scored at each of five levels of proficiency on the literacy scale for each country.

Figure 1.1. Percentage of 16-34 year-old tertiary graduates at the different levels of proficiency in literacy

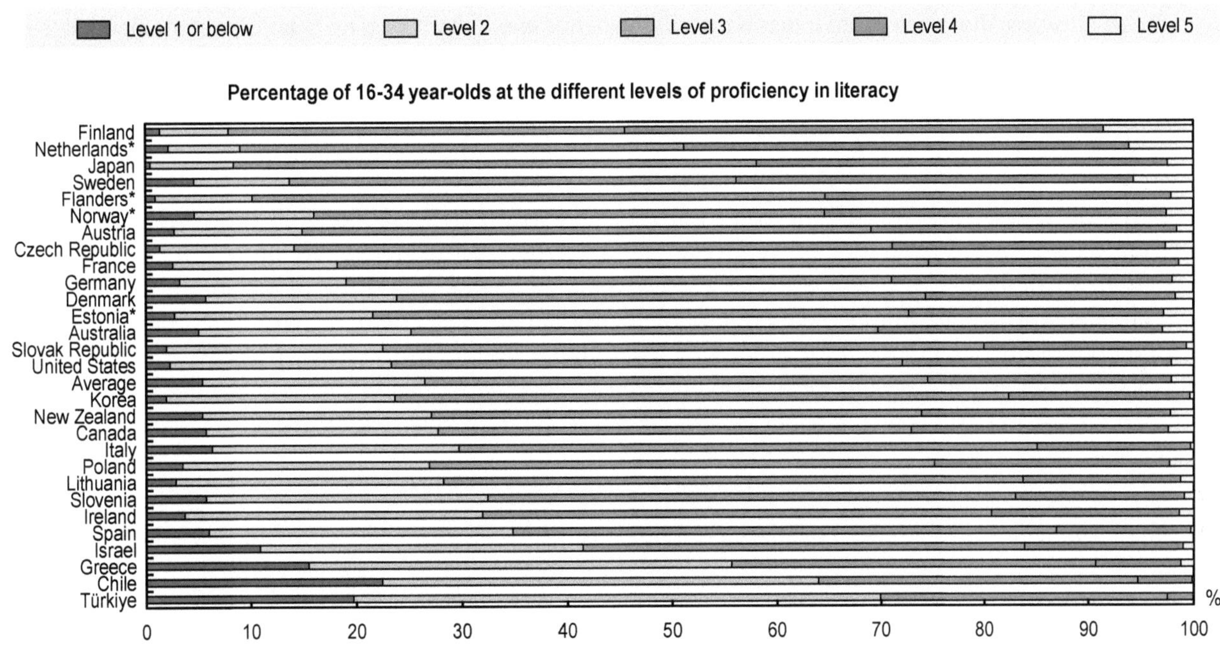

Note: *Participating in the Benchmarking Higher Education System Performance exercise 2017/2018. Countries are ranked in ascending order of the proportion of 16-34 year-olds with higher education who perform below level 2 in literacy proficiency.
Source: OECD (2019b), *Benchmarking Higher Education System Performance*, Higher Education, OECD Publishing, Paris, https://doi.org/10.1787/be5514d7-en (accessed on 1 August 2022) adapted from OECD Survey of Adult Skills, www.oecd.org/skills/piaac/data/.

Two observations can be drawn from these data. First, there is enormous variation in the literacy skills of tertiary education graduates. More than half (54.4%) of Finnish graduates scored at levels 4 or 5 compared with only 2.5% in the Republic of Türkiye. The differences between countries in the distribution of literacy skills does not seem to correlate with the share of the age cohort with a tertiary qualification. Neither massification nor globalisation seem to have had a huge impact on the skills levels of graduates. Evidence of wide differences in skills among tertiary education graduates with a similar level of qualifications contradicts a global convergence of skills equivalent to qualifications.

A second conclusion that can be drawn from these data is that a tertiary qualification does not fully protect against low skills. In many countries, even those with well-developed higher education systems, over 5% of the tertiary-educated 16-34 year-olds only perform at the lowest level of literacy proficiency, with figures higher than 15% in Greece, Chile and Türkiye. On average across OECD countries participating in the Survey of Adult Skills, over 25% of adults with a higher education degree who are younger than 35 do not reach level 3 in literacy, which can be considered as the baseline level for functioning well in the economy and society. A high share of graduates scoring at low levels of proficiency indicates that a higher education degree is not a good signal of the foundational literacy proficiency of graduates.

It is true that literacy skills are foundation skills that are not primarily supposed to be acquired in higher education. Teaching and learning in universities likely have higher added-value in more specialised skills sets. Still, these data are worrisome in that that higher education qualifications do not reliably signal a certain threshold skills level. Neither do they guarantee employers a minimum skills set.

How has the skills level of the tertiary-educated population evolved over time? One would assume that the massive introduction of tertiary qualifications would have increased the general skills level in the population. The OECD Adult Skills Survey, administered in the years 2012-15, and its predecessors, the International Adult Literacy Survey (IALS), administered in the 1990s, and the Adult Literacy and Life Skills Survey (ALL), administered in the 2000s, are the sole data sources that allow empirical testing of that hypothesis. When comparing the literacy performance of the adult population in countries that participated in these surveys, there are more indications of stability or even slight decline than of increasing skill levels (Paccagnella, 2016[7]). Changes in the composition of the populations due to ageing and migration might partly be responsible but one would expect the massive increase in tertiary qualifications to offset these changes and to result in higher skill levels.

Figure 1.2 compares the literacy proficiency change in the adult population between the IALS and PIAAC surveys by educational attainment level. Individuals with an upper secondary or tertiary qualification performed worse in PIAAC than in IALS (with the exception of Australia). The proficiency of adults with less than secondary level attainment increased or remained stable in 5 out of 10 countries. But, strikingly, the proficiency of adults with a tertiary qualification dropped in most countries, with a decline of more than 20 percentage points in Denmark, Ireland, Norway and Sweden. In the United States, Finland and the Flemish Community of Belgium, countries with excellent higher education systems, the decrease exceeds 10 percentage points. Clearly, the increase in tertiary attainment levels did not result in an increase of the skills level in the adult population – on the contrary.

Figure 1.2. Comparing literacy proficiency between IALS and PIAAC by educational attainment

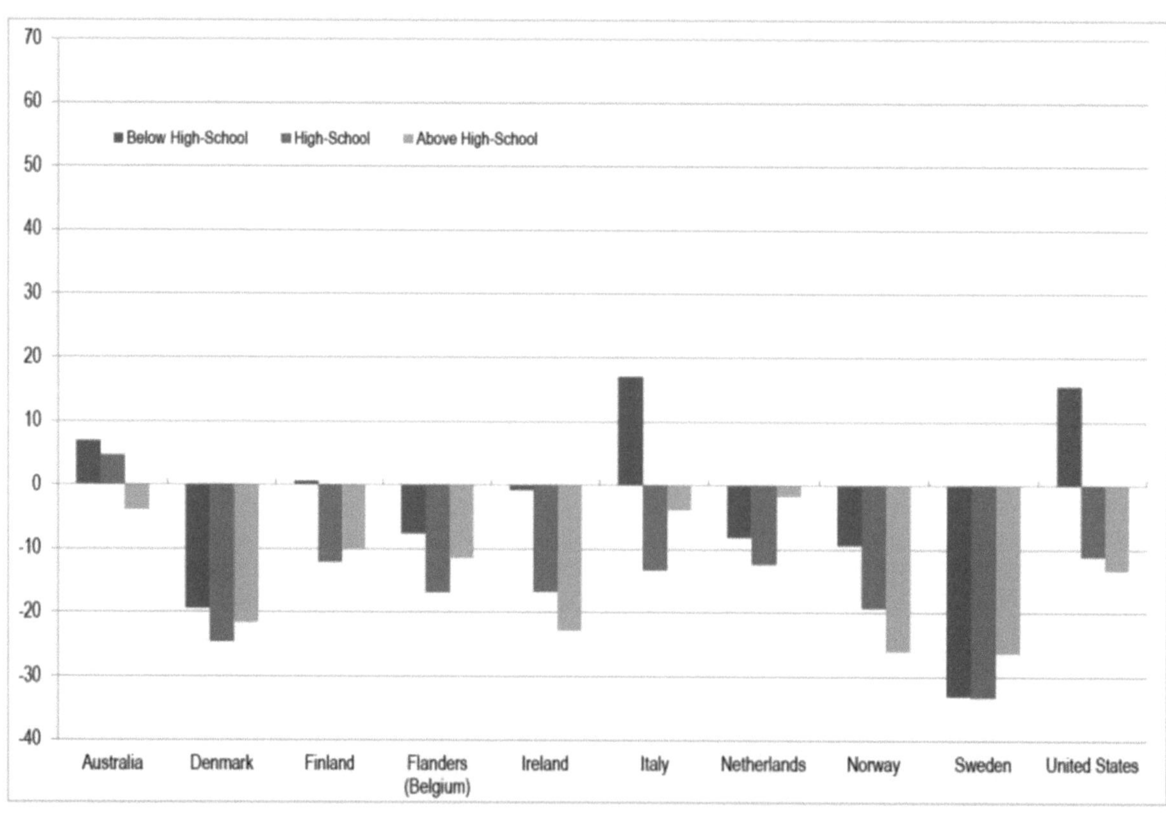

Source: Paccagnella, M. (2016), "Literacy and Numeracy Proficiency in IALS, ALL and PIAAC", *OECD Education Working Papers*, No. 142, OECD Publishing, Paris, https://doi.org/10.1787/5jlpq7qglx5g-en (accessed on 1 August 2022) adapted from International Adult Literacy Survey (IALS) (1994-1998), and Survey of Adult Skills (PIAAC) (2012), www.oecd.org/site/piaac/publicdataandanalysis.htm.

A possible explanation linking the growth of tertiary attainment and the decline of skills in the population can be obtained by looking at the impact of over-qualification on skills. Figure 1.3 shows that tertiary-educated workers in a job for which they have a well-matched qualification have on average higher numeracy skills than workers who work in a job not requiring a tertiary qualification. This could happen either through the recruitment process, which discriminates for skills, or through a process of skill decline or obsolescence when skills are not fully used. High levels of qualification mismatch thus further depreciate the value of tertiary qualifications.

Figure 1.3. Mean numeracy score among adults with ISCED 5A or 6, by selected qualification match or mismatch among workers (2012 or 2015) - Survey of Adult Skills (PIAAC), employed 25-64 year-olds

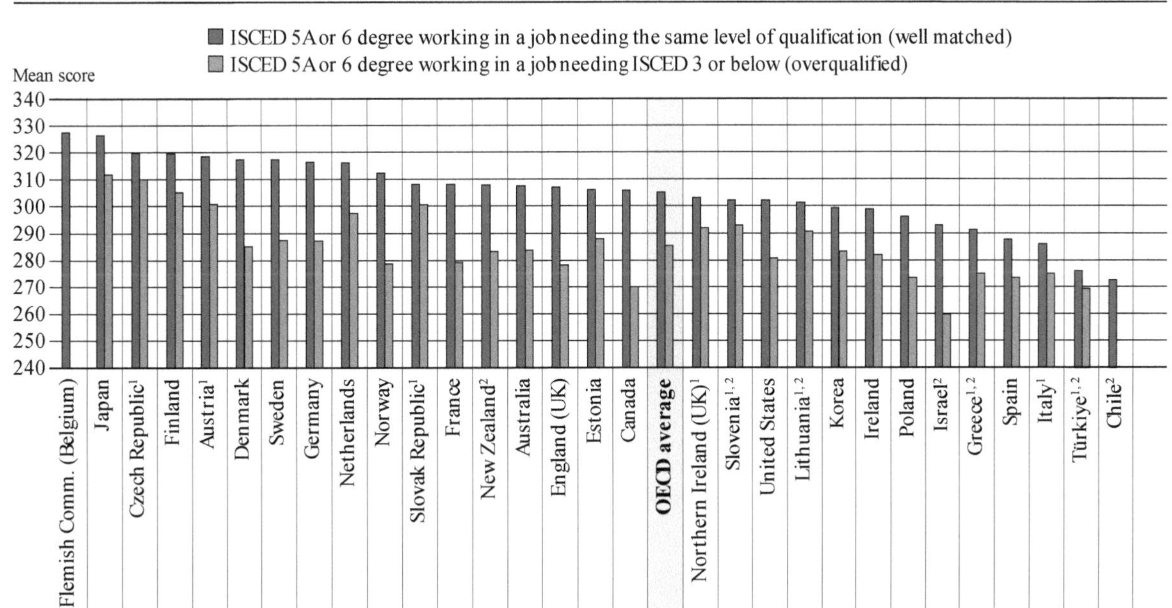

Note: 1. The difference between well-matched and overqualified workers is not statistically significant at 5%. 2. Reference year is 2015; for all other countries and economies the reference year is 2012.
Source: OECD (2018), "Graph A3.b - Mean numeracy score among adults with ISCED 5A or 6, by selected qualification match or mismatch among workers (2012 or 2015): Survey of Adult Skills (PIAAC), employed 25-64 year-olds", in Education at a Glance 2018: OECD Indicators, OECD Publishing, Paris, https://doi.org/10.1787/eag-2018-graph31-en (accessed 1 August 2022).

In conclusion, when comparing human capital growth as measured by two different metrics, educational attainment rates and foundation skill levels, the observations point in opposite directions: growth of qualifications versus decrease in skills. This conclusion further strengthens doubts about the skills equivalent of tertiary qualifications and their ability to provide reliable measures of skills.

Transparency and information asymmetry

To better understand what's at stake here, we need to take a closer look at the nature of higher education. In most countries, higher education systems take a hybrid form, combining elements of 'public good' and markets in a 'quasi-market' arrangement. In recent years, market-oriented elements have become much more important. From essentially nationally steered and 'public good'-oriented structures, higher education systems are increasingly moving towards a 'private consumption'-oriented model. Influenced by economic insights on the private benefits of higher education and the 'new public management' doctrine, policies have strongly supported this transformation by increasing private investment in higher education, encouraging competition for status and resources, supporting internationalisation policies and turning to stronger accountability frameworks. Higher education systems have integrated market elements in their steering but have never completely transformed into real 'capitalist markets' (Marginson, 2013[8]).

Of course, there are still many elements and dimensions of higher education systems that can be characterised as 'public goods', which are critically important to governments. Policy makers still highly value the role of higher education in preserving language and culture; providing equality of opportunity for all students to access higher education; and serving as a vehicle of social mobility. And there are many other considerations that legitimise public policies in higher education.

At the same time, higher education systems also have many 'market failures', the most important one being the well-known problem of 'information asymmetries' (Dill and Soo, 2004[9]; Blackmur, 2007[10]; van Vught and Westerheijden, 2012[11]). From the perspective of students, higher education is an experience good, which will be consumed only vary rarely but which has a huge impact on one's life chances. Information asymmetry seduces providers into maximising their power on the supply side and minimising the role on the demand side. Making the wrong choices can have huge consequences for individuals' lives but also for the economic and social fate of nations. While privatisation of the cost of higher education has increased enormously, the student/consumer has not been empowered to make smarter choices to a similar extent. The availability and quality of information have simply not improved sufficiently to allow students to make smart choices. Instead, and rather cynically, many policy makers reproach students for making too many wrong choices.

Higher education systems and governments have reacted in two opposite ways to this problem. First, they have developed various kinds of paternalistic instruments to protect the consumer interests of students. By acting on behalf of students in making the right decisions for them, they take a 'principal agent' role. Students and their families – and the same mechanism applies to employers – are requested to 'trust' the system's capacity to guarantee basic quality and reliably produce the desired quality and outcomes. In heavily state-driven systems in Europe, this may even take the form of an implicit public denial that there are quality differences among publicly recognised institutions and that a publicly recognised qualification will produce the same outcomes and benefits whatever the institution it comes from.

The second and far more effective way to tackle possible market failure caused by information asymmetry is by producing various instruments that are supposed to improve transparency in the system. In exchange for more institutional autonomy, institutions have been asked to provide more and better data on their performance. Some countries have developed systems of performance management, sometimes linked to funding arrangements. As well, quality assurance arrangements, often based on the trusted academic mechanism of peer review, are supposed to improve the quantity and quality of information available to the general public.

Neither quality assurance systems nor performance management systems have solved the problem of information asymmetry. Performance management systems are essentially bureaucratic tools, meant to inform public policies and steering mechanisms. Their data are often hidden or not understandable by students and the general public. The most commonly used performance indicators have a very poor relationship to the academic quality of students' teaching and learning environments (Dill and Soo, 2004[9]). Surveys of student satisfaction and student evaluation surveys, popular tools for assessing the perceived quality of the teaching and learning experience, bear no relationship to actual student learning (Uttl, White and Gonzalez, 2017[12]).

And quality assurance arrangements, though often conceived as instruments of public accountability, rarely function as information and transparency systems. In many countries, they have moved from a focus on programmes to a focus on the institution's internal management capacity to guarantee quality. Only in the field of research have effective measurement and transparency tools been developed. This is largely due to the fact that in the field of research, sufficient expertise and capacity have been developed to tackle measurement challenges.

In turn, the quality and availability of data on research output have stimulated the emergence of global rankings of higher education institutions. Rankings existed before high-quality research metrics but research bibliometrics have enormously contributed to the development and credibility of rankings. The phenomenon of global rankings and their – sometimes perverse – impact on higher education institutions and systems have been widely analysed and discussed, most notably in the work of Hazelkorn (2011[13]; 2014[14]), or Kehm and Stensaker (2009[15]). Despite resistance and criticism among academics and institutions, rankings have become very powerful and serve as a partial answer to the information needs of students, notably international students. Essentially, it is the lack of alternative, better transparency tools available to students, families, employers and the general public that is responsible for the rise and popularity of university rankings.

The main problem with rankings is their over-reliance on research output data. Information on the actual quality of teaching and learning, however, rely on indirect measures or indicators based on various input factors such as student/staff ratios or per student funding, which often have no evidenced relationship to quality. This has provoked a 'mission drift' towards research as the easiest way for institutions to improve their ranking. Rankings and the research metrics on which they are based have given way to a 'reputation race' among institutions (van Vught, 2008[16]). Rankings have also encouraged the reputation race by relying on reputation surveys to compensate for the lack of reliable teaching and learning metrics. Instead of tackling the information asymmetry problem upfront by opening up the 'black box' of teaching and learning and supporting the development of scientifically sound learning outcomes metrics, institutions have developed 'reputation management' to cope with the new forces in the global higher education order. Institutions have spent more resources on publicity, branding and marketing than genuine efforts to improve teaching and learning environments.

Rankings and reputation metrics also provide little or no incentive to improve teaching and learning. They basically confirm the existing hierarchies in the system. As reputations change very slowly, this jeopardises the dynamism and innovation in the system. In principle, nothing is wrong with reputation metrics. In the Internet economy where consumers are invited to rate all kinds of products and services, these measures lead to aggregate reputation metrics that guide other consumers in their decision making. But in higher education, there are few reputation measures built on reliable data provided by students and graduates. Reputation measures are based on data provided by academics through reputation surveys. They can hardly compensate for the information asymmetry problem in higher education. Yet, there often is no alternative for students, families, employers and the general public.

Distrust

The fact that degrees seem to perform badly in providing information on learning outcomes or skills of graduates further aggravates the transparency problem. It undermines the trust employers, students, policy makers and the general public put in the system. And there are no other proxies than degrees to indicate that individuals have mastered a certain level of skills. It is a rather naïve strategy for the higher education community to be confident in the sustained symbolic power of degrees.

Some observers have noted these signs of distrust in what students learn in college. In their well-known book, *Academically Adrift*, Arum and Roksa (2011[17]) analysed data from the Collegiate Learning Assessment (CLA) instrument administered to a large sample of undergraduate students in the United States. They concluded that 45% of students surveyed demonstrated no significant improvement in complex reasoning and critical thinking skills during the first two years of college. After four years, 36% still failed to show any improvement. In a subsequent report, the same researchers (Arum, Roksa and Cho, n.d.[18]) concluded that "Large numbers of college students report that they experience only limited academic demands and invest only limited effort in their academic endeavours". In a follow-up study. they looked at these students' transition to working life (Arum and Roksa, 2014[19]). They found that, after graduation, poorly performing students in college were more likely to be in unskilled jobs, unemployed or to have been fired from their jobs. The lack of generic, 21st-century workplace skills impeded the employability of graduates – despite their tertiary qualification.

Global corporations and industry leaders are signalling severely decreased levels of trust in university qualifications. The global consultancy firm, Ernst & Young, which is an important graduate recruiter, was one of the first to announce that it would drop degree requirements for its job applicants (Sherriff, 2015[20]). It argued that "there is "no evidence" success at university correlates with achievement in later life." PricewaterhouseCoopers (PwC) quickly followed. Large companies in the information and communication technology (ICT) sector such as Google, Apple and Amazon applied the same policy. The sector had already developed its own alternative credentialing system. Significantly, another knowledge-intensive company, Penguin Random House Publishers, removed any requirement for a university degree from its new job listings (Sherriff, 2016[21]). To back its decision, the publishing group pointed to "increasing evidence that there is no simple correlation" between having a degree and work performance.

Many large companies have followed suit, often with large human resources (HR) departments, which have the capacity to assess job applicants for the skills needed. Small and medium-sized companies, however, still predominantly rely on qualifications as they do not have the resources to conduct assessments in-house. And, public-sector employers and regulated professions are obliged by law to value qualifications (Koumenta and Pagliero, 2017[22]). This shift has had a profound effect on hiring and HR policies, and practices of firms. A research report of hiring practices in the United States by Northeastern University concluded that "skills-based or competency-based hiring appears to be gaining significant interest and momentum, with a majority of HR leaders reporting either having a formal effort to deemphasize degrees and prioritize skills underway (23%) or actively exploring and considering this direction (39%)" (Gallagher, 2018[23]).

Changing skill demand

Rapidly changing skill demand has added to growing employer distrust of tertiary qualifications. Automation and digitalisation have ushered in critical changes in the task input of jobs. This requires different skill sets but higher education institutions have been slow to respond.

There has been a gradual decline in routine tasks. David Autor, economist at the Massachusetts Institute of Technology (MIT), has researched and documented this evolution in the economy of the United States. In 2013, he and his team replicated and expanded their original 2003 analysis (Autor and Price, 2013[24]). They showed (see Figure 1.4) that in a relatively short period of time, the share of routine manual and routine cognitive tasks declined significantly while the share of non-routine analytical and non-routine interpersonal tasks increased. It is clear that routine tasks, even in high-skilled professions, are increasingly automated. Automation does not replace human labour; it complements it. By changing the task content of existing jobs, automation creates entirely new jobs. David Autor (2015[25]) has demonstrated "that the interplay between machine and human comparative advantage allows computers to substitute for workers in performing routine, codifiable tasks while amplifying the comparative advantage of workers in supplying problem-solving skills, adaptability, and creativity". Automation allows the value of the tasks that workers uniquely carry out to be raised by adapting their skills set.

At the higher end of skills distribution, which is the segment for which higher education prepares workers, non-routine tasks are so-called 'abstract' tasks. They require problem solving, intuition, persuasion, and creativity. These tasks are characteristic of professional, managerial, technical and creative occupations such as law, medicine, science, engineering, marketing and design. Workers who are most adept in these tasks typically have high levels of education and analytical capability, and they benefit from computers that facilitate the transmission, organization, and processing of information" (Autor and Price, 2013[24]).

Figure 1.4. Changing task input in the US economy (1960-2009)

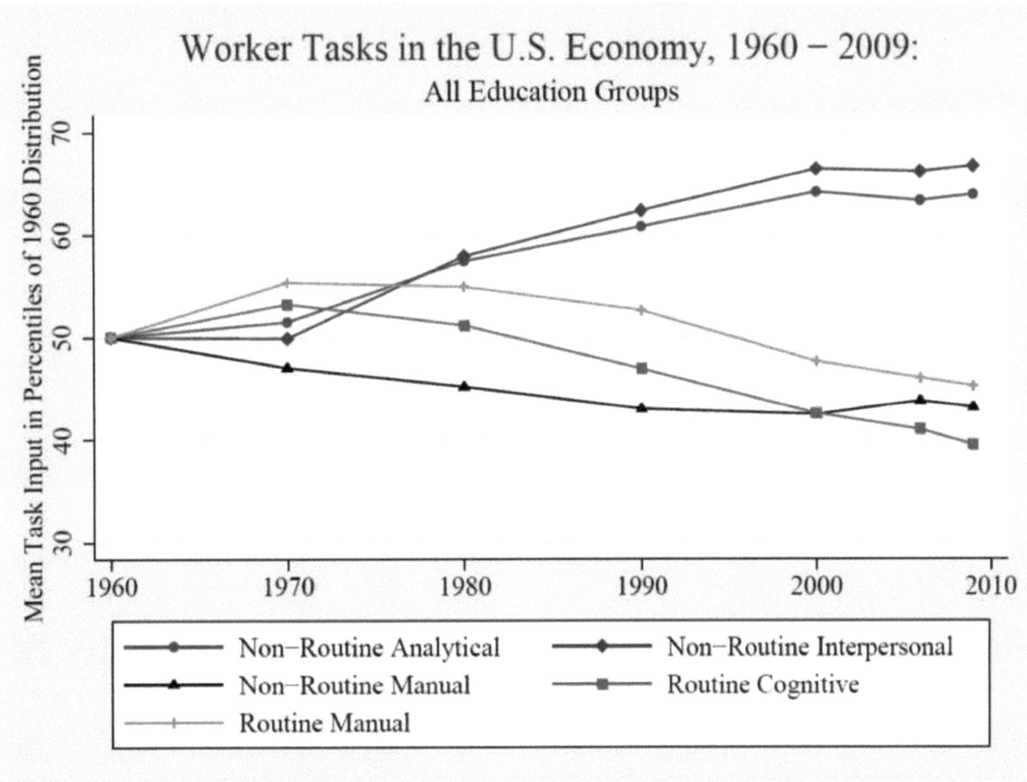

Source: Autor and Price (2013[24]), *The Changing Task Composition of the US Labor Market: An Update of Autor, Levy, and Murnane (2003)*, https://economics.mit.edu/files/9758 (accessed on 1 August 2022).

Another task category that has grown even more significantly than non-routine analytical tasks is non-routine interpersonal tasks. Complex communication tasks requiring highly developed and adaptive social skills have become more important in a wide range of professions. Computers still do poorly at simulating complex human interaction when emotional skills such as empathy come into play. With automation substituting for many tasks, complex interaction and communication tasks have grown in frequency and importance (Deming, 2017[26]). In the United States economy, jobs requiring non-routine communication skills have seen both employment and wage growth, and social skills have yielded increasing returns on the labour market (Deming, 2017[26]; Fernandez and Liu, 2019[27]).

In a number of recent reports, the OECD has developed country-level indicators on non-routine job content and its relationship with digital intensity (Marcolin, Miroudot and Squicciarini, 2016[28]; OECD, 2017[29]; OECD, 2019a[30]). On the basis of PIAAC data, these analyses show a correlation between digitalisation of the work place and industries, and growth in non-routine jobs. Figure 1.5 shows the country-level correlation of these two indicators in manufacturing industries, with increased ICT task intensity going hand-in-hand with a rise in the share of non-routine employment.

Figure 1.5. Share of non-routine employment and ICT task intensity, manufacturing industries, 2012 or 2015

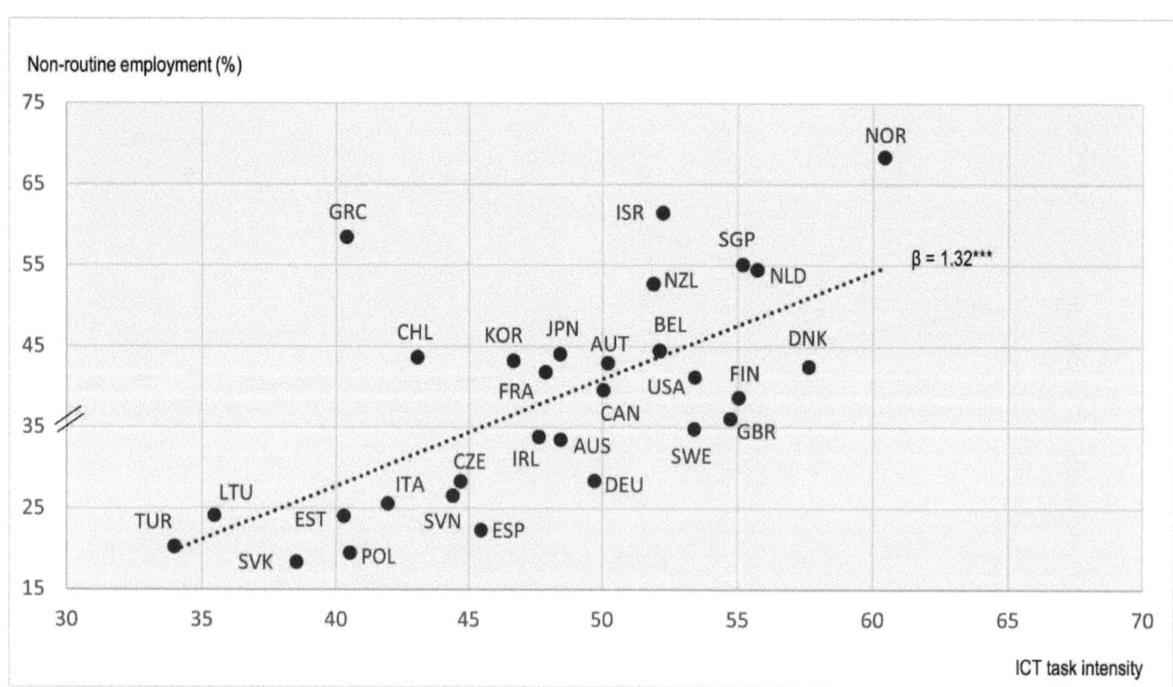

Source: OECD (2017[29]), *OECD Science, Technology and Industry Scoreboard 2017: The digital transformation*, OECD Publishing, Paris, https://doi.org/10.1787/9789264268821-en (accessed on 1 August 2022).

These changes in skill demand have already had a long-standing impact on the jobs of tertiary-educated professionals. Based on an analysis of data in the Reflex (2005) and Hegesco (2008) surveys of tertiary graduates, Avvisati, Jacotin and Vincent-Lancrin (2014[31]) looked into the skill requirements of graduates working in highly innovative jobs. They found that the critical skills that distinguish innovators most from non-innovators are creativity ("come up with new ideas and solutions" and the "willingness to question ideas"); the "ability to present ideas in audience"; "alertness to opportunities"; "analytical thinking", "ability to coordinate activities"; and the "ability to acquire new knowledge". These skills clearly align with what has been labelled non-routine skills.

Changes in the task-content of jobs have also impacted skill demand. Numerous surveys indicate that employers are aware that skills like creativity and analytical thinking have now become dominant in their hiring and recruitment policies (see, for example: (Hart Research Associates, 2013[32]; Kearns, 2001[33])). Terms used to denote skills necessary for successfully performing non-routine tasks include '21st- century skills', 'soft skills', 'generic skills', 'transferable skills', 'transversal skills', etc. These categories usually include critical thinking, creativity, problem solving, communication, team-working and learning-to-learn skills. These skills differ from each other but they are pragmatically put under the umbrella of '21st-century skills'.

Fuelled by the debate on the impact of automation and digitalisation on jobs, discussions are now multiplying on what skills are needed for the future job market. In 2018, the World Economic Forum's Future of Jobs survey of chief executive officers and chief human resource officers of multinational and large domestic companies identified analytical thinking, innovation, complex problem solving, critical thinking and creativity as the most important skills (Avvisati, Jacotin and Vincent-Lancrin, 2014[31]).

In a couple of recent papers, OECD analysts have used the Burning Glass Technologies database of online job postings and applied machine-learning technology to explore the information contained in these job postings (OECD, 2019a[30]; Blömeke et al., 2013[34]). These analyses provide overwhelming evidence of the frequency of 21st-century skill requirements in job postings. In an analysis of online job postings in the United Kingdom between 2017 and 2019, for instance, communication, teamwork, planning, problem solving, and creativity were mentioned as transversal.

Employers' interest in generic or 21st-century skills is also related to ongoing concerns about the impact of qualification and field-of-study mismatch for graduate employability, to which we referred earlier in this chapter. The numbers of graduates in specific fields of study often do not align well with the actual demand for qualifications on the labour market. In OECD countries, an average of 36% of workers are mismatched in terms of qualifications (17% of workers reported in the PIAAC survey that they are overqualified, 19% that they are underqualified) (OECD, 2018[35]). Some 40% of workers are also working in a different field than the one they studied and thus fall under 'field-of-study mismatch' (Montt, 2015[36]). Economists consider mismatch to be a significant obstacle to labour productivity growth. High levels of mismatch has prompted discussions on co-ordination between education and the labour market. On graduate employability, the idea of perfect alignment has been discarded. Instead, employers now look to education to develop foundation skills and the transversal, generic skills needed for employability. More technical skill development is now shared between education and on-the-job training in the workplace. Thus, the mismatch issue has contributed to growing interest in generic, 21st-century skills.

Do we know whether higher education institutions foster generic skills such as critical thinking and problem solving? Again, the answer is: We don't know. What students learn in universities is still generally attuned to routine cognitive tasks and procedural knowledge. Knowledge and skills that can be easily automated continue to dominate curricula. Nevertheless, universities have increased efforts on curriculum reform in response to external demands and pressures. Curriculum reform is generally in the direction of competency-based and interdisciplinary curriculum development. And in curriculum documents one finds statements emphasising the importance of generic skills valued in the workplace. But to know whether universities are fostering students' learning of 21st-century skills, we need much better assessment systems.

Assessing generic skills

The voice of employers, concerns about graduate employability and growing interest in generic skills have influenced curriculum development, course design and teaching and learning practices in higher education institutions. There are three important dimensions in current educational reform in higher education (Zahner et al., 2021[37]): The shift from lecture format to a student-centred approach emphasising students' active class participation; shift from curricular and textbook content to case- and problem-based materials requiring students to apply what they know to novel situations; innovation in assessment instruments from multiple-choice tests that are best used for measuring the level of content absorbed by students to open-ended assessments.

Although many higher education institutions and systems have made significant advances on the first two dimensions of this education reform movement, assessment has lagged behind. As universities focus increasingly on developing their students' generic skills, assessments need to be able to measure how well students are learning – and institutions are teaching – them. Multiple-choice and short-answer assessments remain the dominant testing regime not only for facts but also generic skills. As a result, the testing regime is not assessing the most critical skills required of students in the workplace and – just as importantly – is not supporting the other two dimensions of reform. For educational reform to be in synch with today's knowledge economy, open-ended, performance-based assessments are required. These have become standard practice in the workplace and contemporary human resources management approaches to recruitment, selection and upskilling.

If performance assessments are integrated into accountability systems, this should positively impact classroom practice. Class time spent preparing students to apply knowledge, analysis, and problem-solving skills to complex, real-world problems is time well spent. It will be worthwhile to investigate whether performance assessment for accountability purposes has a desirable effect on teaching and learning. It will be useful as well to investigate the perceived level of effort required to use performance assessments regularly in the classroom.

A critical shortcoming of today's principal educational assessment regime is that it pays little attention to how much an institution contributes to developing the competencies students will need after graduation. The outcomes that are typically looked at by higher education accreditation arrangements such as an institution's retention and graduation rates, and the percentage of its faculty in tenured positions say nothing about how well the school fosters the development of its students' analytic reasoning, problem solving, and communication skills. This situation is unfortunate because the ways in which institutions are evaluated significantly affects institutional priorities. If institutions were held accountable for student learning gains and student achievement, they would likely direct greater institutional resources and effort toward improving teaching and learning. Assessment has an enormous potential for driving change.

Developments in assessing higher education learning outcomes

Over the past decades, several research initiatives and experimental programmes to assess the learning outcomes of students in higher education have been initiated (Douglass, Thomson and Zhao, 2012[38]; Hattie, 2009[39]; Blömeke et al., 2013[34]; Wolf, Zahner and Benjamin, 2015[40]; Coates, 2016[41]; Coates and Zlatkin-Troitschanskaia, 2019[42]). An overview of the field by the OECD identified assessment practices in six countries (Nusche, 2008[43]). In the United States, the Council for Aid for Education has developed the CLA and its more recent variant CLA+, which will be discussed in this book. The University of California has developed the Student Experience in the Research University Survey. The testing company Educational Testing Service (ETS) has developed the HEIghten™ Outcomes Assessment Suite (Liu et al., 2016[44]). The European Commission, through the Tuning initiative, has endorsed the CALOHEE project (Wagenaar, 2019[45]). Germany has initiated a large and cross-disciplinary study for modelling and measuring competencies in higher education (KoKoHs) (Blömeke et al., 2013[34]). In the United Kingdom, the Teaching Excellence Framework includes several projects on the assessment of learning outcomes in universities. And there are probably many more national and local initiatives.

In 2008, mandated by a decision of education ministers gathered in Athens in 2006, the OECD embarked on the Assessment of Higher Education Learning Outcomes (AHELO) Feasibility Study (Coates and Richardson, 2012[46]; Ewell, 2012[47]). The study, which lasted until 2013, was the first international initiative for the assessment of higher education learning outcomes. It involved 248 higher-education institutions and 23 000 students in 17 countries or economies. It included a generic skills strand for which the CLA instrument was used, and two discipline-specific strands (engineering and economics). The results, outcomes and experiences were reported in three volumes (Tremblay, Lalancette and Roseveare, 2012[48]; AHELO, 2013a[49]; AHELO, 2013b[50]). The main conclusion of the AHELO Feasibility Study was that an international assessment of students' learning outcomes, which some people referred to as "a PISA for higher education", was feasible, despite considerable conceptual, methodological and implementation challenges.

In 2015, the OECD proposed to member countries to move to an AHELO Main Study. Several programme proposals were discussed by the Education Policy Committee but no consensus could be reached to embark on a Main Study. At the time, the political debate around AHELO was very heated (Van Damme, 2015[51]). Strong voices of support could be heard in media such as *The Economist* (2015) and the *Times Higher Education* (Morgan, 2015a[52]; Morgan, 2015b[53]; Usher, 2015[54]). At the same time, higher education experts and organisations representing the higher education community denounced the initiative

(Altbach, 2015[55]). Leading universities and university associations expressed strong concerns and outright opposition.

A serious criticisms of the OECD's AHELO proposal is that the higher education system is too diverse to apply common measures of learning outcomes. This would immediately standardise and homogenise teaching and learning in universities. In his critique, Phil Altbach (2015[55]) concentrated on this issue. It is certainly true that higher education systems are diversifying. Heterogeneity of the student body requires specific attention when applying standardised assessment instruments (Coates and Zlatkin-Troitschanskaia, 2019[42]). But the interesting point is whether diversity and heterogeneity completely annihilate the 'common core' of global higher education systems. In higher education, opposite tendencies of convergence as well as divergence are at work (Van Damme, 2019[5]). However, convergence is the dominant tendency in how degrees and qualifications grant access to jobs, earnings and status. While diversity and heterogeneity might have an impact on curriculum development, course content, teaching methods and examinations, they do not disqualify the need to prepare students for employability and work (Van Damme, 2021[56]).

Methodological issues

As in the case of PISA for secondary school education, an assessment of learning outcomes should not focus on curricular knowledge and skills but, rather, attributes commonly associated with higher education. Certainly, there are culturally specific elements in how generic academic skills are defined in specific contexts but there are powerful similarities as well, and more so in higher education than school education. After all, changes in skill demand affect all economies though there are differences in each one's skills balance and placement in global value chains. Overcoming cultural bias and diversified institutional missions is a measurement challenge, not a conceptual barrier.

Another important methodological question is whether the assessment of students' learning outcomes should be an absolute measurement of what students have learnt at the end of their study or a relative assessment of progress, 'learning gain' or the value-added through the process. The main argument for a value-added approach is the huge differences in selectivity among institutions and programmes. Universities can realise excellence in students' learning outcomes through initial selectivity or high value-added through the teaching and learning process. That said, a value-added approach complicates assessment methodologically and logistically. If the overall purpose is to provide feedback to institutions and programmes that will improve their quality, a value-added approach seems mandatory. If the overall purpose, however, is to provide reliable information on the level of generic, 21st-century skills students of a university have acquired, an assessment of absolute levels of learning outcomes makes more sense.

The failure of AHELO to establish itself as an international programme for the assessment of higher education learning outcomes did not lead to the disappearance of the idea itself (Coates and Zlatkin-Troitschanskaia, 2019[42]; Coates, 2016[41]). Several international endeavours have continued. The Educational Testing Service (ETS) has promoted the implementation of its HEIghten suite of assessments, including a critical thinking assessment in China and India. The results of their assessment of the critical thinking skills of undergraduate science, technology, engineering and math (STEM) students in these countries, compared to those in the United States, were published in *Nature Human Behaviour* in 2021 (Loyalka et al., 2021[57]). The data revealed limited learning gains in critical thinking in China and India over the course of a four-year bachelor programme, compared to the United States. Students in India demonstrated learning gains in academic skills in the first two years while those in China did not. The project revealed strong differences in learning outcomes and skills development among undergraduate students in these four countries, with consequences for the global competitiveness of STEM students and graduates across nations and institutions.

The New York- based Council for Aid to Education (CAE), which provided the CLA assessment instrument for the generic skills strand in the AHELO Feasibility Study, upgraded its instrument into the CLA+. CAE has started working with countries and organisations outside the United States interested in assessing generic skills (Wolf, Zahner and Benjamin, 2015[40]; Zahner et al., 2021[37]). Italy was a pioneering and particularly interesting case, where the national accreditation agency, ANVUR, implemented the CLA+ instrument in its TECO project to a large sample of Italian university students (Zahner and Ciolfi, 2018[58]); see also Chapter 11 in this volume). Other countries, systems and institutions followed. The OECD, which did not have a mandate to pursue this initiative, provided the convening space and opportunities to interact and co-ordinate for countries participating in this 'CLA+ International Initiative'. This book brings together the data and analysis of systems that participated in this initiative between 2016 and 2021.

References

AHELO (2013a), *Assessment of Higher Education Learning Outcomes (AHELO) Feasibility Report, Vol. 2. Data analysis and national experiences*, OECD, Paris, https://www.oecd.org/education/skills-beyond-school/AHELOFSReportVolume2.pdf. [49]

AHELO (2013b), *Assessment of Higher Education Learning Outcomes (AHELO) Feasibility Report. Vol. 3. Further insights*, OECD, Paris, https://www.oecd.org/education/skills-beyond-school/AHELOFSReportVolume3.pdf. [50]

Altbach, P. (2015), "AHELO: The Myth of Measurement and Comparability", *International Higher Education* 367, https://doi.org/10.6017/ihe.2015.82.8861. [55]

Arum, R. and J. Roksa (2014), *Aspiring Adults Adrift. Tentative Transitions of College Graduates*, Chicago University Press, Chicago, IL. [19]

Arum, R. and J. Roksa (2011), *Academically Adrift. Limited Learning on College Campuses*, Chicago University Press, Chicago, IL. [17]

Arum, R., J. Roksa and E. Cho (n.d.), *Improving Undergraduate Learning: Findings and Policy Recommendations from the SSRC-CLA Longitudinal Project*, Social Science Research Council (SSRC), https://s3.amazonaws.com/ssrc-cdn1/crmuploads/new_publication_3/%7BD06178BE-3823-E011-ADEF-001CC477EC84%7D.pdf. [18]

Autor, D. (2015), "Why are there still so many jobs? the history and future of workplace automation", Vol. 29(3), pp. 3-30, https://doi.org/10.1257/jep.29.3.3. [25]

Autor, D. and B. Price (2013), *The Changing Task Composition of the US Labor Market: An Update of Autor, Levy, and Murnane (2003)*, https://economics.mit.edu/files/9758 (accessed on 1 August 2022). [24]

Avvisati, F., G. Jacotin and S. Vincent-Lancrin (2014), "Educating Higher Education Students for Innovative Economies: What International Data Tell Us", *Tuning Journal for Higher Education*, Vol. 1/1, pp. 223-240, https://doi.org/10.18543/tjhe-1(1)-2013pp223-240. [31]

Barone, C. and L. Ortiz (2011), "Overeducation among European University Graduates: A comparative analysis of its incidence and the importance of higher education differentiation", *Higher Education*, Vol. 61/3, pp. 325-337, https://doi.org/10.1007/s10734-010-9380-0. [3]

Blackmur, D. (2007), "The Public Regulation of Higher Education Qualities: Rationale, Processes, and Outcomes", in Westerheijden, D. (ed.), *Higher Education Dynamics*, Springer, Dordrecht, https://doi.org/10.1007/978-1-4020-6012-0_1. [10]

Blömeke, S. et al. (2013), *Modeling and measuring competencies in higher education: Tasks and challenges*, Sense, Rotterdam, https://doi.org/10.1007/978-94-6091-867-4. [34]

Brüning, N. and P. Mangeol (2020), "What skills do employers seek in graduates?: Using online job posting data to support policy and practice in higher education", *OECD Education Working Papers, No. 231*, https://doi.org/10.1787/bf533d35-en. [68]

Coates, H. (2016), "Assessing student learning outcomes internationally: insights and frontiers", *Assessment and Evaluation in Higher Education*, Vol. 41/5, pp. 662-676, https://doi.org/10.1080/02602938.2016.1160273. [41]

Coates, H. and S. Richardson (2012), "An international assessment of bachelor degree graduates' learning outcomes", *Higher Education Management and Policy*, Vol. 23/3, https://doi.org/10.1787/hemp-23-5k9h5xkx575c. [46]

Coates, H. and O. Zlatkin-Troitschanskaia (2019), "The Governance, Policy and Strategy of Learning Outcomes Assessment in Higher Education", *Higher Education Policy*, Vol. 32/4, pp. 507-512, https://doi.org/10.1057/s41307-019-00161-1. [42]

Deming, D. (2017), "The growing importance of social skills in the labor market", *Quarterly Journal of Economics*, Vol. 132/4, pp. 1593-1640, https://doi.org/10.1093/qje/qjx022. [26]

Dill, D. and M. Soo (2004), "Transparency and Quality in Higher Education Markets", in Teixeira, P. et al. (eds.), , Higher Education Dynamics, Kluwer, https://doi.org/10.1007/1-4020-2835-0_4. [9]

Douglass, J., G. Thomson and C. Zhao (2012), "The learning outcomes race: The value of self-reported gains in large research universities", *Higher Education*, Vol. 64/3, pp. 317-335, https://doi.org/10.1007/s10734-011-9496-x. [38]

Economist (2015), "Having it All, Special Report on Universities", http://www.economist.com/news/special-report/21646990-ideas-deliveringequity-well-excellence-having-it-all (accessed on 11 August 2015). [59]

Ewell, P. (2012), "A World of Assessment: OECD's AHELO Initiative", *Change: The Magazine of Higher Learning*, Vol. 44/5, pp. 35-42, https://doi.org/10.1080/00091383.2012.706515. [47]

Fernandez, F. and H. Liu (2019), "Examining relationships between soft skills and occupational outcomes among U.S. adults with—and without—university degrees", *Journal of Education and Work*, Vol. 32/8, pp. 650-664, https://doi.org/10.1080/13639080.2019.1697802. [27]

Gallagher, S. (2018), *Educational credentials come of age: a survey on the use and value of educational credentials in hiring*, Northeastern University, https://cps.northeastern.edu/wp-content/uploads/2021/03/Educational_Credentials_Come_of_Age_2018.pdf. [23]

Hart Research Associates (2013), *It takes more than a major: Employer priorities for college learning and student success*, Washington, DC, https://www.aacu.org/leap/documents/2013_EmployerSurvey.pdf. [32]

Hattie, J. (2009), "The black box of tertiary assessment : An impending revolution", in Meyer, L. et al. (eds.), *Tertiary Assessment & Higher Education Outcomes: Policy, Practice & Research Excerpt taken from Hattie (pp.259-275)*, Ako Aotearoa, Wellington, New Zealand. [39]

Hazelkorn, E. (2014), "Reflections on a Decade of Global Rankings: What we've learned and outstanding issues", *European Journal of Education*, Vol. 49/1, pp. 12-28, https://doi.org/10.1111/ejed.12059. [14]

Hazelkorn, E. (2011), *Rankings and the reshaping of higher education: The battle for world-class excellence*, Palgrave-MacMillan, Basingstoke, https://doi.org/10.1057/9780230306394. [13]

Kearns, P. (2001), *Review of research-generic skills for the new economy*, https://www.ncver.edu.au/research-and-statistics/publications/all-publications/generic-skills-for-the-new-economy-review-of-research (accessed on 1 August 2022). [33]

Kehm, B. and B. Stensaker (2009), *University Rankings, Diversity and the New Landscape of Higher Education*, Vol.18, Sense, Global Perspectives on Higher Education, Rotterdam. [15]

Klein, S. et al. (2007), "The collegiate learning assessment: Facts and fantasies", *Evaluation Review*, Vol. 31/5, pp. 415-439, https://doi.org/10.1177/0193841X07303318. [64]

Klein, S. et al. (2005), "An Approach to Measuring Cognitive Outcomes across Higher Education Institutions", *Research in Higher Education*, Vol. 46/3, pp. 251-76, https://www.jstor.org/stable/40197345. [63]

Koumenta, M. and M. Pagliero (2017), *Measuring Prevalence and Labour Market Impacts of Occupational Regulation in the EU*, European Commission, Brussels, https://ec.europa.eu/docsroom/documents/20362/attachments/1/translations/en/renditions/native. [22]

Liu, O. et al. (2016), "Assessing critical thinking in higher education: the HEIghten™ approach and preliminary validity evidence", *Assessment & Evaluation in Higher Education*, Vol. 41/5, pp. 677-694, https://doi.org/10.1080/02602938.2016.1168358. [44]

Loyalka, P. et al. (2021), "Skill levels and gains in university STEM education in China, India, Russia and the United States", *Nature Human Behaviour*, Vol. 5/7, pp. 892-904, https://doi.org/10.1038/s41562-021-01062-3. [57]

M. Rostan and M. Vaira (ed.) (2011), "The New World Order in Higher Education", *Questioning Excellence in Higher Education*, Vol. 3, pp. 3-20. [60]

Marcolin, L., S. Miroudot and M. Squicciarini (2016), "The Routine Content Of Occupations: New Cross-Country Measures Based On PIAAC", *OECD Trade Policy Papers, No. 188*, https://doi.org/10.1787/5jm0mq86fljg-en. [69]

Marcolin, L., S. Miroudot and M. Squicciarini (2016), "The Routine Content Of Occupations: New Cross-Country Measures Based On PIAAC", *OECD Trade Policy Papers*, No. 188, OECD Publishing, Paris, https://doi.org/10.1787/5jm0mq86fljg-en. [28]

Marginson, S. (2019), "Limitations of human capital theory", *Studies in Higher Education*, Vol. 44/2, pp. 287-301, https://doi.org/10.1080/03075079.2017.1359823. [70]

Marginson, S. (2013), "The impossibility of capitalist markets in higher education", *Journal of Education Policy*, Vol. 28/3, pp. 353-370, https://doi.org/10.1080/02680939.2012.747109. [8]

Montt, G. (2015), "The causes and consequences of field-of-study mismatch: An analysis using PIAAC", *OECD Social, Employment & Migration Working Papers* 167, https://doi.org/10.1787/5jrxm4dhv9r2-en. [36]

Morgan, J. (2015a), "OECD's AHELO Project Could Transform University Hierarchy", *Times Higher Education*, https://www.timeshighereducation.co.uk/news/oecds-ahelo-project-could-transform-university-hierarchy/2020087.article. [52]

Morgan, J. (2015b), "World's University 'Oligopoly' Accused of Blocking OECD Bid to Judge Learning Quality", *Times Higher Education*, https://www.timeshighereducation.co.uk/news/world%E2%80%99s-university-%E2%80%98oligopoly%E2%80%99-accused-blocking-oecd-bid-judge-learning-quality. [53]

Nusche, D. (2008), "Assessment of Learning Outcomes in Higher Education: a comparative review of selected practices", *OECD Education Working Papers*, No. 15, OECD Publishing, Paris, https://doi.org/10.1787/244257272573. [43]

OECD (2021), *Education at a Glance 2021: OECD Indicators*, OECD Publishing, Paris, https://doi.org/10.1787/b35a14e5-en. [1]

OECD (2018), *Good Jobs for All in a Changing World of Work: The OECD Jobs Strategy*, OECD Publishing, Paris, https://doi.org/10.1787/9789264308817-en. [35]

OECD (2017), *OECD Science, Technology and Industry Scoreboard 2017: The digital transformation*, OECD Publishing, Paris, https://doi.org/10.1787/9789264268821-en. [29]

OECD (2015), "How is the global talent pool changing (2013, 2030)?", *Education Indicators in Focus*, No. 31, OECD Publishing, Paris, https://doi.org/10.1787/5js33lf9jk41-en. [2]

OECD (2013), *OECD Skills Outlook. First Results from the Survey of Adult Skills*, OECD, Paris, https://www.oecd-ilibrary.org/education/oecd-skills-outlook-2013_9789264204256-en. [73]

OECD (ed.) (2009), *The New Global Landscape of Nations and Institutions*, OECD Publishing, Paris. [65]

OECD (2019b), *Benchmarking Higher Education System Performance*, Higher Education, OECD Publishing, Paris, https://doi.org/10.1787/be5514d7-en. [61]

OECD (2019a), *OECD Skills Outlook 2019: Thriving in a Digital World*, OECD Publishing, Paris, https://doi.org/10.1787/df80bc12-en. [30]

Paccagnella, M. (2016), "Literacy and Numeracy Proficiency in IALS, ALL and PIAAC", *OECD Education Working Papers*, No. 142, OECD Publishing, Paris, https://doi.org/10.1787/5jlpq7qglx5g-en. [7]

Paccagnella, M. (2015), "Skills and Wage Inequality: Evidence from PIAAC", *OECD Education Working Papers*, No. 114, OECD Publishing, Paris, https://doi.org/10.1787/5js4xfgl4ks0-en. [6]

Rosen, Y., S. Derrara and M. Mosharraf (eds.) (2016), *Mitigation of Test Bias in International, Cross-National Assessments of Higher-Order Thinking Skills*, IGI Global, Hershey, PA, https://doi.org/10.4018/978-1-4666-9441-5.ch018. [66]

Saavedra, A. and J. Saavedra (2011), "Do colleges cultivate critical thinking, problem solving, writing and interpersonal skills?", *Economics of Education Review*, Vol. 30/6, pp. 1516-1526, https://doi.org/10.1016/j.econedurev.2011.08.006. [71]

Sherriff, L. (2016), "Penguin Random House Publishers Has Just Announced It's Scrapping Degree Requirements For Its Jobs", *The Huffington Post UK*, https://www.huffingtonpost.co.uk/2016/01/18/penguins-random-house-scrapping-!degree-requirements-jobs_n_9007288.html?1453113478 (accessed on 18 January 2016). [21]

Sherriff, L. (2015), "Ernst & Young Removes University Degree Classification From Entry Criteria As There's 'No Evidence' It Equals Success", *The Huffington Post UK*, https://www.huffingtonpost.co.uk/2016/01/07/ernst-and-young-removes-degree-classification-entry-criteria_n_7932590.html (accessed on 7 January 2016). [20]

The Economist (2016), "Going to university is more important than ever for young people. But the financial returns are falling", *The Economist*, https://www.economist.com/international/2018/02/03/going-to-university-is-more-important-than-ever-for-young-people (accessed on 3 February 2016). [4]

Tremblay, K., D. Lalancette and D. Roseveare (2012), "Assessment of Higher Education Learning Outcomes (AHELO) Feasibility Study", *Feasibility study report*, Vol. 1, https://www.oecd.org/education/skills-beyond-school/AHELOFSReportVolume1.pdf (accessed on 1 August 2022). [48]

Usher, A. (2015), "Universities Behaving Badly", *Inside Higher Education*, https://www.insidehighered.com/blogs/world-view/universities-behaving-badly. [54]

Uttl, B., C. White and D. Gonzalez (2017), "Meta-analysis of faculty's teaching effectiveness: Student evaluation of teaching ratings and student learning are not related", *Studies in Educational Evaluation*, Vol. 54, pp. 22-42, https://doi.org/10.1016/j.stueduc.2016.08.007. [12]

Van Damme, D. (2021), "Transforming Universities for a Sustainable Future", in *The Promise of Higher Education (pp. 431-438)*, Springer International Publishing, https://doi.org/10.1007/978-3-030-67245-4_64. [56]

Van Damme, D. (2019), "Convergence and Divergence in the Global Higher Education System: The Conflict between Qualifications and Skills", *International Journal of Chinese Education*, Vol. 8/1, pp. 7-24, https://doi.org/10.1163/22125868-12340102. [5]

Van Damme, D. (2015), "Global higher education in need of more and better learning metrics. Why OECD's AHELO project might help to fill the gap", *European Journal of Higher Education*, Vol. 5/4, pp. 425-436, https://doi.org/10.1080/21568235.2015.1087870. [51]

Van Damme, D. (2009), "The Search for Transparency: Convergence and Diversity in the Bologna Process", in F. Van Vught (ed.), *Mapping the higher education landscape: towards a European classification of higher education*, Springer, Dordrecht, https://doi.org/10.1007/978-90-481-2249-3_3. [74]

van Vught, F. (2008), "Mission Diversity and Reputation in Higher Education", *Higher Education Policy*, Vol. 21/2, pp. 151-174, https://doi.org/10.1057/hep.2008.5. [16]

Van Vught, F. and F. Ziegele (eds.) (2012), *Transparency, Quality and Accountability*, Higher Education Dynamics 37, Springer, Dordrecht. [11]

Vincent-Lancrin, S. (2019), *Fostering Students' Creativity and Critical Thinking: What it Means in School, Educational Research and Innovation*, OECD Publishing, Paris, https://doi.org/10.1787/62212c37-en. [75]

Wagenaar, R. (2019), *Reform! Tuning the Modernisation Process of Higher Education in Europe: A blueprint for student-centred learning*, Tuning Academy, Groningen, https://research.rug.nl/en/publications/reform-tuning-the-modernisation-process-of-higher-education-in-eu-2. [45]

Weingarten, H., M. Hicks and A. Kaufman (eds.) (2018), *The Role of Generic Skills in Measuring Academic Quality*, McGill-Queen's UP, Kingston, ON. [62]

Wolf, R., D. Zahner and R. Benjamin (2015), "Methodological challenges in international comparative post-secondary assessment programs: lessons learned and the road ahead", *Studies in Higher Education*, Vol. 40/3, pp. 471-481, https://doi.org/10.1080/03075079.2015.1004239. [40]

Zahner, D. and A. Ciolfi (2018), "International Comparison of a Performance-Based Assessment in Higher Education", in *Assessment of Learning Outcomes in Higher Education, Methodology of Educational Measurement and Assessment*, Springer International Publishing, Cham, https://doi.org/10.1007/978-3-319-74338-7_11. [58]

Zahner, D. et al. (2021), "Measuring the generic skills of higher education students and graduates: Implementation of CLA+ international.", in *Assessing undergraduate learning in psychology: Strategies for measuring and improving student performance.*, American Psychological Association, Washington, https://doi.org/10.1037/0000183-015. [37]

Zlatkin-Troitschanskaia, O., H. Pant and H. Coates (2016), *Assessing student learning outcomes in higher education: challenges and international perspectives*, https://doi.org/10.1080/02602938.2016.1169501. [72]

Zlatkin-Troitschanskaia, O., R. Shavelson and C. Kuhn (2015), "The international state of research on measurement of competency in higher education", *Studies in Higher Education*, Vol. 40/3, pp. 393-411, https://doi.org/10.1080/03075079.2015.1004241. [67]

2 The Collegiate Learning Assessment – a performance-based assessment of generic skills

Doris Zahner, Council for Aid to Education (United States)

Tess Dawber, Council for Aid to Education (United States)

Kelly Rotholz, Council for Aid to Education (United States)

Educators and employers clearly recognise that fact-based knowledge is no longer sufficient and that critical thinking, problem solving, and written communication skills are essential for success. The opportunity to improve students' essential skills lies in identification and action. Assessments that provide educators with the opportunity to help students identify their strengths as well as areas where they can improve are fundamental to developing the critical thinkers, problem solvers and communicators who will be essential in the future. With close and careful attention paid toward students' essential skills, even a small increase in the development of these skills could boost future outcomes for students, parents, institutions and the overall economy.

Introduction

The Collegiate Learning Assessment (CLA+) is an assessment of higher education students' generic skills, specifically critical thinking, problem solving and written communication. These are skills and learning outcomes espoused by most higher education institutions (Association of American Colleges and Universities, 2011[1]; Arum and Roksa, 2011[2]; 2014[3]; Liu, Frankel and Roohr, 2014[4]; Wagner, 2010[5]), yet there is a lack of evidence on the extent to which improvement on them is actually achieved (Benjamin, 2008a[6]; 2008b[7]; 2012[8]; Bok, 2009[9]; Klein et al., 2007[10]).

A recent special report on higher education students' career paths (Zinshteyn, 2021[11]) indicated the importance for institutions of higher education to acknowledge, understand and address the existing skills gap and mismatch and to prepare students for the world of work. This report echoes previous research (Montt, 2015[12])on the skills mismatch issue, which has been identified as globally problematic.

While content knowledge is a requisite part of a student's education, alone it is insufficient for a student to thrive academically and professionally (Capital, 2016[13]; Hart Research Associates, 2013[14]; National Association of Colleges and Employers, 2018[15]; Rios et al., 2020[16]; World Economic Forum, 2016[17]). Most students (approximately 80%) consider themselves proficient in the essential college and career skills of critical thinking, problem solving and written communication. However, the percentage of employers who rate recent graduates as proficient in these skills differs greatly: 56% for critical thinking/problem solving and 42% for communication (National Association of Colleges and Employers, 2018[15]).

Specifically, essential college and career skills such as critical thinking, problem solving and communication are the abilities that hiring managers value most (Capital, 2016[13]; Hart Research Associates, 2013[14]; National Association of Colleges and Employers, 2018[15]; Rios et al., 2020[16]; World Economic Forum, 2016[17]). More than content knowledge, these are the skills that can help students entering higher education achieve better outcomes, such as a higher cumulative GPA during their college tenure (Zahner, Ramsaran and Zahner, 2012[18]). However, these essential skills are often not explicitly taught as part of college curricula, nor are they reflected on a college transcript.

The Council for Aid to Education's (CAE) research shows that approximately 60% of entering students are not proficient in these skills, and since these skills are seldom explicitly taught as part of college curricula, most students have little structured opportunity to improve their proficiency. Identifying and supporting students who may be at risk due to insufficient proficiency in these essential skills upon entry to higher education should be one component to helping improve persistence, retention, and graduation rates. Improving students' essential skills in secondary education to better prepare them for higher education should be another important component. Measuring these essential skills can be best accomplished by using an authentic, valid, and reliable assessment.

Educators and employers clearly recognise that fact-based knowledge is no longer sufficient and that critical thinking, problem solving, and written communication skills are essential for success. The opportunity to improve students' essential skills lies in identification and action. Assessments that provide educators with the opportunity to help students identify their strengths as well as areas where they can improve are fundamental to developing the critical thinkers, problem solvers and communicators who will be essential in the future. With close and careful attention paid toward students' essential skills, even a small increase in the development of these skills could boost future outcomes for students, parents, institutions and the overall economy.

CLA+

The Collegiate Learning Assessment (CLA /CLA+) is a performance-based assessment of critical thinking and written communication. Traditionally, the CLA was an institutional-level assessment that measured student learning gains within a university (Klein et al., 2007[10]). The CLA employed a matrix sampling approach under which students were randomly distributed either a Performance Task (PT) or an Analytic Writing Task for which students were allotted 90 minutes and 75 minutes, respectively. The CLA PTs presented real-world situations in which an issue, problem or conflict was identified and students were asked to assume a relevant role to address the issue, suggest a solution or recommend a course of action based on the information provided in a document library. Analytic Writing Tasks consisted of two components – one in which students were presented with a statement around which they had to construct an argument (Make an Argument), and another in which students were given a logically flawed argument that they had to then critique (Critique an Argument).

In its original form, the utility of the CLA was limited. Because the assessment consisted of just one or two responses from each student, reliable results were only available at the institutional level, and students' results were not directly comparable. Likewise, reporting for the CLA was restricted to the purposes of its value-added measure, and institutions were not eligible for summary results unless they had tested specified class levels in the appropriate testing windows.

Thus, the CLA+ was created with a PT similar to the original CLA PT as the anchor of the assessment. The CLA+ also includes an additional set of 25 selected-response questions (SRQs) to increase the reliability of the instrument (Zahner, 2013[19]) for reporting individual student results. The SRQ section is aligned to the same construct as the PT and is intended to assess higher-order cognitive skills rather than the recall of factual knowledge. Similar to the PT, this section presents students with a set of questions as well as one or two documents to refer to when answering each question. The supporting documents include a range of information sources such as letters, memos, photographs, charts, and newspaper articles. Each student receives both components (PT and SRQ) of the assessment.

The CLA+ has six separate subscores. The open-ended student responses from the PT are scored on three subscores, which have a range from 1 – 6: Analysis and Problem Solving (APS), Writing Effectiveness (WE) and Writing Mechanics (WM). The SRQs consist of three subsections: Scientific and Quantitative Reasoning (SQR), Critical Reading and Evaluation (CRE) and Critiquing an Argument (CA). Students have 60 minutes to complete the PT and 30 minutes to complete the SRQs. There is a short demographic survey following the assessment, which should be completed within 15 minutes.

Additionally, CLA+ includes a metric in the form of mastery levels. The mastery levels are qualitative categorisations of total CLA+ scores, with cut scores that were derived from a standard-setting study (Zahner, 2014[20]). The mastery level categories are: Emerging, Developing, Proficient, Accomplished and Advanced.

Sample CLA+ documents can be found at the end of this chapter. These include PT and SRQ documents and questions, the scoring rubric, a sample institutional report and a sample student report.

CLA+ Scoring

All student PT responses are double-scored, one by an AI scoring engine, and the other by a trained human scorer.

Scoring process

For CLA+, all student responses are double-scored, once by a human rater and once through an AI scoring engine. The training for the scoring process is directed by the CAE Measurement Science team. All scorer candidates are selected for their experience with teaching and grading university student writing and have at least a master's degree in an appropriate subject (e.g., English). Once selected, to become a CLA+ scorer, they must undergo rigorous training aligned with best practices in assessment.

A lead scorer is identified for each PT and is trained in person or virtually by CAE measurement scientists and editors. Following this training, the lead scorer conducts an in-person or virtual (but synchronous) training session for the scorers assigned to his or her particular PT. A CAE measurement scientist or editor attends this training as an observer and mentor. After this training session, homework assignments are given to the scorers in order to calibrate the entire scoring team. All training includes an orientation to the prompt and scoring rubrics/guides, repeated practice grading a wide range of student responses, and extensive feedback and discussion after scoring each response. Because each prompt may have differing possible arguments or relevant information, scorers receive prompt-specific guidance in addition to the scoring rubrics. CAE provides a scoring homework assignment for any PT that will be operational before the onset of each testing window to ensure that the scorers are properly calibrated. For new Performance Tasks (i.e. pilot testing), a separate training is first held to orient a lead scorer to the new PT, and then a general scorer training is held to introduce the new PT to the scorers. After participating in training, scorers complete a reliability check where they score the same set of student responses. Scorers with low agreement or reliability (determined by comparisons of raw score means, standard deviations, and correlations among the scorers) are either further coached or removed from scoring.

During pilot testing of any new PTs, all responses are double-scored by human scorers. These double-scored responses are then used for future scorer trainings, as well as to train a machine-scoring engine for all future operational test administrations of the PT.

Until 2020, CAE used Intelligent Essay Assessor (IEA) for its machine scoring. IEA is the automated scoring engine developed by Pearson Knowledge Technologies to evaluate the meaning of a text, not just writing mechanics. Pearson designed IEA for CLA+ using a broad range of real CLA+ responses and scores to ensure its consistency with scores generated by human scorers. Thus, human scorers remain the basis for scoring the CLA+ tasks. However, automated scoring helps to increase scoring accuracy, reduce the amount of time between a test administration and reports delivery, and lower costs. The automated essay scoring technique that CLA+ uses is known as Latent Semantic Analysis (LSA), which extracts the underlying meaning in written text. LSA uses mathematical analysis of at least 800 student responses per PT and the collective expertise of human scorers (each of these responses must be accompanied by two sets of scores from trained human scorers), and applies what it has learned from the expert scorers to new, unscored student responses. Beginning in 2021, CAE engaged a new partner, MZD for delivery and scoring of PTs. MZD's platform has an integrated automatic scoring engine, EMMA (Powers, Loring and Henrich, 2019[21])which functions very similarly to IEA. In fact, CAE conducted a comparison of the two AI-scoring platforms and found the results between EMMA and IEA to be comparable.

Once tasks are fully operational, CLA+ uses a combination of automated and human scoring for its Performance Tasks. In almost all cases, IEA provides one set of scores and a human provides the second set. However, IEA occasionally identifies unusual responses. When this happens, the flagged response is automatically sent to the human scoring queue to be scored by a second human instead of by IEA. For any given response, the final PT subscores are simply the averages of the two sets of scores, whether one human set and one machine set or two human sets.

To ensure continuous human scorer calibration, CAE developed the calibration system for the online scoring interface. The calibration system was developed to improve and streamline scoring. Calibration of scorers through the online system requires scorers to score previously scored results, or "verification papers," when they first start scoring, as well as throughout the scoring window. The system will periodically present verification papers to scorers in lieu of student responses, though they are not flagged to the scorers as such. The system does not indicate when a scorer has successfully scored a verification paper; however, if the scorer fails to accurately score a series of verification papers, he or she will be removed from scoring and must participate in a remediation process. At this point, scorers are either further coached or removed from scoring.

Using data from the CLA, CAE used an array of Performance Tasks to compare the accuracy of human versus automated scoring. For all tasks examined, AI engine-scores agreed more often with the average of multiple experts (r = .84-.93) than two experts agreed with each other (r = .80-.88). These results suggest that computer-assisted scoring is as accurate as–and in some cases, more accurate than–expert human scorers (Steedle and Elliot, 2012[22]).

CLA+ psychometrics

Test design

The test design of the CLA+ assessment is shown in Table 2.1. The numbers of items and points are given for both test components and for the total test. The three SRQ subscores – SQR, CRE, and CA – are reporting categories that consist of items measuring a similar set of skills.

Student responses to the PT are scored with three rubrics, each scored from 1 to 6. The subscores given for the PTs are APS, WE, and WM.

Table 2.1. CLA+ test design

Component	Subscore	Items	Points
Selected-Response Questions (SRQs)	SQR	10	10
	CRE	10	10
	CA	5	5
	Total	25	25
Performance Task (PT)	APS	1	6
	WE	1	6
	WM	1	6
	Total	3	18
Total test		28	43

Note: SQR = Scientific and Quantitative Reasoning; CRE = Critical Reading and Evaluation; CA = Critique an Argument; APS = Analysis and Problem Solving; WE = Writing Effectiveness; WM = Writing Mechanics.

CAE uses a matrix sampling design. Multiple SRQ sets and PTs are randomly spiralled across the students during a given administration. As a result, the reliability analyses are performed by subscore for the SRQ sets and by PTs rather than by form. The data summarised below are based on the CLA+ administrations with domestic students.

Reliability

Reliability refers to the consistency of students' test scores on parallel forms of a test. A reliable test is one that produces relatively stable scores if the test is administered repeatedly under similar conditions. Reliability was evaluated using the method of internal consistency, which provides an estimate of how consistently examinees perform across items within a test during a single test administration (Crocker and Algina, 1986[23]).

The reliability of raw scores was estimated using Cronbach's coefficient alpha, which is a lower-bound estimate of test reliability (Cronbach, 1951[24]). Reliability coefficients range from 0 to 1, where 1 indicates a perfectly reliable test. Generally, a longer test is expected to be more reliable than a shorter test.

Because the PT scores consist of ratings rather than sets of items, the reliability of the ratings is summarised by rater consistency indices. These are rater agreement and correlations between rater scores.

SRQ reliability

The average internal consistency results for the SRQ sets available for operational use are 0.58 for the SQR, 0.59 for the CRE and 0.48 for the CA. The reliabilities are higher for the two ten-item sets compared to the five-item set.

PT reliability

The rater consistency is summarised for exact agreement and exact plus adjacent agreement on ratings, and for correlations between rater scores for the APS, WE and WM ratings. Across PTs and administrations, the exact agreement rates for the three ratings are between 59 and 61 percent and the exact plus adjacent agreement rates are 97 percent or higher. Correlations between rater scores are in the 0.60 to 0.70 range.

Correlations between scale scores

The correlations between the CLA+ total scale score and the component scale scores (i.e. PT, SRQ) are in the 0.80 to 0.90 range. The correlations between the PT and the SRQ scale scores generally are between 0.40 and 0.50. The correlations between the PT and the SRQ subscores of SQR, CRE and CA tend to be between 0.30 and 0.40 for SQR and CRE (both ten-point sets) and between 0.25 and 0.40 for CA (five-point set).

Computing scale scores

SRQ subscores are assigned based on the number of questions answered correctly. The value is adjusted to account for item difficulty, and the adjusted value is converted to a common scale. The scale has a mean of 500 and a standard deviation of 100. SRQ subscores range from approximately 200 to 800. The weighted average of the SRQ subscores is transformed using the scaling parameters to place the SRQ section scores on the same scale.

PT subscores are assigned on a scale of 1 to 6 according to the scoring rubric. The PT subscores are not adjusted for difficulty because they are intended to facilitate criterion-referenced interpretations outlined in the rubric. The PT subscores are added to produce a total raw score, which is then converted to a common scale using linear transformation. The conversion produces scale scores that maintain comparable levels of performance across PTs.

The CLA+ total scores are calculated by taking the average of the SRQ and the PT scale scores. The mastery level cut scores are applied to the CLA+ total score to assign mastery levels to the student scores.

Technical information about the linear equating procedure (Kolen and Brennan, 2004[25]) is provided in the Annex to this chapter.

Establishing mastery levels

The total test scale scores are contextualised by assigning mastery, or performance, levels. A standard-setting workshop was held in December 2013 to set the performance standards for Developing, Proficient and Advanced. A fourth performance standard, Accomplished, was added in November 2014 using the same methodology and panellists.

Panellist discussions were based on the knowledge, skills and abilities required to perform well on the CLA+. The purpose of the activity was to develop consensus among the panellists regarding a narrative profile of the knowledge, skills and abilities required to perform at each mastery level. Then, during the rating activities, panellists relied on these descriptions to make their judgments based on the items and student performance. Table 2.2 shows the CLA+ cut scores used to assign mastery levels.

Table 2.2. CLA+ mastery level cut scores

Mastery level	Scale score
Developing	963
Proficient	1097
Accomplished	1223
Advanced	1368

Figure 2.1. Sample CLA+ PT

Performance Task: Social Media

Instructions

This is an example of a CLA+ Performance Task. In the course of this practice Performance Task, you will prepare a written response to a hypothetical but realistic situation. The Performance Task is made up of an introductory scenario, a question, and six documents/information sources. You will use information from the Document Library in carrying out the task.

While your personal values and experiences are important, you should base your response solely on the evidence provided in the documents.

Scenario

Imagine you are starting a social media company with a partner. The company, called "PenPals," would be an online forum for aspiring writers and journalists to network with employers, share their writing, and connect with other writers. Your business partner has drafted a business plan but cannot decide the best way to make a profit from the online business. Your partner suggests several possibilities: selling advertising space and member information to advertisers, charging members to use the service, charging employers to search for potential employees using the service, or some combination of these three options. Read the business plan and other supporting documents to analyze the strengths and limitations of each funding option.

Prompt

Your task is to write a recommendation to your business partner evaluating the possible funding options and suggesting the best option for the needs and limitations of your business. Consider how financial trends, legal issues, and customer preferences would impact each option. Make sure to address the strengths and/or limitations of each option and support your statement with information found in the documents.

There is no "correct" answer. Your written recommendation should clearly describe all the details necessary to support your position. Your answers will be judged, not only on the accuracy of the information you provide, but also on how clearly the ideas are presented, how thoroughly the information is covered, how effectively the ideas are organized, and how well your writing reflects the conventions of standard written English.

Write your response in the space provided. Write as much as you need to fulfill the requirements on the task; you are not limited by the size of the response area.

Document Library

Document 1: Penpals Draft Business Plan
Document 2: Memo from Nelson Fareira, J.D.
Document 3: Statistics on Internet Apps and Internet Ads.
Document 4: Business Universe Online Discussion Forum
Document 5: Article from Bottom Line Magazine
Document 6: Email from Imani Willis, ReCrucial Recruiting Website

Figure 2.2. Document 1: Penpals Draft Business Plan

Draft for Business Plan

Business Name: Penpals®

Description of Services: PenPals is an online social media service for students and budding professionals in the field of journalism and writing. When members join PenPals®, they will be able to connect with employers or with people looking to hire freelance writers, and can also apply directly to jobs through the site. In addition, PenPals® has created a vibrant community of users that provides professional networking as well as a platform for discussions about freelance writing experiences. Furthermore, PenPals® includes active online forums where the art and skill of writing, as well as professional development, are discussed.

Target Demographic: Freelance or unemployed writers and students—those who are trying make connections or learn how to improve their writing, as well as established news companies and organizations who are looking to hire new writers. We want to appeal to a wide range of people in the writing and journalism fields, including academics and professionals. At the same time, we want to create a platform that has more focus and provides better content than many of the professional social media options currently available.

Funding Options:

- sell advertising space that would show up on the screen before members can access the service
- sell member information to advertisers who would use their information to create user-specific advertising and online mailing lists
- allow members to join for free, but charge members varying rates for most services. (In this case, we would still need to have on-screen advertising, but members would be able to pay a fee to opt out of advertising altogether.)
- charge all members a flat monthly rate for the service
- charge employers and publications a fee for advertising jobs and opportunities on our site
  a combination of the above options

Figure 2.3. Document 2: Memo from Nelson Fareira. J.D.

Thank you for contacting our offices about legal issues surrounding your online business. If you would like to schedule an in-depth consultation, I am happy to meet with you. In the meantime, I am including a statement--free of charge--with a general consultation regarding issues that may affect your business planning. Please feel free to contact me with any further questions.

Respectfully yours,

Nelson Fareira, J.D.

Memo

Legal Risks and Ramifications Involved in Online Business and Social Media

Social media businesses are vulnerable to the following primary legal threats:

1. Breaches of security by third parties. Online platforms are vulnerable to being manipulated and used by cyber criminals to steal information about the host company or users. These breaches are exceptionally serious in instances where users share financial information.

2. Online businesses are at risk of legal action from users for leaking confidential information about individuals for third-party use. This may be in the form of sharing or selling information with or to businesses or governmental third parties, without explicit consent from users.

3. Copyright issues. If users post copyrighted information, the service may be legally liable.

Based on the above legal issues, we recommend that you work with one of our attorneys to develop clear Terms of Use that all users must accept before using your site. Your Social Media Policy should make your information-sharing practices transparent and clear, as well as encourage respectful behavior by all users.

Fareira, Fulton, and Holmes
Business Law Firm

Figure 2.4. Document 3: Statistics on Internet Apps and Internet Ads.

These graphs reflect social media use, user spending, and advertising. All statistics are gathered by IntelFind Data Group.

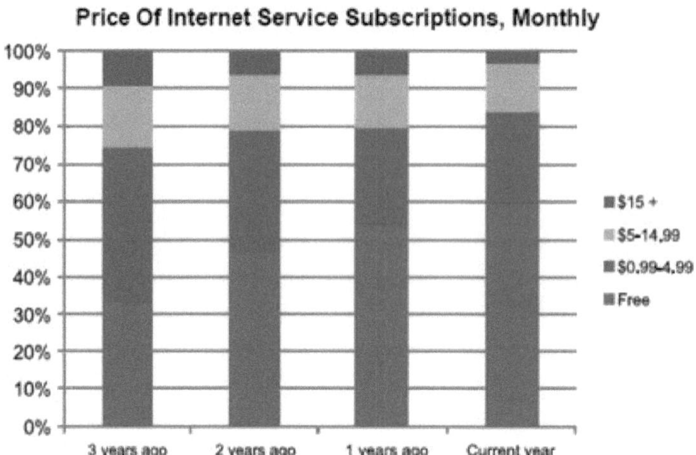

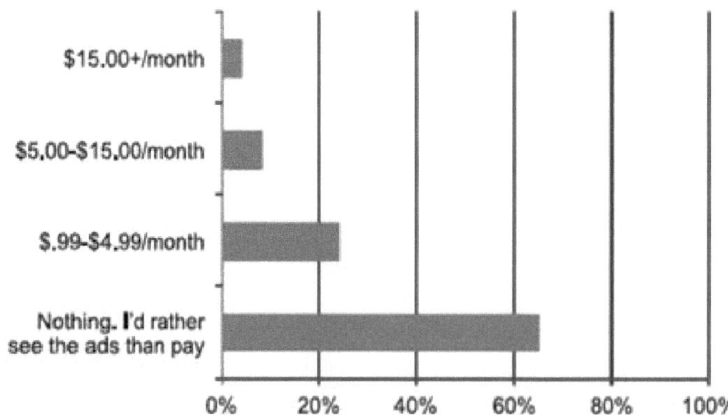

Figure 2.5. Document 4: Business Universe Online Discussion Forum

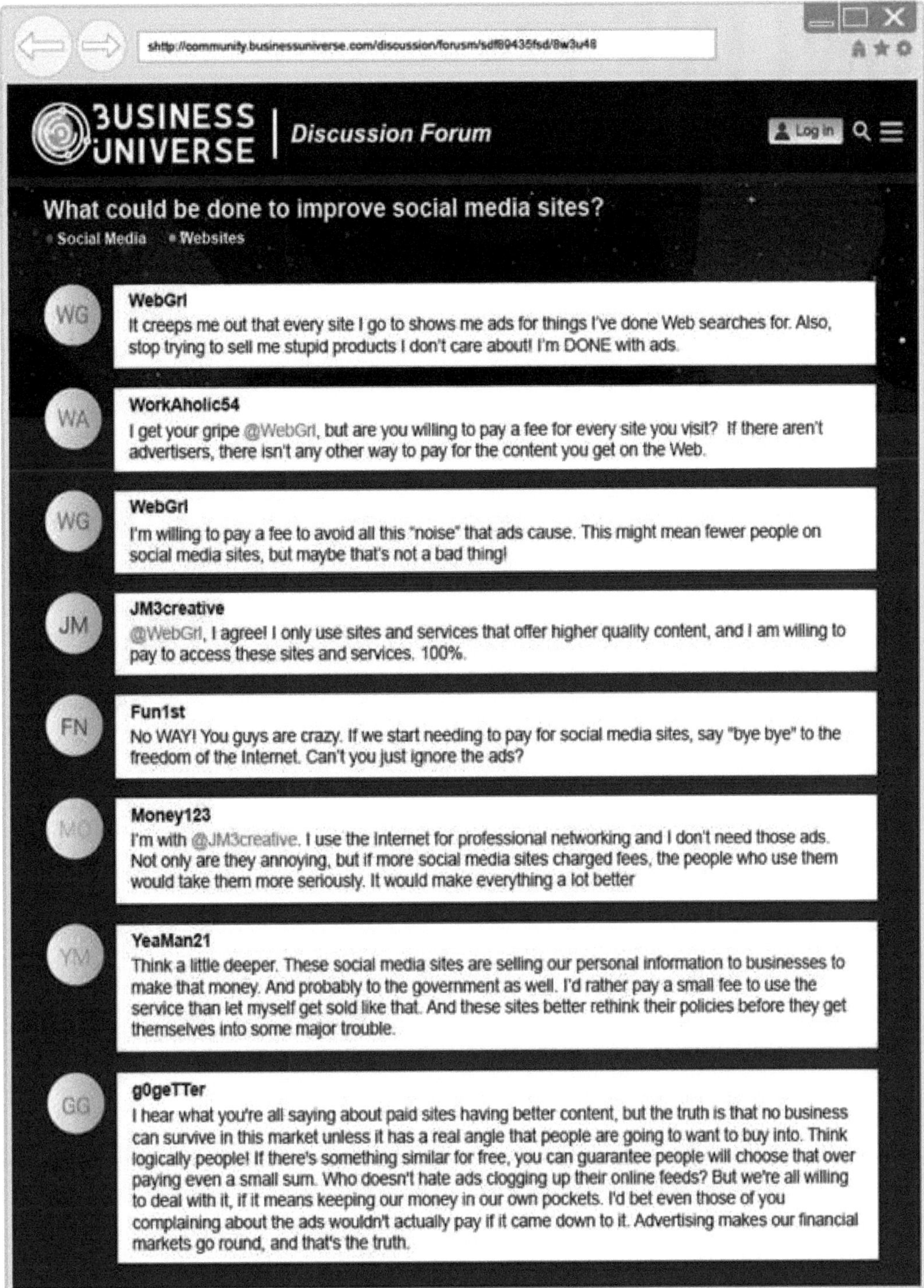

Figure 2.6. Document 5: Article from Bottom Line Magazine

ONLINE PROFITING

by Dina Fowler
Business Consultant and Contributing Writer

The Internet is a fertile and mysterious territory for small business owners and entrepreneurs. Its potential is endless, as well as daunting, and the profit streams are not always obvious. They do exist, but they require some strategic planning to make the most of—and require an understanding of—the global online economy. In general, diversifying your revenue streams is a wise approach, and, luckily, the World Wide Web provides a variety of opportunities that can work in combination with each other.

It is possible to tap into one of the many Internet-based revenue streams to ignite financial fires for your online business. It really depends on what your business has to offer. One of the more straightforward profit sources is to sell a product or service that exists outside of the virtual world, like a clothing business or design company, for example. In these cases, you are utilizing the Internet to promote your products or services, network with other companies, advertise, and offer promotions or deals. Much of the business exchange can take place via social media or on your website, which can help to expedite and expand your profit-making influence.

You need to be more creative, though, when you don't have a physical product to offer. If you're offering online content or resources, the most obvious and direct form of revenue is to charge users a fee for accessing your online presence. This works if you are offering a unique online resource that provides explicit benefits to the user. Good models for this are dating websites, newspapers with online subscription fees, and job or apartment search engines. Even with these types of services, however, the more that people have to pay, the less likely they are to visit your site.

Selling promotional space in the form of pop-ups, banners, and sidebars to advertisers is a classic approach adopted from non-Internet based media, such as newspapers and magazines. The benefit, of course, is that your content remains free to users and your profit comes from the advertisers. The problem is that it's not always as profitable as one might think. Typically, the way that pay-per-click advertising works, a site needs an average of one million views per month in order to actually make a profit. The danger in this approach is that with the popular distaste for pop-up ads and banners, you may be driving away viewers with these advertisements rather than bringing them in. More effective approaches to online advertising include selling customer information to advertisers and providing targeted advertisements, where marketers have access to user information and develop ads based on users' Internet behavior.

The wisest approach for online business entrepreneurs is to match form to function. Choose the revenue streams that best fit your business model. If you're a high traffic site, then advertising will be well worth it. If you can find the right partners, make it a joint venture. And as always, diversify your profits. It's the best security for any business, online or off. ∎

Figure 2.7. Document 6: Email from Imani Willis, ReCrucial Recruriting Website

PenPals Team

From:	Imani Willis
Sent:	Februay 2
To:	PenPals Team
Cc:	
Subject:	ReCrucial data

Dear PenPals Team,

Thanks for reaching out to us about how our Web service maintains financial viability through the solicitation of funding from employers. As you know, ReCrucial consistently places in the top five recruiting sites across multiple industries in the US.

You asked for information about the purchasing patterns of employers who post open jobs on ReCrucial. The charts below show that data for the last two years. Our team is working to help create more stable revenue streams for the future.

Feel free to contact me with any other questions.

Best regards,

Imani Willis
Chief Marketing Officer

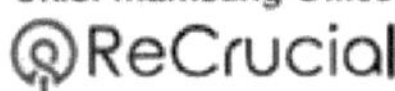

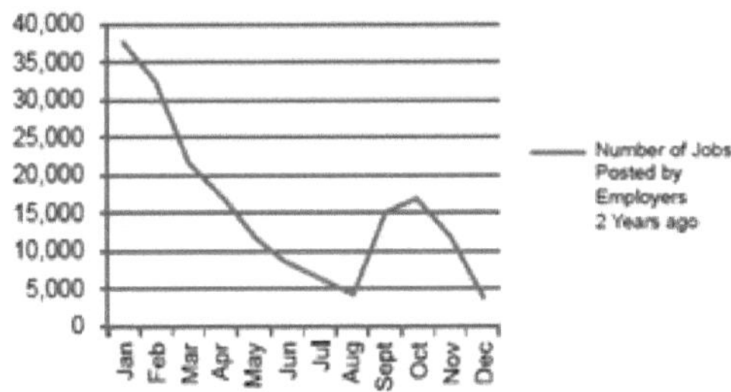

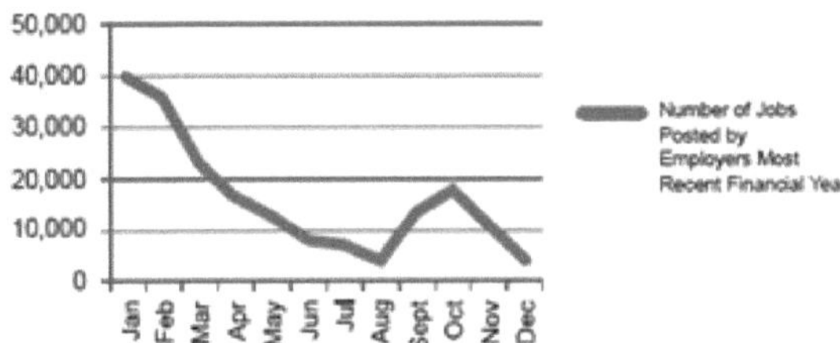

Figure 2.8. Sample CLA+ SRQ (Part 1)

Critical Reading & Evaluation: Document 1

Dear Nord County School Board,

We urge you to consider a ban on serving coffee in the Nord High School cafeteria. This is important for protecting and promoting good health practices in our teenagers. Caffeine is a harmful drug for growing brains and bodies. Many adults struggle to break their own addiction to coffee so allowing the teenagers at Nord High School to begin drinking coffee on a regular basis is a dangerous idea. Teenagers have less self-control and common sense about their own health than their adult counterparts.

There may be parents and researchers who claim that a daily cup or two of coffee for a teenager is not dangerous, but this is a misconception that is easily erased by simply looking at the facts. Teenagers need more sleep than most adults because their minds and bodies are still developing. Caffeine consumption disrupts their sleep cycles and leads to sleepiness during the school day. One study found that teenagers who fell asleep during class consumed 76% more caffeine than those who did not sleep during the school day. Additionally, caffeine consumption can lead to mood swings, impulsiveness, and loss of control. These are issues that many parents deal with. Serving coffee in the Nord High School cafeteria only worsens these problems and threatens the healthy functioning of our high school students.

Ban coffee from Nord High School and help Nord teenagers lead healthier lives.

Sincerely,

Garret Ricci

Garret Ricci
Parent of Nord High School students

Figure 2.9. Sample CLA+ SRQ (Part 2)

Critical Reading & Evaluation: Document 2

PETITION TO KEEP COFFEE IN OUR SCHOOL CAFETERIA

To all Nord High School students:

Due to complaints from some parents, the Nord School Board is now considering a ban on coffee in our high school cafeteria. This would be an injustice to our school community! We have a right to make our own choices about our bodies and our consumption habits. Coffee is a healthy drink in moderation and is an important part of the school day for students who lead busy lives, balancing homework, friends, work, and extra-curricular activities. Just one cup of coffee during the day can help busy students stay alert and focused.

It's time that the Nord School Board treats high school students like the young adults that we are. They must give us the responsibility of making smart choices, and we will rise to the occasion. We must demand respect for our choices and our needs.

Oppose the ban on coffee in the Nord High School cafeteria by signing the petition below. Protect our rights!

Sincerely yours,
Lisa Browning
Nord High School Senior Class President

Figure 2.10. Sample CLA+ SRQ (Part 3)

Critical Reading & Evaluation: Questions

1. Which of the following statements, if true, would most seriously weaken Garret Ricci's claim?

    A. Teenagers who are prone to mood swings and impulsiveness consume caffeine at the same rate as their peers.
    B. Adults who consume a small amount of caffeine daily are able to multitask more efficiently.
    C. Adults who consume caffeine regularly were not necessarily coffee drinkers as teenagers.
    D. Eighty percent of caffeine consumed by teenagers is consumed in the form of soda and other caffeinated non-coffee beverages.

2. Which of the following is a significant flaw in the Garret Ricci's argument?

    A. The author assumes that teenagers have less self-control than adults, without any evidence.
    B. The author claims that sleeping during class is caused by caffeine consumption, while it may be that caffeine consumption is a result of sleepiness.
    C. The author associates sleep and mood with health, without explaining the connection.
    D. The author uses anecdotal evidence from parents and teenagers, rather than a substantial body of research.

3. On which point do Garret Ricci and Lisa Browning most clearly disagree?

    A. the ability of teenagers to make reasonable judgments about their own health
    B. the usefulness of coffee as a replacement for sleep
    C. the effects of coffee on the human brain and body
    D. the prevalence of coffee in a variety of cultural and commercial settings

4. It can be inferred that Lisa Browning would **most likely** agree with which of the following statements?

    A. The School Board should not be allowed to make decisions about anything that affects the daily life of students.
    B. The job of a class president is to protect the rights of students and represent their voices.
    C. Parents who complain about coffee in the cafeteria have a negative view of teenagers.
    D. Every high school student should enjoy the physical and mental benefits of coffee by drinking it daily.

5. Which of the following statements could be used as a counterargument to Garret Ricci's claim?

    A. Coffee needs to be available in high school cafeterias for the teachers and staff members who rely on it.
    B. Because of its bitter taste, most teenagers are unlikely to consume coffee, whether or not it is served in their high school cafeterias.
    C. Teenagers will be exposed to coffee elsewhere, so it is important that they learn to consume it in school, with self-control and moderation.
    D. It is the parents' job, not the school's, to determine whether their teenagers should consume caffeine.

Figure 2.11. CLA+ scoring rubric

cla+ Scoring Rubric	1	2	3	4	5	6
Analysis and Problem Solving Making a logical decision or conclusion (or taking a position) and supporting it by utilizing appropriate information (facts, ideas, computed values, or salient features) from the Document Library	May state or imply a decision/conclusion/ position Provides minimal analysis as support (e.g., briefly addresses only one idea from one document) or analysis is entirely inaccurate, illogical, unreliable, or unconnected to the decision/conclusion/ position	States or implies a decision/conclusion/ position Provides analysis that addresses a few ideas as support, some of which is inaccurate, illogical, unreliable, or unconnected to the decision/conclusion/ position	States or implies a decision/conclusion/position Provides some valid support, b omits or misrepres ents critical information, suggesting only superficial analysis and partial comprehension of the documents May not account for contradictory information (if applicable)	States an explicit decision/conclusion/ position Provides valid support that addresses multiple pieces of relevant and credible information in a manner that demonstrates adequate analysis and comprehension of the documents; some information is omitted May attempt to address contradictory information or alternative decisions/ conclusions/ positions (if applicable)	States an explicit decision/conclusion/ position Provides strong support that addresses much of the relevant and credible information, in a manner that demonstrates very good analysis and comprehension of the documents Refutes contradictory information or alternative decisions/conclusions/ positions (if applicable)	States an explicit decision/conclusion/ position Provides comprehensive support, including nearly all of the relevant and credible information, in a manner that demonstrates outstanding analysis and comprehension of the documents Thoroughly refutes contradictory evidence or alternative decisions/conclusions/ positions (if applicable)
Writing Effectiveness Constructing organized and logically cohesive arguments. Strengthening the writer's position by providing elaboration on facts or ideas (e.g., explaining how evidence bears on the problem, providing examples, and emphasizing especially convincing evidence)	Does not develop convincing arguments; writing may be disorganized and confusing Does not provide elaboration on facts or ideas	Provides limited, invalid, over-stated, or very unclear arguments; may present information in a disorganized fashion or undermine own points Any elaboration on facts or ideas tends to be vague, irrelevant, inaccurate, or unreliable (e.g., based entirely on writer's opinion); sources of information are often unclear	Provides limited or somewhat unclear arguments. Presents relevant information in each response, but that information is not woven into arguments Provides elaboration on facts or ideas a few times, some of which is valid; sources of information are sometimes unclear	Organizes response in a way that makes the writer's arguments and logic of those arguments apparent but not obvious Provides valid elaboration on facts or ideas several times and cites sources of information	Organizes response in a logically cohesive way that makes it fairly easy to follow the writer's arguments Provides valid elaboration on facts or ideas related to each argument and cites sources of information	Organizes response in a logically cohesive way that makes it very easy to follow the writer's arguments Provides valid and comprehensive elaboration on facts or ideas related to each argument and clearly cites sources of information
Writing Mechanics Demonstrating facility with the conventions of standard written English (agreement, tense, capitalization, punctuation, and spelling) and control of the English language, including syntax (sentence structure) and diction (word choice and usage)	Demonstrates minimal control of grammatical conventions with many errors that make the response difficult to read or provides insufficient evidence to judge Writes sentences that are repetitive or incomplete, and some are difficult to understand Uses simple vocabulary, and some vocabulary is used inaccurately or in a way that makes meaning unclear	Demonstrates poor control of grammatical conventions with frequent minor errors and some severe errors Consistently writes sentences with similar structure and length, and some may be difficult to understand Uses simple vocabulary, and some vocabulary may be used inaccurately or in a way that makes meaning unclear	Demonstrates fair control of grammatical conventions with frequent minor errors Writes sentences that read naturally but tend to have similar structure and length Uses vocabulary that communicates ideas adequately but lacks variety	Demonstrates good control of grammatical conventions with few errors Writes well-constructed sentences with some varied structure and length Uses vocabulary that clearly communicates ideas but lacks variety	Demonstrates very good control of grammatical conventions Consistently writes well-constructed sentences with varied structure and length Uses varied and sometimes advanced vocabulary that effectively communicates ideas	Demonstrates outstanding control of grammatical conventions Consistently writes well-constructed complex sentences with varied structure and length Displays adept use of vocabulary that is precise, advanced, and varied

Figure 2.12. Sample CLA+ institutional report

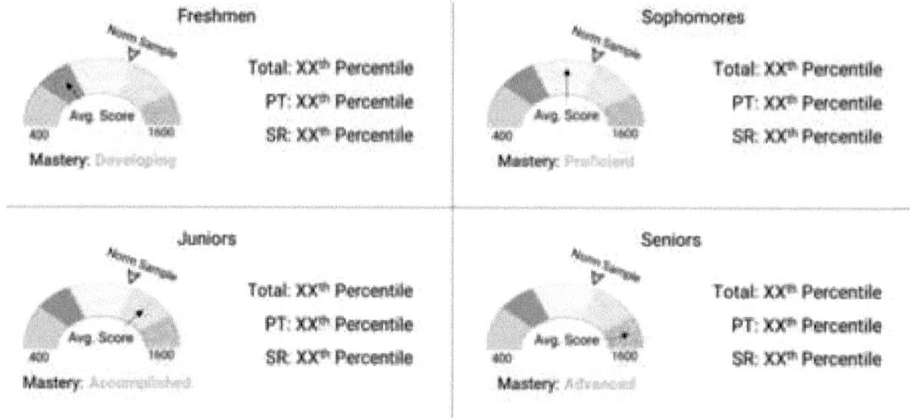

Figure 2.13. Sample CLA+ student report

Username: Student123
Your Institution
Fall 2020 Next Step Report

Total Selected-Response Score: **1050**
Mastery Level: **Accomplished**
Percentile Rank: **92%**

Your CLA+ Scores

	Your Score	Percentile Rank	Institution Average
Overall CLA+ Score	1083	92%	1060
Performance Task Score	1100	95%	1072
Selected-Response Score	1050	84%	1035

Your CLA+ Mastery Level

	Your Mastery	Average Mastery Level at Your Institution
Total CLA+ Mastery Level	Accomplished	Developing

Understanding Your Results

- Your **Total CLA+ Score** is comprised of two components: your Performance Task section score and your Selected-Response Question section score.

- The **Performance Task** section score summarizes your performance on the first part assessment. In the Performance Task section, you were asked to address a real-world issue and recommend a course of action to take in a purposeful written response by making use of information provided in a Document Library.

- The **Selected-Response Question** section score summarizes your performance on the second part of the assessment. In this part of the assessment, you received 25 document-based selected-response questions.

- Your **Mastery Level** describes your level of performance based on your Total CLA+ Score. There are five CLA+ Mastery Levels, shown below:

© 2021, Council for Aid to Education, Inc.   1

References

Arum, R. and J. Roksa (2014), *Aspiring Adults Adrift. Tentative Transitions of College Graduates*, Chicago University Press, Chicago, IL. [3]

Arum, R. and J. Roksa (2011), *Academically Adrift. Limited Learning on College Campuses*, Chicago University Press, Chicago, IL. [2]

Association of American Colleges and Universities (2011), "The LEAP Vision for Learning: Outcomes, Practices, Impact, and Employers' Views", Vol. 26/3, p. 34. [1]

Benjamin, R. (2012), "The Seven Red Herrings About Standardized Assessments in Higher Education", *National Institute for Learning Outcomes Assessment* September, pp. 7-14. [8]

Benjamin, R. (2008a), "The Case for Comparative Institutional Assessment of Higher-Order Thinking Skills", *Change: The Magazine of Higher Learning*, Vol. 40/6, pp. 50-55, https://doi.org/10.3200/chng.40.6.50-55. [6]

Benjamin, R. (2008b), *The Contribution of the Collegiate Learning Assessment to Teaching and Learning*, Council for Aid to Education, New York. [7]

Bok, D. (2009), *Our Underachieving Colleges: A Candid Look at How Much Students Learn and Why They Should Be Learning More*, https://doi.org/10.1111/j.1540-5931.2007.00471.x. [9]

Capital, P. (2016), *2016 Workforce-Skills Preparedness Report*, http://www.payscale.com/data-packages/job-skills. [13]

Crocker, L. and J. Algina (1986), *Introduction to Classical and Modern Test Theory*, Wadsworth Group/Thomson Learning, Belmont, CA. [23]

Cronbach, L. (1951), "Coefficient alpha and the internal structure of tests", *Psychometrika*, Vol. 16/3, pp. 297-334, https://doi.org/10.1007/BF02310555. [24]

Hart Research Associates (2013), "It takes more than a major: Employer priorities for college learning and student success", *Liberal Education*, Vol. 99/2. [14]

Klein, S. et al. (2007), "The collegiate learning assessment: Facts and fantasies", *Evaluation Review*, Vol. 31/5, pp. 415-439, https://doi.org/10.1177/0193841X07303318. [10]

Kolen, M. and R. Brennan (2004), *Test Equating, Scaling, and Linking: Methods and Practices, 2nd Ed.*, Springer, New York. [25]

Liu, O., L. Frankel and K. Roohr (2014), "Assessing Critical Thinking in Higher Education: Current State and Directions for Next-Generation Assessment", *ETS Research Report Series*, Vol. 2014/1, pp. 1-14, https://doi.org/10.1002/ets2.12009. [4]

Montt, G. (2015), "The causes and consequences of field-of-study mismatch: An analysis using PIAAC", *OECD Social, Employment & Migration Working Papers* 167. [12]

National Association of Colleges and Employers (2018), *Are college graduates "career ready"?*, https://www.naceweb.org/career-readiness/competencies/are-college-graduates-career-ready/ (accessed on 19 February 2018). [15]

Powers, S., M. Loring and Z. Henrich (2019), *Essay Machine Marking Automation (EMMA) Research Report*, MZD. [21]

Rios, J. et al. (2020), "Identifying Critical 21st-Century Skills for Workplace Success: A Content Analysis of Job Advertisements", *Educational Researcher*, Vol. 49/2, pp. 80-89, https://doi.org/10.3102/0013189X19890600. [16]

Steedle, J. and S. Elliot (2012), *The efficacy of automated essay scoring for evaluating student responses to complex critical thinking performance tasks*, Council for Aid to Education, New York, NY. [22]

Wagner, T. (2010), *The Global Achievement Gap: Why Even Our Best Schools Don't Teach the New Survival Skills Our Children Need – and What We Can Do about It*, Basic Books, New York, NY. [5]

World Economic Forum (2016), *Global Challenge Insight Report: The Future of Jobs: Employment, Skills and Workforce Strategy for the Fourth Industrial Revolution*, World Economic Forum, http://www3.weforum.org/docs/WEF_Future_of_Jobs.pdf. [17]

Zahner, D. (2014), *CLA+ Standard Setting Study Final Report*, Council for Aid to Education, New York, NY. [20]

Zahner, D. (2013), *Reliability and Validity – CLA+*, Council for Aid to Education, New York, NY. [19]

Zahner, D., L. Ramsaran and D. Zahner (2012), "Comparing alternatives in the prediction of college success", *Annual Meeting of the American Educational Research Association*. [18]

Zinshteyn, M. (2021), "Careers in a Changing Era: How Higher Ed Can Fight the Skills Gap and Prepare Students for a Dynamic World of Work", *Inside Higher Ed.*. [11]

Annex 2.A. Linear equating procedure

CAE uses linear equating to transform the scores to the reporting scale. The following technical information is obtained from Kolen and Brennan (2004[25]).

In linear equating, scores that are equal distance from their means in standard deviation units are set to be equal. Linear equating can be viewed as allowing for the scale units, as well as the means, of the two forms to differ.

Define $\mu(X)$ as the mean on Form X and $\mu(Y)$ as the mean on Form Y for a population of examinees.

Define $\sigma(X)$ as the standard deviation of Form X and $\sigma(Y)$ as the standard deviation of Form Y.

The linear conversion is defined by setting standardised deviation scores (z-scores) on the two forms to be equal such that:

$$\frac{x - \mu(X)}{\sigma(X)} = \frac{y - \mu(Y)}{\sigma(Y)}$$

One way to express the linear equation for converting observed scores on Form X to the scale of Form Y is the following:

$$ly(x) = y = \frac{\sigma(Y)}{\sigma(X)} x + \left[\mu(Y) - \frac{\sigma(Y)}{\sigma(X)} \mu(X) \right]$$

The expression is a linear equation of the form slope (x) + intercept with:

$$slope = \frac{\sigma(Y)}{\sigma(X)}, \text{ and } intercept = \mu(Y) - \frac{\sigma(Y)}{\sigma(X)} \mu(X)$$

The CLA+ equating procedures are described below.

The SRQ raw subscores (SQR, CRE, CA) undergo a scaling process to correct for different levels of difficulty of the subscore sections. The scaled mean and standard deviation for each subscore are approximately 500 and 100, respectively. The SRQ total score is computed by taking a weighted average of the SRQ subscores, with weights corresponding to the number of items of each subscore section. The SRQ total score then undergoes a linear transformation to equate it to the scores obtained by our norm population of college freshmen on the original set of SRQs. This process ensures that SRQ scores can be compared with one another regardless of which SRQ set was administered or in which year the test was taken.

The PT raw subscores are summed to produce a single raw PT total score. The raw PT total score undergoes a linear transformation to equate it to the scores obtained by our norm population of college freshmen on the original set of PTs. This ensures that PT scores can be compared with one another regardless of which PT was administered or in which year the test was taken. The CLA+ total scale score is computed by averaging the SRQ and PT scale scores. All three scale scores (SRQ, PT, total) range from 400 to 1 600, the normal SAT Math and Critical Reading score scale.

Because the CLA+ is administered in different languages, separate scalings are performed based on language of administration. For example, the linear transformations applied for the Spanish tests administered in Mexico and Chile were the same for a given SRQ set or PT, as were the linear transformations applied for the English tests administered in the US and the UK.

3 CLA+ International

Doris Zahner, Council for Aid to Education (United States)

Kelly Rotholz, Council for Aid to Education (United States)

This chapter explores the Memorandum of Understanding executed by the Council for Aid to Education (CAE) and the OECD in order for both organisations to continue collaborating on assessing higher education students' generic skills.

Introduction

Using the lessons learnt from the Assessment of Higher Education Learning Outcomes (AHELO) feasibility study (Dias and Amaral, 2014[1]; Ewell, 2012[2]; Lalancette, 2013[3]; Tremblay, 2013[4]; Wolf and Zahner, 2016[5]; Wolf, Zahner and Benjamin, 2015[6]), the Council for Aid to Education (CAE) and the OECD executed a Memorandum of Understanding (MOU), which allowed the two organisations to continue collaborating on assessing higher education students' generic skills. The intent of the MOU was for the collaboration between the OECD Directorate for Education and Skills and CAE to enable tertiary education institutions and jurisdictions to develop and implement innovative performance-based assessments to measure the generic skills of higher education students (Table 3.1). The collaboration included activities such as:

- marketing and recruiting
- translations and adaptations of CLA+
- test administration
- scoring training
- scoring and reporting
- international benchmarking
- publications and presentations.

Table 3.1. Responsibilities and contributions for the project for CAE and the OECD as outlined in the MOU

Contribution	Organisation	Notes
Develop test instruments in collaboration with participating jurisdictions and the OECD	CAE	Completed translation and adaptation of three forms of CLA+ International
Administer tests over secure Internet platforms	CAE	Completed administration of CLA+ International to participating institutions in the UK, Mexico, Chile and Finland
Train national scorers recruited by each entity that implements the test	CAE	Completed scorer training for the UK, Mexico, Chile and Finland
Compile scores and analyses and prepare reports (and other research if entities request it) at the individual student and institutional levels in collaboration with the OECD	CAE	Completed score reports for the UK, Mexico, Chile and Finland
Provide standard setting for country-based criterion-referenced mastery levels for individual student badges if countries request it	CAE	Participating institutions decided to use CLA+ levels of mastery for their badges
Develop a transparent system of cost-sharing among participating jurisdictions	CAE	This has occurred in Latin America where individual institutions are being recruited
Support jurisdiction participation in the Programme	OECD	Possibly interested OECD member countries and partners have been approached
Advise on possible measures to optimise the comparability of the assessment results	OECD	In process
Conduct research on assessment results provided by jurisdictions participating in the Programme at their option	OECD	In process
Publish OECD reports on the OECD's analysis of the test data results, findings and recommendations	OECD	In process

Convene jurisdictions participating in the Programme and others to share knowledge and experiences in improving learning outcomes	OECD	CLA+ International meetings in September 2016 (Paris), February 2017 (Cambridge, UK), September 2018 (Paris), 30 March 2020 (Virtual) February 2021 (Virtual)
Engage in a long-term process of development and improvement of the assessment instruments in accordance with the needs and aspirations of participating jurisdictions	OECD	In process

The MOU stipulated that for its execution no financial transactions were supposed to happen between CAE and the OECD. Financial arrangements were bilaterally concluded between the participating jurisdictions and CAE without any involvement of the OECD. The limited expenses at the OECD, mainly to compensate for the time spent by staff, were covered by grants from countries from the AHELO feasibility study.

CLA+ International recruitment

Two approaches were used for recruiting participants in CLA+ international: top-down and bottom-up. For the top-down strategy, CAE collaborated with the OECD, as outlined in the MOU for ministry-level participation. The OECD approached representatives from possibly interested OECD member countries and partners for jurisdiction participation. The OECD also hosted a series of conferences which convened all participants in the initiative as well as interested jurisdictions. A total of six conferences were convened (Table 3.2).

Table 3.2. CLA+ International Global Conferences

Conference Title	Date	Location
OECD/CAE International Programme for Tertiary Assessment	20 January 2016	OECD Conference Centre
Inaugural Meeting of the CAE-OECD International Programme for Tertiary Assessment	3 – 5 October 2016	OECD Conference Centre
Using Assessments for Evidence-Based Policy Decisions	2 – 3 February 2017	Cambridge, UK
OECD/CLA+ International Initiative: Using Assessment for Evidence-Based Policy Decisions	14 September 2018	OECD Conference Centre
OECD/CLA+ International Initiative: Assessing Generic Skills in Tertiary Education – Progress Report	30 March 2020	Virtual
First results of the Finnish CLA+ International study	17 February 2021	Virtual

For the bottom-up strategy, CAE engaged CAE Fellows to recruit individual institutions or regional organisations and consortia. The CAE Fellows assist CAE by introducing and supporting CLA+ for their regions. CAE Fellows are selected based on their expertise in the fields of education and assessment. Their responsibilities include recruitment of institutions, presenting at regional conferences, and reporting regional updates during project meetings. CAE staff and leadership are also an integral part of recruiting and presentations (Table 3.3).

Table 3.3. CLA+ International Regional Conferences

Presentation Title	Date	Conference/Location
A Case Study of an International Performance-Based Assessment of Critical Thinking Skills	4 April 2014	AERA Philadelphia, PA
International Testing of a Performance-Based Assessment	12 April 2016	AERA Washington, DC
International Assessment of Student Learning Outcomes Initiative:	17 October 2016	Post-secondary Education Quality Assessment Board, Toronto, Canada
An Application of Pasteur's Quadrant	26 September 2017	Lima, Peru
CLA+ International, OECE/CAE Initiatives	13 April 2018	AERA, New York, NY
International Testing of a Performance-Based Assessment in Higher Education	12 October 2018	Post-secondary Education Quality Assessment Board, Toronto, Canada
International Assessment of Generic Skills	15 May 2019	CINDA, Santiago, Chile
Measuring Generic Skills in an International Context	3 June 2021	INQAAHE Virtual
Measurement of Learning Outcomes Achievement	7 – 8 October 2021	INQAAHE Barcelona, Spain

CLA+ International collaborators

The first collaboration, starting in 2013, was between CAE and the Italian National Agency for the Evaluation of Universities and Research Institutes (ANVUR). ANVUR's decision to participate in CLA+ International was a direct result of AHELO. Italy participated only in the engineering strand of the feasibility study and was interested in assessing the generic skills of their students.

This was followed by student learning gain studies with the University of Guadalajara (23 campuses), a consortium of four "post-1992" (Hannah, 1996[7]) institutions and a public university in the United Kingdom, several individual institutions across Chile, and 18 universities and universities of applied sciences in a study sponsored by the Ministry of Culture and Education of Finland. Most recently, a large, private university system in Mexico with six campuses joined the initiative with the intention of assessing over 2 200 students and focusing on measuring student learning gains both within individual campuses and fields of study, as well as across the entire system.

The purposes of individual countries and institutions participating in CLA+ International varies from needing individual students assessed in order to meet university graduation requirements to understanding the level and quality of students' generic skills within the higher education system. Individual chapters in Part III of this manuscript provide detailed information on each participating country or region.

Prior studies of CLA+ International have been published about individual countries or institutions (Shek et al., 2016[8]; Zahner and Ciolfi, 2018[9]; Zahner and Kostoris, 2016[10]; Zahner et al., 2020[11]; Zlatkin-Troitschanskaia et al., 2018[12]). However, this is the first research study aggregating all CLA+ International data and reporting results within and across countries/regions. Results from individual countries, regions, and institutions can be found in Part III of this manuscript. Perspective and potential future projects using CLA+ International can be found in Part IV.

CLA+ International assessment development and administration

Since CLA+ was an existing valid and reliable instrument (Zahner, 2013[13]): Chapter 3) and had already been developed for students in the United States, no new versions of the assessment were made for CLA+

International. Rather, Performance Tasks (PTs) and Selected-Response Questions (SRQs) were selected by a committee of CAE measurement scientists and international higher education educators and administrators to be translated, adapted and administered internationally.

Performance Task (PT) and Selected-Response Question (SRQ) selection

Three PTs and three sets of SRQs were selected for international use. These PTs and SRQs were chosen because the topics were relevant and relatable across multiple cultures and contexts, and performed well operationally when used in the United States. Ministries or large consortiums who participated in CLA+ International had the opportunity to select the PT and sets of SRQs to be used for their international participation. CAE presented the three options to them and recommended a single set if the group was interested in internationally comparable results. All consortiums opted to use the set that allowed for internationally comparable data.

In the case of Latin America, CAE worked with individual institutions directly to deliver CLA+ International. In this circumstance, CAE selected the items to be used and oversaw the process of translation and adaptation.

Translation and adaptation

The translation and adaptation process was led by CAE and its translation partner cApStAn in collaboration with country team members, following industry best practices (Geisinger, 1994[14]; Hambleton and Li, 2005[15]). The translation and adaptation of a performance assessment is a more complex process than simple word-for-word replacement from one language to another. At CAE, translation and adaptation experts ensure that the translated and adapted assessments are consistent with the original version in the source language and, just as importantly, will be interpreted by students in their native language as intended. CAE's experts confirm that the assessment topics possess the same authenticity, context and meaning for the target student population as they do for the original student population for which the tasks were initially developed. CAE uses an internationally accepted five-step translation process in compliance with International Translation Committee (ITC) guidelines, the same guidelines used for the localisation process of major international studies such as the Programme for International Student Assessment (PISA), Trends in International Mathematics and Science Study (TIMMS), Progress in International Reading Literacy Study (PIRLS), Programme for the International Assessment of Adult Competencies (PIAAC), and AHELO. This process includes:

1. Translatability review: Source material is reviewed to confirm that the text will adapt well into member languages and cultures. Particular attention is paid to disambiguation of source, respecting key correspondences between stimuli and questions, and determining what should or should not be adapted to local context.

2. Double translation and reconciliation: Two translators independently review the text and provide translations. The translations are reconciled and sent to country teams for review.

3. Member Team Review: Members are provided with an opportunity to review the translated work and provide input and recommendations.

4. Focused Verification: The verification process ensures that the translated and adapted assessment is consistent with the context and intent of the original assessment.

5. Cognitive Labs, as appropriate: With CAE's guidance, members conduct cognitive labs with a small sample of student participants to ensure that the translated and adapted assessment is clear and consistent with the context and intent of the original assessment.

CAE followed this process for translation and adaptation for use in Italy, Finland and Mexico. For the first translation and adaptation of the CLA+ International in Spanish for Spanish-language countries in addition to Mexico, a modified adaptation process was used given the short timeline for this first administration.

cApStAn reviewed the translation that was completed for the Mexican Spanish test content and made adaptation recommendations that are regionally appropriate for use in Chile. These recommendations were reviewed and approved by the measurement science team at CAE.

Cognitive labs

Following best practices in translating and adapting assessments (Geisinger, 1994[14]; Hambleton and Li, 2005[15]), cognitive labs (Leighton, 2017[16]; Zucker, Sassman and Case, 2004[17]) were recommended to improve and verify the quality of translated and adapted assessments. Additionally, the cognitive labs were used to confirm that the cognitive processes and reasoning elicited by the translated and adapted CLA+ International assessment were consistent with and aligned to the constructs measured by CLA+. More specifically, the cognitive labs were intended to ensure that the translation and adaptation of CLA+ from English into additional languages: 1) did not alter the constructs measured; 2) was interpreted by the participants in the ways originally intended; and 3) was not more difficult for the country's participants to read and understand than it would have been had the tasks been originally written in the participant's native language.

In-country project staff assigned an interviewer to conduct the cognitive labs with voluntary participants using the printed version of the assessment. If deemed necessary, a revised version of each translated and adapted assessment was prepared based on information taken from the cognitive labs.

The CLA+ International cognitive labs were carried out in three stages:

1. Training, in which the interviewer explained the purpose of the cognitive lab and trained participants to think aloud with small tasks.
2. Think-aloud, in which participants provided concurrent verbal reports of their thinking as they engaged in the task. During the think-aloud, the interviewer took notes about reasoning processes as well as potential translation and/or adaptation issues.
3. Follow-up interview, in which the interviewer asked scripted questions with the intent of eliciting additional information on the clarity of the translation and adaptation of the assessment, translation and adaptation issues and participants' strategies for coming up with their answer or solution.

In addition to the interviewer's note-taking, the cognitive lab for each participant was audio recorded. Project staff working in teams listened to the recordings to identify potential unintended challenges that may have resulted from the translation and adaptation. Based on the analysis of the participants' think-aloud protocols and responses to follow-up questions, the project staff identified ways in which the translation and adaptation of the assessment needed improvement. These findings were shared with CAE, and all necessary adjustments and edits were implemented.

Test administration and associated activities

Following the translation and adaptation, and cognitive lab processes, CAE worked with all participating institutions to finalise the assessment prior to test administration. CAE provided guidance to participating members on improving student recruitment efforts, proctor training and test day administration preparations. CAE also provided technical support before, during and after test administration.

Important milestones and activities

- CAE's secure, scalable online test platform was translated into the appropriate language.
- All test materials and scoring rubrics were translated into the appropriate language.
- Administrative instructions and guides were provided to member teams.
- Cognitive labs were performed with CAE oversight.

- Exemplary best practices, communications materials, training, and logistics guidance were provided.
- Student recruitment was carried out with CAE support.
- Test was administered using a secure online testing platform.
- Training of Lead Scorers was carried out by CAE.
- Member scorers were scored using CAE's secure online scoring platform.
- CAE review and analysis of data was followed by preparation of member reports.
- Individual student reports and secure badges/certificates were prepared and distributed by CAE and/or the member.

Administration

CLA+ International is administered through an Internet-based testing platform. Test-takers enter the exam through a secure browser that locks down unnecessary computer functions and distributes a 60-minute PT and a 30-minute, 25-item SRQ section to each student.

- The PT asks students to craft a written response to an open-ended question about a hypothetical but realistic scenario using a library of relevant documents (Document Library).
- The SRQs ask students to choose the best response to questions in the categories of Scientific and Quantitative Literacy, Critical Reading and Evaluation, and Critiquing an Argument.

All testing sessions require a proctor to authorise students into the interface and manage the testing environment. The assessment is designed to be completed in approximately 90 minutes. At the beginning of the testing session, there is an optional tutorial that students can scroll through or bypass if they so choose. The assessment requires standardised administration to ensure consistent testing conditions for all students. CAE provides training materials for Institutional Administrators and Proctors.

Scoring process

For CLA+ International, all student responses were double-scored by human scorers fluent in the native language of the student. The training for the scoring process was directed by the CAE Measurement Science team and started with a group training for all Lead Scorers from all participating members/institutions. Trainings were most often conducted in-country as a two-day in-person training.

CAE recommended appointing a Lead Scorer and an Assistant Lead (or Co-lead) Scorer to attend this training to better distribute the information and responsibilities that followed. In-person training was conducted for participants in the UK, Italy, Mexico, and Finland. Colleagues in Mexico opted for CAE to oversee the scoring process for their participation. The training occurred once per test administration. This training was conducted in English, utilising American student exemplary responses. All scoring took place and was monitored on CAE's platform. Data analyses and reporting then followed. The Lead Scorer and Assistant Lead Scorer underwent rigorous training to become part of the CLA+ International scorer team.

The scoring training for the PTs included:

- an orientation to the prompts and scoring rubrics/guides
- repeated practice grading a wide range of student responses
- extensive feedback and discussion after scoring each response.

Following this training, CAE team members acted as a resource for the Lead Scorer and Assistant Lead Scorer, who were responsible for recruiting and training the member's team of scorers. This ensured quality and consistency both within and across countries. The scorers were recruited from participating institutions according to their ability to judge university student generic skills. Institutions often appointed professors, institutional research fellows, post-doctoral associates or doctoral students to score the student responses. Scorers were often remunerated by the participating member universities at their discretion. CAE scorers for the Spanish student responses were remunerated at the same rate as the scorers who worked on the American English student responses.

All scoring took place and was monitored on CAE's secure platform. Trained scorers received a randomised selection of anonymised student responses within the relevant language and entered their score results directly into CAE's Internet-based scoring platform. The scorers did not know the institution to which each student belonged. CAE's system automatically monitored human scorer calibration and inter-rater reliability and notified the Lead Scorers of any scorers who were not appropriately calibrated.

A calibration verification system was developed to improve and streamline scoring. Calibration of scorers through the system required scorers to score previously scored results, or "Verification Papers", when they first start scoring, as well as throughout the scoring window. The system periodically presented Verification Papers to scorers in lieu of student responses though they were not flagged to the scorers as such. The system did not indicate when a scorer had successfully scored a Verification Paper but if the scorer failed to accurately score a series of Verification Papers, the scorer was removed from scoring and had to participate in a remediation process. At this point, scorers were either further coached or removed from scoring.

Scoring and equating

In order to provide students with scale scores, CAE converted the raw scores to scale scores using a procedure called equating. The purpose of equating is to have a common scale of measurement. Equating permits comparisons of student groups across time, regardless of the sets of items that were administered. The equating procedure that CAE used was linear transformation. The result was a set of equating constants that convert the raw scores to scale scores for a PT or a given set of SRQs. Details of the procedure are described in the Appendix of Chapter 3. The same steps are followed for the domestic and international student groups.

Reporting

Each country or association received its own set of reports and data files, including a report showing how, overall, its participating universities performed as a group. Additionally, individual university reports were prepared for each participating university. CAE provided all members with comparative information from CAE's domestic national data from the United States. Finally, CAE prepared individual student reports for all participating students and issued badges for those whose scores merited a proficient, accomplished, or advanced score.

Part II of this manuscript offers detailed insight into the combined CLA+ International data set.

References

Blömeke, S. (ed.) (2013), "OECD Assessment of Higher Education Learning Outcomes (AHELO): Rationale, challenges and initial insights from the feasibility study", *Modeling and measuring and initial insights from the feasibility study*, pp. 113-126.　[4]

Dias, D. and A. Amaral (2014), "Assessment of Higher Education Learning Outcomes (AHELO): An OECD Feasibility Study", pp. 66-87, https://doi.org/10.1057/9781137374639_5.　[1]

Ewell, P. (2012), "A World of Assessment: OECD's AHELO Initiative", *Change: The Magazine of Higher Learning*, Vol. 44/5, pp. 35-42, https://doi.org/10.1080/00091383.2012.706515.　[2]

Frisby, C. and C. Reynolds (eds.) (2005), *Translation and Adaptation Issues and Methods for Educational and Psychological Tests*, John Wiley and Sons, Hoboken, NJ.　[15]

Geisinger, K. (1994), "Cross-Cultural Normative Assessment: Translation and Adaptation Issues Influencing the Normative Interpretation of Assessment Instruments", *Psychological Assessment*, Vol. 6/4, p. 304, https://doi.org/10.1037/1040-3590.6.4.304.　[14]

Hannah, S. (1996), "The higher education act of 1992: Skills, constraints, and the politics of higher education", *Journal of Higher Education*, Vol. 67/5, pp. 498-527, https://doi.org/10.1080/00221546.1996.11780274.　[7]

Lalancette, D. (2013), *OECD assessment of higher education learning outcomes (AHELO): Rationale, challenges and initial insights from the feasibility study*, McGill-Queen's University Press, Montreal, https://doi.org/10.1007/978-94-6091-867-4.　[3]

Leighton, J. (2017), *Using Think-Aloud Interviews and Cognitive Labs in Educational Research*, Oxford University Press, Oxford, https://doi.org/10.1093/acprof:oso/9780199372904.001.0001.　[16]

Rosen, Y., S. Derrara and M. Mosharraf (eds.) (2016), *Mitigation of Test Bias in International, Cross-National Assessments of Higher-Order Thinking Skills*, IGI Global, Hershey, PA, https://doi.org/10.4018/978-1-4666-9441-5.ch018.　[5]

Shek, D. et al. (2016), "Assessing learning gains of university students in Hong Kong adopting the Collegiate Learning Assessment Plus (CLA+)", *International Journal on Disability and Human Development*, Vol. 15/3, p. 331, https://doi.org/10.1515/ijdhd-2015-6001.　[8]

Wolf, R., D. Zahner and R. Benjamin (2015), "Methodological challenges in international comparative post-secondary assessment programs: lessons learned and the road ahead", *Studies in Higher Education*, Vol. 40/3, pp. 471-481, https://doi.org/10.1080/03075079.2015.1004239.　[6]

Zahner, D. (2013), *Reliability and Validity – CLA+*, Council for Aid to Education, New York, NY.　[13]

Zahner, D. and A. Ciolfi (2018), "International Comparison of a Performance-Based Assessment in Higher Education", in Olga Zlatkin-Troitschanskaia et al. (eds.), *Assessment of Learning Outcomes in Higher Education: Cross-National Comparisons and Perspectives*, Springer, New York, https://doi.org/10.1007/978-3-319-74338-7_11.　[9]

Zahner, D. and F. Kostoris (2016), *International Testing of a Performance-Based Assessment in Higher Education*, Council for Aid to Education, Washington, DC.　[10]

Zahner, D. et al. (2020), "Measuring the generic skills of higher education students and graduates: Implementation of CLA+ international", in *Assessing undergraduate learning in psychology: Strategies for measuring and improving student performance*, https://doi.org/10.1037/0000183-015. [11]

Zlatkin-Troitschanskaia, O. et al. (2018), "Adapting and Validating the Collegiate Learning Assessment to Measure Generic Academic Skills of Students in Germany: Implications for International Assessment Studies in Higher Education", Springer, Cham, https://doi.org/10.1007/978-3-319-74338-7_12. [12]

Zucker, S., C. Sassman and B. Case (2004), *Cognitive Labs*, Harcourt Assessment, San Antonio, TX. [17]

4 Ensuring cross-cultural reliability and validity

Doris Zahner, Council for Aid to Education (United States)

Katri Kleemola, University of Helsinki (Finland)

Heidi Hyytinen, University of Helsinki (Finland)

Jani Ursin, University of Jyväskylä (Finland)

Olivia Cortellini, Council for Aid to Education (United States)

The purpose of this chapter is to present a reliability and validity case study investigating the scoring of the Collegiate Learning Assessment (CLA+) of higher education students in Finland as well as the United States. This study contributes to the overall literature on establishing equivalency for an international assessment of students' critical thinking and written communication skills. Two prior studies, similar in nature, both found that results from a translated and adapted performance-based assessment are comparable (Zahner and Steedle, 2014[1]; Zahner and Ciolfi, 2018[2]). This chapter presents a third case using CLA+ across two languages and cultures.

Introduction

One of the main concerns surrounding an international assessment is the reliability and validity of the process, particularly because the translation and adaptation of the assessment is especially challenging (Geisinger, 1994[3]; Hambleton, 2004[4]; Wolf, Zahner and Benjamin, 2015[5]; Zlatkin-Troitschanskaia, Shavelson and Kuhn, 2015[6]). Although international assessments such as the Organisation for Economic and Co-operation Development's (OECD) own Programme for International Student Assessment (PISA) and Programme for the International Assessment of Adult Competencies (PIAAC) are well-established and widely adopted, international assessments in higher education are especially challenging because differences across countries (e.g., educational systems, level of autonomy of higher education institution, socio-economic status) increase the complexity of testing (Blömeke et al., 2013[7]). This becomes even more challenging when using performance-based assessments, which require higher education students to generate a unique response as opposed to selecting one from a set of options.

However, this global research collaboration has created an opportunity to investigate cross-cultural comparisons of a performance-based assessment of generic skills. One such opportunity is through the translation and adaptation of assessments into students' native languages to be administered and scored across countries. Due to differences in culture, language, and other demographics, one important study is to examine the reliability of such translations and adaptations, particularly for a performance-based assessment that includes writing. In order to draw valid score inferences, it is assumed that individuals who earn the same observed score on these instruments have the same standing on the construct regardless of the language in which they were assessed. The evaluation of several criteria could aid in meeting the assumption:

1. The construct measured exists across nations.
2. The construct is measured in the same manner across nations.
3. Items that are believed to be equivalent across nations are linguistically and statistically equivalent.
4. Similar scores across different culturally adapted versions of the assessment reflect similar degrees of proficiency.

The purpose of this chapter is to present a reliability and validity case study investigating the scoring of the Collegiate Learning Assessment (CLA+) of higher education students in Finland as well as the United States. This study contributes to the overall literature on establishing equivalency for an international assessment of students' critical thinking and written communication skills. Two prior studies, similar in nature, both found that results from a translated and adapted performance-based assessment are comparable (Zahner and Steedle, 2014[1]; Zahner and Ciolfi, 2018[2]). This chapter presents a third case using CLA+ across two languages and cultures.

Theoretical background

Performance tasks and scoring

In a Performance Task (PT), students are asked to generate their own answers to questions as the evidence of skill attainment (Hyytinen and Toom, 2019[8]; Shavelson, 2010[9]). PTs are typically based on the criterion-sampling approach (Hyytinen and Toom, 2019[8]; McClelland, 1973[10]; Shavelson, 2010[9]; Shavelson, Zlatkin-Troitschanskaia and Mariño, 2018[11]). In that sense, their aim is to elicit what students know and can do (McClelland, 1973[10]; Shavelson, 2010[9]; Zlatkin-Troitschanskaia et al., 2019[12]). That is, PTs engage students in applying their skills in genuine or "authentic" contexts, not simply memorising a body of factual knowledge or recognising the correct answer from a list of options. A PT, with its open-ended questions, requires the integration of several skills, for example, analysing, evaluating, and synthesising information and justifying conclusions by utilising the available evidence (Hyytinen et al., 2015[13]; Shavelson, 2010[9]).

Recently, several challenges relating to the use, reliability, and interpretation of PTs have been reported (Attali, 2014[14]; Shavelson, Zlatkin-Troitschanskaia and Mariño, 2018[11]; Zlatkin-Troitschanskaia et al., 2019[12]). Answering a PT takes time and effort from students. Thus, relatively few constructs can be observed and assessed within one PT compared to multiple-choice tests (Zlatkin-Troitschanskaia et al., 2019[12]). Another challenge relates to scoring. The way in which students' responses are scored plays a crucial role in assessment validity (Solano-Flores, 2012[15]). The scoring criteria of PT responses need to be developed and defined so that they are in line with the construct measured (Zlatkin-Troitschanskaia et al., 2019[12]). Moreover, students' written responses are typically scored by using human evaluation. Therefore, it has been suggested that the scoring of PTs is open to bias (Hyytinen et al., 2015[13]; Popham, 2003[16]).

In scoring, the scorers analyse the quality of the response based on a scoring rubric that describes the characteristics of typical features at each score level. It has been assumed that it is very difficult for scorers to converge on a single scoring standard (Attali, 2014[14]; Braun et al., 2020[17]). Disagreements about the quality of the response across the scorers result in inconsistencies in scoring. However, most of the inconsistencies stem from incorrect interpretation of the scoring rubric (Borowiec and Castle, 2019[18]). Extensive scorer training and rubric development via cognitive interviews have been proposed as solutions for ensuring consistent scoring (Borowiec and Castle, 2019[18]; Shavelson, Baxter and Gao, 1993[19]); see also Zlatkin-Troitschanskaia et al (2019[12]). Consequently, the use of PTs is considered time-consuming and expensive, as a large amount of time and effort is needed to train scorers and to score the responses consistently (Attali, 2014[14]; Braun, 2019[20]).

Cross-cultural challenges in PT scoring

Cross-cultural assessments may have challenges due to cultural and linguistic differences or technical and methodological issues (Hambleton, 2004[4]; Solano-Flores, 2012[15]). This case study focuses on cross-cultural challenges in the scoring of PTs. To our knowledge, cross-cultural scoring presents two types of possible challenges. First, the scoring rubric may not meet the conventions of the second culture, in this case Finnish. Second, scorers may interpret responses and the scoring rubric in a different way than originally intended due to cultural differences (Braun et al., 2020[17]). For instance, in Finland there is no substantive assessment culture: there are hardly any high-stakes assessments in schools or higher education institutions (e.g., (Sahlberg, 2011[21])), and therefore, scorers may have limited experience with such evaluation.

Furthermore, Finnish is inherently different from English, which is the original language of the present assessment. Finnish belongs to the Finno-Ugric language group, distinct from English and Indo-European languages. This means the languages are structurally very different. It also seems that linguistic conventions are different between the two languages. For instance, it has been found that Finnish has different rhetoric practices compared to English (Mauranen, 1993[22]). These differences between languages may influence how scorers from each country interpret responses and scoring principles.

It has been noted that often in cross-cultural assessments, the same individuals do not establish the content to be assessed, write and develop the task, create the scoring rubric, and score students' answers. Therefore, it is important that there is a shared understanding of the elements of the assessment among different contributors in order to make sure that the constructs are measured and scored in the same manner across cultures (Solano-Flores, 2012[15]).

Method

This case study stems from a national project that investigated the level of Finnish undergraduate students' generic skills, what factors are connected with the level of generic skills, and to what extent these skills develop during higher education studies (Ursin et al., 2015[23]) (Chapter X). The participants were students at the initial and final stages of their undergraduate degree programmes. During the 2019 -2020 academic year, 2 402 students from 18 participating Finnish institutions completed a translated and culturally adapted version of the CLA+ that included a PT and a set of 25 selected-response questions (SRQs). This case study investigates a subset of the students' PT responses.

CLA+

As described in detail in Chapter 2, CLA+ is a performance-based assessment of analytic reasoning and evaluation, problem solving, and written communication skills. It consists of two sections: a PT, which requires students to generate a written response to a given scenario, and SRQs. Students have 60 minutes to complete the PT and 30 minutes for the SRQs.

United States context

In the United States, most participating institutions of higher education have traditionally used CLA+ for value-added purposes. To this end, they assess a sample of entering first-year students typically during the fall semester and compare those students to a sample of exiting fourth-year students typically assessed during the spring semester. The demographic characteristics of the student population in the USA are presented in Table 4.1.

Table 4.1. Demographics of U.S. CLA+ students

Gender	55% Female	40.8% Male	4.2% Decline to state	
Race/Ethnicity	52.7% White	13.1% Latinx	12.5% Black	10.9% Asian
Primary language	83.1% English			
Highest parental education	23.4% HS or less	23.3% Some college	52.7% Higher education degree	

Note: Only the most common race/ethnicity groups are reported. Other groups (including "decline to state") represent approximately 11% of the student population.

Finnish context

The main feature of evaluation in Finnish higher education is that it is enhancement-oriented so that the focus is on providing support and information to further enhance the quality of the programmes and institutions. Consequently, the evaluation of Finnish higher education favours more formative ways of evaluation as opposed to summative evaluation focusing on the achievement of specified targets (Ursin, 2020[24]). Hence, the use of standardised tests, such as CLA+, is not typical in Finnish higher education institutions, and this case study was the first of this calibre to utilise a standardised test to investigate generic skills of Finnish undergraduate students. Nonetheless, similar to the United States, the 18 participating higher education institutions from Finland tested entering first-year students typically in the fall semester and exiting third-year students typically during the spring semester. The Finnish sample consisted of 2 402 students (1 538 entering and 864 exiting students) from the 2019-2020 academic year (Table 4.2).

Table 4.2. Demographics of Finland CLA+ students

Gender	48% Female	49% Male	3% Decline to state
Primary language	93% Finnish	4% Swedish	3% Other
Highest parental education	39% HS or less	9% Vocational	52% Higher education degree
Gender	48% Female	49% Male	3% Decline to state

PTs

For the PT, students are given an engaging, real-world scenario along with a set of documents such as research articles, newspaper and magazine articles, maps, graphs, and opinion pieces pertaining to the scenario. They are asked to make a decision or recommendation after analysing these documents and to write a response justifying their decision/recommendation by providing reasons and evidence both for their argument and against the opposing argument(s). There is no one correct answer for any PT. Rather, students are scored on how well they support and justify their decision with the information provided in the documents. No prior knowledge of any particular domain is necessary to do well, nor is there an interaction between the topic of the PT and the students' field of study (Steedle and Bradley, 2012[25]).

The CLA+ scoring rubric (Chapter 2) for the PT has three subscores: Analysis and Problem Solving (APS), Writing Effectiveness (WE), and Writing Mechanics (WM).

The APS subscore measures students' ability to interpret, analyse, and evaluate the quality of the information that is provided in the document library. This entails identifying information that is relevant to a problem, highlighting connected and conflicting information, detecting flaws in logic and questionable assumptions, and explaining why information is credible, unreliable, or limited. It also evaluates how well students consider and weigh information from discrete sources to make decisions, draw conclusions, or propose a course of action that logically follows from valid arguments, evidence, and examples. Students are also expected to consider the implications of their decisions and suggest additional research when appropriate.

The WE subscore evaluates how well students construct an organised and logically cohesive argument by providing elaboration on facts or ideas. For example, students can explain how evidence bears on the problem by providing examples from the documents and emphasising especially convincing evidence.

The WM subscore measures how well students follow the grammatical and writing conventions of the native language. This includes factors such as vocabulary, diction, punctuation, transitions, spelling, and phrasing.

Each student receives a raw score from 1-6 on each of the subscores, so, in this study, student total scores ranged from 3-18. If a student failed to respond to the task or gave a response that was off topic, a score of 0 (the equivalent of N/A) was given for all three subscores, and these student responses were eliminated from any subsequent analyses.

The rubric was also translated from English into Finnish. The scoring rubric was originally developed to be specific to each PT (Klein et al., 2007[26]; Shavelson, 2008[27]). However, this method of using unique rubrics for individual tasks created an issue with the standardisation, and thus validity, of the assessment. In 2008, a standardised version of the scoring rubric was introduced to address this threat to validity. The standardised version was designed to measure the underlying constructs assessed (i.e., analytic reasoning and evaluation, problem solving, writing effectiveness, and writing mechanics) that are applicable to all versions of the PT. This method of using a common rubric for PTs was found to be useful for improving students' skills (with feedback) across multiple fields of study (Cargas, Williams and Rosenberg, 2017[28]).

In fact, having a common rubric for a performance-based assessment of domain-agnostic skills was one of the reasons the CLA was selected to be the anchor for the "generic skills strand" of the Assessment of

Higher Education Learning Outcomes (AHELO) project, an international feasibility study sponsored by the OECD (AHELO, 2012[29]; 2014[30]; Tremblay, Lalancette and Roseveare, 2012[31]) to measure higher education students' "generic" skills using PTs in a global context. The results from this feasibility study indicated that it was indeed possible to validly and reliably assess students' critical thinking and written communication skills with a common, translated and culturally adapted PT and rubric (Zahner and Steedle, 2014[1]). This result was replicated in a subsequent international comparative study between American and Italian higher education students (Zahner and Ciolfi, 2018[2]).

SRQs

CLA+ includes a set of 25 SRQs that are also document-based and designed to measure the same construct as the APS subscore of the PT. Ten measure Data Literacy (DL) (e.g. making an inference); ten, critical reading and evaluation (CRE) (e.g. identifying assumptions); and five measure critiquing arguments (CA) (e.g. detecting logical fallacies). This section of the assessment was not analysed for this project as it was automatically machine-scored.

Translation and adaptation

CLA+ is translated and culturally adapted using the internationally accepted five-step translation process that is in compliance with International Test Commission (Bartram et al., 2018[32]) guidelines. The Council for Aid to Education (CAE) follows the guidelines used for the localisation process of major international studies such as PISA, Trends in International Mathematics and Science Study (TIMSS), Progress in International Reading Literacy Study (PIRLS), PIAAC, and AHELO. The process includes a translatability review, double translation and reconciliation, client review, focused verification, and cognitive labs.

During the translatability review, source material is reviewed to confirm that the text will adapt well to the native language and culture. Particular attention is paid to disambiguation of source, respecting key correspondences between stimuli and questions, and deciding what should or should not be adapted to local context. Two independent translators then review the text and provide translations. The translations are reconciled and sent to the lead project manager for review and an opportunity to provide minor suggestions. The translated CLA+ items are sent for a focused verification. Cognitive labs are then carried out with the assistance of participating institutions and the institutional teams to ensure the translation and adaptation process was effective.

The CLA+, including the rubric used in this study, was translated into Finnish and Swedish, which are the two main official languages of Finland. The adaptation and translation of both language versions of the task included several phases, as described above. Firstly, the test instruments were translated from English into the target language. Then, two translators (who had knowledge of English-speaking cultures but whose native language was the primary language of the target culture) independently checked and confirmed the translations. Subsequently, the research team in Finland reconciled and verified the revisions. The translations were then pretested in cognitive labs among 20 Finnish undergraduate students, with final modifications incorporated, as necessary. The use of cognitive labs with think-aloud protocols and interviews made it possible to ensure that the translation and adaptation process had not altered the meaning or difficulty of the task (Hyytinen et al., 2021[33]; Leighton, 2017[34]).

This case study only investigated a subset of Finnish student responses. Finnish was specifically selected due to its differences from English as well as the significantly larger number of student responses in Finnish compared to Finnish-Swedish.

CLA+ was administered online via a secure testing platform during an assigned testing window ranging from August 2019 into March 2020. In September 2019, a CAE measurement science team member went to Finland to conduct a two-day in-person scorer training. The first day consisted of an introduction to the PT, an overview of the online scoring interface, a thorough review of the PT and all of the associated documents, and a review of the scoring handbook, followed by initial scoring and calibration of the training papers. As part of scoring the calibration papers, each scorer independently scored a student's response to the PT. Each scorer then shared their three subscores (APS, WE, and WM) with the group. The CAE colleague then revealed the CAE-verified score for the training paper. A discussion of the CAE score compared to the Finnish scores followed each paper. On the second day, the group completed the scoring of the preselected calibration papers as well as discussed a plan for completing the scoring process.

Following this in-person meeting, the two lead scorers in Finland double-scored the first batch of student responses and selected their calibration papers based on their agreement and the distribution of scores. Fifty calibration papers were selected to be inputted into the scoring queue in order to check for consistency of scoring. A scorer would receive one of these calibration papers every 15 or 20 responses. If they did not score within the appropriate range of the previously scored paper, they would enter into a separate training queue of more previously scored validity papers. If they failed again, they would need remediation, which is one-on-one consultation with the lead scorer. Following remediation, the scorer would once again need to pass a set of training papers before being allowed back into the scoring queue. Remediation occurred once for the Finnish scoring team. As a point of reference, the American scorers, in any given administration of this PT, require remediation an average of 1.7 times per semester, although the volume of student responses is much larger for the American scorers.

Once scoring commenced, there was an internal calibration meeting for the Finnish team as well as a meeting with CAE as many months had passed between the training and scoring.

Scoring equivalency case study

In order to assess the equivalency of scoring across countries, we sought to answer two research questions. The first was how well does a translated and culturally adapted performance-based assessment requiring students to generate a written response get scored across countries and languages? The second was whether equivalence can be established across the two forms of the assessment.

As part of this case study, two sets of scoring equivalency papers were selected and scored. Both sets were selected from a larger pool of responses that had perfect agreement between the initial two scorers in the system. Since mid-level scores were overrepresented in this reduced response pool, the final sample was selected by randomly selecting 1-4 responses from each score level.

Sample A consisted of 20 papers initially written in English that had previously been scored by American scorers. For this case study, these papers were scored by Finnish scorers who had mastery of the English language (Table 4.3). Sample B consisted of 20 papers that were initially written in Finnish and scored by Finnish scorers that were subsequently translated into English and scored by American scorers. In the translation of these Sample B papers from Finnish into American English, all the typos and other errors in the original student response were included as much as possible, given the differences between the two languages. These student responses were scored by American scorers.

Table 4.3. Samples A and B by test language and scorer native language

Test Language	Scorer Native Language	
	English	Finnish
English		Sample A
Finnish	Sample B	

For this equivalency case study, scorers from both countries who scored the cross-country responses were blind to the scores from the other pair of scorers. Scorer agreement within countries was examined by calculating correlations between scorers. The scoring equivalence data were analysed by comparing mean scores on common sets of translated responses across countries.

Results

Scoring equivalency case study

This case study investigated whether PT results could be reliably scored in a standardised international testing environment. Analyses were conducted to investigate whether student responses received the same scores regardless of language or country. "Sameness" was examined in two ways: relative and absolute. The first refers to whether the relative standings of the responses were consistent (i.e. highly correlated) regardless of language or country. The second reflects whether the mean scores of the responses were equal.

Relative Quality of Scores: How well does a translated and culturally adapted performance-based assessment requiring students to generate a written response get scored across countries and languages?

To determine whether the scorers agreed with one another about the relative quality of the responses, correlation coefficients among pairs of scorers, both within and across countries, were calculated. The within-country analyses showed that student responses could be reliably scored within each country. The data presented in Table 4.4 and Table 4.5 show the inter-rater correlations for double-scoring U.S. students by U.S. scorers and Finnish students by Finnish scorers, respectively. These data are presented to show the results of the operational testing.

Table 4.4. Within-country correlations for Performance Task (PT) total score and subscores between two scorers: United States (*n* = 141 233)

		Scorer 2			
		Total2	APS2	WE2	WM2
Scorer 1	Total1	**.844**	.783	.794	.765
	APS1	.797	**.761**	.750	.700
	WE1	.804	.750	**.763**	.718
	WM1	.765	.682	.714	**.730**

Note: APS = Analysis and Problem Solving; WE = Writing Effectiveness; WM = Writing Mechanics.

Table 4.5. Within-country correlations for Performance Task (PT) total score and subscores between two scorers: Finland (*n* = 2 402)

		Scorer 2			
		Total2	APS2	WE2	WM2
Scorer 1	Total1	.809	.754	.742	.713
	APS1	.739	.713	.683	.615
	WE1	.750.	.700.	.707	.634
	WM1	.728.	.629	.644	.705

Note: APS = Analysis and Problem Solving; WE = Writing Effectiveness; WM = Writing Mechanics.

For the scoring equivalency case study, each student response was scored by a total of four scorers: two from the United States and two from Finland. As shown in Table 4.6, the inter-country correlations of the total scores, for two scorers, in each country were high, with r = .95 for Sample A and r = .93 for Sample B. The correlation of .95 indicates that the two Finnish scorers that scored the 20 U.S. PTs had a strong linear relationship. The correlation of .93 indicates that the two U.S. scorers that scored the 20 Finnish PTs that were translated into English also had a strong linear relationship.

Table 4.6. Inter-country scorer agreement for total score, by sample

	Sample A: Finland	Sample B: Finland
Sample A: U.S.	.95	
Sample B: U.S.		.93

Note: Sample A = English; Sample B = Finnish to English.

Correlations between the two teams for the subscores were not as high as they were for total score, ranging from r = .88–.92 for Sample A and r = .89–.91 for Sample B (Table 4.7).

WM may need to be discussed in more detail because the Finnish scorers were not native English speakers and the Finnish papers that were back-translated into English may not have captured all of the language nuances of Finnish.

Table 4.7. Inter-country scorer agreement by subscore and sample

	Subscores	Sample A: Finland			Sample B: Finland		
		APS	WE	WM	APS	WE	WM
Sample A: U.S.	APS	0.92					
	WE		0.94				
	WM			0.88			
Sample B: U.S.	APS				.91		
	WE					.89	
	WM						.89

Note: A = English; B = Finnish to English; APS = Analysis and Problem Solving; WE = Writing Effectiveness; WM = Writing Mechanics.

Absolute Quality of Scores: Can equivalency be established across the two forms of the assessment?

To determine whether the scorers agreed with one another on the absolute quality of the scores, the mean scores across countries were analysed. Figure 4.1 illustrates the mean total scores for each country for Sample A and Sample B.

Figure 4.1. Mean total scores for each sample

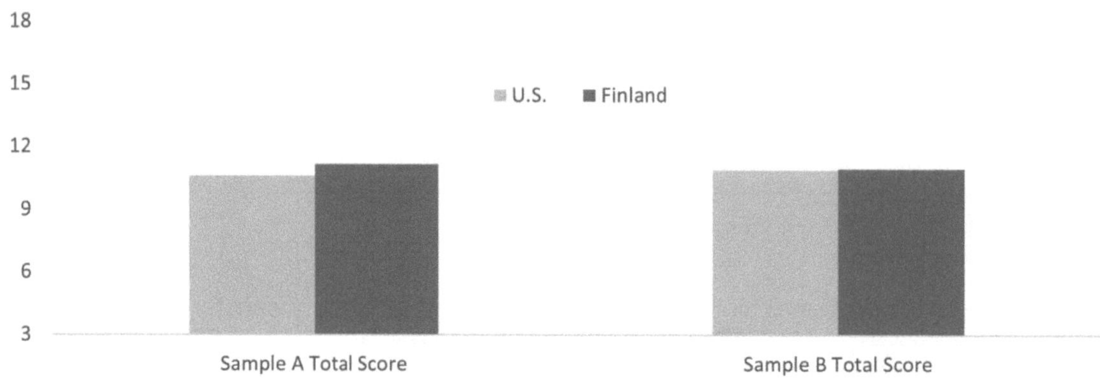

Note: A = English; B = Finnish to English.

There was no significant difference in the mean total scores for both sets of 20 papers in Sample A (t_{19} = -1.70; p = .11) and Sample B (t_{19} = -0.14; p = .89). The pattern of mean scores suggests that translating responses did not affect the perceived response quality or that there was no difference in scorer leniency across countries.

The individual subscores were also analysed. For Sample A (Figure 4.2), the difference between the two groups of scorers was not significant for APS and WE, but for WM, there was a significant difference between the two groups (MUSA = 3.55, MFin = 4.03; p = .004). One possible explanation is that the Finnish scorers, although familiar with American English, were scoring student responses in a language that was not their native language.

Figure 4.2. Mean subscores for sample A (English)

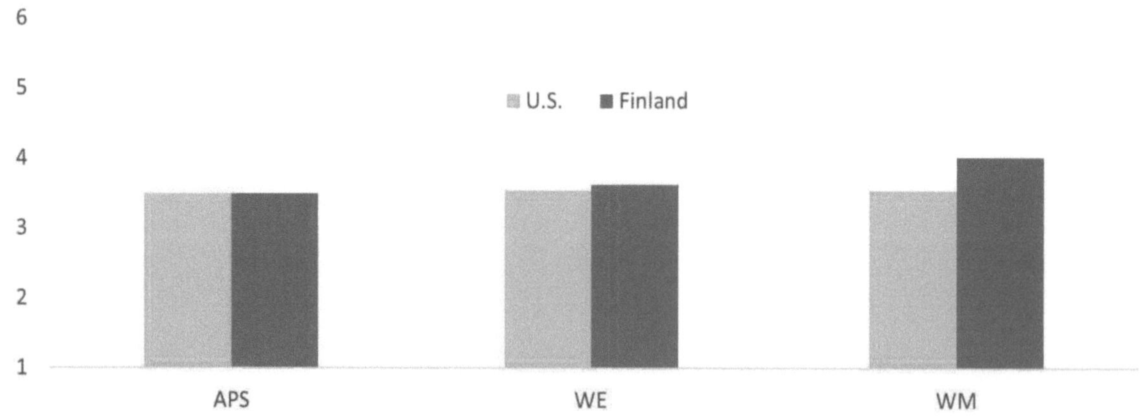

Note: APS = Analysis and Problem Solving; WE = Writing Effectiveness; WM = Writing Mechanics.

There were no significant differences in the average subscores across the two teams for Sample B (Figure 4.3), where the Finnish student responses were translated and culturally adapted into English. The observed difference in means for Sample A for WM was not seen in Sample B.

Figure 4.3. Mean subscores for Sample B (Finnish to English)

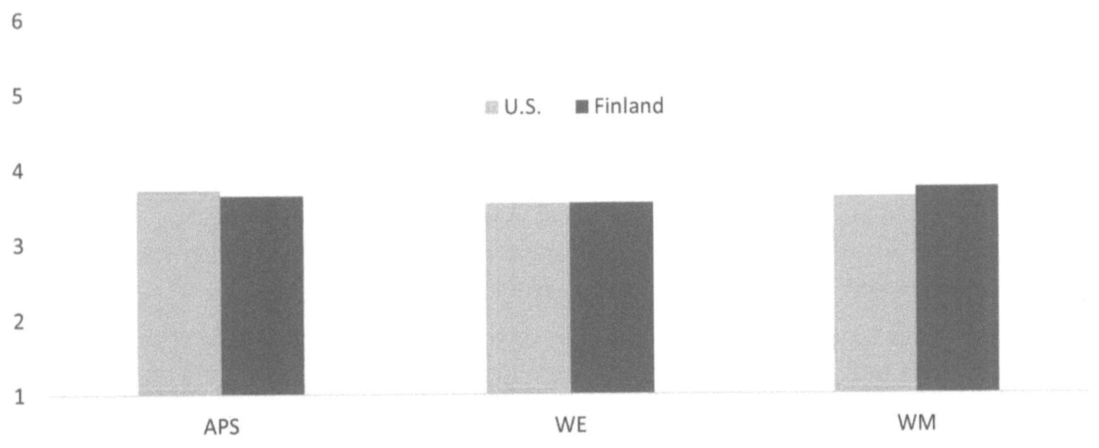

Note: APS = Analysis and Problem Solving; WE = Writing Effectiveness; WM = Writing Mechanics.

The results suggest that translated responses are scored the same as responses originally composed in the native language of the scorer.

Conclusion

This case study of scoring equivalency across languages and countries provides several findings of interest to international assessment programmes. The first is that scoring reliability within countries was high, indicating that scorer training was effective within each country participating in the case study (cf. (Borowiec and Castle, 2019[18]; Shavelson, Baxter and Gao, 1993[19]; Zlatkin-Troitschanskaia et al., 2019[12]). Thus, students can be assessed on their higher order skills using an open-ended performance-based assessment within a given country. Similarly, when comparing results across countries, there were no notable between-country differences in the judgment of the absolute quality of the students' PT responses.

The scores assigned to responses were highly consistent within a country (Table 4.4 and Table 4.5) as well as across countries (Table 4.6 and Table 4.7). The results indicate that with appropriate training and calibration, it is possible to achieve scoring reliability across countries.

A final finding from this case study is that it is feasible to develop, translate, administer, and score the responses to a computer-based, college-level, open-ended assessment of general knowledge, skills, and abilities that are applicable to many countries. Scores from an international testing programme can be calibrated to recognise relative response quality, as well as absolute response quality. The scores on such tests can provide valid and reliable data for large-scale international studies. Results from these types of assessments can be used in large-scale assessment programmes globally. With the increasing popularity of performance-based assessments and a global interest in critical thinking skills, it makes sense to further investigate international assessment of these skills.

Although the results indicate a high correlation between the two countries, there may be additional cultural variables that are not reflected in the results. The papers from the two countries were unique in some respects, leading the team to conclude that there is additional research into the cross-cultural context that needs to be explored (e.g., (Braun et al., 2020[17])).

Language-wise, the samples were not equal, which is often a necessity in a cross-cultural investigation, but it is also a limitation. Sample A (English) was scored by the Finnish team, who are not native speakers of English. While fluent, they are not familiar with all conventions of the English language. This was the probable cause in the difference between the team scores in WM in Sample A. Furthermore, Sample B (Finnish) comprised responses that were translated to English to enable the American team to score. Translated texts generally have been found to be different from original texts in terms of vocabulary and structural aspects (e.g., (Eskola, 2004[35])). However, no significant differences were found between the team scores in WM in Sample B. While it is clear that some of the errors in the responses were lost in translation, it is plausible that high correlation of different error types explained the agreement. In other words, errors that could be translated, such as typos, were strong indicators of other, more language-specific errors. More research is needed to understand if the international scoring rubric captures all characteristics of languages other than English (e.g., Finnish) in terms of WM.

Another limitation of this case study concerns the sample size. A rather small sample of students' answers from only two countries was analysed. This may indicate the risk of potential bias in the results. In addition, the results may not be applicable to other cultures or languages.

Although the findings should be interpreted with caution, this case study provides new insights into PT scoring across two different countries and languages. The results can be utilised as a basis for more extensive empirical studies. In the future, we hope to complete the study by including additional countries in our analyses. Additionally, we hope to develop tools to help individual students identify and improve their areas of strength and opportunity. This can be accomplished through more detailed student and institutional reports that provide pathways to success as well as verified micro-credentials for essential university and workplace success skills such as those measured by CLA+.

Acknowledgements

This chapter and the research behind it would not have been possible without the support of the authors' institutions, their colleagues, and the Finnish Ministry of Education and Culture. We would especially like to thank Tess Dawber, Kari Nissinen, Kelly Rotholz, Kaisa Silvennoinen, Auli Toom, and Zac Varieur.

References

AHELO (2014), *Testing student and university performance globally: OECD's AHELO*, OECD, http://www.oecd.org/edu/skills-beyond-school/testingstudentanduniversityperformancegloballyoecdsahelo.htm. [30]

AHELO (2012), *AHELO feasibility study interim report*, OECD. [29]

Attali, Y. (2014), "A Ranking Method for Evaluating Constructed Responses", *Educational and Psychological Measurement*, Vol. 74/5, pp. 795-808, https://doi.org/10.1177/0013164414527450. [14]

Bartram, D. et al. (2018), "ITC Guidelines for Translating and Adapting Tests (Second Edition)", *International Journal of Testing*, Vol. 18/2, pp. 101-134, https://doi.org/10.1080/15305058.2017.1398166. [32]

Blömeke, S. et al. (2013), *Modeling and measuring competencies in higher education: Tasks and challenges*, Sense, Rotterdam, https://doi.org/10.1007/978-94-6091-867-4. [7]

Borowiec, K. and C. Castle (2019), "Using rater cognition to improve generalizability of an assessment of scientific argumentation", *Practical Assessment, Research and Evaluation*, Vol. 24/1, https://doi.org/10.7275/ey9d-p954. [18]

Braun, H. (2019), "Performance assessment and standardization in higher education: A problematic conjunction?", *British Journal of Educational Psychology*, Vol. 89/3, pp. 429-440, https://doi.org/10.1111/bjep.12274. [20]

Braun, H. et al. (2020), "Performance Assessment of Critical Thinking: Conceptualization, Design, and Implementation", *Frontiers in Education*, Vol. 5, https://doi.org/10.3389/feduc.2020.00156. [17]

Cargas, S., S. Williams and M. Rosenberg (2017), "An approach to teaching critical thinking across disciplines using performance tasks with a common rubric", *Thinking Skills and Creativity*, Vol. 26, pp. 24-37, https://doi.org/10.1016/j.tsc.2017.05.005. [28]

Eskola, S. (2004), "Untypical frequencies in translated language: A corpus-based study on a literary corpus of translated and non-translated Finnish", in *Translation universals: do they exist?*. [35]

Geisinger, K. (1994), "Cross-Cultural Normative Assessment: Translation and Adaptation Issues Influencing the Normative Interpretation of Assessment Instruments", *Psychological Assessment*, Vol. 6/4, p. 304, https://doi.org/10.1037/1040-3590.6.4.304. [3]

Hambleton, R. (2004), "Issues, designs, and technical guidelines for adapting tests into multiple languages and cultures", in *Adapting Educational and Psychological Tests for Cross-Cultural Assessment*, Lawrence Erlbaum, https://doi.org/10.4324/9781410611758. [4]

Hyytinen, H. et al. (2015), "Problematising the equivalence of the test results of performance-based critical thinking tests for undergraduate students", *Studies in Educational Evaluation*, Vol. 44, pp. 1-8, https://doi.org/10.1016/j.stueduc.2014.11.001. [13]

Hyytinen, H. and A. Toom (2019), "Developing a performance assessment task in the Finnish higher education context: Conceptual and empirical insights", *British Journal of Educational Psychology*, Vol. 89/3, pp. 551-563, https://doi.org/10.1111/bjep.12283. [8]

Hyytinen, H. et al. (2021), "The dynamic relationship between response processes and self-regulation in critical thinking assessments", *Studies in Educational Evaluation*, Vol. 71, p. 101090, https://doi.org/10.1016/j.stueduc.2021.101090.   [33]

Klein, S. et al. (2007), "The collegiate learning assessment: Facts and fantasies", *Evaluation Review*, Vol. 31/5, pp. 415-439, https://doi.org/10.1177/0193841X07303318.   [26]

Leighton, J. (2017), *Using Think-Aloud Interviews and Cognitive Labs in Educational Research*, Oxford University Press, Oxford, https://doi.org/10.1093/acprof:oso/9780199372904.001.0001.   [34]

Mauranen, A. (1993), "Cultural differences in academic discourse - problems of a linguistic and cultural minority", in *The Competent Intercultural Communicator: AFinLA Yearbook*.   [22]

McClelland, D. (1973), "Testing for competence rather than for "intelligence"", *The American psychologist*, Vol. 28/1, https://doi.org/10.1037/h0034092.   [10]

Popham, W. (2003), *Test Better, Teach Better: The Instructional Role of Assessment*, ASCD, https://www.ascd.org/books/test-better-teach-better?variant=102088E4.   [16]

Sahlberg, P. (2011), "Introduction: Yes We Can (Learn from Each Other)", in *FINNISH LESSONS: What can the world learn from educational change in Finland?*.   [21]

Shavelson, R. (2010), *Measuring college learning responsibly: Accountability in a new era*, Stanford University Press, https://www.sup.org/books/title/?id=16434.   [9]

Shavelson, R. (2008), *The collegiate learning assessment*, Forum for the Future of Higher Education, https://www.researchgate.net/publication/271429276_The_collegiate_learning_assessment.   [27]

Shavelson, R., G. Baxter and X. Gao (1993), "Sampling Variability of Performance Assessments", *Journal of Educational Measurement*, Vol. 30/3, pp. 215-232, https://doi.org/10.1111/j.1745-3984.1993.tb00424.x.   [19]

Shavelson, R., O. Zlatkin-Troitschanskaia and J. Mariño (2018), "International Performance Assessment of Learning in Higher Education (iPAL): Research and Development", https://doi.org/10.1007/978-3-319-74338-7_10.   [11]

Solano-Flores, G. (2012), *Smarter Balanced Assessment Consortium: Translation accommodations framework for testing English language learners in mathematics*, Smarter Balanced Assessment Consortium (SBAC), https://portal.smarterbalanced.org/library/en/translation-accommodations-framework-for-testing-english-language-learners-in-mathematics.pdf.   [15]

Steedle, J. and M. Bradley (2012), *Majors matter: Differential performance on a test of general college outcomes [Paper presentation]*, Annual Meeting of the American Educational Research Association, Vancouver, Canada.   [25]

Tremblay, K., D. Lalancette and D. Roseveare (2012), "Assessment of Higher Education Learning Outcomes (AHELO) Feasibility Study", *Feasibility study report*, Vol. 1, https://www.oecd.org/education/skills-beyond-school/AHELOFSReportVolume1.pdf (accessed on 1 August 2022).   [31]

Tremblay, K., D. Lalancette and D. Roseveare (2012), *Assessment of higher education learning outcomes feasibility study report: Design and implementation*, OECD, Paris, http://hdl.voced.edu.au/10707/241317. [36]

Ursin, J. (2020), "Assessment in Higher Education (Finland)", in *Bloomsbury Education and Childhood Studies*, https://doi.org/10.5040/9781350996489.0014. [24]

Ursin, J. et al. (2015), "Problematising the equivalence of the test results of performance-based critical thinking tests for undergraduate students", *Studies in Educational Evaluation*, Vol. 44, pp. 1-8, https://doi.org/10.1016/j.stueduc.2014.11.001. [23]

Ursin, J. et al. (2021), *Assessment of undergraduate students' generic skills in Finland: Finding of the Kappas! Project (Report No. 2021: 31)*, Finnish Ministry of Education and Culture. [37]

Wolf, R., D. Zahner and R. Benjamin (2015), "Methodological challenges in international comparative post-secondary assessment programs: lessons learned and the road ahead", *Studies in Higher Education*, Vol. 40/3, pp. 1-11, https://doi.org/10.1080/03075079.2015.1004239. [5]

Zahner, D. and A. Ciolfi (2018), "International Comparison of a Performance-Based Assessment in Higher Education", in Olga Zlatkin-Troitschanskaia et al. (eds.), *Assessment of Learning Outcomes in Higher Education: Cross-National Comparisons and Perspectives*, Springer, New York, https://doi.org/10.1007/978-3-319-74338-7_11. [2]

Zahner, D. and J. Steedle (2014), *Evaluating performance task scoring comparability in an international testing programme [Paper presentation]*, The 2014 National Council on Measurement in Education, Philadelphia, PA. [1]

Zlatkin-Troitschanskaia, O., R. Shavelson and C. Kuhn (2015), "The international state of research on measurement of competency in higher education", *Studies in Higher Education*, Vol. 40/3, pp. 393-411, https://doi.org/10.1080/03075079.2015.1004241. [6]

Zlatkin-Troitschanskaia, O. et al. (2019), "On the complementarity of holistic and analytic approaches to performance assessment scoring", *British Journal of Educational Psychology*, Vol. 89/3, pp. 468-484, https://doi.org/10.1111/bjep.12286. [12]

Part II CLA+ International Database

5 General CLA+ International results

Olivia Cortellini, Council for Aid to Education (United States)

Tess Dawber, Council for Aid to Education (United States)

The CLA+ International Database comprises data from studies conducted by the Italian National Agency for the Evaluation of Universities and Research Institutes (ANVUR) covering 23 campuses of exiting students from the University of Guadalajara system; entering and exiting students from a consortium of four "post-1992" (Hannah, 1996[1]) institutions and a public university in the United Kingdom; several individual institutions across Chile; and entering and exiting students from 18 universities and universities of applied sciences in a study sponsored by the Ministry of Culture and Education of Finland. The dataset also includes all of the entering and exiting students in the United States between fall 2015 and spring 2020. This section presents the results from the aggregated database of all student participants. Some analyses separate students by those from, and those outside, the United States due to disparity in sample size. Part III provides information on each participating country or region.

Introduction

Chapter 5 addresses the distribution of scores and mastery levels across the student population. Before discussing the scores and mastery levels, information about the data are provided. Table 5.1 shows the number of students for each country by year and administration. As you can see, the United States has data for all the administrations from 2015 to 2020 and has the largest total sample by far. All countries except Italy have participated in multiple administrations of the Collegiate Learning Assessment (CLA+).

Table 5.1. CLA+ samples by country and administration

Year	Admin	Chile	Finland	Italy	Mexico	United Kingdom	United States	Total
2015	Spring			6 589			11 974	18 563
2015	Fall					141	12 418	12 559
2016	Spring					702	8 458	9 160
2016	Fall					730	12 734	13 464
2017	Spring					167	8 376	8 543
2017	Fall				2 793	212	11 172	14 177
2018	Spring	499			2 548	135	7 116	10 298
2018	Fall				3 249	154	9 808	13 211
2019	Spring	729					6 580	7 309
2019	Fall		1 469				5 824	7 293
2020	Spring		831				1 854	2 685
2020	Fall	1 727					1 926	3 653
Total		2 955	2 300	6 589	8 590	2 241	98 240	120 915

Table 5.2 shows the number of students for each country by entering (Year 1) and exiting (Year 4) university status. Overall, 52% of the sample are entering students, and 48% of the sample are exiting students. However, the entering and exiting percentages varied greatly by country. There are more entering than exiting students for each country, except for Italy, which only tested exiting students. The countries with a high percentage of entering students in the sample are the United Kingdom and Chile (93 and 81, respectively). In contrast, 52% of the U.S. sample are entering students.

Table 5.2. Sample by country and year of study

Country	Entering	Exiting	Total
Chile	2 387	568	2 955
Finland	1 469	831	2 300
Italy	0	6 589	6 589
Mexico	6 551	2 039	8590
United Kingdom	2 086	155	2 241
United States	50 809	47 431	98 240
Total	63 302	57 613	120 915

Because the countries have differing numbers of participants, the summary information is based on equal weighting of the countries, so the results are not heavily influenced by countries with higher student counts. That is, the mean scores presented are the average of the six country means. We assume that the population variances are equal across countries, so the standard deviations presented are the average of the country standard deviation values.

Mastery levels

Entering students in the combined international dataset received, on average, a total CLA+ score of 1 086 (*SD* = 134; see Table 5.3), which corresponds with the Developing mastery level. Exiting students, on average, received a total CLA+ score of 1097 (*SD* = 138), which corresponds with the Proficient mastery level. Although the effect size is small (*d* = .10), it is pertinent to note that the average score for exiting students passed the criterion-referenced threshold for "proficient" performance, whereas the entering students' average total score did not. Furthermore, it is important to acknowledge that the entering and exiting student samples differed across countries, given that institutions in different countries tested different student populations. Nevertheless, it is encouraging to see the improvement in average mastery level. Further results broken down by section score are reported in Table 5.3. Given widely varying participation rates across countries, Table 5.3 reports the grand mean computed from each country mean and the mean standard deviation rather than basing the results on all students in the dataset to prevent the large U.S. sample from skewing the results.

Table 5.3. Average total CLA+ scores and section scores, by class

	Total CLA+ score	Performance Task score	Selected-Response Question score
Entering	1 086	1 095	1 076
	(134)	(160)	(168)
Exiting	1 097	1 106	1 088
	(138)	(165)	(169)

Note: Standard deviations are listed below means, in parentheses.

Using the integrated international database, results are presented for the proportion of students classified into the five CLA+ mastery levels for all students (Table 5.4) and for all students by class (Table 5.5). Table 5.4 shows the average percentage of students within the countries at each performance level. The minimum and maximum values represent individual country percentages. For example, the average percentage of students classified as Emerging was about 21% across the six countries. To show the range, one country had 13% of students (Minimum column) and one country had 42% of students (Maximum column) classified as Emerging. The results highlight the variability of student performance across countries.

Table 5.4. Mastery level distribution

Level	Average percentage	Minimum	Maximum
Emerging	20.9%	13.4%	41.7%
Developing	34.1%	28.5%	37.6%
Proficient	30.0%	17.4%	34.7%
Accomplished	13.3%	4.5%	19.4%
Advanced	1.7%	0.2%	3.7%

Distribution of mastery levels was somewhat similar between class levels, as indicated in Table 5.5. Like the results in Table 5.4, the average for entering and exiting students is the average of the country percentages rather than the average across students. Overall, a slightly lower percentage of exiting students performed below the Proficient mastery level compared to entering students, and a slightly higher percentage of exiting students performed above the Proficient mastery level compared to entering students. At both class levels, student scores were clustered around the Developing and Proficient mastery levels.

Table 5.5. Mastery level, by class

Level	Entering students			Exiting students		
	Average	Minimum	Maximum	Average	Minimum	Maximum
Emerging	18.4%	14.4%	27.1%	17.5%	6.5%	41.7%
Developing	34.2%	29.0%	38.6%	32.3%	22.6%	37.7%
Proficient	31.9%	26.6%	34.3%	30.6%	17.4%	36.3%
Accomplished	13.8%	9.5%	18.6%	16.8%	4.5%	30.3%
Advanced	1.8%	0.1%	3.4%	2.8%	0.2%	8.4%

CLA+ total scores

Overall, total CLA+ score distributions were similar for entering and exiting students. The distribution of CLA+ scale scores for entering students and exiting students are presented in Figure 5.1 and Figure 5.2, respectively. The exiting student distribution shifted slightly to the right compared to the entering student distribution, suggesting some improvement in the CLA+ total scores for the exiting university students.

Figure 5.1. CLA+ total score distribution, entering students

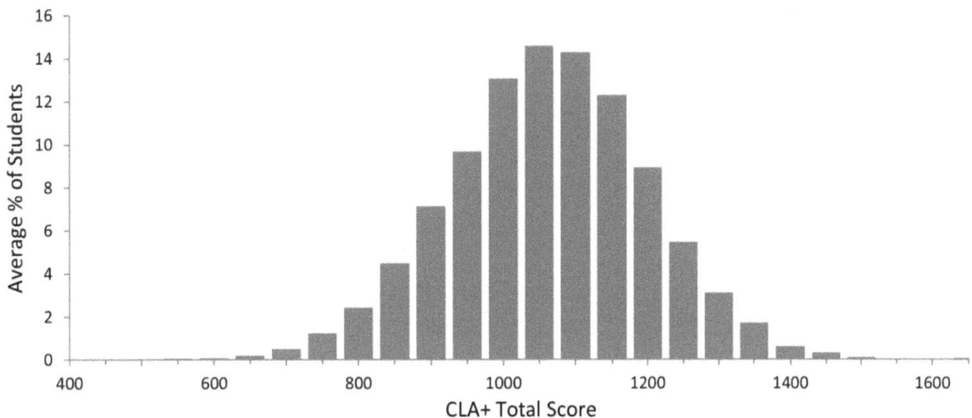

Figure 5.2. CLA+ total score distribution, exiting students

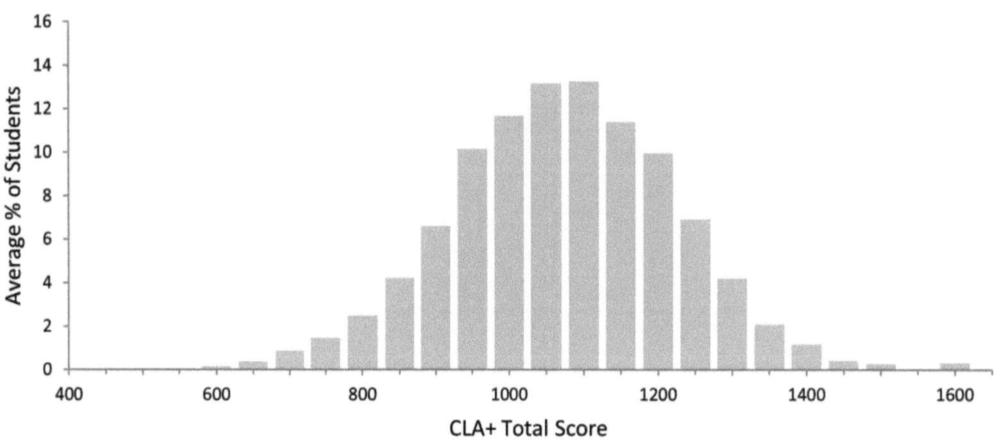

CLA+ subscores

In addition to receiving total and section scores, students who complete CLA+ also receive subscores for each section. For the Performance Task (PT), students receive subscores for Analysis and Problem Solving (APS), Writing Effectiveness (WE) and Writing Mechanics (WM). PT subscores range from 1-6 points each. Among entering students, the average subscores for APS, WE and WM, respectively, were 3.3 (*SD* = 0.8), 3.2 (*SD* = 0.8) and 3.6 (*SD* = 0.7). Among exiting students, subscores were slightly higher and slightly more variable. The average for APS was 3.4 (*SD* = 0.8), the average for WE was 3.4 (*SD* = 0.8) and the average for WM was 3.7 (*SD* = 0.8). These findings, illustrated in Figure 5.3, show that exiting students obtained slightly higher PT subscores.

Figure 5.3. Performance Task subscores among entering and exiting students

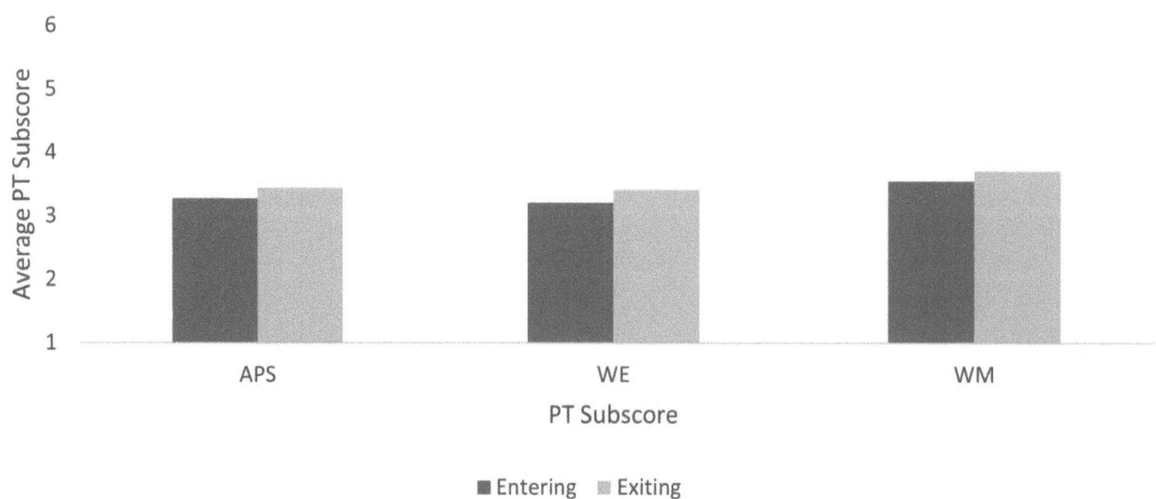

Note: PT = Performance Task; APS = Analysis and Problem Solving; WE = Writing Effectiveness; WM = Writing Mechanics

Like the PT, the Selected-Response Question (SRQ) section is composed of three subscores. The subscores are Scientific and Quantitative Reasoning (SQR), Critical Reading and Evaluation (CRE) and Critique an Argument (CA). For both the SQR and CRE subscores, exiting students outperformed entering students. Entering students received an average score of 521 (*SD* = 101) on the SQR section, compared to exiting students who scored on average 532 (*SD* = 103). In the CRE section, entering students received an average score of 507 (*SD* = 100), whereas exiting students received an average score of 513 (*SD* = 100). On the CA section, entering students, with an average score of 522 (*SD* = 98), slightly outperformed exiting students, who scored on average 512 (*SD* = 102). Results are illustrated in Figure 5.4. Although the results are not as consistent as the PT subscore results, the exiting students obtained slightly higher scores on two of the three subscores compared to the entering students.

Figure 5.4. Selected-Response Question subscores among entering and exiting students

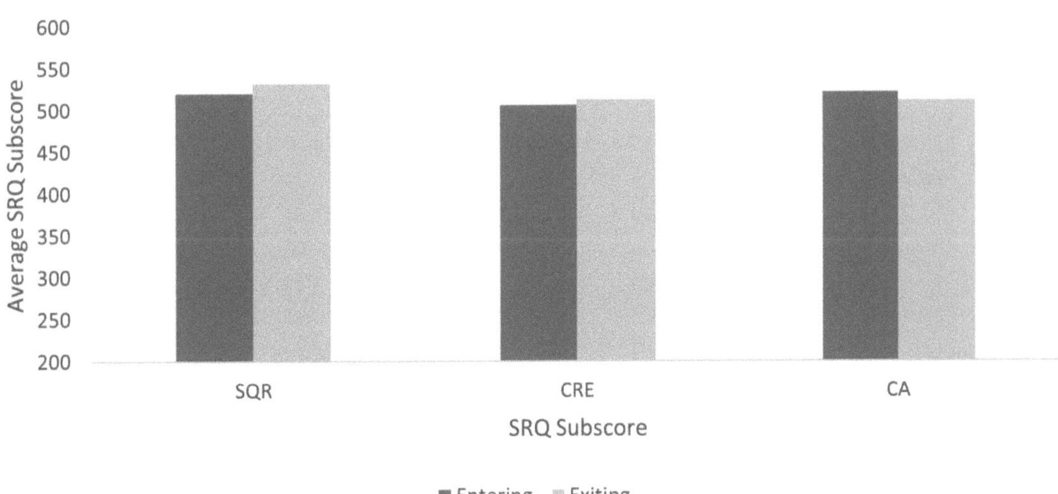

Note: SRQ = Selected-Response Question; SQR = Scientific and Quantitative Reasoning; CRE = Critical Reading and Evaluation; CA = Critique an Argument

Student self-reported effort and engagement

After students complete the CLA+, they typically receive a questionnaire in which they report the amount of effort they spent on each section of the assessment as well as how engaging they found each section of the assessment was. Both effort and engagement are reported on 5-point Likert scales, with higher values indicating higher levels of effort and engagement. On the PT, the average effort rating given by entering students was 3.6 (*SD* = 0.9), and the average rating given by exiting students was 3.7 (*SD* = 0.9). For the SRQ section, entering students reported an average of 3.1 points on the effort scale (*SD* = 0.9), and exiting students reported an average of 3.3 (*SD* = 0.9.) Table 5.6 summarises the distribution of self-reported effort ratings by class and section. Important to note is that these data are not available for all students because not every country included this survey at the end of the assessment.

Table 5.6. Students' self-reported effort on each CLA+ section

		No effort at all	A little effort	A moderate amount of effort	A lot of effort	My best effort
PT	Entering	1.0%	7.8%	40.6%	34.9%	15.7%
	Exiting	1.0%	7.5%	36.8%	34.9%	19.9%
SRQs	Entering	3.7%	19.1%	46.0%	23.7%	7.5%
	Exiting	2.4%	14.8%	42.1%	29.0%	11.6%

Note: PT = Performance Task; SRQs = Selected-Response Questions

As shown in Table 5.7, for each increase in self-reported effort, there was an increase in the average score on the applicable section. In other words, students who reported making more effort on the PT generally received higher PT scores than those who reported less effort, and students who reported higher levels of effort on the SRQ section tended to score higher on that section than did their peers who reported less effort. One exception to this is that SRQ scores did not increase for students who reported making "[their] best effort" compared to students who reported "a lot of effort". This pattern held for both entering and exiting students. The relationship between CLA+ section score and the amount of effort expended is illustrated in Figure 5.5. The PT results for the exiting students showed a different trend line compared to the other results. A steeper slope was observed from "a little effort" to "a lot of effort" and "best effort", demonstrating a more dramatic increase in PT scores for the highest two effort ratings.

Table 5.7. Average CLA+ section score by self-reported effort

		No effort at all	A little effort	A moderate amount of effort	A lot of effort	My best effort
PT	Entering	927	987	1 070	1 126	1 142
		(188)	(176)	(154)	(147)	(148)
	Exiting	955	1 000	1 107	1 165	1 174
		(148)	(138)	(148)	(150)	(156)
SRQs	Entering	956	1 029	1 082	1 111	1 106
		(147)	(159)	(165)	(165)	(170)
	Exiting	928	1 047	1 101	1 133	1 116
		(125)	(167)	(168)	(161)	(169)

Note: Standard deviations are listed below means, in parentheses. PT = Performance Task; SRQs = Selected-Response Questions

Figure 5.5. Average CLA+ section score by amount of effort

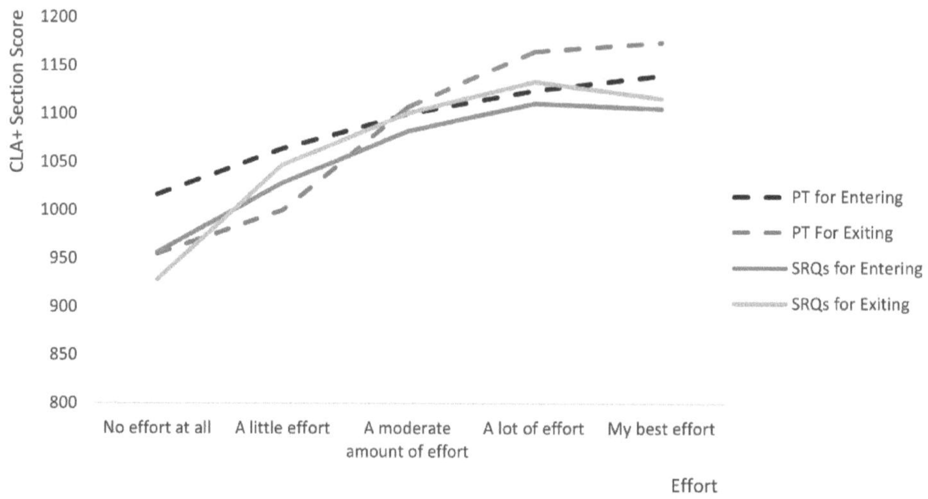

Note: PT = Performance Task; SRQs = Selected-Response Questions

Compared to self-reported effort, there was more variability between the PT and the SRQ section in self-reported engagement. The average rating that entering students reported for their engagement with the PT was 3.1 (SD = 1.0), and that given by exiting students was 3.2 (SD = 1.0). However, entering students reported an average engagement level of 2.6 (SD = 1.0) for the SRQ section, and exiting students reported an average of 2.8 (SD = 1.1). Distributions are summarised in Table 5.8.

Table 5.8. Students' self-reported engagement on each CLA+ section

		Not at all engaging	A little engaging	Moderately engaging	Very engaging	Extremely engaging
PT	Entering	7.4%	19.3%	39.5%	27.6%	6.2%
	Exiting	7.2%	16.1%	33.9%	33.8%	9.1%
SRQs	Entering	17.9%	28.9%	33.6%	15.9%	3.8%
	Exiting	14.0%	25.6%	35.2%	20.3%	5.0%

Note: PT = Performance Task: SRQs = Selected-Response Questions

There was a similar relationship between engagement and CLA+ section score to the previously described relationship between effort and section score. As with effort, students who reported higher levels of engagement on a section tended to receive higher scores on that section than their peers who reported less engagement. Also similar to the previous findings on effort and section score, the pattern did not hold for students who reported being "very engaged" to "extremely engaged" with the SRQ section (see Table 5.9). The mean SRQ scores tended to plateau and decrease for the higher engagement ratings whereas the mean PT scores continued to rise across the range of engagement ratings. The relationship between CLA+ section score and level of engagement is illustrated in Table 5.9.

Table 5.9. Average CLA+ section score by self-reported engagement

		Not at all engaging	A little engaging	Moderately engaging	Very engaging	Extremely engaging
PT	Entering	1 017	1 064	1 100	1 124	1 140
		(176)	(164)	(153)	(152)	(155)
	Exiting	1 038	1 084	1 143	1 163	1 178
		(162)	(163)	(147)	(150)	(155)
SRQs	Entering	1 029	1 074	1 089	1 103	1 089
		(161)	(165)	(168)	(167)	(172)
	Exiting	1 039	1 085	1 119	1 127	1 109
		(165)	(173)	(166)	(156)	(182)

Note: Standard deviations are listed below means, in parentheses. PT = Performance Task; SRQs = Selected-Response Questions

Figure 5.6. Average CLA+ section score by level of engagement

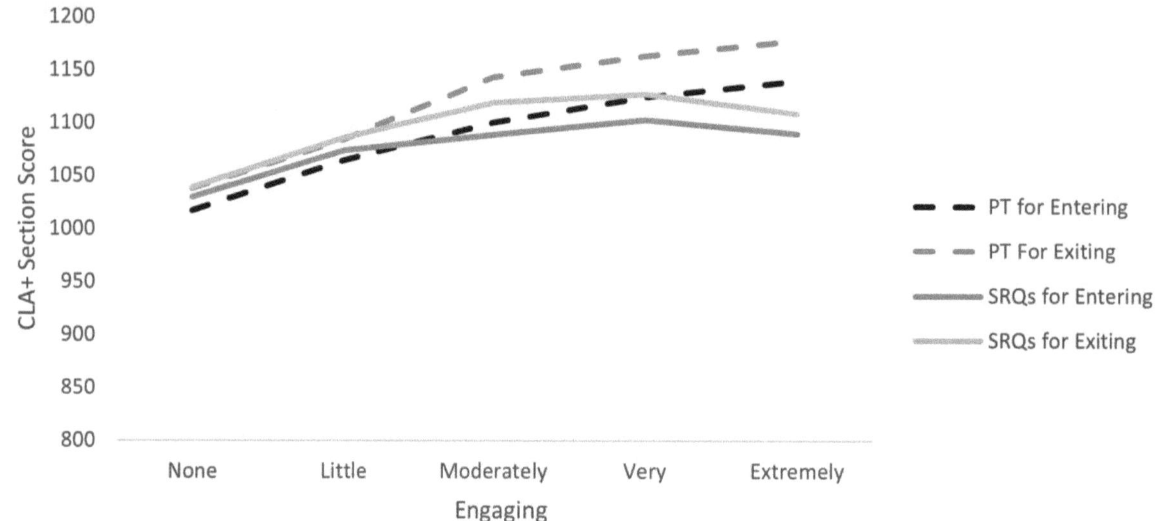

Note: PT = Performance Task; SRQs = Selected-Response Questions

Summary

Chapter 5 addressed the distribution of scores and mastery levels across the student population. Because the countries have differing numbers of participants, the summary information was based on equal weighting of the countries, so the results are not heavily influenced by countries with higher student counts.

Overall, the exiting students performed better than their entering peers on average. This is consistent across all countries in the sample and offers some evidence that higher education contributes to the improvement of students' generic skills. However, the learning gains are not large and there is room for improvement of these skills globally.

Based on mean scores, entering students performed at the Developing mastery level and exiting students performed at the Proficient mastery level. Subscore results showed slightly higher scores for exiting students compared to entering students. The relationship between CLA+ scores and self-reported effort/engagement on each section was examined. Generally, for each rating increase in self-reported effort/engagement, there was an increase in the average score on the applicable section. It is encouraging to see the improvement in scores and to see the linear relationship between effort/engagement and test results.

Reference

Hannah, S. (1996), "The higher education act of 1992: Skills, constraints, and the politics of higher education", *Journal of Higher Education*, Vol. 67/5, pp. 498-527, https://doi.org/10.1080/00221546.1996.11780274.   [1]

6 CLA+ International demographic variables

Olivia Cortellini, Council for Aid to Education (United States)

Tess Dawber, Council for Aid to Education (United States)

This chapter explores relationships between demographic variables and Collegiate Learning Assessment (CLA+) performance. The demographic variables of interest in this dataset are primary language, gender, and parental education level. To allow for inferential analyses, overall means are reported in this chapter rather than grand means of country means. However, due to the large sample from the United States compared to the sample sizes of other participating countries, results for the U.S. domestic data are reported separately from results from the rest of the combined international data.

Primary language

After completing CLA+, most students responded to a series of demographic survey questions. In one question, students were asked to identify whether their primary language was the same as the language of instruction at their institution, or whether their primary language was different from the language of instruction at their university. Tables 6.1-6.4 summarise average total CLA+ score as well as CLA+ section scores broken down by primary language, class level and sample.

Table 6.1. CLA+ score by primary language, entering students: International sample

| | Entering students | | | | Mean difference (language the same minus language different) |
| | Primary language is the same as the language of instruction (n = 8 604) | | Primary language is different from the language of instruction (n = 1 139) | | |
	Mean	Standard deviation	Mean	Standard deviation	
Total CLA+ score	1 095	132	1 057	138	38
PT score	1 107	167	1 073	179	34
SRQ score	1 084	164	1 040	163	44

Note: PT = Performance Task; SRQ = Selected-Response Questions

Table 6.2. CLA+ score by primary language, entering students: U.S. sample

| | Entering students | | | | Mean difference (language the same minus language different) |
| | Primary language is the same as the language of instruction (n = 41 673) | | Primary language is different from the language of instruction (n = 9 104) | | |
	Mean	Standard deviation	Mean	Standard deviation	
Total CLA+ score	1 060	150	1 065	146	-5
PT score	1 041	170	1 052	159	-11
SRQ score	1 078	186	1 077	184	1

Note: PT = Performance Task; SRQ = Selected-Response Questions

Table 6.3. CLA+ score by primary language, exiting students: International sample

| | Exiting students | | | | Mean difference (language the same minus language different) |
| | Primary language is the same as the language of instruction (n = 8 835) | | Primary language is different from the language of instruction (n = 642) | | |
	Mean	Standard deviation	Mean	Standard deviation	
Total CLA+ score	1 031	142	999	151	31
PT score	1 011	176	976	193	35
SRQ score	1 050	173	1 023	172	27

Note: PT = Performance Task; SRQ = Selected-Response Questions

Table 6.4. CLA+ score by primary language, exiting students: U.S. sample

	Exiting students				Mean difference (language the same minus language different)
	Primary language is the same as the language of instruction (n = 40 787)		Primary language is different from the language of instruction (n = 6 615)		
	Mean	Standard deviation	Mean	Standard deviation	
Total CLA+ score	1 110	147	1 062	148	48
PT score	1 095	170	1 058	166	37
SRQ score	1 124	181	1 067	181	57

Note: PT = Performance Task; SRQ = Selected-Response Questions

Independent samples t-tests were used to determine whether any differences in CLA+ scores between primary language groups were significant (see Tables 6.5-6.7). Most t-tests yielded significant results, except for the comparison of Selected-Response Question (SRQ) section scores among entering students from the U.S. domestic dataset. However, although most results were statistically significant, the effect sizes ranged from negligible to small. Generally, small differences were found between primary language groups among international entering students and among U.S. exiting students. In both samples, students whose primary language was the same as the language of instruction on average performed slightly better than their peers who had a different primary language. Among entering U.S. students and exiting international students, any differences found were too small to be practically meaningful.

When examining the differences between primary language groups more closely, it becomes evident that neither portion of the assessment is uniquely driving these differences. However, in subsamples where there were meaningful differences (i.e., international-entering and U.S.-exiting), there were found to be slightly larger effect-sizes with respect to the SRQ section than to the PT section. In some ways this is counterintuitive, as the PT section requires a written response whereas the SRQ section does not. One possible explanation for this unexpected finding is that, on average, students receiving instruction in their non-native language may be more adept at writing in their language of instruction than they are at comprehending documents in their language of instruction. Although both sections are document-based, the content of the PT is broader in scope than that of the SRQ section. Thus, when completing the PT, students may be better able to comprehend the information because they are given more context. Further research is needed to fully investigate the differences in CLA+ performance between students receiving instruction in their primary language versus a different language.

In the international sample, differences between primary language groups were found only among entering students. There are several possible explanations for this finding. One possibility is that students who are receiving instruction in their non-primary language may face a greater learning curve at the beginning of their higher education careers, which they adapt to over the course of their education. Another possibility is that there is an attrition effect. That is, it is possible that, if some students who receive instruction in their non-primary language are struggling more than their peers, they may be less likely to continue in their higher education careers. Thus, the students who were struggling upon entrance would not be included in the exiting student sample.

Meanwhile, students in the United States showed the opposite pattern in CLA+ performance. Specifically, a language-based difference in CLA+ performance emerged only among exiting students in the U.S. sample. Similar to the International sample, it is possible that this result was affected by student attrition. However, further investigation is needed to examine potential factors influencing this unexpected finding.

Table 6.5. Independent samples t-test results: Total CLA+ score by primary language

		t	df	p	Cohen's d
Entering	International sample	9.96	1746	<.001	0.29
	U.S. sample	-2.92	13620	0.004	0.03
Exiting	International sample	5.21	768	<.001	0.21
	U.S. sample	24.16	47400	<.001	0.33

Table 6.6. Independent samples t-test results: Performance Task score by primary language

		t	df	p	Cohen's d
Entering	International sample	6.59	1729	<.001	0.20
	U.S. sample	-6.01	14033	<.001	0.07
Exiting	International sample	4.59	762	<.001	0.20
	U.S. sample	16.81	8991	<.001	0.22

Table 6.7. Independent samples t-test results: Selected-Response score by primary language

		t	df	p	Cohen's d
Entering	International sample	9.60	12381	<.001	0.27
	U.S. sample	0.67	50775	0.504	0.01
Exiting	International sample	3.96	10069	<.001	0.16
	U.S. sample	23.70	47400	<.001	0.31

Gender

Similar to primary language, students also identified their gender after concluding the assessment. The answer options presented to students were: male, female and decline to state. Since the framing of the gender survey question was consistent across participating countries, gender is a key variable for drawing comparisons across the overall sample. However, once again, U.S. data is reported separately from the rest of the international dataset due to the large sample sizes in the United States. Table 6.8-Table 6.11 summarise CLA+ total and section scores by gender, class and dataset.

Table 6.8. CLA+ score by gender, entering students: International sample

	Male (n = 5,873)		Female (n = 4,9676295)		Decline to State (n = 215)	
	Mean	Standard deviation	Mean	Standard deviation	Mean	Standard deviation
Total CLA+ score	1 086	139	1 095	126	1 106	154
PT score	1 089	175	1 116	161	1 100	193
SRQ score	1 084	169	1 074	160	1 112	172

Note: PT = Performance Task; SRQ = Selected-Response Questions

Table 6.9. CLA+ score by gender, entering students: U.S. sample

	Male (*n* = 22,701)		Female (*n* = 27,080)		Decline to state (*n* = 996)	
	Mean	Standard deviation	Mean	Standard deviation	Mean	Standard deviation
Total CLA+ score	1 065	153	1 057	145	1 071	160
PT score	1 040	171	1 045	165	1 041	178
SRQ score	1 090	190	1 068	180	1 101	198

Note: PT = Performance Task; SRQ = Selected-Response Questions

Table 6.10. CLA+ score by gender, exiting students: International sample

	Male (*n* = 4,460)		Female (*n* = 5,558)		Decline to state (*n* = 53)	
	Mean	Standard deviation	Mean	Standard deviation	Mean	Standard deviation
Total CLA+ score	1 042	140	1 017	144	1 081	159
PT score	1 013	178	1 004	177	1 064	213
SRQ score	1 071	171	1 030	172	1 098	184

Note: PT = Performance Task; SRQ = Selected-Response Questions

Table 6.11. CLA+ score by gender, exiting students: U.S. sample

	Male (*n* = 17,966)		Female (*n* = 28,060)		Decline to state (*n* = 1,376)	
	Mean	Standard deviation	Mean	Standard deviation	Mean	Standard deviation
Total CLA+ score	1 107	153	1 102	144	1 082	157
PT score	1 090	175	1 091	166	1 059	177
SRQ score	1 123	188	1 112	178	1 104	194

Note: PT = Performance Task; SRQ = Selected-Response Questions

One-way analysis of variance (ANOVAs) were used to further examine potential gender difference in CLA+ performance (see Table 6.12-Table 6.14). Similar to the findings with primary language, most differences found were statistically significant but negligibly small. In most cases, post-hoc analyses revealed that the difference between males and females was driving the significant results rather than the students who declined to state their gender. This may be due to a relatively small sample of students in the latter group. Overall, there were no consistent patterns found within specific subsets of the sample. In other words, there was not one subsample in which males consistently outperformed females or vice versa. Similarly, for total CLA+ score and Performance Task (PT) score, there was not a consistent pattern of one gender outperforming another across subsamples.

The only consistent finding was the difference in average CLA+ performance on the SRQ section. On the SRQ section, all groups yielded a significant difference in which male students slightly outperformed female students on average. However, in most subsamples, the effect-size between males and females in average SRQ performance was negligible. One exception to this is the International-Exiting subsample, in which there was a small difference between males and females in average SRQ performance.

Overall, there were few clear patterns regarding gender-based differences in CLA+ performance. The one finding of note was the difference between males and females on the SRQ section among exiting international students. Further research is needed to examine the factors that may have contributed to this finding.

104 |

Table 6.12. One-way ANOVA results comparing total CLA+ score by gender

		df	F	$\eta2$	p
Entering	International	2, 12380	7.60	0.001	0.001
	Domestic	2, 50774	20.52	0.001	<.001
Exiting	International	2, 10068	42.44	0.008	<.001
	Domestic	2, 47399	21.20	0.001	<.001

Table 6.13. One-way ANOVA results comparing Performance Task score by gender

		df	F	$\eta2$	p
Entering	International	2, 12380	38.30	0.006	<.001
	Domestic	2, 50774	7.35	0.000	0.001
Exiting	International	2, 10068	6.12	0.001	.002
	Domestic	2, 47399	23.81	0.001	<.001

Table 6.14. One-way ANOVA results comparing Selected-Response score by gender

		df	F	$\eta2$	p
Entering	International	2, 12380	11.9.43	0.002	<.001
	Domestic	2, 50774	93.71	0.004	<.001
Exiting	International	2, 10068	72.62	0.014	<.001
	Domestic	2, 47399	25.55	0.001	<.001

In addition to providing their primary language and gender, students also responded to a survey question about their parents' highest level of education. However, the response options differed based on whether the students tested on the international platform or the domestic platform. For students who tested on the international platform, except for the Italian students, the response options were based on the UK education system. Translations for other countries were kept parallel so that each answer choice would indicate an equivalent level of education to the UK sample. For the purpose of these analyses, response categories have been converted to map onto ISCED levels. Students' average scores by class and parental education level are reported in Figure 6.1-Figure 6.6 for the International and U.S. samples.

CLA+ results by parental level of education were further examined via one-way ANOVAs (see Table 6.15-Table 6.16). Broadly speaking, higher levels of parent education were associated with higher CLA+ scores. In the international sample, each successive level of parent education was often associated with a statistically significant average score increase up until the bachelor's degree level. For degrees beyond a bachelor's, there were fewer significant score differences between education levels. In the U.S. sample, each successive level of parent education was associated with a significant average score increase.

In conclusion, students whose parents had at least a bachelor's degree performed better on CLA+ than did those whose parents had less than a bachelor's degree. In the international sample, the benefit of parent education diminished after the bachelor's degree level. In the U.S. sample, however, the benefit continued to the graduate/post-graduate education level. The difference between the international and U.S. samples may be due to nuances in the relationship between education attainment and socio-economic status. Alternatively, these differences also may result from sampling discrepancies among countries.

Figure 6.1. Average CLA+ score by class and parent education, International Sample

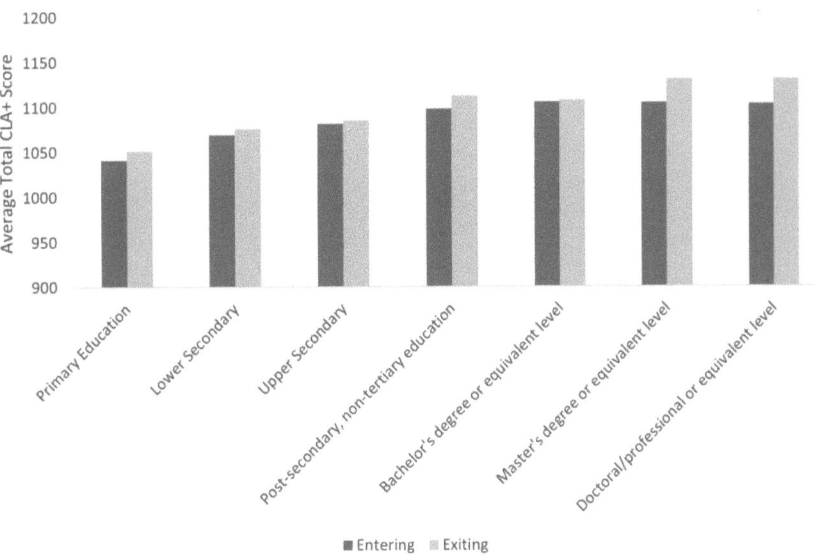

Figure 6.2. Average performance task score by class and parent education, International sample

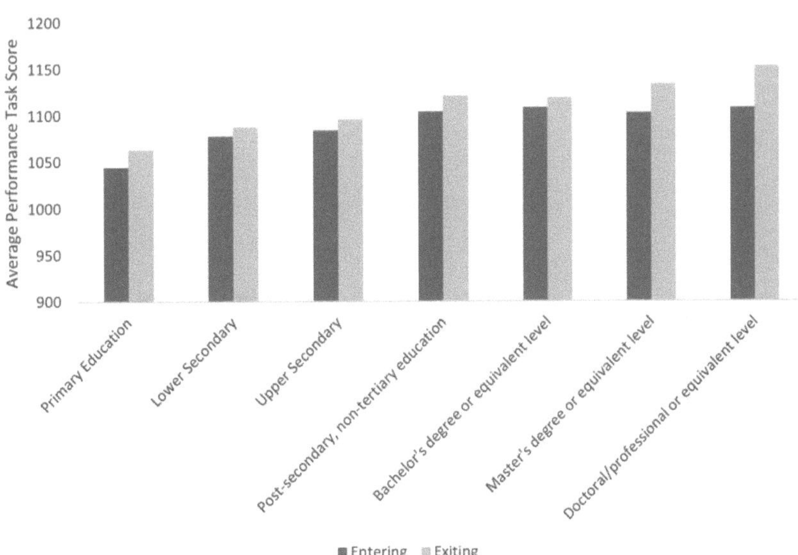

Figure 6.3. Average selected-response score by class and parent education, International sample

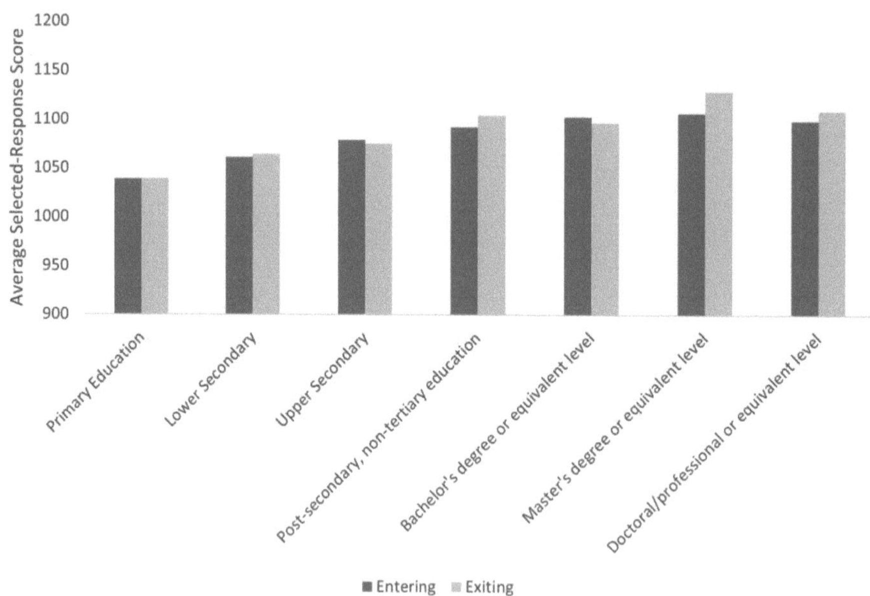

Figure 6.4. Average CLA+ score by class and parent education, U.S. sample

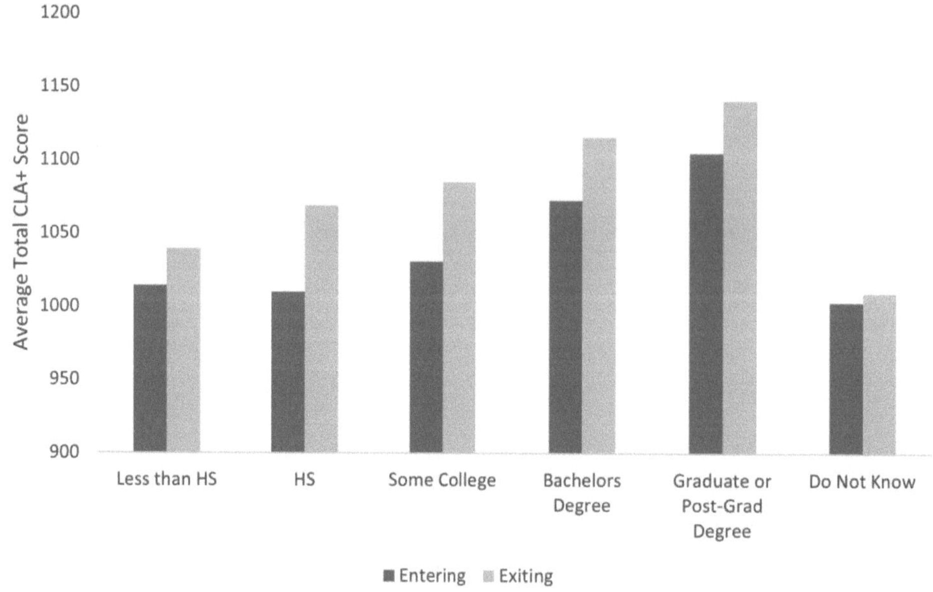

Figure 6.5. Average performance task score by class and parent education, U.S. sample

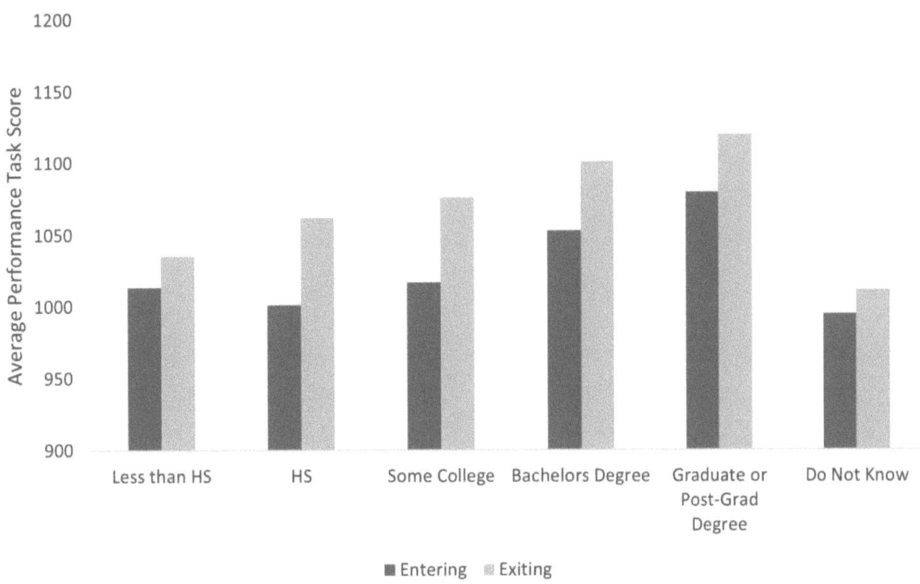

Figure 6.6. Average selected-response score by class and parent education, U.S. sample

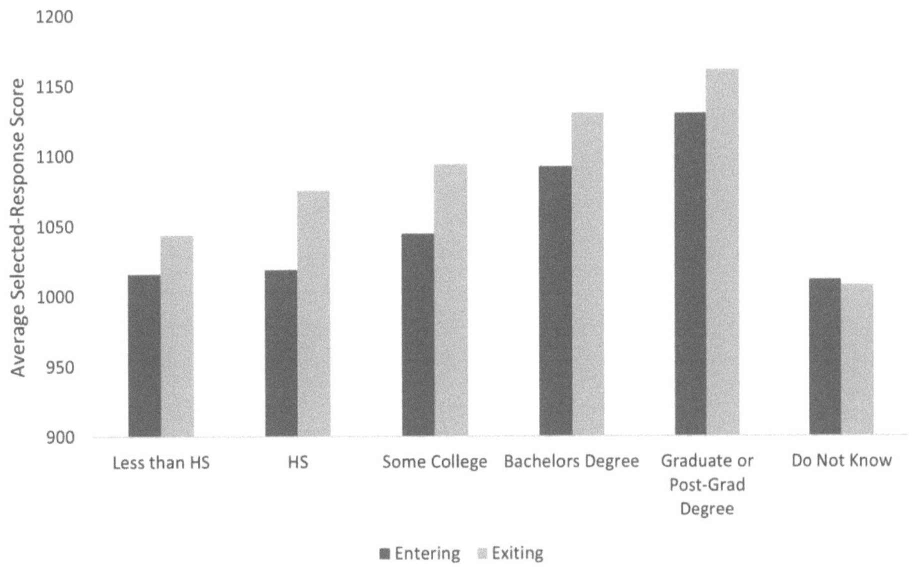

Table 6.15. One-way ANOVA results for comparisons by parent education, international sample

		df	F	$\eta2$	p
Entering	Total CLA+ score	6, 10805	40.17	0.022	<.001
	PT score	6, 10805	23.131	0.013	<.001
	SRQ score	6, 10805	29.09	0.016	<.001
Exiting	Total CLA+ score	6, 3475	18.99	0.032	<.001
	PT score	6, 3475	11.24	0.019	<.001
	SRQ score	6, 3475	13.72	0.023	<.001

Note: PT = Performance Task; SRQ = Selected-Response Questions

Table 6.16. One-way ANOVA results for comparisons by parent education, U.S. sample

		df	F	η2	p
Entering	Total CLA+ score	5, 50771	636.76	0.059	<.001
	PT score	5, 50771	331.73	0.032	<.001
	SRQ score	5, 50771	569.66	0.053	<.001
Exiting	Total CLA+ score	5, 47396	418.05	0.042	<.001
	PT score	5, 47396	207.32	0.021	<.001
	SRQ score	5, 47396	383.89	0.039	<.001

Note: PT = Performance Task; SRQ = Selected-Response Questions

Given the differences found in CLA+ performance based on parent education levels, it is useful to investigate any potential interaction between parent education and CLA+ performance. Specifically, it is important to address the concern that performance differences between entering and exiting students may be due to selection rather than educational effect. Although the available data does not allow for a conclusive causal inference to be made, it does allow for deeper exploration. To disentangle the relationship between parent education and student CLA+ performance, entering and exiting students' average total CLA+ scores were compared after controlling for parent education. The first step of this procedure entailed running a simple regression between parent education and total CLA+ score (see Table 6.17-Table 6.18).

Table 6.17. Simple regression results, international sample

Source	B	SE B	β	t	p
Constant	1046.00	2.77		378.17	<.001
Parent Education	11.70	0.67	0.15	17.56	<.001

Table 6.18. Simple regression results, U.S. sample

Source	B	SE B	β	t	p
Constant	984.43	1.54		637.70	<.001
Parent Education	27.00	0.41	0.21	66.26	<.001

Next, independent-samples t-tests were used to compare entering and exiting students within each sample. The residuals from the simple regressions were used as the dependent variables (see Table 6.19). The t-tests showed significant results for both samples; however, the effect-size for the international sample was negligibly small. From a practical standpoint, these results are inconclusive as to whether performance differences between entering and exiting students can be traced back to selection or education effect. On the one hand, significant differences between class levels after controlling for parent education support the notion that there may be an education effect beyond selection. This is further enhanced by the modest but meaningful effect size seen in the U.S. sample. However, the small effect size among the international sample points to initial selection as a more important indicator than education effect.

Table 6.19. Independent samples t-test results: Total CLA+ score residual by class level

	t	df	p	Cohen's d
International sample	-3.61	14292	<.001	-.07
U.S. sample	-48.45	97048	<.001	-.31

Overall, these results must be interpreted with caution given the limitations of these analyses. Most notably, unlike analyses from previous chapters, the residuals in the international sample were not weighted by country. This may have masked effects that were more prominent in some countries but less prominent than others. Furthermore, there is not sufficient information to draw a causal inference about the impact of education versus selection. Future research is needed to tease out this complex relationship.

7 Predictive validity of CLA+

Doris Zahner, Council for Aid to Education (United States)

Jessalynn James, TNTP (United States)

Jonathan Lehrfeld, ETS (United States)

The research results presented in this chapter are from two studies using a longitudinal data set that examined the validity of CLA+ as a predictor of post-higher education outcomes for students transitioning from higher education to career. CLA+ data from students who graduated in 2014 and 2017 and survey results from their employers and advisors help answer questions about the importance of these skills in post-higher education and whether they can be predicted by CLA+ test scores.

Introduction

Note: The data on the predictive validity of Collegiate Learning Assessment (CLA+) pertain to the data from CLA+ for students from the United States. There is currently insufficient CLA+ International data for a study of the predictive validity of the instrument.

Fact- and content-based knowledge is no longer sufficient for success in higher education and career. Students need generic skills such as critical thinking, problem solving and written communication to achieve their full potential. Although parents and students often believe that gaining admission to higher education is a clear step toward success, today's students face an enormous challenge in successfully navigating higher education, as reflected in national graduation rates within the United States. Only 41% of first-time, full-time higher education students within the United States graduate within four years and only 59% do so within six years (de Brey et al., 2019[1]), statistics that paint a concerning picture. Persistence and retention are long-standing challenges – with little recent improvement – particularly for minority and low-income students (Banks and Dohy, 2019[2]; Hernandez and Lopez, 2004[3]). The most recent data indicate that among students who enrolled in higher education for the first time in fall 2017, only 62% were retained at their original institution in fall 2018 (National Student Clearinghouse Research Center, 2019[4]). Although many students cite non-academic reasons such as financial difficulties, health or family obligations as the primary causes for dropping out or deferring their education (Astin and Oseguera, 2012[5]), academic failure is also a significant factor contributing to lack of persistence and retention of students in higher education.

Once students do graduate, their next challenge is finding a career that leverages their knowledge, skills and abilities. As stated in Chapter 2, while content knowledge is a requisite part of a student's education, it alone is insufficient for a student to thrive academically and professionally (Capital, 2016[6]; Hart Research Associates, 2013[7]; National Association of Colleges and Employers, 2018[8]; Rios et al., 2020[9]; World Economic Forum, 2016[10]). The question of whether these generic skills are empirically predictive of post-higher education outcomes remains. CLA+ data from graduating seniors help answer questions about the importance of these skills and the effectiveness of using CLA+ as a tool for identifying students' strengths and areas of improvement.

The research results presented in this chapter are from two studies using a longitudinal data set that examined the validity of CLA+ as a predictor of post-higher education outcomes for students transitioning from higher education to career. CLA+ data from students who graduated in 2014 and 2017 and survey results from their employers and advisors help answer questions about the importance of these skills in post-higher education and whether they can be predicted by CLA+ test scores.

Study 1: CLA+ Predictive Validity of Post-Higher Education Outcomes

This study examined the validity of CLA+ as a predictor of post-higher education outcomes for students' transitions to their careers. A longitudinal survey was administered to spring 2014 graduates to follow their post-higher education experiences.

Method

Participants

A total of 12 752 seniors tested in spring 2014. They came from 149 four-year institutions of higher education that included a mix of public and private research universities, master's colleges and universities, and baccalaureate colleges. Admissions rates from the 149 institutions ranged from 18% to 100% (median 66%), six-year graduation rates ranged from 19% to 92% (median 55%), and percentage White ranged from 5% to 95% (median 68%). Criterion-referenced standards for the CLA+ were established (Zahner, 2014[11]) using the bookmark methodology (Lewis et al., 1999[12]). Table 7.1 shows the demographic information for the entire cohort and for those who earned the proficient, accomplished, or advanced level of mastery, which was 61.6% of the cohort.

Table 7.1. Demographic descriptive statistics

	All participants	Proficient, Accomplished & Advanced
n	12 752	7 849
% Female	62.3	61.2
% White	60.9	68.6
% English primary language spoken at home	85.7	88.9
% Parent with at least bachelor's degree	52.5	57.7
Mean (St. Dev) cumulative GPA (out of 4.0)	3.22 (.49)	3.34 (.46)

Data sources and materials

CLA+

Students took the CLA+ in spring 2014.

Survey #1

A longitudinal survey was administered to the 2014 cohort to follow their post-higher education experiences. Surveys were administered to participants three, six, and 12 months following graduation. Of approximately 13 000 students, 1 585 agreed to participate in the survey, and 993 persisted through all three phases. It should be noted that the registration for the survey was sent in August, three months after many of the participants had graduated, potentially limiting reach due to defunct or unattended email addresses.

Results

Logistic regressions were used to analyse the predictive validity of CLA+ scores on post-higher education outcomes (Table 7.2). These included:

- positive post-higher education outcomes in general (0 = no, 1 = yes to full- or part-time employment, enrolment in continuing education, military service, or participation in a service or volunteer programme such as AmeriCorps)
- annual salary (0 = below USD 45 000, 1 = above USD 45 000), using the national median for 2014 graduates from higher education (National Association of Colleges and Employers, 2015[13]) to determine the dichotomy
- employment (0 = unemployed, 1 = employed full or part time)
- full-time employment (0 = no, 1 = yes)
- continuing education (0 = not currently enrolled in a programme of continuing education, 1 = enrolled in a programme of continuing education).

The CLA+ score was used to predict the five dichotomous variables in separate analyses. The results are found in Table 7.2. CLA+ was found to be a significant predictor of all post-higher education outcomes for students one year following their graduation.

Table 7.2. Logistic regression results for predicting post-higher education outcomes by CLA+ scores

	General outcomes	Salary	Employment	Full-time employment	Graduate school
	β (SE)	β (SE)	β (SE)	β (SE)	β (SE)
n	969	634	791	705	318
CLA+ score	.002* (.001)	.002* (.001)	.003** (.001)	.001* (.001)	.003** (.001)
Intercept	.10 (.97)	-3.22** (.94)	-.91 (1.14)	-1.15 (.71)	-3.25** (1.14)
-2 Log likelihood	647.81	727.48	453.37	1059.47	386.00

Note: *p < .05; **p < .01

Race/Ethnicity by generic skills by institution competitiveness (Figure 7.1)

Race/ethnicity was self-reported by students in the demographic survey from the CLA+. Four categories were selected for analysis: Asian; African-American/Black, non-Hispanic; Hispanic or Latino; and White, non-Hispanic. Students were also categorised into two groups based on their mastery of the skills measured on CLA+: those proficient in critical thinking and written communication and those with developing or emerging skills. The final variable was whether the student attended a competitive or non-competitive institution (Barron's Profiles of American Colleges, 2014[14]).

Figure 7.1. Distribution of CLA+ proficiency and institution competitiveness by race/ethnicity; n = 12 476.

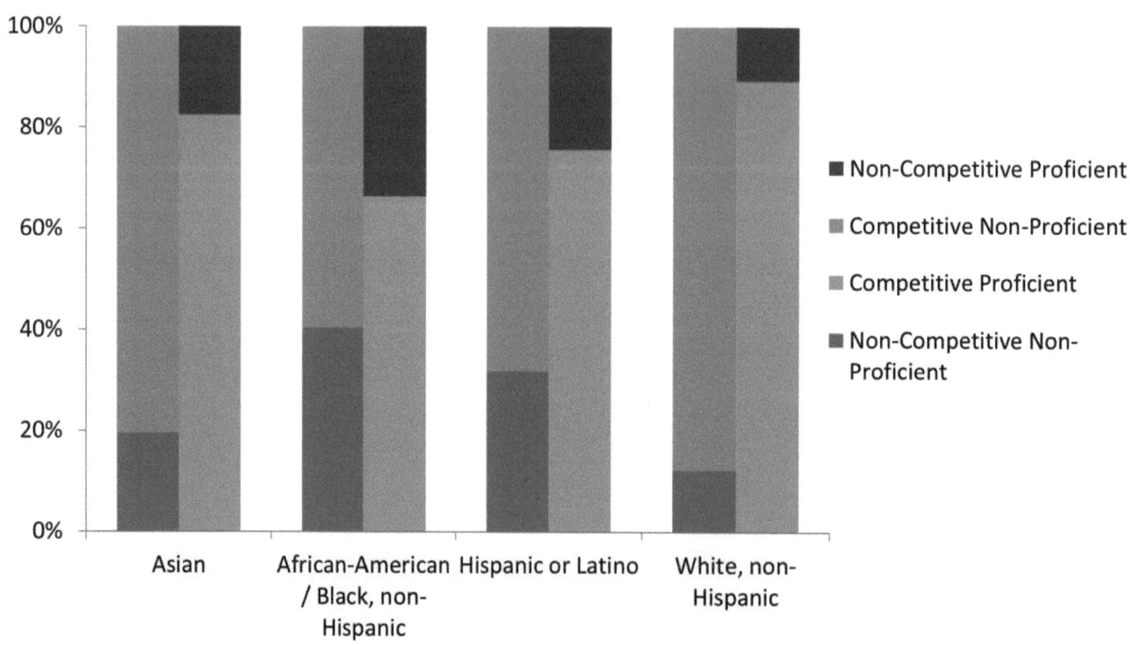

Basically, there are large proportions of minority students who have proficient and above mastery of the critical-thinking and written-communication skills attending non-competitive institutions. Approximately 35% of African-American/Black (non-Hispanic) and 25% of Hispanic or Latino students attending these non-competitive institutions have proficient, accomplished, or advanced skills. Although these proportions may not seem large, the number of minority students in less or non-competitive institutions far exceeds the number who attend the competitive institutions. This means that there is a significantly large group of qualified university graduates from under-represented or minority groups who may be overlooked as viable candidates due to the school they attended.

There are potentially millions of students graduating from less and non-competitive institutions (Benjamin, 2020[15]) who are proficient in the skills that employers say they desire (Hart Research Associates, 2013[7]), (2015[16]). Given that there is increasing enrolment at these less and non-selective institutions, which have higher proportions of minority students (Benjamin, 2020[15]), employers should expand their recruitment searches beyond the elite colleges and universities in order to have a more representative and diverse workforce.

Findings from this study offer support for the conclusion that critical-thinking and written-communication skills are important in predicting career placement and workplace success (Arum and Roksa, 2014[17]). Additionally, CLA+ can serve as both an effective instrument for identifying high-achieving students from less and non-competitive institutions and for making their skills more visible to perspective employees. The high-performing students who attend less and non-competitive institutions (Hoxby and Aver, 2012[18]) do in fact have the same critical-thinking skills as their peers at competitive institutions, which can potentially lead to positive post-college outcomes.

Study 2: CLA+ Predictive Validity of Employers' and Advisors' Assessments

This study follows the first study on the predictive validity of CLA+ on post-higher education outcomes and further answers the question of the importance of generic skills and the utility of an instrument for measuring these skills. In 2015, researchers contacted the employers or graduate advisors of the original student cohort and surveyed them. A second cohort of students from spring 2017 was also contacted for this study. They were not included in Study 1.

Method

Participants

From the spring 2014 cohort, 52 employers and 23 advisors responded to the survey for a total of 75 participants. An additional 10 employers and 4 advisors responded to a separate survey for the 2017 cohort, for a grand total of 89 participants. Given the small sample size, the employers' and advisors' survey results were analysed together. Table 7.3 shows the demographic information of the students whose employers and advisors responded to the survey and for all students who tested in spring 2014 as well as spring 2017.

Table 7.3. Demographic descriptive statistics

	Employer survey students	All participants spring 2014 & spring 2017
n	89	21 513
% Female	66.3	60.0
% White	66.3	59.2
% English primary language spoken at home	89.5	84.5
% Parent with at least bachelor's degree	66.2	51.9
Mean (St. Dev) cumulative GPA (out of 4.0)	3.37 (.45)	3.24 (.48)
Mean (St. Dev) SAT (or converted ACT)	1 114 (153)	1 066 (172)

Analysis

Descriptive statistics and chi-square tests were used to investigate whether employers and advisors care about the skills measured by CLA+. Ordinal logistic regression models were then used to illustrate the relationship between CLA+ total score and employers' and advisors' ratings of the participants on said skills, as well as the relationship between CLA+ total score and employers'/advisors' rating of how the participant ranked compared to other recent higher education graduates in the workplace/graduate programme. The proportional odds assumption was tested by comparing the fit of the ordinal logistic regression models with multinomial regression models. Both sets of models were found to result in very similar fit for each question.

Data sources and materials

Survey #2

In 2015, one year following graduation from university, a survey was administered to employers and advisors of students who took CLA+ in spring 2014. The survey was also administered to employers and advisors from the 2017 cohort. It should be noted that there is bias in the sample since students self-selected to provide their employers' and graduate advisors' information. However, the students did not significantly differ demographically from the total cohort of students (Table 7.3). There were slightly more female students, students who identified as white, students who spoke English as a primary language at home and students with parents with at least an undergraduate degree in the participating group than the total cohort.

The survey consisted of a series of questions (Table 7.4) regarding how important critical thinking and written communication skills are to successful performance by an employee or student, the employer's or advisor's perceptions of how proficient their employee or student is, and how the employee or student ranked in comparison to peers in the workplace or graduate programme.

Table 7.4. Employer survey questions

How important are the following skills to successful performance in the participant's position:	1 = Unimportant	2 = Of little importance	3 = Moderately important	4 = Important	5 = Very important
Analysis and Problem Solving					
Writing Effectiveness					
Writing Mechanics					
How would you rate the participant on the following skills:	1 = Unsatisfactory	2 = Needs improvement	3 = Satisfactory	4 = Good	5 = Outstanding
Analysis and Problem Solving					
Writing Effectiveness					
Writing Mechanics					
Overall, where does the participant's performance rank compared to other recent college graduates in your workplace?	1 = Well below other employees	2 = Below other employees	3 = About the same as other employees	4 = Above other employees	5 = Well above other employees

Results

Importance of CLA+ skills

Results indicate that employers and graduate advisors indeed find critical thinking and written communication skills, as measured by analysis and problem solving, writing effectiveness, and writing mechanics, important. Table 7.5 shows the distribution of responses to the first three questions in Table 7.4. Since only a few employers or graduate advisors responded "Unimportant" or "Of little importance", these two categories and "Moderately important" were collapsed into one "Moderately important or less" category in subsequent analyses. However, for descriptive purposes, we show the original five response categories.

As might be expected given the observed percentages reported in the table, the chi-square tests confirmed that the responses were significantly different from chance (i.e. there was not an equal chance that employers/advisors would choose any of the three responses to each question). Clearly, employers and graduate advisors deemed analysis and problem solving, writing effectiveness, and writing mechanics to be important or very important.

Table 7.5. Distribution of responses to "Importance" questions

Importance of	Unimportant	Of little importance	Moderately important	Important	Very important	$\chi^2(df)$, p
Analysis and Problem Solving	0%	0%	8%	24%	67%	132.96(4), $p < .001$
Writing Effectiveness	2%	4%	13%	34%	47%	63.93(4), $p < .001$
Writing Mechanics	5%	5%	19%	42%	30%	41.78(4), $p < .001$

CLA+ scores predicting participants' workplace or graduate school performance

Next, we used ordinal logistic regression models to examine the predictive ability of CLA+ total score on four ratings given by the participants' employer or graduate advisor (questions 4-7 in Table 7.4). Given that analysis and problem solving, writing effectiveness and writing mechanics are important or very important skills, how well does CLA+ total score predict participants' subsequent use of these skills in the workplace or graduate school? Also, how well does the CLA+ score predict relative rankings of the participants by the employer or graduate advisor?

Table 7.6 shows the ordinal logistic regression coefficients, their standard errors, 95% confidence intervals and the t-statistics ($p < .001$ for all analyses). The regression coefficients can be interpreted as the log-odds of being rated higher given a 1-point increase in CLA+ total score. For instance, in the analysis and problem solving model, the estimated coefficient is given as .0033. Thus, for a 1-point increase in CLA+ total score, the log-odds of "jumping" to a higher rating category ("Good" instead of "Satisfactory or worse", or "Outstanding" instead of "Good") increases by .0033. The regression coefficients are small because CLA+ total scores are on a large scale (400-1600), so one extra point is not expected to make much of a difference. Two factors would increase the interpretability of the results: 1) using a more meaningful score increase, such as 50 points, and 2) converting the log-odds to odds by exponentiating the coefficient. Thus, if one student scores 50 points higher than a second student, the log-odds of being rated one category higher than the second student is 50*.0033 = .165, and the odds are exp (.165) = 1.18. This first student is 18% more likely than the second student to be rated one category higher ("Good" rather than "Satisfactory or worse", or "Outstanding" rather than "Good") due to the higher CLA+ total score.

Table 7.6. Ordinal logistic regression models for predicting participants' post-higher education performance

Covariate	Est. coefficient	Std. error	t-statistic	95% CI	
				Lower	Upper
Analysis and Problem Solving					
CLA+ score	.0033	.0002	14.33	.0029	.0038
Writing Effectiveness					
CLA+ score	.0043	.0002	18.36	.0039	.0048
Writing Mechanics					
CLA+ score	.0046	.0002	19.33	.0041	.0051
Rank comparison of participant					
CLA+ score	.0049	.0002	22.18	.0045	.0053

Note: Estimated coefficients are log-odds of being rated one category higher given a 1-point increase in CLA+ total score.

Conclusion

Employers and advisors find critical thinking and written communication skills to be important or very important for entry-level positions in the workforce and graduate programmes. CLA+ is predictive of positive post-higher education outcomes as measured by employers' survey responses. This is important to note because despite approximately 1.8 million individuals graduating each year, employers are still finding a skills gap (Arum and Roksa, 2014[17]; Capital, 2016[6]; Hart Research Associates, 2013[7]; National Association of Colleges and Employers, 2018[8]; Rios et al., 2020[9]; World Economic Forum, 2016[10]). Recent graduates struggle to find appropriate entry-level jobs and wonder if they are getting a good return on their investment (Abel, Deitz and Su, 2014[19]). And traditional career services and job-search resources typically do not provide students with a platform to demonstrate higher-order skills to employers.

The impact to students who either do not graduate or graduate and are not able to find appropriate employment is huge for students and parents as well as institutions. The most recent data from the US Department of Education indicate that many low- and middle-income families have taken on a substantial amount of debt to finance their child's college education (Fuller and Mitchell, 2020[20]). The OECD (2013[21]) Survey of Adult Skills (PIAAC), assessing foundation skills such as literacy, numeracy and problem solving in digital environments has demonstrated that higher education qualifications, the most commonly used measure of human capital, are a poor indicator of the actual skills level of the population. There is growing evidence that qualifications do not match skills (McGowan and Andrews, 2015[22]). Helping students improve and showcase their critical thinking, problem solving and communication skills improves their chances for positive academic and career outcomes.

Findings from this study offer support for the conclusion that generic skills such as critical thinking and written communication are important in predicting career placement and workplace success. Additionally, the CLA+ can serve as an effective instrument not only for identifying high-achieving students but also for making their critical thinking and written communication skills more visible to prospective employers and graduate school admissions officers.

References

Abel, J., R. Deitz and Y. Su (2014), "Are recent college graduates finding good jobs?", *Current Issues in Economics and Finance*, Vol. 20/1. [19]

Arum, R. and J. Roksa (2014), *Aspiring Adults Adrift*, University of Chicago Press, Chicago, IL. [17]

Astin and L. Oseguera (2012), "Pre-College and Institutional Influences on Degree Attainment", in Seidman, A. (ed.), *College Student Retention: Formula for Student Success*, Rowman & Littlefield Publishers, New York. [5]

Banks, T. and J. Dohy (2019), "Mitigating Barriers to Persistence: A Review of Efforts to Improve Retention and Graduation Rates for Students of Color in Higher Education", *Higher Education Studies*, Vol. 9/1, pp. 118-131, https://doi.org/10.5539/hes.v9n1p118. [2]

Barron's Profiles of American Colleges (2014), *Barron's profiles of American colleges, 31st edition*, Barron's Educational Series. [14]

Benjamin, R. (2020), "Leveling the Playing Field From College to Career", in *Collective Goods and Higher Education Research*, https://doi.org/10.4324/9780429453069-6. [15]

Capital, P. (2016), *2016 Workforce-Skills Preparedness Report*, http://www.payscale.com/data-packages/job-skills. [6]

de Brey, C. et al. (2019), "Status and trends in the education of racial and ethnic groups 2018", *National Center for Educational Statistics*, Vol. NCES 2019-038, https://nces.ed.gov/programs/raceindicators/index.asp. [1]

Fuller, A. and J. Mitchell (2020), "Which Schools Leave Parents With the Most College Loan Debt?", *The wall street journal*, https://www.wsj.com/articles/which-schools-leave-parents-with-the-most-college-loan-debt-11606936947. [20]

Hart Research Associates (2015), *Falling short? College learning and career success*, Hart Research Associates, Retrieved from Washington, DC, http://www.aacu.org/sites/default/files/files/LEAP/2015employerstudentsurvey.pdf. [16]

Hart Research Associates (2013), "It takes more than a major: Employer priorities for college learning and student success", *Liberal Education*, Vol. 99/2. [7]

Hernandez, J. and M. Lopez (2004), "Leaking Pipeline: Issues Impacting Latino/A College Student Retention", *Journal of College Student Retention: Research, Theory & Practice*, Vol. 6/1, pp. 37-60, https://doi.org/10.2190/fbly-0uaf-ee7w-qjd2. [3]

Hoxby, C. and C. Aver (2012), "The Missing One-Offs: The hidden supply of high-achieving, low-income students", *National Bureau of Economic Research Working Paper 18586*. [18]

Lewis, D. et al. (1999), *The Bookmark Standard Setting Procedure*, McGraw-Hill, Monterey, CA. [12]

McGowan, M. and D. Andrews (2015), *Skill mismatch and public policy in OECD countries*, OECD Publishing, Paris. [22]

National Association of Colleges and Employers (2018), *Are college graduates "career ready"?*, https://www.naceweb.org/career-readiness/competencies/are-college-graduates-career-ready/. [8]

National Association of Colleges and Employers (2015), *Average starting salary for college class of 2014*, http://www.naceweb.org/about-us/press/average-starting-salaries-class-2014.aspx. [13]

National Student Clearinghouse Research Center (2019), *First-Year Persistence and Retention for Fall 2017 Cohort*, https://nscresearchcenter.org/snapshotreport35-first-year-persistence-and-retention/. [4]

OECD (2013), *Technical report of the Survey of Adult Skills (PIAAC)*, OECD, Paris, http://www.oecd.org/skills/piaac/_Technical%20Report_17OCT13.pdf. [21]

Rios, J. et al. (2020), "Identifying Critical 21st-Century Skills for Workplace Success: A Content Analysis of Job Advertisements", *Educational Researcher*, Vol. 49/2, pp. 80-89, https://doi.org/10.3102/0013189X19890600. [9]

World Economic Forum (2016), *Global Challenge Insight Report: The Future of Jobs: Employment, Skills and Workforce Strategy for the Fourth Industrial Revolution*, World Economic Forum, http://www3.weforum.org/docs/WEF_Future_of_Jobs.pdf. [10]

Zahner, D. (2014), *CLA+ Standard Setting Study Final Report*, Council for Aid to Education, New York, NY. [11]

8 Fields of study

Tess Dawber, Council for Aid to Education (United States)

Olivia Cortellini, Council for Aid to Education (United States)

This chapter explores the relationships between student performance on the Collegiate Learning Assessment (CLA+) and fields of study at university or college. The fields of study are classified differently for the international and U.S. samples. Therefore, the results are presented separately. In addition, the international survey included questions about the format of instruction. These data are discussed first.

Instructional format

After completing the CLA+, the international students responded to a series of questions, including questions about the format of their instruction. Questions are not mutually exclusive; students were asked to select all that apply.

The table in the Annex shows the number and percentage of students that endorsed each of the instructional formats, shown in the column headings by field of study. The percentages are calculated based on the number of students for a given field of study. For example, reading across the row for liberal arts students, their instruction included lectures (54% of students), art studios (51%), and seminars (41%), to name a few formats. Overall, lectures, seminars and independent study were the most endorsed instruction formats across the fields of study.

Students' performance on the CLA+ was examined for each instructional format. Table 8.1 shows the CLA+ mean scores by instructional format. It is important to note that there is overlap in the samples (e.g., students who participated in seminars may also have participated in independent studies). The mean total scores for students who participated in seminars, science laboratories or lectures were within the Proficient level of mastery. The mean total scores for the other instructional formats were within the Developing mastery level. Lecture and seminar formats are common across all fields of study, but the science laboratories were indicated most often by science students (see Annex). The results suggest that having students engage in seminars, science laboratories or lectures may facilitate the development of critical thinking skills. Figure 8.1 shows the average student CLA+ scores by instructional format.

Table 8.1. CLA+ scores by instructional format: International sample

Instructional Format	N	CLA+ Mean Score		
		Total	PT	SRQ
Seminar	5 497	1 112	1 126	1 097
Lecture	7 526	1 103	1 111	1 095
Distance learning/online class	2 997	1 092	1 084	1 100
Science laboratory	1 458	1 105	1 105	1 105
Art studio	2 662	1 094	1 105	1 083
Service learning/field work	3 510	1 072	1 080	1 064
Independent study	5 713	1 096	1 105	1 087
Other	1 629	1 082	1 083	1 081

Figure 8.1. Average CLA+ scores by instructional format for the international sample

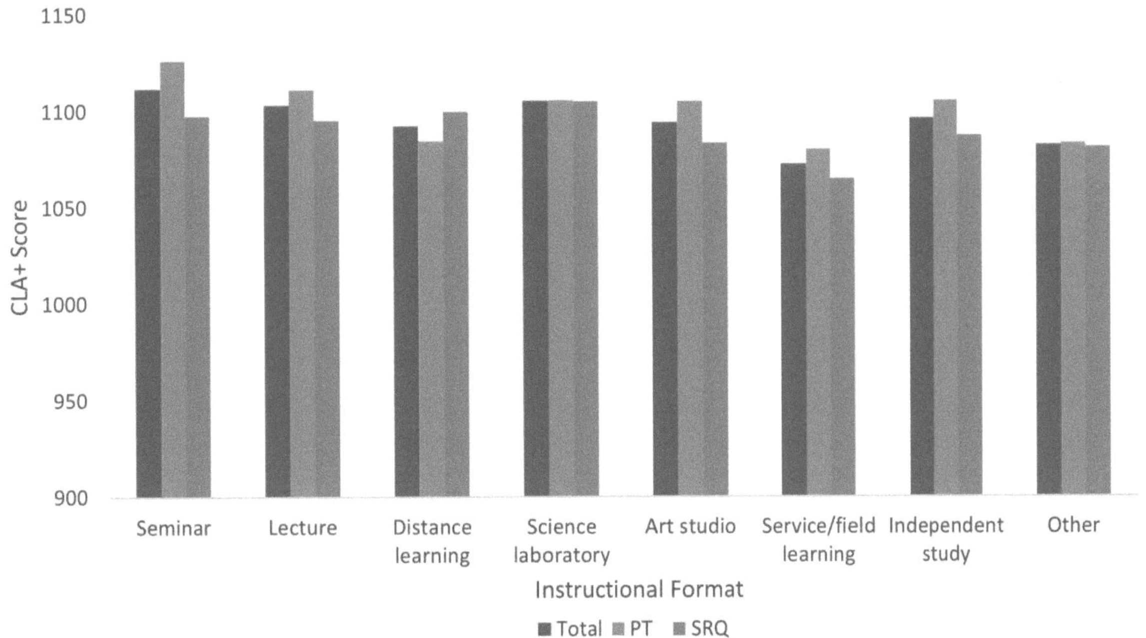

Note: PT = Performance Task; SRQ = Selected-Response Questions

Fields of study for international students

The fields of study response options differed depending on whether students tested on the international platform or the domestic platform. The countries that tested on the international platform were Chile, Finland, Mexico and some United Kingdom students (22%). The domestic platform included the United States only. The average student score results are presented in tables as well as illustrated in figures.

Table 8.2 presents the CLA+ total score and section results by field of study for the international sample. The table shows the average scale score results for the entering and exiting students and the average difference between those scores. When mean difference results are positive, exiting students achieved higher scores on average than entering students; when mean difference results are negative, entering students achieved higher scores on average than exiting students. Generally, the exiting students achieved higher mean scores than entering students, with a few exceptions.

Fields of study with fewer than 100 students for either cohort were excluded to avoid reporting results that are not representative of the student groups. The three fields of study excluded were the general programme (liberal arts), law, and services (social services, nursing) programmes.

Looking at the CLA+ total score results, the average scores for science, humanities or arts, and social sciences were within the Proficient mastery level for entering students. All average scores for exiting students were classified as Proficient except for business and agriculture. The mean difference values show greater growth from entering to exiting status for the health or welfare and not-specified groups. Another observation is that the samples for entering students were much higher than those for the exiting students, roughly between 2 and 4 times higher.

To determine whether there were performance differences across the fields of study for the international students, analysis of variance (ANOVA) was performed. The results in Table 8.3 show that there were significant differences for both cohorts and for each CLA+ score, although the effect sizes were low.

Table 8.2. CLA+ scores by field of study for student cohorts: International sample

Field of Study	Entering students			Exiting students			Mean difference
	Mean	N	SD	Mean	N	SD	
CLA+ Total Score							
Humanities or arts	1 109	2 228	129	1 119	697	134	9
Social sciences	1 098	1 188	129	1 109	326	133	12
Business	1 057	1 269	131	1 055	412	131	-2
Science	1 113	1 580	135	1 117	417	126	5
Engineering, manufacturing, architecture, or construction	1 092	2 155	124	1 106	576	124	14
Agriculture	996	425	122	991	177	111	-5
Health or welfare (social services, nursing)	1 076	1 158	116	1 098	616	125	22
Not known or not otherwise specified	1 075	379	124	1 113	139	114	38
CLA+ Performance Task							
Humanities or arts	1 120	2 228	158	1 137	697	163	17
Social sciences	1 099	1 188	166	1 123	326	166	24
Business	1 084	1 269	179	1 065	412	176	-19
Science	1 103	1 580	162	1 124	417	149	21
Engineering, manufacturing, architecture, or construction	1 088	2 155	151	1 100	576	148	12
Agriculture	975	425	167	986	177	149	11
Health or welfare (social services, nursing)	1 086	1 158	142	1 120	616	156	34
Not known or not otherwise specified	1 073	379	151	1 116	139	133	44
CLA+ Selected-Response Questions							
Humanities or arts	1 099	2 228	163	1 101	697	164	2
Social sciences	1 097	1 188	159	1 096	326	170	-1
Business	1 030	1 269	154	1 044	412	154	14
Science	1 123	1 580	172	1 111	417	168	-12
Engineering, manufacturing, architecture, or construction	1 096	2 155	161	1 113	576	164	16
Agriculture	1 018	425	143	997	177	134	-21
Health or welfare (social services, nursing)	1 065	1 158	157	1 075	616	158	10
Not known or not otherwise specified	1 077	379	156	1 109	139	177	32

Note: "Mean difference" is calculated by subtracting the mean for "Entering" from the mean for "Exiting".

To determine whether there were performance differences across the fields of study for the international students, ANOVA analyses were performed. The results in Table 8.3 show that there were significant differences for both cohorts and for each CLA+ score, although the effect sizes were low.

Table 8.3. One-way ANOVA for CLA+ scores across fields of study for international students

Cohort	CLA+ Score	df	F	$\eta2$	p
Entering	Total CLA+ score	7, 10381	63.46	0.041	<.001
	Performance Task score	7, 10381	45.95	0.030	<.001
	Selected-Response score	7, 10381	51.76	0.034	<.001
Exiting	Total CLA+ score	7, 3359	29.60	0.058	<.001
	Performance Task score	7, 3359	24.73	0.049	<.001
	Selected-Response score	7, 3359	17.03	0.034	<.001

Bonferroni post hoc comparisons were conducted using a significance level of 0.05. For the CLA+ total score, the science and humanities students performed better than all or most of the other fields of study and all or most of the other fields of study performed better than business and agriculture for the entering cohort. For the exiting cohort, the humanities and science students outperformed the business and agriculture students, and all groups performed better than the agriculture group.

The CLA+ PT results show that humanities and arts students performed better than all other fields of study and all other fields of study performed better than agriculture for the entering cohort. For the exiting cohort, all fields of study outperformed the business and agriculture groups.

The CLA+ SRQ results show science students performed better than all other groups, and the business and agriculture students received lower scores on average than the other fields of study for the entering cohort. For the exiting cohort, engineering students performed better than health and welfare, business, and agriculture students; business performed better than agriculture but lower than most other groups, and agriculture students performed lower than all other groups.

These results suggest that there are consistent and meaningful differences across the fields of study. The business and agriculture students were found to have relatively low scores and the humanities, science and social science students were found to have relatively high scores compared to their peers in other fields of study. The implication of these findings is that students, particularly business and agriculture students, may benefit from some instructional workshops on critical thinking and written communication skills to increase their skills to the level of other fields of study.

Figure 8.2-Figure 8.4 show the international student results for the CLA+ total, PT, and SRQ scores, respectively.

Figure 8.2. International students' CLA+ total scores by field of study

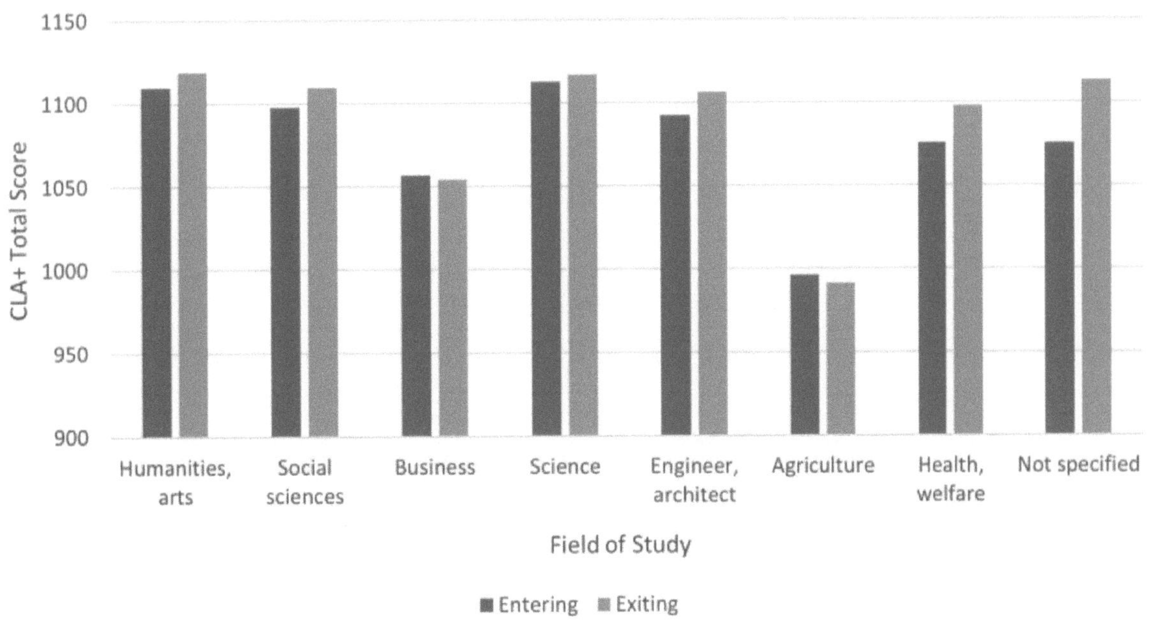

Figure 8.3. International students' performance task scores by field of study

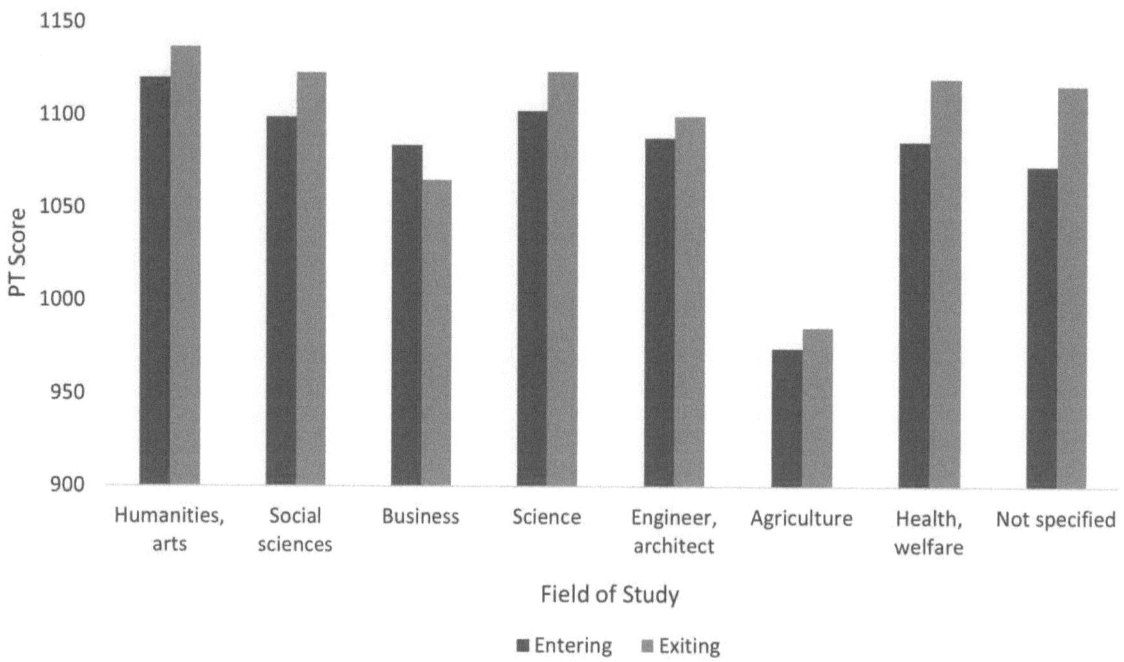

Figure 8.4. International students' selected response scores by field of study

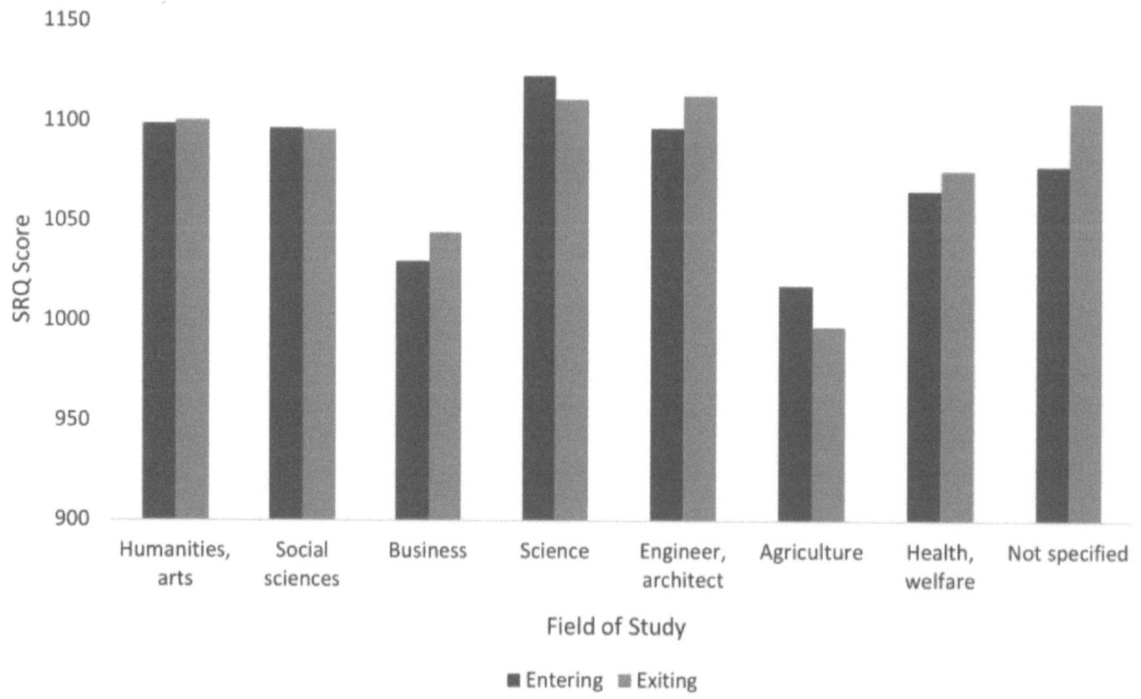

Fields of study for U.S. students

The fields of study for the United States consisted of five categories. Table 8.4 presents the results by cohort and field of study for each CLA+ score. The mean difference results are shown as well.

Looking at the CLA+ total score results for entering students, only the average score for sciences and engineering students was at the Proficient mastery level, and the average scores for the other fields of study were at the Developing mastery level. In contrast, the average scores for the exiting students were in the Proficient range for sciences and engineering, social sciences, and humanities and languages students, and in the Developing range for business and helping/services. It is interesting to note that the ranking of the fields of study remained the same for the entering and exiting students across all three CLA+ scores. Science and engineering students obtained the highest mean score, followed by social science, humanities and languages, business, and helping/services.

The mean difference results were positive for all CLA+ scores and fields of study, indicating that the exiting students consistently achieved higher scores on average than the entering students. The highest mean difference was observed for the helping/services field across all three CLA+ scores, which may suggest that studies in the helping/services area contribute to acquiring critical thinking and written communication skills.

Table 8.4. CLA+ scores by field of study for student cohorts: U.S. Sample

Field of Study	Entering students			Exiting students			Mean difference
	Mean	N	SD	Mean	N	SD	
Total Score							
Business	1 046	8 572	146	1 087	10 611	143	41
Helping/Services	1 018	11 239	139	1 078	11 191	143	61
Humanities and Languages	1 069	4 057	148	1 110	6 327	149	41
Sciences and Engineering	1 097	16 290	146	1 143	10 015	146	45
Performance Task							
Business	1 033	8572	166	1 079	10 611	168	46
Helping/Services	1 010	11 239	164	1 068	11 191	166	58
Humanities and Languages	1 052	4 057	168	1 100	6 327	170	48
Sciences and Engineering	1 069	16 290	164	1 116	10 015	167	47
Social Sciences	1 055	5 078	174	1 106	6 871	172	51
Selected-Response Score							
Business	1 059	8 572	181	1 095	10 611	177	35
Helping/Services	1 025	11 239	172	1 089	11 191	176	64
Humanities and Languages	1 086	4 057	184	1 119	6 327	184	34
Sciences and Engineering	1 125	16 290	184	1 169	10 015	181	44
Social Sciences	1 090	5 078	186	1 130	6 871	183	39

To determine whether there were significant performance differences across the fields of study for the U.S. students, ANOVA analyses were performed. The results in Table 8.5 show that there were significant differences for both cohorts for each CLA+ score although the effect sizes were relatively low. Figure 8.5, Figure 8.6 and Figure 8.7 show the mean scale score results for each CLA+ score by fields of study for the U.S. sample.

Table 8.5. One-way ANOVA for CLA+ scores across fields of study for U.S. students

Cohort	CLA+ score	df	F	η2	p
Entering	Total CLA+ score	4, 45231	536.83	0.045	<.001
	Performance Task score	4, 45231	229.00	0.020	<.001
	Selected-Response score	4, 45231	548.18	0.046	<.001
Exiting	Total CLA+ score	4, 45010	318.44	0.028	<.001
	Performance Task score	4, 45010	140.46	0.012	<.001
	Selected-Response score	4, 45010	330.66	0.029	<.001

Bonferroni post hoc tests were conducted at the 0.05 significance level. The same pattern of results emerged for both cohorts and for all CLA+ test scores. Specifically, sciences and engineering, and social sciences students outperformed all or most other fields of study; business and helping/services students performed lower than all or most other fields of study.

Figure 8.5. U.S. students' CLA+ total scores by field of study

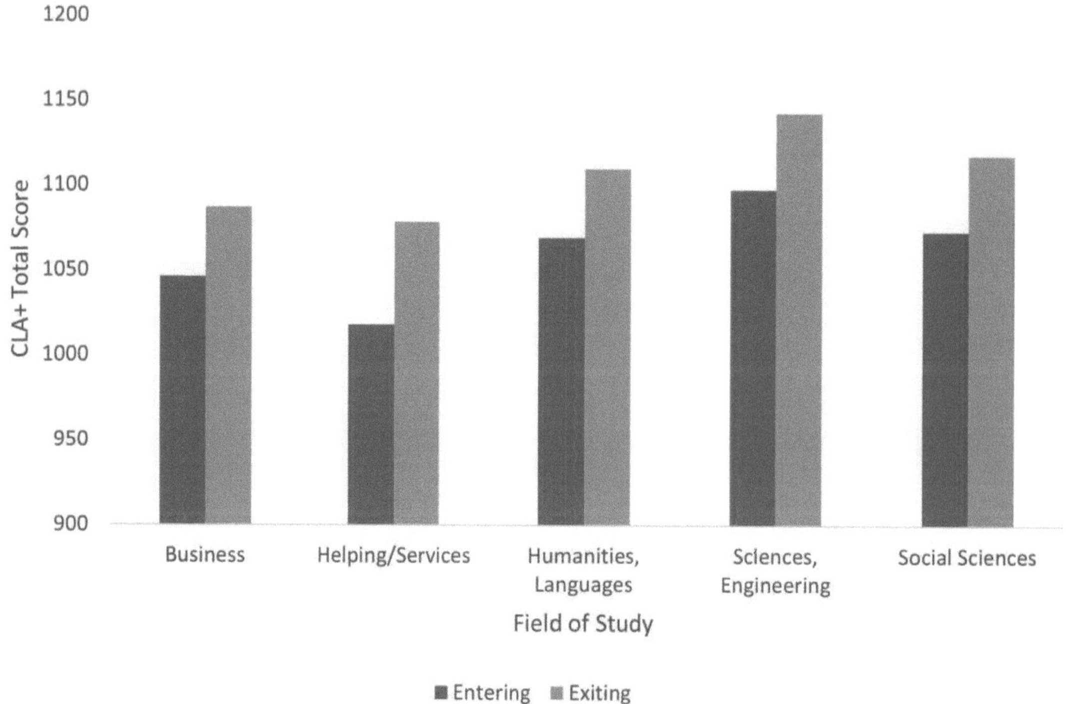

Figure 8.6. U.S. students' performance task scores by field of study

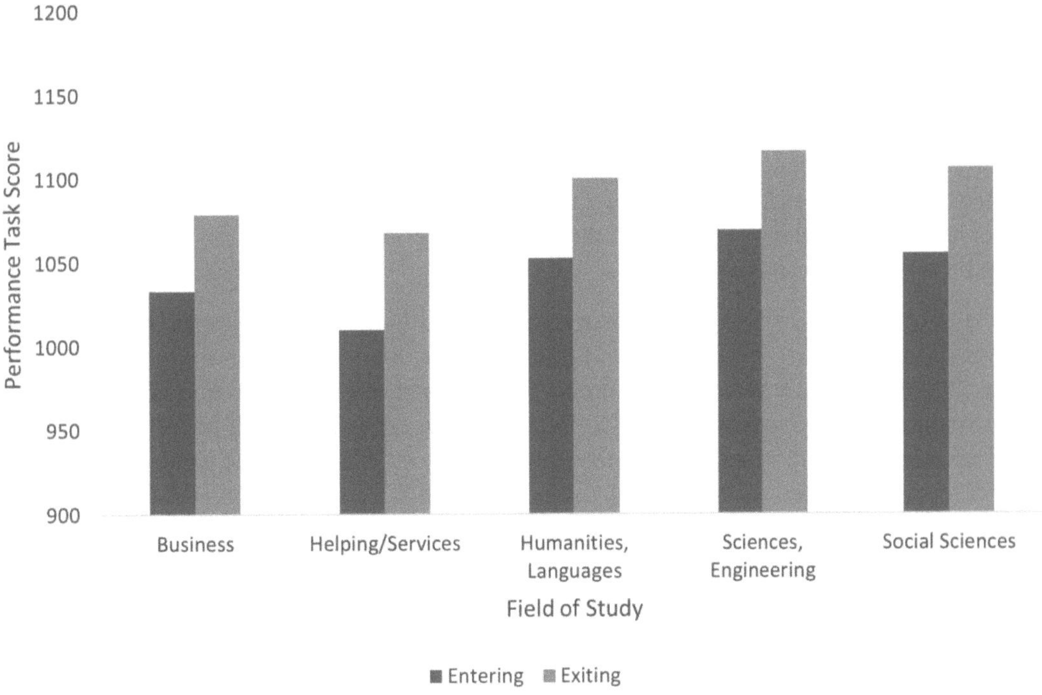

Figure 8.7. U.S. students' selected response scores by field of study

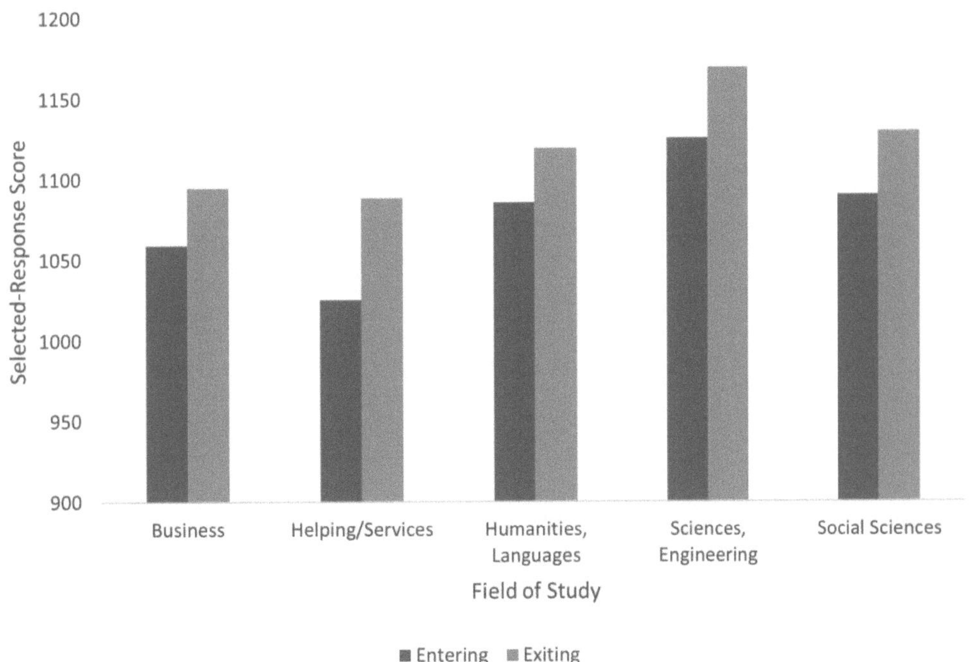

Conclusion

This chapter explored the relationships between student performance on the CLA+ and fields of study at university or college. In addition, students' performance on the CLA+ was examined for each instructional format. On average, CLA+ scores for students who participated in seminars, science laboratories or lectures were within the Proficient level of mastery.

The fields of study for the international students were different from those for the U.S. students. For the international students, the science and humanities students tended to outperform their peers in other fields of study. For the U.S. sample, the sciences and engineering students, and the social science students outperformed their peers on average.

These results suggest that there are consistent and meaningful differences across the fields of study for the international and U.S. samples. The international sample is more diverse than the U.S. sample. As noted in Part III of this book, the chapters from Italy, Finland, the United Kingdom, Mexico and Latin American describe the introduction of the CLA+ within a specific context and for a specific purpose. Regardless of educational policies and accountability programmes, student groups may benefit from instruction to facilitate developing their critical thinking and written communication skills.

Annex 8.A. International sample: Instructional format by fields of study

Annex Table 8.A.1. Instructional format by fields of study for the international sample

		Seminars		Lectures		Distance Learning/ Online Classes		Science Laboratories		Art Studios		Service Learning/ Field Work		Independent Study		Other	
		N	%	N	%	N	%	N	%	N	%	N	%	N	%	N	%
General programme (liberal arts)	161	80	49.7%	115	71.4%	35	21.7%	5	3.1%	27	16.8%	29	18.0%	44	27.3%	22	13.7%
Humanities or arts	2 925	1 209	41.3%	1 591	54.4%	312	10.7%	86	2.9%	1 481	50.6%	702	24.0%	1195	40.9%	286	9.8%
Social sciences	1 514	740	48.9%	999	66.0%	342	22.6%	70	4.6%	126	8.3%	334	22.1%	564	37.3%	131	8.7%
Business	1 681	722	43.0%	920	54.7%	431	25.6%	42	2.5%	96	5.7%	395	23.5%	652	38.8%	133	7.9%
Science	1 997	813	40.7%	993	49.7%	415	20.8%	533	26.7%	192	9.6%	381	19.1%	807	40.4%	256	12.8%
Engineering, manufacturing, architecture, or construction	2 731	818	30.0%	1 163	42.6%	650	23.8%	394	14.4%	445	16.3%	541	19.8%	1104	40.4%	425	15.6%
Agriculture	602	159	26.4%	230	38.2%	92	15.3%	79	13.1%	77	12.8%	298	49.5%	224	37.2%	78	13.0%
Health or welfare (social services, nursing)	1 774	681	38.4%	980	55.2%	550	31.0%	217	12.2%	115	6.5%	620	34.9%	807	45.5%	160	9.0%
Services (personal, transport, environmental, security)	272	77	28.3%	155	57.0%	55	20.2%	7	2.6%	10	3.7%	52	19.1%	106	39.0%	29	10.7%
Not known or not otherwise specified	518	146	28.2%	288	55.6%	73	14.1%	23	4.4%	89	17.2%	138	26.6%	156	30.1%	100	19.3%
Total	14 175	5 445		7 434		2 955		1 456		2 658		3490		5 659		1 620	

Note: Percentages in the orange cells are between 25 and 50 percent; percentages in the grey cells are greater than 50 percent.

9 Benchmarking countries

Tess Dawber, Council for Aid to Education (United States)

Olivia Cortellini, Council for Aid to Education (United States)

Chapter 9 addresses the benchmarking of countries. Although Chapter 5 summarises the mastery levels across countries, equally weighting the countries because of sample size differences, the current chapter discusses the results by country without disclosing the nationalities. The countries are labelled A through E for anonymity. The data presented include only countries that tested entering and exiting students, which are Chile, Finland, Mexico, the United Kingdom and the United States. Italy tested exiting students only and, therefore, is not included in these results.

Introduction

The first section of the chapter presents the mastery levels for entering and exiting students by country. The second section of the chapter covers the summary statistics for entering and exiting students by country. Both sections together provide insight into student performance on the CLA+ by examining patterns of performance across countries.

Mastery levels by country

Table 9.1 presents the percentage of entering and exiting students at each mastery level by country. The difference between the percentage of exiting and entering students is shown in the row labelled "Difference" (exiting minus entering). The expectation is that exiting students would perform better than entering students given that exiting students have completed several years of post-secondary education. We would expect to see a lower percentage of exiting students classified into the Emerging and Developing mastery levels (negative difference) and a higher percentage of exiting students classified into the Proficient, Accomplished and Advanced mastery levels (positive difference). The results show this is generally the case for four of the five countries. Country C shows small percentage differences across the mastery levels, some of which are in the direction opposite to what is expected (e.g. a slightly higher percentage of students in the exiting cohort are classified as Developing compared to entering students). The results for Country C suggest that students' performance on the CLA+ was similar for entering and exiting students.

Table 9.1. Mastery level by country and cohort

Country	Cohort	Mastery level				
		Emerging	Developing	Proficient	Accomplished	Advanced
A	Entering	14.4%	35.9%	33.3%	14.6%	1.8%
	Exiting	9.3%	32.0%	35.9%	20.2%	2.5%
	Difference	-5.1%	-3.9%	2.6%	5.6%	0.7%
B	Entering	18.1%	38.6%	33.8%	9.5%	0.1%
	Exiting	12.4%	35.9%	36.3%	14.7%	0.7%
	Difference	-5.7%	-2.7%	2.5%	5.2%	0.6%
C	Entering	17.4%	36.2%	31.5%	12.9%	2.0%
	Exiting	17.1%	37.7%	30.9%	12.0%	2.4%
	Difference	-0.3%	1.5%	-0.6%	-0.9%	0.4%
D	Entering	14.8%	29.0%	34.3%	18.6%	3.4%
	Exiting	6.5%	22.6%	32.3%	30.3%	8.4%
	Difference	-8.3%	-6.4%	-2.0%	11.7%	5.0%
E	Entering	27.1%	31.5%	26.6%	13.3%	1.5%
	Exiting	17.9%	29.3%	30.5%	19.3%	2.9%
	Difference	-9.2%	-2.2%	3.9%	6.0%	1.4%

Note: "Difference" is calculated by subtracting the percentage for "Entering" from the percentage for "Exiting".

Figure 9.1. Mastery level by country and cohort

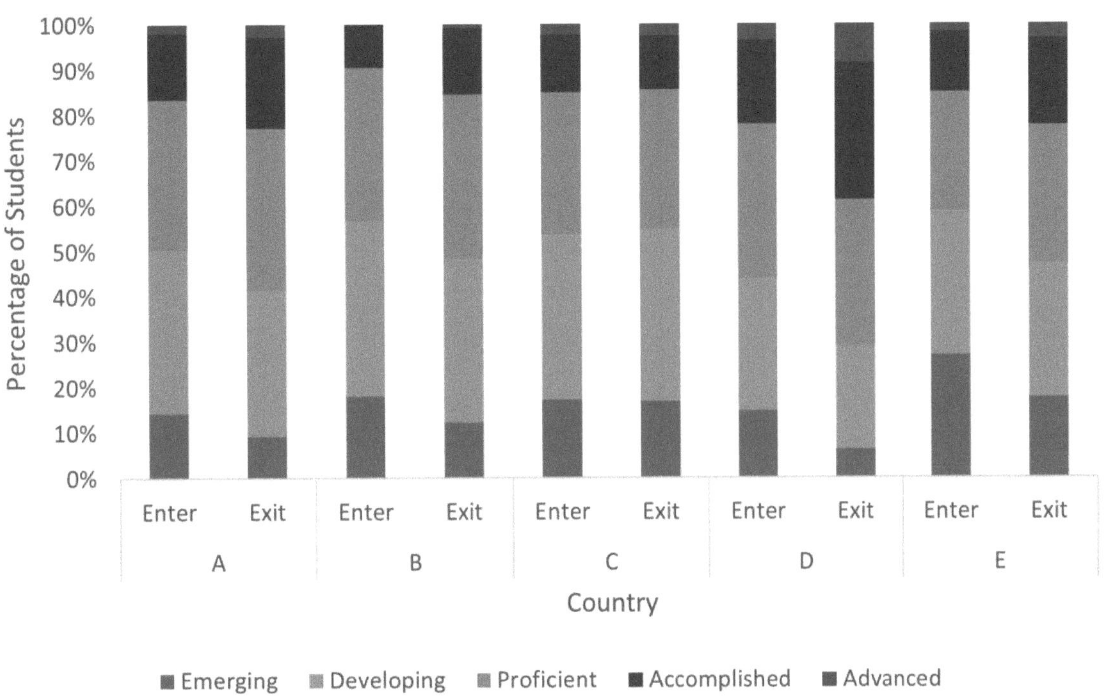

Figure 9.2 shows a different perspective. It presents the mastery level percentage difference values (exiting minus entering) found in Table 9.1 by country and mastery level. Although the patterns are the same for Countries A, B, D and E, the results for Countries D and E show more dramatic changes than Countries A and B. That is, the percentage of students classified into each mastery level differs to a greater extent based on entering and exiting status.

Figure 9.2. CLA+ total score percentage difference between exiting and entering students

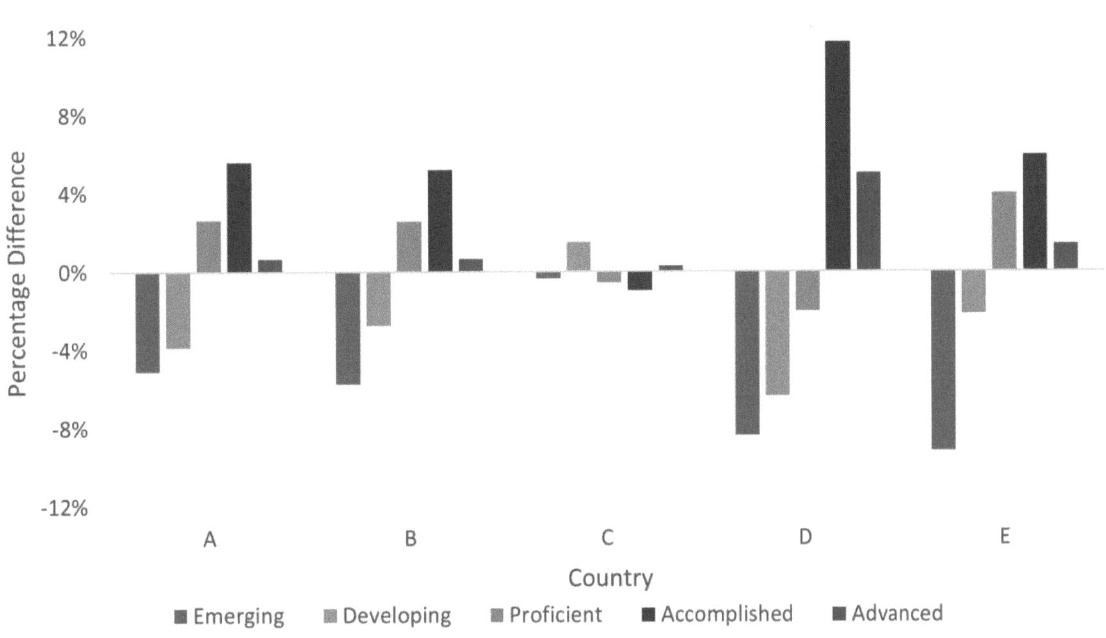

Several factors come into play when interpreting cross-country results:

- Do post-secondary education systems support the development of critical thinking skills?
- Are there systematic differences in the entering and exiting student groups? High-achieving entering students and low-achieving exiting students will show smaller differences than low-achieving entering students and high-achieving exiting students.
- Were students motivated to perform well on the test?

Given that each country's education system and political environment are unique, the other chapters in the book provide insight into the purposes and goals for administering the CLA+ to the samples of students chosen to participate. The growth between entering and exiting students' skills may be interpreted in the context of those factors.

The importance of effort and engagement on CLA+ scores was highlighted in Chapter 5. Students who reported high interest and engagement in the Selected-Response Question (SRQ) and Performance Task (PT) sections achieved higher section scores. The results tended to be linear. With each successive endorsement of a higher rating of effort and engagement, there was an incremental increase in PT and SRQ section scores.

Another means of assessing effort and motivation is to look at whether students used all the allotted time to complete the SRQ and PT sections. Typically, we find that most students do not use all the time. On occasion, some of the students do not answer the final few questions on the SRQ section. Between time use and question response, we hypothesise that motivation may be a factor for some students.

Summary statistics

This section presents CLA+ summary results by country and cohort. Table 9.2 shows the mean, the 25th and 75th percentile rank scores, and the interquartile range for entering and exiting students. The difference between the mean exiting and entering student scores is presented in the last column (mean difference). These percentile rank scores convey variability in student scores that is not subject to the outlier values.

Surprisingly, the average CLA+ total scores across countries were relatively similar. For example, the lowest and highest average CLA+ total scores for entering students were 1 060 and 1 111, respectively. However, the lowest value was classified as the Developing mastery level and the highest value was classified as the Proficient mastery level. The largest mean differences between exiting and entering students were observed for Countries D and E for each CLA+ test component. These results provide a consistent picture with the results presented above. There were greater score gains from the entering to exiting cohorts for Countries D and E compared to the other countries. The mean difference values for Country C indicate that the performance of entering and exiting students was similar.

The interquartile ranges were widest for the CLA+ SRQ score for each country. Recall that the SRQ section is out of 25 raw score points, compared to 18 raw score points for the PT. However, the largest mean difference values were observed for the PT section scores, indicating a gain in written communication skills measured by the CLA+ assessment.

Table 9.2. CLA+ scores by country and cohort

Country	Entering students				Exiting students				Mean difference
	Mean	25th perc. rank	75th perc. rank	Inter-quartile range	Mean	25th perc. rank	75th perc. rank	Inter-quartile range	
CLA+ total score									
A	1 099	1 018	1 186	168	1 127	1 038	1 214	177	28
B	1 072	996	1 153	157	1 101	1 022	1 185	163	29
C	1 086	999	1 173	174	1 085	996	1 169	173	-1
D	1 111	1 020	1 210	190	1 176	1 070	1 277	207	64
E	1 060	952	1 168	216	1 103	1 001	1 210	209	42
CLA+ PT score									
A	1 096	1 001	1 181	180	1 130	1 046	1 226	180	35
B	1 062	989	1 148	159	1 099	1 021	1 180	159	37
C	1 088	1 001	1 181	180	1 099	1 001	1 181	180	10
D	1 188	1 084	1 290	206	1 263	1 155	1 372	217	74
E	1 043	931	1 159	228	1 090	976	1 207	231	47
CLA+ SRQ score									
A	1 101	978	1 220	242	1 123	998	1 250	252	21
B	1 082	966	1 195	229	1 102	984	1 224	240	20
C	1 084	969	1 191	222	1 071	951	1 176	225	-13
D	1 034	919	1 150	231	1 089	982	1 205	223	55
E	1 078	938	1 217	279	1 116	985	1 253	268	38

Note: "Mean difference" is calculated by subtracting the mean scale score for "Entering students" from the mean scale score for "Exiting students". PT = Performance Task; SRQ = Selected-Response Question

To get a sense of how these values compare across countries, Figure 9.3, Figure 9.4 and Figure 9.5 illustrate the scale scores at the 25th and 75th percentile ranks by cohort and country for the CLA+ total test score, PT section score and SRQ section score, respectively. The first thing to notice across the figures is the variability across countries. The differences are more pronounced for the PT section compared to the SRQ section and total test score. For example, compare Countries D and E for the PT results. Educational systems may place different emphasis on written communication skills, resulting in higher achievement for some countries. Overall, these results suggest that different countries tend to have different strengths on the PT and SRQ sections.

Figure 9.3. CLA+ total score results by country and student cohort

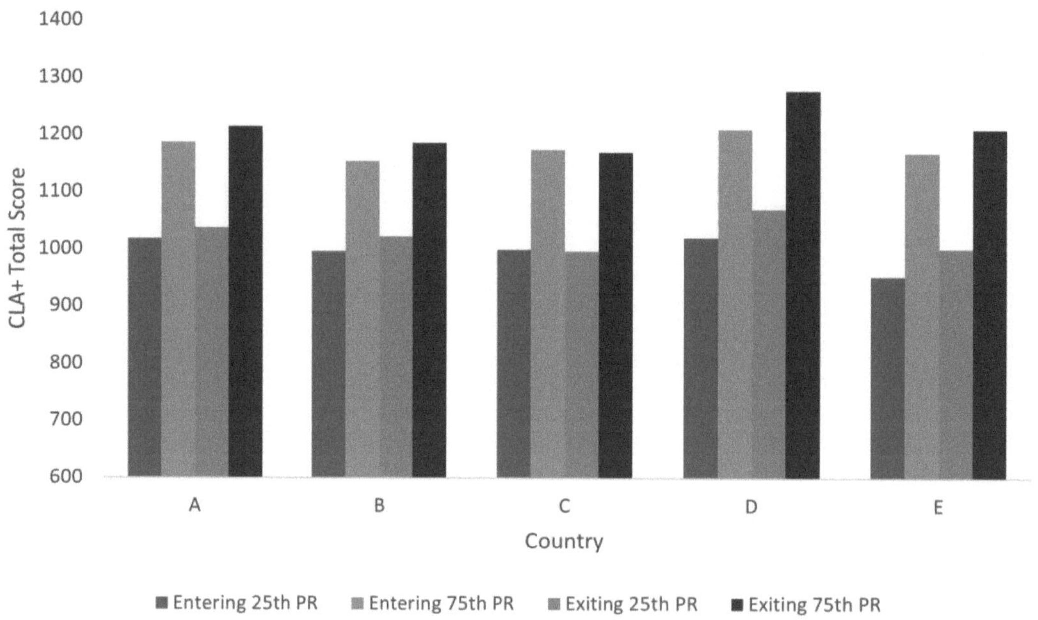

Note: PR = percentile rank

Figure 9.4. CLA+ Performance Task (PT) score results by country and student cohort

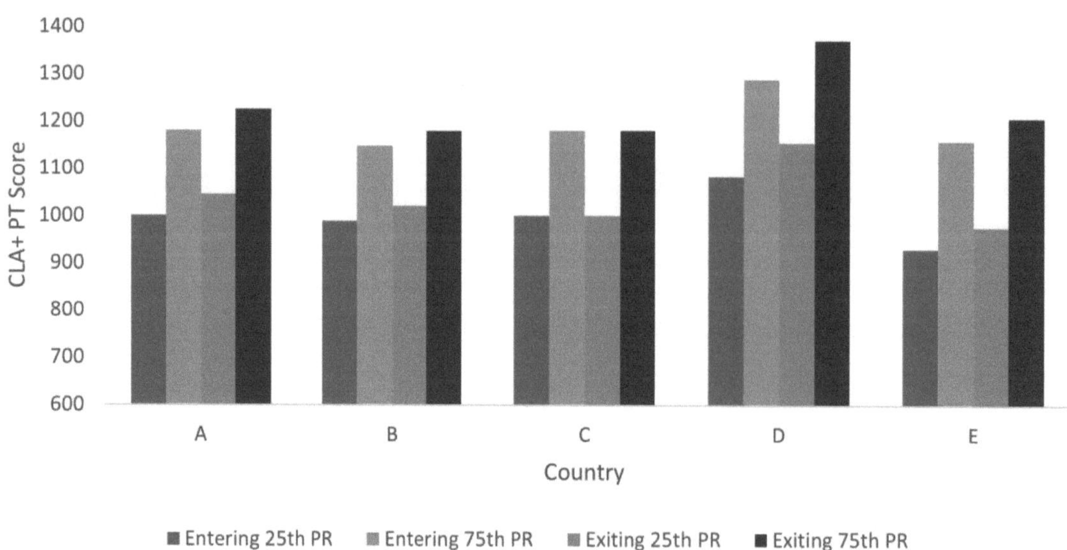

Note: PR = percentile rank

Figure 9.5. CLA+ Selected-Response Question (SRQ) score results by country and student cohort

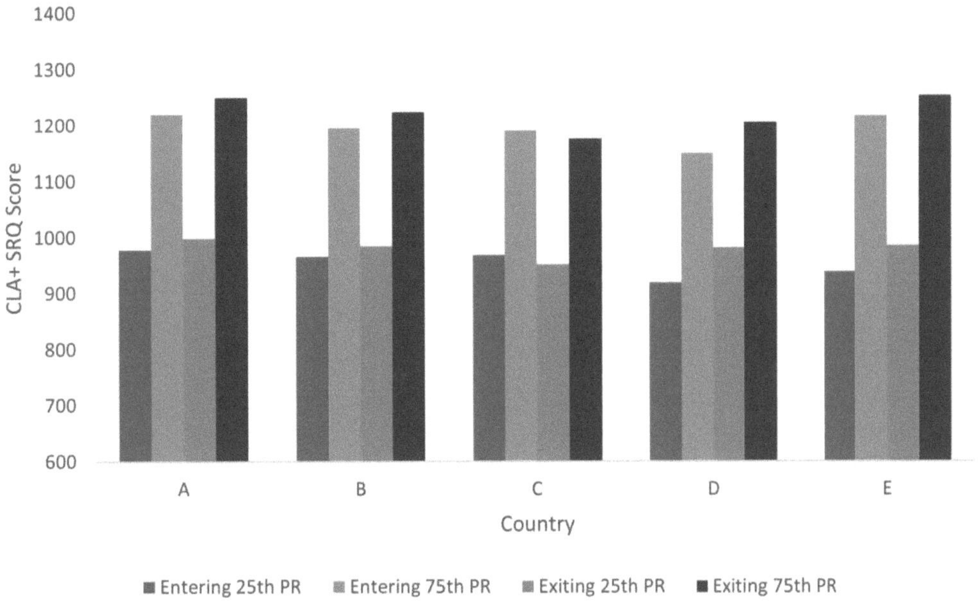

Note: PR = percentile rank

Conclusion

Chapter 9 addressed the benchmarking of countries by discussing the country-level results without disclosing the nationalities. These results provide insight into the patterns of performance on the CLA+ across countries. The first section of the chapter presented the mastery levels for entering and exiting students by country. As expected, a lower percentage of exiting students were classified into the Emerging and Developing mastery levels and a higher percentage of exiting students classified into the Proficient, Accomplished and Advanced mastery levels compared to their entering university peers. One exception was observed. Student performance was similar for the entering and exiting students for one country.

The second section of the chapter presented summary statistics for entering and exiting students by country. The 25th and 75th percentile rank values showed variability across countries. Differences were more pronounced for the Performance Task (PT section) compared to the Selected-Response Question (SRQ) section and total test scores. Overall, these results suggest that the five countries display different levels of variability in CLA+ scores and display relative strengths and weaknesses on the PT and SRQ sections.

Part III The CLA+ assessment in participating countries

10 CLA+ in the United States

Doris Zahner, Council for Aid to Education (United States)

Olivia Cortellini, Council for Aid to Education (United States)

Kelly Rotholz, Council for Aid to Education (United States)

Tess Dawber, Council for Aid to Education (United States)

Part III of this report discusses the assessment in each of the six participating countries. Each chapter reviews policy context, test administration, mastery levels, score distribution and data regarding effort and engagement. This chapter discusses the CLA+ assessment in the United States, where it has a long history and has acquired strong status and recognition.

Introduction

The original higher education institutions in the United States, modelled after the Oxford-Cambridge system in the United Kingdom (Miller and Rudolph, 1962[1]; Thelin, 2012[2]) to educate and train ministers, have evolved over time and become a complex, if not globally the most complex, higher education system. Currently, there are 4 360 degree-granting institutions (Snyder, de Brey and Dillow, 2019[3]) of which 2 832 are four-year and 1 528 are two-year. Bachelor's degrees are typically awarded by public or private institutions as part of a four-year study programme. Associate's degrees are usually two years in length and awarded through community colleges, technical colleges and vocational schools.

The denominations of "college" and "university", although often colloquially used interchangeably within the United States, do have some differences. While there are no national standards, which is a theme within higher education in the United States, universities are typically institutions that provide both undergraduate and graduate degrees and have larger student enrolment. Colleges, on the other hand, tend to only offer undergraduate (associate's and bachelor's) degrees and often have fewer students than universities. Universities may designate certain programmes as colleges within the university. For example, the Colleges of Agricultural Life Sciences; Architecture, Art and Planning; Arts and Sciences; Engineering; and Human Ecology are all part of Cornell University. Both colleges and universities can be public or private institutions. And within the private institution sector, they can be categorised as non-profit or for-profit entities. A third, and much smaller, category of higher education institutions uses titles such as "institute", "academy", "union", "conservatory" and "school".

As with many other countries, there are publicly and privately funded institutions. Within the private sector, there is further division with non-profit and for-profit institutions. Public institutions are mainly funded by the state and federal governments (Ginder, Kelly-Reid and Mann, 2017[4]) and are non-profit organisations. Private institutions rely more heavily on endowments (Kaplan, 2020[5]) and, particularly for the for-profit institutions, student tuition, which can be up to 90% of the funding (Ginder, Kelly-Reid and Mann, 2017[4]). Public institutions comprise 37% (1 623 out of 4 260) of the higher education institutions within the United States (Snyder, de Brey and Dillow, 2019[3]). Within the private sector, which consists of approximately 63% of all higher education institutions, 61.5% (1 682 of 2 727) of them are non-profit (Snyder, de Brey and Dillow, 2019[3]).

As of autumn 2020, 16.7 million undergraduate students are projected to attend colleges and universities in the United States (De Brey et al., 2021[6]). Of these students, the majority (74%) are attending public institutions, 83.4% are attending four-year institutions, 57.1% are women and 38.3% are persons of colour (De Brey et al., 2021[6]). During the 2020/21 academic year, almost two million bachelor's degrees were awarded (De Brey et al., 2021[6]).

However, despite the upward trend in college enrolment over the last two decades, college graduation rates remain relatively low within the United States. According to the National Center of Education Statistics (Hussar et al., 2020[7]), as of spring 2020, nearly 40% of students who began seeking a bachelor's degree at a four-year institution in 2012 have yet to receive their degree. Furthermore, year-to-year retention rates vary considerably across institutions. Between 2017 and 2018, although highly selective institutions had high student retention rates of 97%, less selective and open-admissions schools retained a substantially smaller percentage (62%) of their students during this same period (Hussar et al., 2020[7]). Contrary to an oft-perpetuated notion that student retention is a "first-year" problem, student attrition remains a risk for students at all class levels, with approximately one-third of college dropouts having obtained at least three-quarters of the credits required for graduation (Mabel and Britton, 2018[8]). Although many students cite non-academic reasons such as financial difficulties, health or family obligations as the primary causes for dropping out or deferring their college education (Astin and Oseguera, 2012[9]), academic failure is also a significant factor contributing to lack of persistence and decreased retention of students in higher education.

Student attrition from higher education institutions can lead to a number of financial consequences. Students who do not obtain a bachelor's degree tend to have poorer career outcomes, as measured by salary and employment, than their more educated peers. According to the US Bureau of Labor Statistics (2020[10]), there is an increase in median annual salary for each successive level of education completed. Similarly, unemployment varies inversely with degree attainment, meaning those who are less educated are more likely to be unemployed. Important to note is that career outcome setbacks for non-degree holders are not limited to those who have never enrolled in college. Those who were at one time enrolled in higher education and unsuccessful in completing their undergraduate education also experience career outcome setbacks.

Prior findings are mixed as to whether non-degree holders who have completed some college fare better financially than those who did not continue their education after receiving a high-school diploma (e.g. Baum (2014[11]), Giani, Attewell and Walling, (2019[12]), Shapiro et al. (2014[13])). However, there is little dispute that students who complete their bachelor's degree fare better than those who enrol in college but never graduate (Giani, Attewell and Walling, 2019[12]). Like college graduates, college students who never complete their degree tend to face substantial financial costs of accumulating debt while forgoing monetary earnings. However, unlike degree-holding peers, college dropouts experience the burden of these costs without eventually gaining the social capital (i.e. networks of relationships) that comes with a higher education degree. In fact, this problem even extends to students who take more than the standard four years to graduate college as they accrue increased financial costs over the years with diminishing returns (Sullivan, 2010[14]).

Higher education institutions have employed numerous strategies to increase student retention and graduation rates, with mixed results. Some programmes that have shown success at increasing retention and graduation rates include "methods of inquiry" critical thinking courses (Ahuna, Tinnesz and VanZile-Tamsen, 2010[15]) and targeted study skills courses for returning students who are on academic probation due to their low grade point averages (GPAs) (Engle, Reilly and Levine, 2004[16]). Conversely, Johnson and Stage (2018[17]) reviewed universities' use of the 10 high-impact practices for student success as identified by the Association of American Colleges and Universities: freshman seminars, core curricula, learning communities, writing courses, collaborative assignments, undergraduate research, study abroad, service learning, internships and capstone or senior projects (Kuh, 2008[18]). The quantity of practices offered on campus showed no relation to either four- or six-year graduation rates. Of the 10 practices, only internships and freshman seminars showed predictive relationships with graduation rate, both of which were weak and negative. Internships had a negative relationship with four-year graduation rate but not six-year graduation rate, indicating that internships may prolong the amount of time needed to complete all required credits while not discouraging graduation itself.

Johnson and Stage (2018[17]) suggest that the negative relationship they found between inclusion of freshman seminars and graduation rate may stem from a lack of targeted instruction. That is, schools that require freshman seminars for all students may be investing too heavily in the seminars rather than allocating their resources to students with a higher need. Indeed, Potts and Shultz (2008[19]) found no significant effect of freshman seminars on student retention when considering an entire student body, but they did find a significant positive effect on retention for students who lived off-campus and for students whose high-school profiles were below the typical standard of their school. Similarly, Engle, Riley and Levine (2004[16]) found a positive effect of targeted retention programmes for students who had performed poorly in their first or second year of college.

Interestingly, despite the noted importance of academic experiences to student integration and thus retention, little research to date has examined the role of critical thinking skills in student retention. Critical thinking skills have, however, been linked with other college and post-college outcomes. Some examples include career outcomes such as employment status and salary (Arum and Roksa, 2014[20]): Chapter 7), and educational outcomes such as graduate school enrolment (Arum and Roksa, 2014[20]; Mullen, Goyette and Soares, 2003[21]).

Given the positive findings regarding programmes and courses that target and cater to students' specific needs, it is important to better understand methods that can be used to target students effectively. Although there is evidence that courses designed to enhance critical thinking skills can positively impact student retention (e.g. (Ahuna, Tinnesz and VanZile-Tamsen, 2010[15])), there is a relative lack of literature investigating the importance of critical thinking skills as predictors of student retention compared to more traditional predictors like high-school grade point average (HSGPA). If universities wish to introduce programming that targets critical thinking skills, it follows that students should be identified and selected based on their critical thinking proficiency.

From a theoretical perspective, Mah (2016[22]) touts the benefits of critical thinking skills, learning analytics and digital badges to student retention, suggesting that these constructs and practices not only benefit student retention individually but also interact with one another. An assessment of critical thinking skills, then, has the potential to serve different functions in promoting an increase in student retention. First, at the institution level, it has the potential to help identify students who would benefit most from targeted remediation. Second, at the student level, it can help students understand their own strengths and weaknesses and thereby seek the appropriate guidance and resources to meet their needs. This is not only for students who are not proficient in these skills. Those who are proficient can also benefit from further improvement of their skills. Third, providing feedback on critical thinking performance may increase students' motivation to further their own critical thinking skills and thus enhance their academic engagement.

Policy context

In 2006, under the Commission of the Future of Higher Education, the Voluntary System of Accountability (VSA) was established in order to provide a way to compare and report evidence of student learning at higher education institutions via the College Portrait (Jankowski et al., 2012[23]; McPherson and Shulenburger, 2006[24]; Miller, 2007[25]). The Spellings Commission, named after then-Secretary of Education Margaret Spellings, convened a panel of experts to develop a strategy to ensure that higher education was accessible and affordable, and that it adequately prepared students for the global economy. The VSA was developed by the Association of Public and Land-grant Universities (APLU) and the American Association of State Colleges and Universities (AASCU) as a way for higher education institutions to measure the requirements outlined by the Spellings Commission and avoid the growing concern that the federal government was going to mandate a single metric for institutional accessibility, affordability and accountability. The VSA provides a framework to meet these requirements (Keller and Hammang, 2008[26]). As part of the VSA initiative, assessments of student outcomes and evaluating institutional effectiveness are necessary (Liu, 2017[27]; 2011[28])

In 2008, a study funded by the Fund for the Improvement of Postsecondary Education (FIPSE) examined whether assessments of higher education students' general education learning outcomes provided comparable information (Klein et al., 2009[29]; Steedle, Kugelmass and Nemeth, 2010[30]). Findings from this study led to the use of three assessments of generic skills – ACT's Collegiate Assessment of Academic Proficiency (CAAP), Council for Aid to Education's (CAE) Collegiate Learning Assessment (CLA) and Educational Testing Service's (ETS) Measure of Academic Proficiency and Progress (MAPP) – as part of the VSA initiative for institutional accountability.

The CLA became one of the assessments that institutions could use to report student learning outcomes on the VSA's College Portrait. Institutions administered the CLA for VSA reporting for either benchmarking or value-added as a measure of institutional growth. And although this was a partial solution to the quality assurance and accountability recommendation from the Spellings Commission, this solution was insufficient for measuring individual student learning gains of these essential college and career skills such as critical thinking, problem solving, and written communication.

Process of implementation of the CLA+

Since 2002, CAE has pioneered the use of performance-based assessments for assessing students' essential college and career readiness skills. To date, over 700 institutions, both in the United States and internationally, and over 650 000 students have participated in the CLA. The CLA was designed as an institutional measure of student's critical thinking skills, providing cross-sectional growth estimates and norm-referenced data. In 2013, CAE transitioned to the next iteration of CLA, CLA+. CLA+ includes a selected-response section, which provides additional subscores and allows CLA+ to provide student level reliability.

The assessment is designed to be completed in approximately 90 minutes and includes an optional tutorial, a Performance Task (PT), Selected-Response Questions (SRQs), and a demographic survey. The CLA+ is administered through a secure browser that distributes the PT and 25 SRQs to each student. The assessment instruments must be administered under standardised, controlled testing conditions, with all students monitored by a proctor. In Spring 2020, CAE introduced remote proctoring as a response to the COVID-19 pandemic. Remote proctoring allowed higher education institutions to administer CLA+ to students online and proctor via web conferencing software. Results from a study measuring the difference between students who were administered CLA+ and were proctored remotely versus in-person found no significant differences between students' PT scores and only marginally significant differences for SRQ scores (Zahner and Cortellini, 2021[31]). Students in the remote proctoring condition performed slightly better on the SRQs than those in the in-person proctoring condition.

The standard cross-sectional model for assessing institutional growth involves testing a sample of 100 or more entering students during the fall testing window (typically mid-August through early November), and then testing a sample of 100 or more exiting students during the spring testing window (typically early February through mid-May). All testing sessions require a proctor to approve students into the interface and manage the testing environment.

Test administration steps:

1. Receive welcome email from CLA+ team with instructional materials.
2. Verify testing plans.
3. Review instructional materials and complete technology testing.
4. Administer CLA+ exam to students.
5. Confirm with CAE that testing is complete.
6. Submit registrar data to confirm student's class level.
7. Receive reports through a secure file-sharing service.

Cross-sectional results include growth estimates (in the form of effect sizes and value-added scores) and normed data such as percentile rankings. Cross-sectional reports also include information such as summary scores, subscores, and mastery levels.

If an institution only wishes to assess a single cohort or does not want institutional growth metrics, it can opt to receive mastery level results. Mastery level results include statistics only for the students tested within a specific administration; they do not include growth estimates or normed data and have less stringent sampling requirements. These results include summary scores, subscores, and mastery levels. Students do not need to test within a specific administration in order to be included in the institutional sample for this type of reporting.

Results

Total CLA+ scores and section scores among entering and exiting students

Table 10.1 presents the average score and standard deviation (in parentheses) for each CLA+ score by cohort. Entering students in the United States received an average total CLA+ score of 1 060 (*SD* = 149), which corresponds with the Developing mastery level. Exiting students on average scored 43 points higher, with an average score of 1 103 (*SD* = 148), which corresponds to the Proficient mastery level. Independent samples t-tests found a small, significant difference between entering and exiting students on total CLA+ score (Table 10.2). As seen by the score differences summarised in Table 10.1 as well as the t-test results shown in Table 10.2, the increase in total CLA+ score in between class levels seems to be driven in part by the difference in the respective classes' average performance on the PT. There was a 47-point average score increase between entering and exiting students on the PT (Cohen's *d* = .28) whereas there was a 38-point average score increase between classes on the SRQ section (Cohen's *d* = .21).

Table 10.1. Average total CLA+ scores and section scores, by class

	Total CLA+ score	Performance Task score	Selected-Response score
Entering (*n* = 50,809)	1 060 (149)	1 043 (168)	1 078 (186)
Exiting (*n* = 47,431)	1 103 (148)	1 090 (170)	1 116 (182)
Score difference (exiting - entering)	+43	+47	+38

Table 10.2. Independent samples t-test results for entering vs. exiting students

	t	*df*	*p*	Cohen's d
Total CLA+ score	-44.76	97894	<.001	.29
Performance Task score	-43.63	97627	<.001	.28
Selected-Response score	-32.27	97972	<.001	.21

CLA+ mastery levels and score distributions

Overall distribution of CLA+ mastery levels is summarised in Table 10.3. As shown in Figure 10.1, the distributions varied between entering and exiting students. Chi-square analysis revealed these differences to be statistically significant (*df* = 4, χ^2 = 1835.19, p < .001, Cramer's *V* = .137). Overall, higher percentages of entering than exiting students fell into the non-proficient mastery levels (i.e. "Emerging" and "Developing"), and higher percentages of exiting than entering students fell into the mastery levels that meet and exceed the "Proficient" threshold (i.e. "Proficient", "Accomplished" and "Advanced"). The most notable difference between entering and exiting students regarding mastery levels was the 9-percentage-point difference found at the Emerging level of mastery. Whereas 27% of entering students performed at this level (meaning that they lacked even basic critical thinking skills), 18% of exiting students performed at the Emerging level. The trend between entering and exiting students in mastery level distribution was further reflected in the distribution of total CLA+ scores (Figure 10.2-Figure 10.3). Although scores were normally distributed at both class levels, the distribution of exiting student scores fell slightly more than that of entering student scores.

Table 10.3. Mastery level distribution

Level	Percentage
Emerging	22.7%
Developing	30.4%
Proficient	28.5%
Accomplished	16.2%
Advanced	2.2%

Figure 10.1. CLA+ mastery level distribution, by class

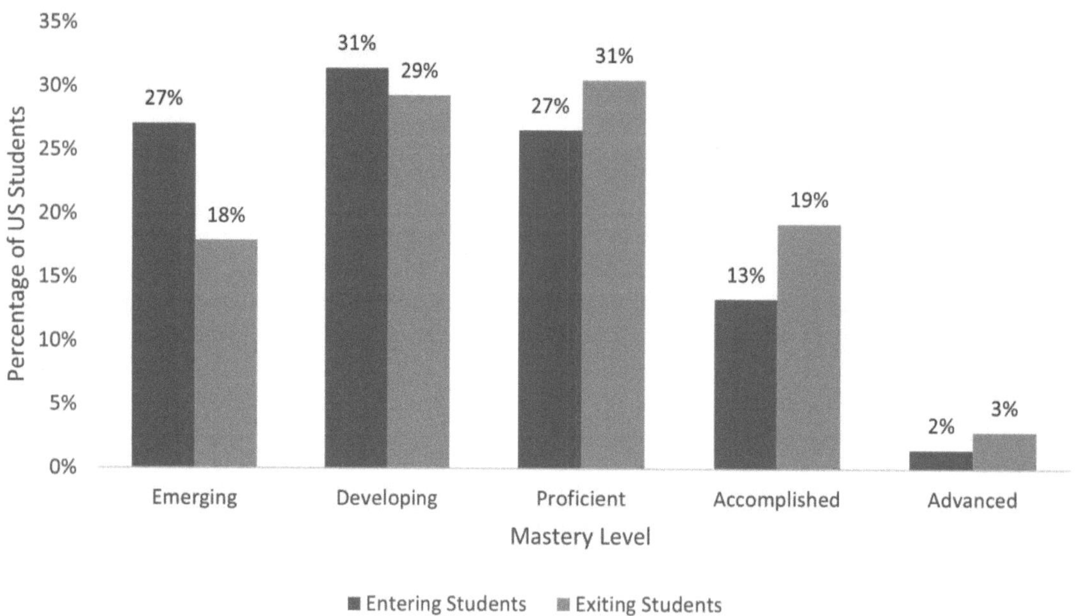

Figure 10.2. Total CLA+ score distribution, entering students

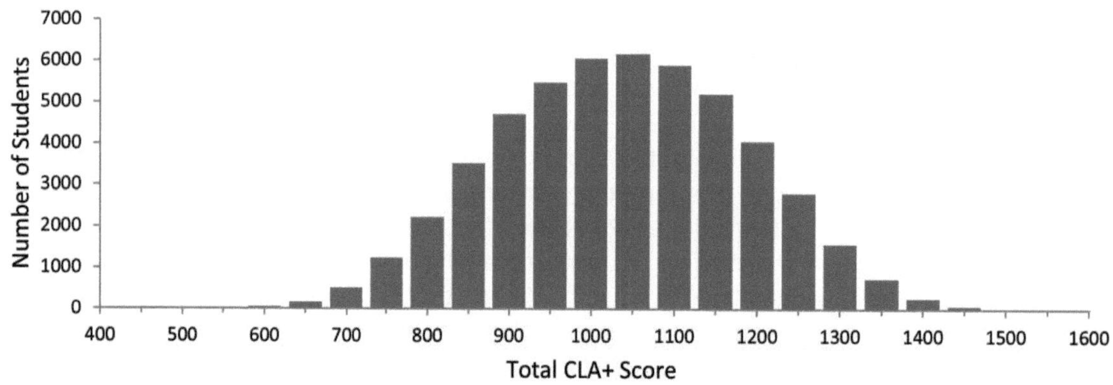

Figure 10.3. Total CLA+ score distribution, exiting students

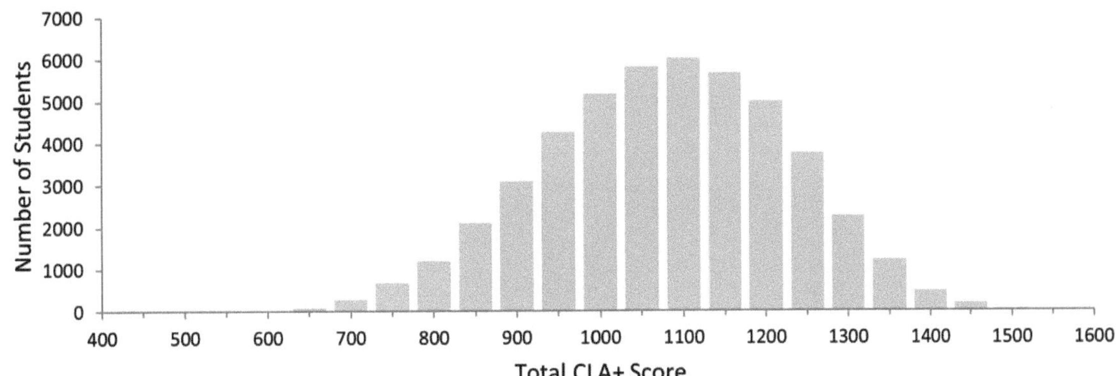

CLA+ subscores

In addition to the comparison of total CLA+ scores and score distributions, PT and SRQ subscores were also analysed. On all three PT subscores – Analysis and Problem Solving (APS), Writing Effectiveness (WE) and Writing Mechanics (WM) – exiting students on average outperformed entering students. The differences between entering and exiting student scores were significant but small (Figure 10.4; Table 10.4). The same pattern held for the three SRQ subscores: Scientific and Quantitative Reasoning (SQR), Critical Reading and Evaluation (CRE) and Critique an Argument (CA). However, the difference in SRQ subscores, though significant, was negligibly small (Figure 10.5; Table 10.4).

Figure 10.4. Performance Task subscores, by class

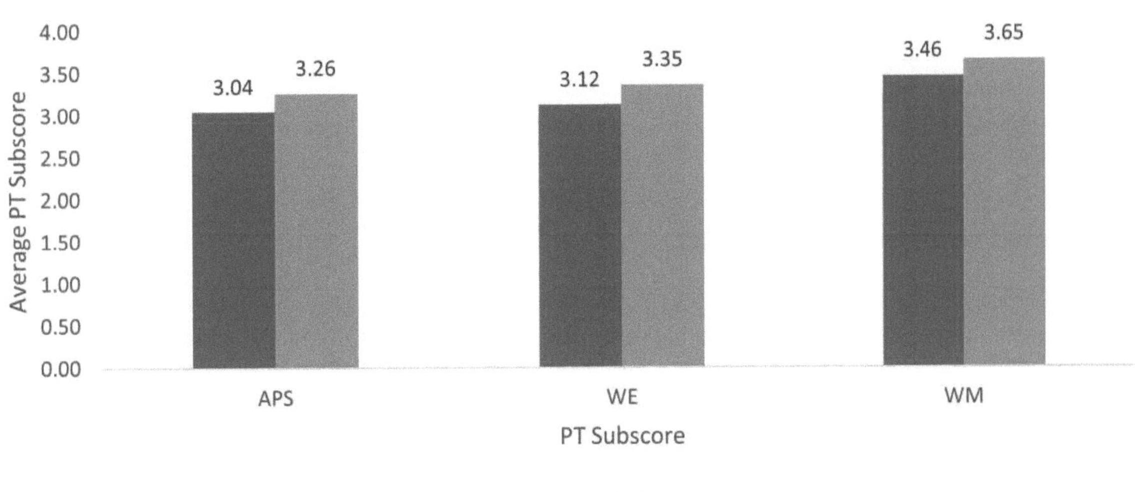

Note: APS = Analysis and Problem Solving; WE = Writing Effectiveness; WM = Writing Mechanics

Figure 10.5. Selected Response subscores, by class

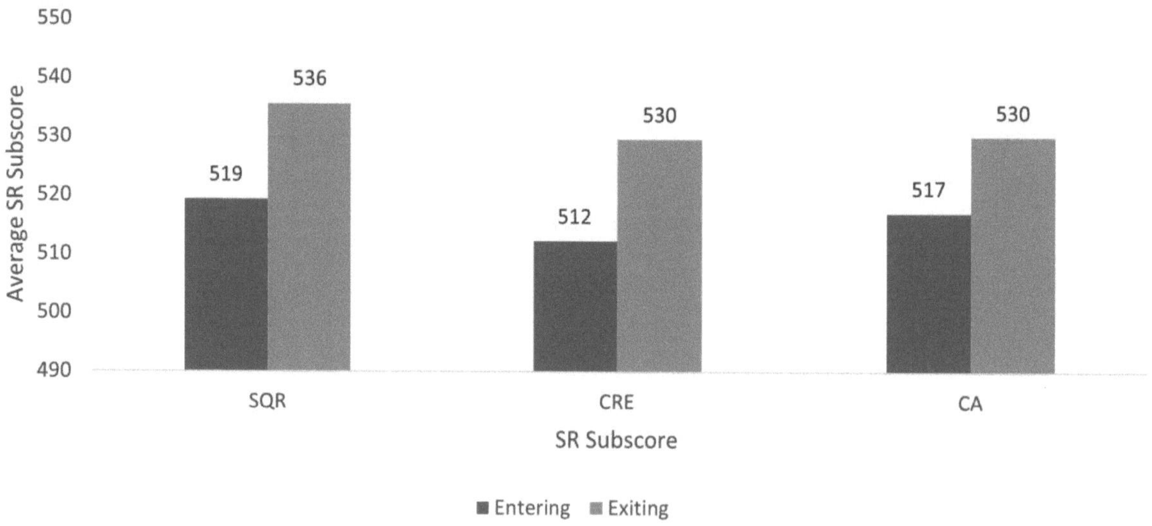

Note: SQR = Scientific and Quantitative Reasoning; CRE = Critical Reading and Evaluation; CA = Critique an Argument

Table 10.4. Independent samples t-test results for entering vs. exiting students

	t	df	p	Cohen's d
APS	-40.63	97024	<.001	0.25
WE	-44.66	96903	<.001	0.28
WM	-44.27	97401	<.001	0.27
SQR	-25.31	97858	<.001	0.16
CRE	-27.93	98042	<.001	0.18
CA	-20.24	97257	<.001	0.13

Note: APS = Analysis and Problem Solving; WE = Writing Effectiveness; WM = Writing Mechanics; SQR = Scientific and Quantitative Reasoning; CRE = Critical Reading and Evaluation; CA = Critique an Argument

Self-reported effort and engagement

Upon completion of CLA+, all U.S. domestic students reported their perceived effort and engagement for each section of the assessment via 5-point Likert scales (Table 10.5). On the PT, entering students gave an average effort rating of 3.7 (SD = 0.9). The average rating given by exiting students was 3.7 (SD = 0.9). For the SRQ section, entering students reported an average of 3.2 points on the effort scale (SD = 1.0) and exiting students reported an average of 3.3 (SD = 1.0.) Table 10.5 summarises the distribution of self-reported effort ratings by class and section. Paired-samples t-tests showed that entering students reported spending more effort on the PT section than on the SRQ section (t(50776) = 126.61, p < .001, Cohen's d = .54). The same was true for exiting students (t(47401) = 99.19, p < .001, Cohen's d = .41). For both class levels, the effect size was moderate.

Table 10.5. Students' self-reported effort on each CLA+ section

		No effort at all	A little effort	A moderate amount of effort	A lot of effort	My best effort
PT	Entering	0.5%	5.5%	38.5%	34.9%	20.5%
	Exiting	0.7%	6.3%	36.1%	32.4%	24.5%
SRQ	Entering	3.3%	17.2%	45.8%	23.7%	10.0%
	Exiting	2.8%	14.2%	43.0%	25.3%	14.7%

Note: PT = Performance Task; SRQ = Selected-Response Questions

Compared to self-reported effort, students' ratings of their engagement with the assessment tended to fall lower on the scale. However, the differences between students' reported engagement with the PT and the SRQ section mirrored those previously seen with self-reported effort. The average PT engagement rating among entering students was 3.0 (SD = 1.0), and that among exiting students was 3.1 (SD = 1.0). In contrast, entering students reported an average engagement level of 2.4 (SD = 1.0) for the SRQ section, and exiting students reported an average of 2.6 (SD = 1.1). At both class levels, there was a significant difference between the two sections regarding student engagement. The effect size was moderate for both entering students ($t(50776)$ = 117.27, p < .001, Cohen's d = .41) and exiting students ($t(47401)$ = 99.67, p < .001, Cohen's d = .49). Distributions are summarised in Table 10.6.

Table 10.6. Students' self-reported engagement on each CLA+ section

		Not at all engaging	A little engaging	Moderately engaging	Very engaging
PT	Entering	8.2%	19.0%	40.1%	26.9%
	Exiting	8.3%	17.5%	37.9%	29.2%
SRQ	Entering	21.5%	30.5%	33.2%	12.3%
	Exiting	18.1%	27.3%	36.0%	15.3%

Note: PT = Performance Task; SRQ = Selected-Response Questions

CLA+ section scores, by effort and engagement

At both class levels, there was found to be an association between self-reported effort/engagement and CLA+ performance. Broadly speaking, average scores tended to increase with each successive level of effort and engagement (Table 10.7-Table 10.8). Indeed, multiple regression analysis shows that both effort and engagement were significant predictors of PT score (Table 10.9) at both class levels. The total variation in the PT scores explained by effort and engagement was 12% for entering students and 14% for exiting students. The exception to this is self-reported engagement on the SRQ section. Although both effort and engagement emerged as significant predictors of SRQ score among exiting students, only effort emerged as a significant predictor among entering students (Table 10.10). The total variation in the SRQ scores explained by effort and engagement was lower than that found in the PT regression results. Only 6% of variation in the SRQ scores was explained by effort and engagement for both entering and exiting student results.

Table 10.7. Average CLA+ section score by self-reported effort

		No effort at all	A little effort	A moderate amount of effort	A lot of effort	My best effort
PT	Entering	840	896	1 001	1 080	1 104
		(180)	(163)	(159)	(153)	(159)
	Exiting	819	932	1 046	1 130	1 150
		(165)	(161)	(158)	(152)	(160)
SRQ	Entering	904	1 010	1 084	1 123	1 122
		(147)	(179)	(181)	(177)	(179)
	Exiting	902	1 039	1 119	1 157	1 154
		(148)	(179)	(175)	(172)	(179)

Note: PT = Performance Task; SRQ = Selected-Response Questions

Table 10.8. Average CLA+ section score by self-reported engagement

		Not at all engaging	A little engaging	Moderately engaging	Very engaging	Extremely engaging
PT	Entering	945	996	1 051	1 082	1 096
		(168)	(167)	(163)	(157)	(160)
	Exiting	982	1 039	1 096	1 131	1 135
		(177)	(171)	(162)	(158)	(160)
	Entering	1 024	1 086	1 096	1 103	1 082
		(180)	(184)	(186)	(179)	(184)
	Exiting	1 055	1 120	1 136	1 135	1 113
		(183)	(180)	(179)	(179)	(181)

Note: PT = Performance Task; SRQ = Selected-Response Questions

Table 10.9. Regression results: Effort/engagement and Performance Task score

	Entering				Exiting			
Variable	B	$SE (B)$	β	p	B	$SE (B)$	β	p
Effort	52.53	0.90	0.27	<.001	56.22	0.92	0.31	<.001
Engagement	19.90	0.78	0.12	<.001	16.44	0.82	0.10	<.001

Table 10.10. Regression results: Effort/engagement and Selected-Response score

	Entering				Exiting			
Variable	B	$SE (B)$	β	p	B	$SE (B)$	β	p
Effort	47.49	0.99	0.24	<.001	46.98	0.97	0.25	<.001
Engagement	-0.24	0.90	0.00	0.792	-2.28	0.91	-0.01	0.012

Policy implications and lessons learnt

Higher education institutions in America have a long track record of resilience and innovation: perhaps the most familiar example is how colleges and universities embraced the GI bill1[1] and implemented the largest expansion of access to post-secondary education in the world (Olson, 1973[32]). The COVID-19 pandemic poses a new and daunting challenge, leading many educators and analysts to wonder if higher education will ever return to what it once was, more specifically, in-person or on-campus teaching and learning. Indeed, some critics of the American system (at all levels), borrowing the perhaps tired cliché about not letting a good crisis go to waste, hope the current challenge will lead to fundamental reforms. One education leader sees it as a "Sputnik-like opportunity" (Reville, 2020[33]).

Whether and how the system continues to adapt will depend on a combination of political will, economic constraints, technological possibilities and commitment to core values of teaching and learning. Meanwhile, changes are already apparent: classrooms are moving to remote or hybrid formats requiring adaptations by faculty and staff; administrators are considering alternative semester schedules to ease congestion and enable "social distancing"; and admissions offices are modifying requirements to make standardised tests optional in an effort to ease burdens on students already struggling to complete high school (or college) successfully.

If the national goal for higher education institutions is to achieve higher levels of educational attainment (Bowen, Mcpherson and Ream, 2018[34]), then the role of assessment within this context is essential. At the centre of educational attainment is retention, persistence and graduation. Given the positive findings regarding programmes and courses that target and cater to students' specific needs, it is important to better understand methods that can be used to target students effectively. Although there is evidence that courses designed to enhance critical thinking skills can positively impact student retention (e.g. (Ahuna, Tinnesz and VanZile-Tamsen, 2010[15])), there is a relative lack of literature investigating the importance of critical thinking skills as predictors of student retention compared to more traditional predictors like high-school grade point average. If universities wish to introduce programming that targets critical thinking skills, it follows that students should be identified and selected based on their critical thinking proficiency.

Upon attaining a higher education degree, if graduates are unable to find appropriate employment, the impact is immense for students, their parents and their institutions. The most recent data from the US Department of Education reveal that many low- and middle-income families have taken on a substantial debt to finance their child's college education (Fuller and Mitchell, 2020[35]). According to analysis by the Federal Reserve Bank of New York (2018[36]), as of December 2020, 40% of recent college graduates were underemployed – that is, they were working in jobs that typically do not require a college degree, impacting their personal financial health and that of the broader economy.

Thus, there is a need to identify and improve students' generic skills because it is these skills that employers deem essential for career success (Capital, 2016[37]; Hart Research Associates, 2013[38]; National Association of Colleges and Employers, 2018[39]; Rios et al., 2020[40]; World Economic Forum, 2016[41]).

Next steps

Since 2019, CAE has pivoted away from using CLA+ solely as a higher education accountability and quality assurance instrument. Currently, in addition to providing institutions with information about institutional value-added, CAE also makes it possible for educators to use CLA+ results as a student diagnostic to identify students' strengths and areas of improvement as well as for longitudinal and efficacy studies. The instrument can be used to answer institutional research questions such as:

- How ready are students for, and where do they need support in, their next step?

- How well is the institution developing essential skills in students?
- How much are students growing from year to year?
- How has a new curriculum improved students' essential skills?

Additionally, CAE has renamed the Scientific and Quantitative Reasoning (SQR) subscore of the SRQ section Data Literacy (DL) as it more accurately reflects the skills measured on the assessment. All reports from the autumn 2021 academic year will reflect this updated language. No changes to the actual construct have been made. This was solely a change in the naming of the subsection.

Next Step Platform

In 2021, CAE introduced the Next Step Platform, which incorporates the client-facing applications used throughout the assessment process, including support assistance and account management, through one login. To better engage students, technology-enhanced elements such as video stimuli and responses, simulations, and drag-and-drop options can be embedded in performance-based assessments. New reporting capabilities will allow students and educators to better understand students' readiness for their next step.

For educators, the Next Step Platform offers a convenient way to deliver CLA+. The platform also allows custom assessments to be easily designed, developed and administered on the same platform, reducing time and effort.

Students can complete assessments within the platform, and results can be quickly provided due to enhanced artificial intelligence (AI) scoring. The Next Step Platform will also offer students an opportunity to earn micro-credentials, an evidence-based measure of real-world skills that they can share with colleges and prospective employers.

SSA+

In 2020, CAE introduced the Success Skills Assessment (SSA+) as a formative assessment of students' generic skills. Ideally, institutions would assess students using SSA+ as they enter university, and would receive the students' score reports shortly, if not immediately, following completion of the assessment. Following the assessment of students, institutions could implement courses of study or other curricular support to help students improve their skills.

SSA+, a 60-minute assessment, is aligned to the same constructs that are measured on CLA+, but uses technology-enhanced and other items to scaffold students' generic skills rather than just asking students to write a single essay. There is still a written portion to the SSA+ PT, scored on the same rubric as the CLA+ PT. However, the SSA+ PT is meant to be more formative than the CLA+, allowing educators to work directly with students in the classroom on improving their skills.

The impetus for this development was based on requests from CLA+ clients who wanted a shorter assessment that returned student results more quickly and used technology-enhanced and more modern item types to measure their students' skills. The students' written responses are scored primarily with an automated scoring engine, and technology-enhanced and selected-response items are also automatically scored.

CAE believes that using a formative assessment of generic skills like SSA+, followed by curricular support to improve these skills, and ending with a summative assessment such as CLA+ will lead to better learning outcomes for higher education students. Any higher education institutions in the United States who are interested in using an assessment to measure students' generic skills are encouraged to reach out to CAE for more information on how to implement a testing plan for this purpose.

Prospects

Educators can use students' assessment scores and mastery levels of generic skills to help identify strengths and developmental support required for improvement. Being assessed this way is particularly valuable for those students who are most at risk of dropping out due to academic difficulty. Identifying students who might benefit from additional academic intervention early in their tenure may lead to an increase in student retention, persistence, and graduation rates. Furthermore, improving these skills would increase the likelihood that the individual student will have better higher education and post-higher education outcomes, such as higher GPA (Zahner, Ramsaran and Zahner, 2012[42]), appropriate employment, higher salary, and enrolment in a graduate programme (Zahner and James, 2016[43]; Zahner and Lehrfeld, 2018[44]).

Educators and employers clearly recognise that fact-based knowledge is no longer sufficient and that generic skills such as critical thinking, problem solving, and written communication skills are essential for success. The opportunity to improve students' essential skills lies in identification and action. This can be further highlighted with the use of verified digital badges or a micro-credential, which is a movement that has been slowly gaining momentum (Mah, Bellin-Mularski and Ifenthaler, 2016[45]; Lemoine and Richardson, 2015[46]; Lemoine, Wilson and Richardson, 2018[47]; Rottmann and Duggan, 2021[48]). Assessments that are coupled with verified digital badges or micro-credentials provide educators with the opportunity to help students identify their strengths as well as areas where they can improve. This is fundamental to developing the critical thinkers, problem solvers, and communicators who will be essential in the future. With close and careful attention paid to students' essential generic skills, even a small increase in the development of these skills could boost future outcomes for students, parents, institutions, and the overall economy.

References

Ahuna, K., C. Tinnesz and C. VanZile-Tamsen (2010), ""Methods of Inquiry": Using Critical Thinking to Retain Students", *Innovative Higher Education*, Vol. 36/4, pp. 249-259, https://doi.org/10.1007/s10755-010-9173-5. [15]

Arum, R. and J. Roksa (2014), *Aspiring Adults Adrift: Tentative Transitions of College Graduates*, University of Chicago Press, Chicago. [20]

Astin and L. Oseguera (2012), "Pre-College and Institutional Influences on Degree Attainment", in *College Student Retention: Formula for Student Success*, Rowman & Littlefield Publishers, New York. [9]

Baum, S. (2014), "Higher Education Earning Premium Value, Variation, and Trends", *Urban Institute* February Issue, https://www.urban.org/research/publication/higher-education-earnings-premium-value-variation-and-trends (accessed on 5 August 2022). [11]

Bowen, W., M. Mcpherson and T. Ream (2018), "Lesson Plan: An Agenda for Change in American Higher Education", *The Review of Higher Education*, Vol. 41/2. [34]

Capital, P. (2016), *2016 Workforce-Skills Preparedness Report*, http://www.payscale.com/data-packages/job-skills (accessed on 28 April 2021). [37]

De Brey, C. et al. (2021), *Digest of Education Statistics 2019 (NCES 2021-009)*, https://nces.ed.gov/pubs2021/2021009.pdf (accessed on 5 August 2022). [6]

Engle, C., N. Reilly and H. Levine (2004), "A Case Study of an Academic Retention Program", *Journal of College Student Retention: Research, Theory & Practice*, Vol. 5/4, pp. 365-383, https://doi.org/10.2190/jp0w-5358-y7dj-14b2. [16]

Federal Reserve Bank (2018), *The Labor Market for Recent College Graduates*, https://www.newyorkfed.org/research/college-labor-market/college-labor-market_underemployment_rates.htm (accessed on 5 August 2022). [36]

Fuller, A. and J. Mitchell (2020), "Which schools leave parents with the most college loan debt?", *The Wall Street Journal*, https://www.wsj.com/articles/which-schools-leave-parents-with-the-most-college-loan-debt-11606936947 (accessed on 3 December 2020). [35]

Giani, M., P. Attewell and D. Walling (2019), "The Value of an Incomplete Degree: Heterogeneity in the Labor Market Benefits of College Non-Completion", *The Journal of Higher Education*, Vol. 91/4, pp. 514-539, https://doi.org/10.1080/00221546.2019.1653122. [12]

Ginder, S., J. Kelly-Reid and F. Mann (2017), "Enrollment and Employees in Postsecondary Institutions, Fall 2016; and Financial Statistics and Academic Libraries, Fiscal Year 2016 First Look (Provisional Data)", *First Look (Provisional Data) (NCES 2015-012). U.S. Department of Education. Washington, DC: National Center for Education Statistics*, https://nces.ed.gov/pubs2018/2018002.pdf (accessed on 5 August 2022). [4]

Hart Research Associates (2013), "It takes more than a major: Employer priorities for college learning and student success", *Liberal Education*, Vol. 99/2. [38]

Hussar, B. et al. (2020), "The condition of education 2020", *Institute of Education Sciences*, Vol. 5/1, https://nces.ed.gov/pubs2020/2020144.pdf (accessed on 5 August 2022). [7]

Jankowski, N. et al. (2012), *Transparency and Accountability: An Evaluation of the VSA College Portrait Pilot, A Special Report from the National Institute for Learning Outcomes Assessment for the Voluntary System of Accountability,*, National Institute for Learning Outcomes Assessment, Champaign, IL, https://www.learningoutcomesassessment.org/wp-content/uploads/2019/02/VSA_Report.pdf. [23]

Johnson, S. and F. Stage (2018), "Academic Engagement and Student Success: Do High-Impact Practices Mean Higher Graduation Rates?", *The Journal of Higher Education*, Vol. 89/5, pp. 753-781, https://doi.org/10.1080/00221546.2018.1441107. [17]

Kaplan, A. (2020), *Voluntary Support of Education: Key Findings from Data Collected for the 2018-19 Academic Fiscal Year for US Higher Education Institutions*, Council for Advancement and Support of Education, Washington, DC. [5]

Keller, C. and J. Hammang (2008), "The voluntary system of accountability for accountability and institutional assessment", *New Directions for Institutional Research*, Vol. 2008/S1, pp. 39-48, https://doi.org/10.1002/ir.260. [26]

Klein, S. et al. (2009), *Test Validity Study (TVS) Report*, ETS Technical Report, Electronic Testing Services, Princeton, NJ, https://www.ets.org/research/policy_research_reports/publications/report/2009/iddk. [29]

Kuh, G. (2008), *High-Impact Educational Practices: What They Are, Who Has Access to Them, and Why They Matter*, Association of American Colleges and Universities, Washington, DC. [18]

Lemoine, P. and M. Richardson (2015), "Micro-Credentials, Nano Degrees, and Digital Badges: New Credentials for Global Higher Education.", *International Journal of Technology and Educational Marketing*, Vol. 5/1, pp. 36-49. [46]

Lemoine, P., W. Wilson and M. Richardson (2018), *Marketing Micro-Credentials in Global Higher Education: Innovative Disruption*, IGI Global, https://doi.org/10.4018/978-1-5225-5673-2.ch007. [47]

Liu, O. (2017), "Ten Years After the Spellings Commission: From Accountability to Internal Improvement", *Educational Measurement: Issues and Practice*, Vol. 36/2, pp. 34-41, https://doi.org/10.1111/emip.12139. [27]

Liu, O. (2011), "Outcomes Assessment in Higher Education: Challenges and Future Research in the Context of Voluntary System of Accountability", *Educational Measurement: Issues and Practice*, Vol. 30/3, pp. 2-9, https://doi.org/10.1111/j.1745-3992.2011.00206.x. [28]

Mabel, Z. and T. Britton (2018), "Leaving late: Understanding the extent and predictors of college late departure", *Social Science Research*, Vol. 69, pp. 34-51, https://doi.org/10.1016/j.ssresearch.2017.10.001. [8]

Mah, D. (2016), "Learning Analytics and Digital Badges: Potential Impact on Student Retention in Higher Education", *Technology, Knowledge and Learning*, Vol. 21/3, pp. 285-305, https://doi.org/10.1007/s10758-016-9286-8. [22]

Mah, D., N. Bellin-Mularski and D. Ifenthaler (2016), *Foundation of digital badges and micro-credentials: Demonstrating and recognizing knowledge and competencies*, https://doi.org/10.1007/978-3-319-15425-1. [45]

McPherson, P. and D. Shulenburger (2006), *Toward a Voluntary System of Accountability Program (VSA) for Public Universities and Colleges*, National Association of State Universities and Land-Grant Colleges, Washington, DC.   [24]

Miller, M. (2007), "Editorial: The Commission on the Future of Higher Education", *Change: The Magazine of Higher Learning*, Vol. 39/1, pp. 8-9, https://doi.org/10.3200/chng.39.1.8-9.   [25]

Miller, R. and F. Rudolph (1962), "The American College and University: A History", *AAUP Bulletin*, Vol. 48/4, https://doi.org/10.2307/40222930.   [1]

Mullen, A., K. Goyette and J. Soares (2003), "Who Goes to Graduate School? Social and Academic Correlates of Educational Continuation after College", *Sociology of Education*, Vol. 76/2, pp. 143-169, https://doi.org/10.2307/3090274.   [21]

National Association of Colleges and Employers (2018), *Are college graduates "career ready"?*, https://www.naceweb.org/career-readiness/competencies/are-college-graduates-career-ready/ (accessed on 19 February 2018).   [39]

Olson, K. (1973), "The G. I. Bill and Higher Education: Success and Surprise", *American Quarterly*, Vol. 25/5, pp. 596-610, https://doi.org/10.2307/2711698.   [32]

Potts, G. and B. Schultz (2008), "The freshman seminar and academic success of at-risk students", *College Student Journal*, Vol. 42/2, pp. 647-658.   [19]

Reville, P. (2020), *Coronavirus gives us an opportunity to rethink K-12 education*, https://www.bostonglobe.com/2020/04/09/opinion/coronavirus-gives-us-an-opportunity-rethink-k-12-education/ (accessed on 9 April 2020).   [33]

Rios, J. et al. (2020), "Identifying Critical 21st-Century Skills for Workplace Success: A Content Analysis of Job Advertisements", *Educational Researcher*, Vol. 49/2, pp. 80-89, https://doi.org/10.3102/0013189x19890600.   [40]

Rottmann, A. and M. Duggan (2021), *Micro-credentials in higher education*, IGI Global.   [48]

Shapiro, D. et al. (2014), *Some college, no degree: A national view of students with some college enrollment, but no completion, Signature Report No.7*, National Student Clearinghouse Research Cener, Herndon, VA.   [13]

Snyder, T., C. de Brey and S. Dillow (2019), "Digest of Education Statistics 2017", *National Center for Education Statistics*, https://nces.ed.gov/pubs2018/2018070.pdf (accessed on 5 August 2022).   [3]

Steedle, J., H. Kugelmass and A. Nemeth (2010), "What Do They Measure? Comparing Three Learning Outcomes Assessments", *Change: The Magazine of Higher Learning*, Vol. 42/4, pp. 33-37, https://doi.org/10.1080/00091383.2010.490491.   [30]

Sullivan, D. (2010), "The Hidden Costs of Low Four-Year Graduation Rates", *Liberal Education*, Vol. 96 (Summer 2010), pp. 24-31.   [14]

Thelin, J. (2012), *A History of American Higher Education: Third Edition*, Johns Hopkins University Press, Athens, MD.   [2]

U.S. Bureau of Labor Statistics (BLS) (2020), *Learn more, earn more: Education leads to higher wages, lower unemployment*, https://www.bls.gov/careeroutlook/2020/data-on-display/education-pays.htm (accessed on May 2020).	[10]

World Economic Forum (2016), *Global Challenge Insight Report: The Future of Jobs: Employment, Skills and Workforce Strategy for the Fourth Industrial Revolution*, World Economic Forum, http://www3.weforum.org/docs/WEF_Future_of_Jobs.pdf.	[41]

Zahner, D. and O. Cortellini (2021), *The role and effect of remote proctoring on assessment in higher education*, Proceedings of the 2021 American Educational Research Association, Washington, DC.	[31]

Zahner, D. and J. James (2016), *Predictive validity of a critical thinking assessment of post-college outcomes [Paper presentation]*, 2016 Conference of the American Educational Research Association, Washington, DC,.	[43]

Zahner, D. and J. Lehrfeld (2018), *Employers' and advisors' assessments of the importance of critical thinking and written communication skills post-college [Paper presentation]*, 2018 Conference of the American Educational Research Association, New York, NY.	[44]

Zahner, D., L. Ramsaran and D. Zahner (2012), "Comparing alternatives in the prediction of college success.", *Annual Meeting of the American Educational Research Association*.	[42]

Note

[1] The Servicemen's Readjustment Act of 1944, often referred to as the G. I. Bill, was a law that provided a range of benefits for returning World War II veterans.

11 Assessing university students' learning outcomes: The Italian experience with TECO

Alberto Ciolfi, National Agency for the Evaluation of Universities and Research Institutes (ANVUR) (Italy)

Morena Sabella, National Agency for the Evaluation of Universities and Research Institutes (ANVUR) (Italy)

As discussed in this chapter, Italy was the first country outside the United States to implement the CLA+ assessment as part of its nation-wide TECO project and its decision to move towards a different assessment approach.

Introduction

Since its inception in 1999, Italy has been part of the Bologna Process, which seeks to bring coherence to higher education systems across Europe. The European Higher Education Area (EHEA) was established to facilitate student and staff mobility, and to make European higher education more inclusive, accessible, attractive and competitive worldwide.

One of the outcomes of the process was the development of the Qualifications Framework for the European Higher Education Area (QF for the EHEA). All participating countries agreed to introduce a three-cycle higher education system consisting of bachelor's, master's and doctoral studies (PhDs).

Accordingly, the Italian Qualification Framework has been structured in three cycles: each cycle corresponds to a specific academic qualification (degree) that allows you to continue your studies, and participate in public calls to enter the labour market. All study programmes are structured in credits, called "*credito formativo universitario*" (CFU). This system is equivalent to the European Credit Transfer and Accumulation System (ECTS). A CFU corresponds approximately to a 25-hour workload for the student, including time for individual study. The average amount of work done by a full-time student during an academic year is conventionally set at 60 CFU/ECTS.

Figure 11.1. The Italian university system

Sistema universitario italiano

The Italian University System

3° ciclo / 3rd cycle: Dottorato di Ricerca — PhD — Diploma di Specializzazione; Master universitario di II livello

2° ciclo / 2nd cycle — 120 CFU/ECTS: Laurea Magistrale a ciclo unico (single cycle); Laurea Magistrale — Master's; Master universitario di I livello

1° ciclo / 1st cycle — 180 CFU/ECTS: Laurea — Bachelor's

Scuola secondaria di 2° grado (5 anni) - *Upper Secondary Education (5 years)*

Scuola secondaria di 1° grado (3 anni) - *Lower Secondary Education (3 years)*

Scuola primaria (5 anni) - *Primary Education (5 years)*

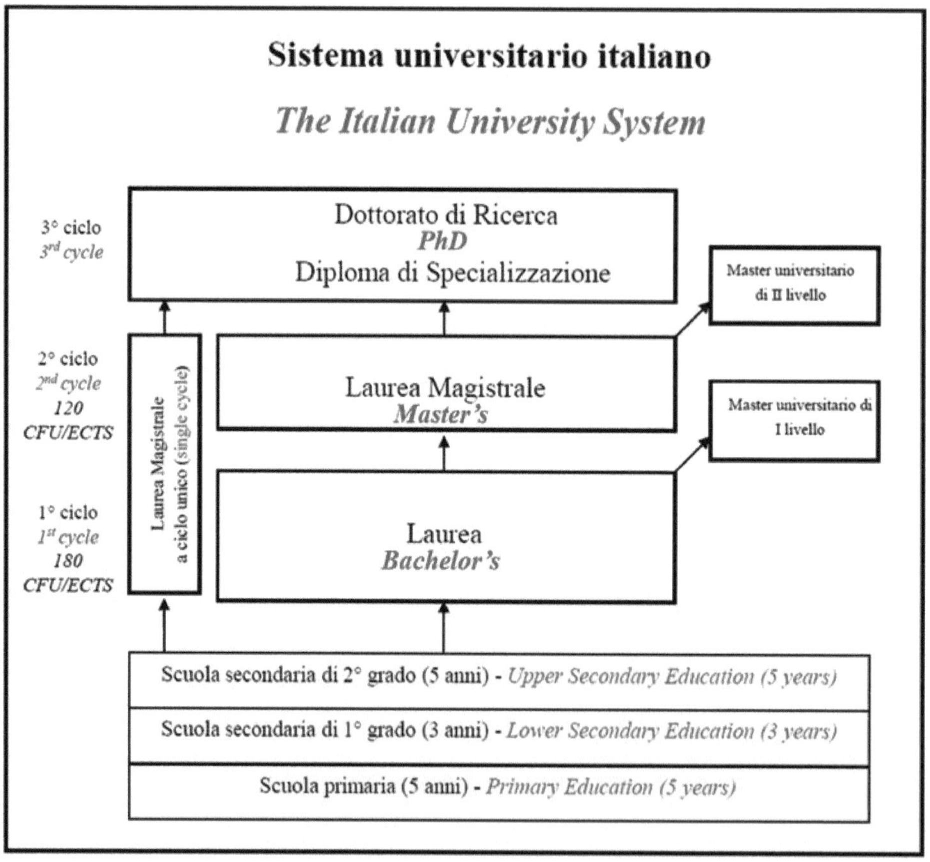

Source: ANVUR

The Italian higher education system currently includes 97 universities: 61 public universities, 19 private universities, 11 private online universities (e-learning programmes only), and six special tertiary education schools, which only provide doctoral training. Moreover, the national system also includes higher education in Art, Music and Dance (AFAM), which currently totals 159 institutions that carry out teaching, artistic production and research in visual arts, music, dance, drama and design, and deliver university-level degrees. The AFAM sector is not included in the Italian experience of assessing students' generic learning outcomes.

Policy context

The learning outcomes common to all qualifications of the same cycle adhere to a set of general descriptors. They reflect the wide range of disciplines and profiles, and must be able to summarise the variety of features of each national higher education system. The Dublin Descriptors are general statements about the ordinary outcomes that are achieved by students after completing a curriculum of studies and obtaining a qualification. The descriptors are conceived to describe the overall nature of the qualification. Furthermore, they are not to be considered disciplines and they are not limited to specific academic or professional areas.

The Dublin Descriptors consist of: Knowledge and understanding; Applying knowledge and understanding; Making judgements; Communication skills; and Learning skills. The learning outcomes of the Italian first- and second-cycle degree courses are structured according to the Dublin Descriptors.

Notably, between 2012 and 2013, the National Agency for the Evaluation of Universities and Research Institutes (hereinafter referred to as ANVUR) carried out an experimental assessment of the generic learning outcomes shown by students graduating from Italian universities by means of the TECO (*TEst sulle COmpetenze*) test. This pilot test was designed taking as a reference point the OECD feasibility study called AHELO – Assessing Higher Education Learning Outcomes. It is consistent with the European Standards and Guidelines for Quality Assurance (ESG, 2015[1]) that promote student-centred learning, accompanied by the analysis of learning outcomes, across the European Higher Education Area (EHEA).

ANVUR is an Italian independent public body that oversees the national higher education system and whose primary objective is to enhance its overall quality. The evaluation tasks of the agency, which has been operating since 2012, span the full range of higher education institutions' activities: teaching and learning; research; impact of social initiatives ("third mission"); and administrative performance. Both output and process evaluation methodologies are applied with broad use of informative tools developed by/in collaboration with ANVUR.

Reasons for TECO

Different reasons impelled ANVUR to undertake this pilot test, beginning in 2013. Legislative Decree n. 19 of 27 January 2012 governing the system of Self-Assessment and Periodic Assessment and Accreditation in higher education (hereinafter referred to as AVA) introduced a system of the initial and periodic accreditation of universities and their study programmes; a periodic assessment of the quality, efficiency and outcomes of universities' teaching activities; and the enhancement of the mechanisms underpinning the self-assessment of the quality and effectiveness of universities' activities.

Within this framework, the TECO pilot test supplements the assessment process via indicators that allow self-evaluation of the quality of learning achieved by students during their studies. Specifically, TECO enables self-evaluation of generic competences students possess upon graduating from university. It does so by constructing indicators that estimate the skill levels of university students. These indicators also allow for the periodic evaluation and accreditation of universities and their study programmes.

It is also the case that principal stakeholders (employers, universities, students and their families, taxpayers, and the government) are interested in an ever-improving quality of education in Italian universities. At the beginning, the pilot TECO test aimed to measure cross-disciplinary competences: the critical thinking needed to solve a problem or make a decision; the ability to represent and communicate a given fact; and the ability to learn new knowledge related to areas not necessarily connected with the particularities of the scientific discipline being studied. These competences are not monitored, assessed or certified by universities because they are not the subject of specific teaching activities; rather, they are part of that intangible stock of knowledge and skills that all teachers should pass on to students simply by teaching their subject. These are detected through TECO-T, a test designed to evaluate transversal skills. Disciplinary skills acquired by students in various bachelor's programmes are evaluated through TECO-D.

The Italian experiment with the CLA+ (TECO 2013-2015)

In the design of the TECO pilot test, ANVUR established a series of criteria dictated both by the awareness that it was an experiment (tight deadlines, limited budget, voluntary student participation) and by the need to collect as much data as possible (contextual variables) for a more complete understanding of test results:

1. Using the same test for all university courses, which would be evaluated in a uniform way with regard to all students because generic competences are by their nature independent of the specific field of study – they depend on how you study, not on what is being studied.

2. Using a test consisting of a) an open-response part that enables a check of reading ability, the critical analysis of texts and the ability to make coherent decisions therefrom as well as writing effectiveness and technique, and b) a closed-response part to evaluate the quality of scientific-quantitative reasoning.

3. Identifying eligible students (graduating students) i.e. those entitled to participate in the test if they are in a defined range of progress and maturity along the study path.

4. Limiting the objective to assessing acquired generic competences (the actual level of learning) and not the added-value of university education. This implies excluding freshmen from the test but allows for significant information to be delivered to stakeholders with shorter lead times. In principle, a longitudinal analysis (of the same people at the beginning and at the end of university studies) would be the best choice to determine university added-value but this would require a wait of at least 3-4 years.

5. Using contextual variables to enable filtering out of individual outcomes of the TECO (rebranded CLA+) that depend on both individual characteristics of the student population – for example, of a personal or family nature – and collective characteristics – for example, the rate of growth in the region of origin or the region where the university is located. This filters out individual characteristics that may account for certain students' rapid and successful completion of studies. And it allows the added-value to be statistically estimated by analysing what remains of various multiple regressions.

2013 testing

Almost 30 universities offered to participate in the TECO pilot test. The following 12 (a pre-defined limit) were selected for the 2013 pilot: Eastern Piedmont (PO), Padua (PD), Milan (MI), Udine (UD), Bologna (BO), Florence (FI), Rome La Sapienza (RM1), Rome Tor Vergata (RM2), Naples Federico II (NA), Salento (LE), Cagliari (CA) and Messina (ME). This ensured universities with a mix of size characteristics and adequate regional representation (4 from the North, 4 from the Centre and 4 from the South plus islands); and excluded non-multidisciplinary universities.

Regarding the administration of the test, it was known that the people entitled to take the CLA+ were just under 20% of all students from the third and fourth years – excluding courses for the health professions – enrolled in the 12 participating universities, i.e. a population of 21 872 in academic year 2012-2013. In fact, 14 907 people pre-registered for the test – including numerous extraneous persons not eligible for the test – and, among those eligible and pre-registered, only about 5 900 students actually came to sit the test.

The 2013 TECO pilot test carried out by ANVUR was the first-ever attempt to assess the level of generic competences acquired by university students in Italy (Zahner and Ciolfi, 2018[2]). The mean proportion of eligible candidates out of students from the third and fourth year (regularity index, R) and the mean proportion of those who came to sit the test out of those eligible (participation index, P) range very broadly across the 25 disciplinary groups and the 12 participating universities.

2015 testing

In 2015, the same pilot experiment was carried out by ANVUR with the participation of 26 universities and over 6 000 students. Regarding the participation, the multivariate analysis carried out on some independent variables (such as age, average diploma grade, number of exams, average exam grade) showed that the student's age, the grade obtained at the high school diploma, and average exam grades, were in all cases significant (<0.05). In other words, the younger the student's age and higher their grade at the diploma and university exams, the greater their participation in TECO. In addition to verifying the levels of generalist competencies through an additional specific questionnaire, the TECO pilots also provided for some background variables (such as demographic, environmental, socio-economic and cultural background-related data) of the participating students. These variables were in part collected during the registration phase of the CLA+ (basic information) and in part the day they took the test (mostly socio-economic and cultural background information).

The analysis showed a systematic downwards correlational relationship between the CLA+ result and the variables of age, female gender (versus male) and residence outside the region of the university's location. There was an upwards relationship relative to the variables of time since diploma obtained, coming from a "classical studies" high school (compared to other types of high schools), mean diploma and university grades, Italian citizenship and Italian spoken at home (versus non-Italian citizenship and language). The influence of parents appears in the sense that an absent mother (not father) lowers the CLA+ score, all other things being equal, and having a father employed in a managerial/professional position (but not a mother) raises it.

The effect of the socio-cultural condition was much stronger in simple correlations because in multiple regressions it is also exercised through diploma and university grades as well as in the choice of secondary school. Some contextual variables – such as, for example, family status – lose value once others are controlled. This is specifically because family status helps to predict the type of secondary school diploma, diploma grade, type of course of study chosen and average university grade in addition to predicting the result on the CLA+ test. On the other hand, in simple correlations, parents' high professional and cultural status strongly correlated with success in the CLA+: when, regardless of the father's position, the mother has a managerial/professional position or a white-collar job, university degree or high-school diploma, results above the mean and the median were observed; and this applies equally to the father. The absence of at least one parent is the worst deprivation condition and is much worse than having a father or mother who is a manual labourer, unemployed or without qualifications.

The examination of simple correlations between all contextual variables and the result on the CLA+ test or its two components, complemented at times by looking at indirect correlation (e.g. with diploma and university grades), yielded some broad generalisations, not necessarily applicable to all the geographical macro-areas of Italy. Looking at the variables for family data, it was somewhat surprising that the cases where there are siblings at the university or not were observationally equivalent and likewise for living off-site with respect to the university or not. The size of the family seemed instead to have a negative effect, and likewise for the travel time required to reach university. Students with more technological equipment on average performed better, as well as those who go on at least one trip per year outside the region or abroad; this did not seem to influence the mean diploma grade but, rather, the mean grade on university exams.

2013 and 2015 critical issues

Both CLA+ 2013 and 2015 experiments have highlighted some critical issues. The first was the self-selection bias of the universities and the students that joined the project and took the test, respectively. In the case of universities, the composition of the sample was defined more on the basis of the expression of their availability than on their representativeness. Regarding the selection of students, in addition to the criteria of the minimum number of ECTS obtained by students enrolled in the third year of a given university, the self-selection of the same students was also added, with an average participation rate of 20%, which prevented extrapolating the observations obtained to the entire student population.

The second critical issue was related to the scoring of the answers provided by the students. The open answers of the Performance Task (PT) test were codified by 239 scorers, identified among the faculty of the universities participating in the pilot, who evaluated the students' tests completely free of charge. For each university, a professor was identified as the Lead Scorer. After being trained by the Council for Aid to Education (CAE), the Lead Scorer had the responsibility of training and monitoring the assigned working group on scoring. In the Italian experience this multi-level training weakened the assessment system, increasing the gap in the coding, as indicated by a low correlation coefficient between the same scorers. On the basis of predefined quality parameters, a third evaluation was necessary in 52% of cases.

Redefining the TECO

These critical issues led ANVUR to redefine the entire TECO in 2016. This included reference areas, related frameworks, methodological approach and tools. Regarding student participation, it comprised all students enrolled in the first cycle and single-cycle courses at a specific point in their career as they were more numerous (and therefore more relevant for public policy purposes), less self-selected (in respect to master's degrees) and more likely to enter the labour market.

Another important change concerned the timing of the delivering of the TECO: the number of CFU as a selection criterion was abandoned. Instead, the only administrative criterion was that students be enrolled. This choice was congruent with a value-added approach, which reflects the skills development during the university training and not just the initial characteristics of the students.

Unlike previously, the new TECO contained only closed-ended questions to facilitate coding and reduce variability between different scorers. And developing the test in-house overcame the problem of test adaptability to the Italian sample (Ciolfi et al., 2016[3]).

Finally, the already mentioned subdivision of the project into two parallel strands, TECO *transversal* (TECO-T) and TECO *disciplinary* (TECO-D), was another aspect on which ANVUR wanted to focus when redefining the project.

It was clear that TECO should continue to refer to transversal skills such as *Literacy, Numeracy, Problem solving, Civics* (intended as civic and political knowledge, and skills). Given their transversal nature, the assessment of these skills for university students could not reflect disciplinary knowledge acquired in the various bachelors' programmes. However, ANVUR believes that transversal skills can be improved during university studies, and they are not the end state of an individual's cognitive development (Benadusi and Stefano, 2018[4]).

In particular, the TECO-T was carried out by the agency with a top-down process that involved groups of selected experts, consisting mainly of university professors. The detection of disciplinary skills was granted by autonomous disciplinary-focused working groups, supported by ANVUR. Briefly, after analysing and identifying the core disciplinary content of a study programme, they organised them with respect to the five Dublin Descriptors. After this preliminary phase, each working group was responsible for drafting the actual discipline-specific TECO-D.

Figure 11.2. Different content and approaches of the TECO-T and the TECO-D

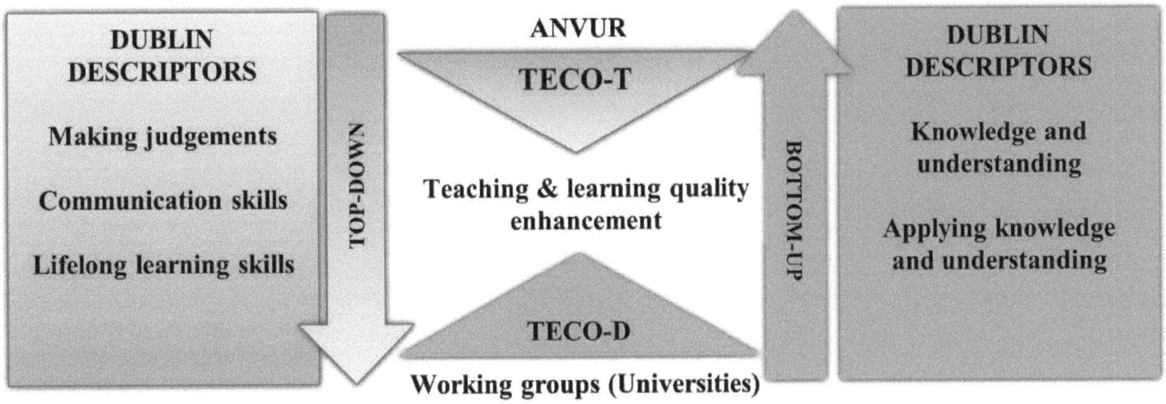

Source: ANVUR

Participation in the project was still voluntary for universities, study programmes and students. The tests were aimed at students enrolled in the first and last year of the study programme. The results of the tests were communicated individually to the participating students and anonymously to programme managers and did not affect any assessment by the faculty or the final grade of the degree.

TECO-T and transversal skills

The skills assessed in TECO-T are *Literacy, Numeracy, Problem Solving* and *Civics*. The working hypothesis is that these skills draw on a generalist training background. They can be trained in university, regardless of discipline-related content, and the skills are therefore comparable between universities and/or study programmes (Rumiati et al., 2018[5]). The agency carried out the TECO-T tests with the collaboration of experts consisting mainly of university professors, following a top-down process.

The first tests carried out and validated (I and II field trials in 2016) were Literacy and Numeracy.

The *Literacy* test was designed to assess students' ability levels in understanding, interpreting and reflecting on a text that was not directly related to a specific disciplinary content or a subject area, using two types of tests: a text followed by closed-ended questions and a short text in which some words had been deleted (Cloze test) that the student must re-enter.

The *Numeracy* test measures students' ability levels in understanding and solving logical-quantitative problems through a short text accompanied by graphs and tables followed by some questions or an infographic picture followed by some short questions.

During the 2019 edition, two new TECO-T were validated: *Problem Solving and Civics.*

The *Problem Solving* test evaluates the level of understanding and ability to solve simple and complex problems as well as the ability to achieve objectives in a given context where they cannot be achieved with direct actions or with known chains of actions and operations (Checchi et al., 2019[6]).

Finally, the *Civics* test evaluates personal, interpersonal and intercultural skills that concern forms of behaviour that characterise people that participate actively and constructively in social and working life, and can resolve conflicts where necessary. At the base, there is the understanding of concepts such as democracy, justice, equality, citizenship and civil rights.

TECO-D and disciplinary skills

The so-called disciplinary skills, unlike transversal ones, are closely linked to the specific contents of study programmes and can only be compared between programmes of a similar disciplinary field.

The development of TECO-D was coordinated by ANVUR but carried out by working groups appointed by the governing board of ANVUR. Members of those working groups were university professors and researchers in a specific disciplinary field who voluntarily participated in the project. They were selected to represent the whole of academia and scientific organisations.

TECO-D working groups determined the core disciplinary contents of a group of homogeneous programmes to develop a comprehensive disciplinary test.

Joining the TECO-D presents innovative aspects for the academic community for various reasons:

- It stimulates a shared definition of core disciplinary contents and their organisation with respect to the Dublin Descriptors;
- It fosters the drafting of tests with shared content at the level of homogenous groups of study programmes, allowing inter- and intra-university comparisons for self-assessment purposes;
- It guarantees centralised and certified management by ANVUR (delivering, data collection and analysis).

To help disciplinary working groups reach their objectives, ANVUR prepared two main tools containing useful information for:

- how to determine core disciplinary content according to the Dublin Descriptors (Working document n.1).
- how to correctly prepare a test (Working document n.2).

The agency also provided technical-scientific support to the working groups for the validation of the prepared tests.

TECO-T and TECO-D (2016-2019)

Since 2016, each year ANVUR proposes specific time windows for the delivering of the TECO-T and TECO-D tests, generally between October and December. The activity is co-ordinated by the disciplinary groups and the tests are delivered using an online platform managed by CINECA1[1]. Once the delivering window is closed, ANVUR proceeds with the analysis. Meanwhile, every participating student can download their personal certificate of achievement by accessing a dedicated portal with the same personal credentials used to access the test. The single result (average 200 and standard deviation 40) is calculated by standardising the scores obtained by all respondents on the basis of the two-parameter Rasch probabilistic model, which allows both the ability of the respondent and the difficulty of each question to be considered.

The results obtained in the TECO are not recorded in the student's university career.

TECO 2016

The first TECO experiment developed by ANVUR (with the collaboration of a group of experts) was a pilot of the TECO-T (Literacy and Numeracy only). ANVUR delivered it at the end of 2016 in order to validate the tests through a field trial. The pilot took place in five universities involving specific students: University of Messina (Economics), University of Padua (Psychology), University of Rome "Tor Vergata" (Medicine), University of Salento (Literature) and the Polytechnic of Turin (Engineering). This first pilot involved 854 students enrolled in the first and third year of the first cycle (bachelor's). The consequent analysis by

ANVUR showed that all individual items measured specific skills, represented different levels of difficulty and were able to distinguish the most competent students from others.

In particular, regarding the *Literacy* test (booklets 1 to 6), a good internal consistency was measured by the Cronbach's Alpha, meaning that the tests were able to measure a single competence. The items in the different booklets were similar in difficulty, reflecting the test design criteria.

Table 11.1. TECO-T Literacy field trial

	Literacy 1	Literacy 2	Literacy 3	Literacy 4	Literacy 5	Literacy 6
Number of valid tests (students)	144	142	142	142	142	142
Mean Score	19.85	18.71	21.05	18.03	19.39	19.04
Std. Dev.	4.04	3.70	4.79	4.44	3.81	3.63
Variation coefficient - CV	20.3	19.7	22.8	24.6	19.7	19.1
Cronbach's Alpha	0.777	0.675	0.796	0.766	0.664	0.689
Ease Mean	0.66	0.62	0.70	0.60	0.65	0.63
Point biserial correlation	0.39	0.31	0.39	0.39	0.32	0.32
Number of revised items	10	8	7	9	7	10

Source: ANVUR analysis

Regarding the Numeracy test (booklets 1 to 4), the Cronbach's Alpha is near 0.8, meaning that the tests were able to measure a single competence. The items in the different booklets were similar in difficulty, reflecting the test design criteria.

Table 11.2. TECO-T Numeracy field trial

	Numeracy 1	Numeracy 2	Numeracy 3	Numeracy 4
Number of valid tests (students)	214	214	213	213
Mean Score	13.31	15.91	14.99	15.59
Std. Dev.	4.81	4.50	4.87	5.17
Variation coefficient - CV	36.1	28.3	32.5	33.2
Cronbach's Alpha	0.848	0.799	0.829	0.837
Ease Mean	0.53	0.64	0.60	0.62
point biserial correlation	0.41	0.40	0.42	0.45
Number of revised items	6	5	4	2

Source: ANVUR analysis

After the analysis, ANVUR revised all booklets in order to solve some minor problems related to specific items (see tables). During the Spring of 2017, the final versions of the *Literacy* and *Numeracy tests* were delivered to 1 759 students enrolled in the first and third year of the first cycle (bachelor's) in five other universities (Bari, Bologna, Firenze, Milano "Bicocca", Palermo), taking into account only five disciplinary areas selected by ANVUR (Biology, Education, Psychological Sciences, Economics and Health Professions).

In Spring 2017, the TECO additionally delivered (at the end of the test) a questionnaire that provided useful information about students' family background and other personal experiences related to university and working daily life.

After test validation, a national TECO pilot took place between November 2017 and March 2018. With the TECO-T (*Literacy* and *Numeracy*) the following TECO-Ds were delivered to students enrolled in those specific study programmes after the TECO-T: Physiotherapy, Nursing, Medical Radiology. Overall, this pilot involved 27 universities across the country and a total of 12 510 students on a voluntary basis. A total of 481 test sessions were activated on the CINECA platform and 146 classroom tutors appointed by the participating universities monitored delivery.

Since it was not possible to set up an adequate number of test rooms equipped with computers for some universities, a paper-based method of test delivering was provided to allow all the universities to participate in the pilot.

The overall results for all students (without distinguishing them by university or study programme) showed that the differences between the mean scores are statistically significant between first- and third-year students for both *Literacy* and *Numeracy*. A statistically significant increase in the students' skills during their university studies was observed, albeit with a progressive growth for the Literacy-related ones, and with a significant decrease for the Numeracy-related ones between second and third year. It should be noted that at the beginning of their studies, students recorded a level below the set average value (200) in both areas (198.6 for *Literacy* and 197.6 for *Numeracy*) (Ciolfi and Sabella, 2018[7]).

Figure 11.3. Mean scores and confidence intervals of Literacy and Numeracy tests, by academic year of enrolment

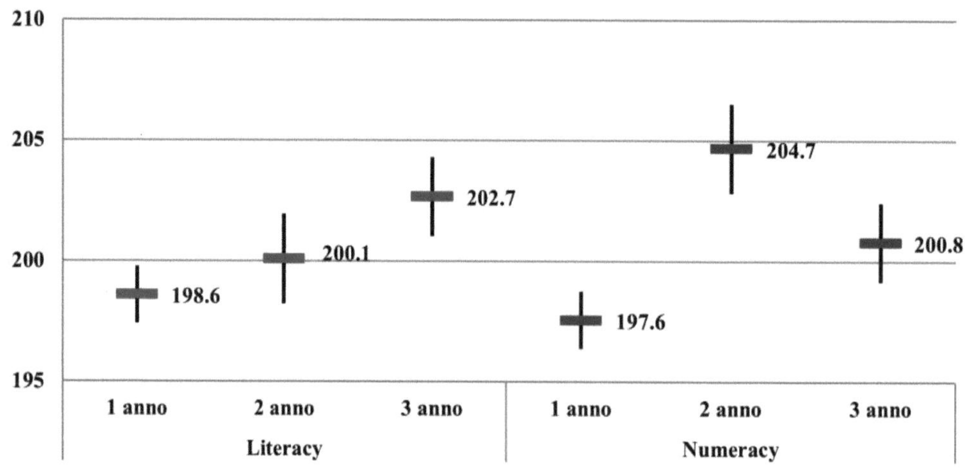

Note: 1 anno = first year, 2 anno = second year, 3 anno = third year
Source: ANVUR analysis

The following figure shows the same results by gender, suggesting that girls, while showing the same trend as boys over the three years, reach significantly lower levels, in particular for *Numeracy*. Notably, by separating the data by gender, the differences between the first and third year for *Literacy* are not statistically significant.

Figure 11.4. Mean scores and confidence intervals of Literacy and Numeracy tests, by academic year of enrolment and gender

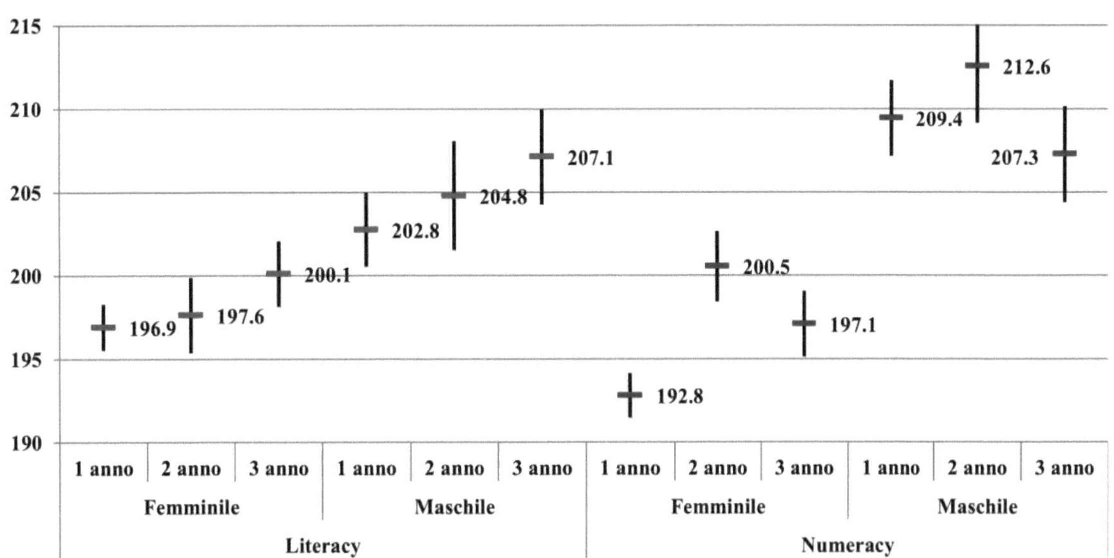

Note: Femminile = female, Maschile = male
Source: ANVUR analysis

During the pre-enrolment phase for TECO, students were asked to answer a questionnaire relating to their parents' educational qualifications, profession and type of occupation and other background information. With this information it was possible to calculate a status index inspired by the Index of Economic, Cultural, and Social Status (ESCS) used in the OECD's Programme for International Student Assessment (PISA) reports. The ESCS is one of the most common used variables in the analysis of data from the PISA programme. It is based on student responses to a context questionnaire, built to achieve information about educational opportunity and inequalities. The calculation for the TECO involves the synthesis by Principal Component Analysis (ACP) of two variables: the score attributed to the highest occupational status of the parents (Ganzeboom and Treiman, 1996[8]) and the highest number of years of education achieved by the parents. Based on the quartiles, four classes were identified, the aggregate results of which are shown in the table below. It clearly emerges that the family context (with the related cultural and / or economic stimuli) affects the skills development of students, in particular for students with advantaged backgrounds (Ciolfi and Sabella, 2018[7]).

Figure 11.5. Mean scores and confidence intervals of Literacy and Numeracy tests, by year and cultural status

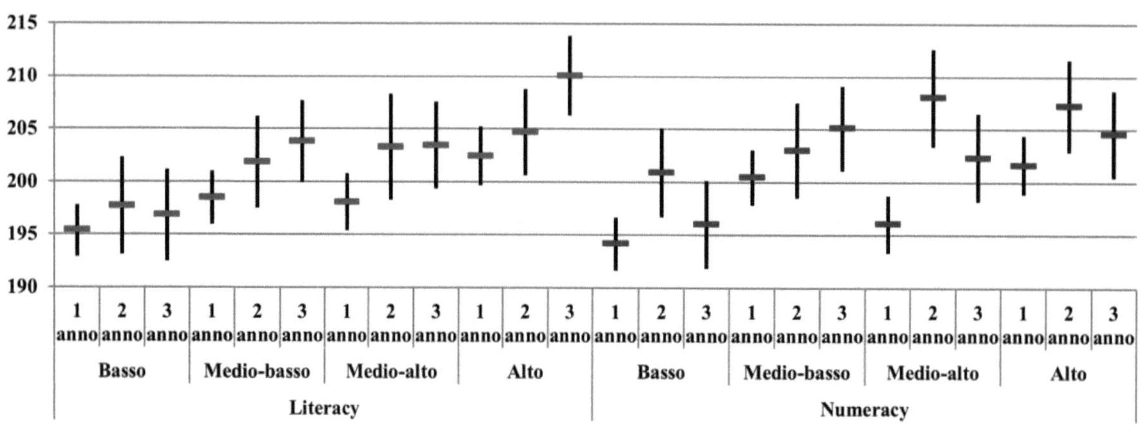

Note: basso = bottom quartile, medio-basso = second quartile, medio-alto = third quartile, alto = top quartile.
Source: ANVUR analysis

TECO 2018

The 2018 TECO pilot had the same characteristics as the TECO-T (*Literacy* and *Numeracy*) and the Nursing, Physiotherapy, and Medical Radiology TECO-Ds that were delivered to students enrolled in those specific study programmes (Galeoto et al., 2019[9]).

Overall, this pilot involved 26 universities across the country and a total 10 148 students on a voluntary basis. A total of 450 test sessions were activated on the CINECA platform and 153 classroom tutors appointed by the participating universities monitored the delivery.

Nursing students were the most numerous in absolute number (7 557), followed by those in Physiotherapy (1 655) and Medical Radiology (936).

TECO 2019

During the TECO 2019 edition, which took place between September and December, 47 universities participated throughout the country, with a total of 21 929 students. The participating students were enrolled in 12 different first-level study programmes in the medical-health area2[2]. A specific TECO-D was developed and delivered for each one. In addition, two new TECO-T areas were statistically validated: *Problem Solving* and *Civics*. More specifically, a selected group of 4 050 students answered the new *Problem Solving* or *Civics* test. Students were from 41 universities, enrolled in the Medical Radiology, Philosophy and Education Sciences study programmes. The validation of the tests showed good reliability and validity for both tests.

TECO 2020

Starting with the TECO 2020 edition, students were given a single TECO-T booklet containing tests for all the four validated areas *Literacy, Numeracy, Problem Solving* and *Civics*.

Figure 11.6. The development of TECO

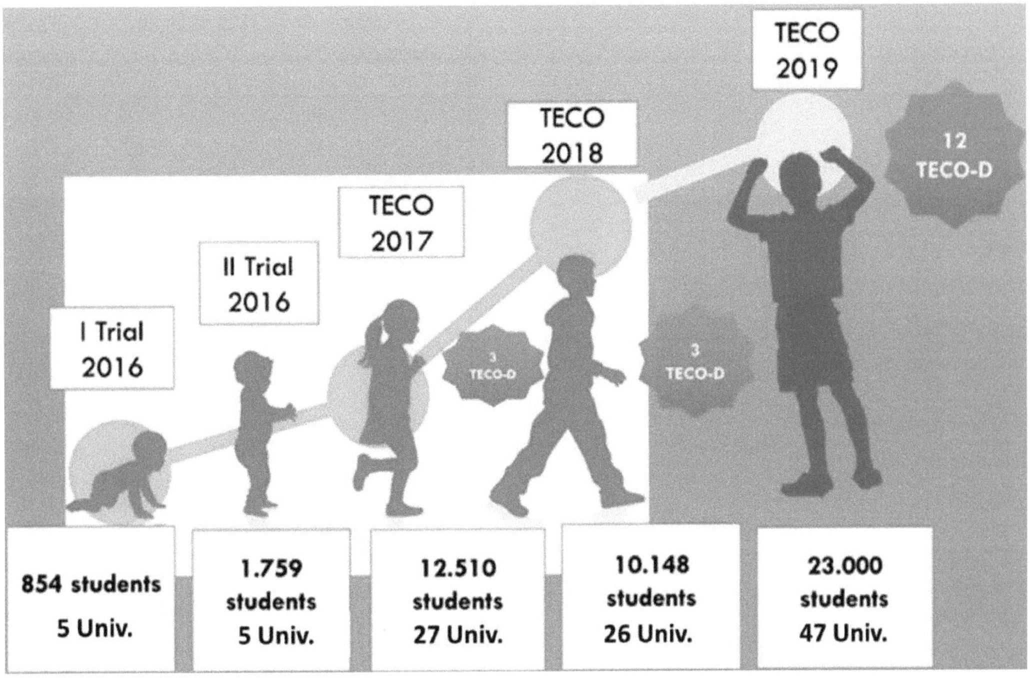

Delivering TECO during the COVID-19 pandemic

For the TECO 2020/2021 edition a new delivery system was developed in compliance with current regulations to prevent the spread of the COVID-19 pandemic.

ANVUR decided to carry out the delivery of the test remotely, meaning that every student was connected from home with their personal device. The students' recognition system, the block of web pages during the test and the management of virtual classrooms (with the help of an online tutor) were defined together with CINECA.

To allow for easy organisation of the TECO, two delivery windows were defined instead of one: the first was from 20 October to 31 December 2020, the second from 1 March to 31 May 2021.

The TECO 2020/2021 was organised in two distinct parts as in previous years: a TECO-T and TECO-D (if available for the study programme in which the student was enrolled). Each student had to complete both parts. Only students who completed the TECO-T would be able to take the TECO-D. In any case, a break was guaranteed between the two phases.

The TECO-T is a single 50-minute test with reference to *Literacy, Numeracy, Problem Solving* and *Civics*. Two different sets of the TECO-T were randomly assigned to students, also within the same virtual classroom.

The TECO-Ds all last 90 minutes. During the first window (October-December 2020) Health Professions, Education and Psychology were delivered; during the second window (March-May 2021) Philosophy, Psychology, Education, Classics and Modern Letters and Medicine TECO-Ds were administered.

Some 19 292 students from 54 universities participated in the first window (October-December 2020). The tests were carried out in 48 days for a total of 1 282 test sessions (an average of 26.7 sessions per day) for an average of 402 tests per day.

Table 11.3. TECO 2020 participation

Disciplines	N. of virtual classrooms	N. of students	Participating universities/total universities*
Dietetics	42	510	12/22
Physiotherapy	104	1 868	17/41
Nursing	451	10 204	21/42
Childhood nursing	11	192	6/8
Speech therapy	36	557	9/29
Neuro and Psychomotricity of the developmental age	29	646	8/12
Obstetrics	74	1 222	17/33
Education	155	1 155	20/42
Psychology	253	1 186	28/42
Biomedical laboratory techniques	53	675	16/35
Medical radiology techniques	69	820	20/39
Occupational therapy	19	257	7/8
Total	**1 296**	**19 292**	

Note: *Number of participating universities / number of universities that offer that study programme.
Source: ANVUR analysis

For students who participated in the second window (March-May 2021), the week 19-22 April 2021 was dedicated exclusively to students enrolled in Medicine and Surgery single-cycle master's programmes (Bacocco et al., 2020[10]). The whole operation was carried out in four days for a total of 5 924 students from 29 universities with 721 virtual classroom tutors.

Table 11.4. TECO 2021 Medicine and Surgery participation

University	N. of students
TORINO	768
Napoli Federico II	713
ROMA "La Sapienza"	630
CATANIA	534
BRESCIA	315
MILANO-BICOCCA	300
FIRENZE	289
MOLISE	289
MILANO	287
ROMA "Tor Vergata"	201
PISA	163
TRIESTE	163
PADOVA	158
BOLOGNA	140
PIEMONTE ORIENTALE "Amedeo Avogadro"-Vercelli	134
SALERNO	113
INSUBRIA Varese-Como	97
MODENA e REGGIO EMILIA	90
FERRARA	86
VERONA	83
"Campus Bio-Medico" di ROMA	81
MESSINA	74

"Magna Graecia" di CATANZARO	54
L'AQUILA	37
Campania "Luigi Vanvitelli"	36
FOGGIA	35
PARMA	22
"G. d'Annunzio" CHIETI-PESCARA	20
BARI ALDO MORO	12
Total	**5 924**

Source: ANVUR analysis

Currently, ANVUR is focusing on the analysis of this last Medicine and Surgery field trial. Once the analysis is completed, each student can download their certificate of achievement certified by ANVUR.

Possible next steps and prospects

Over the last few years, the main political decision maker in the field of higher education (namely, the Ministry of Education, University and Research) has been characterised by deep and continuous changes in top management and internal organisation due to the instability of the national government.

These changes have not favoured the continuity of dialogue between the government, ANVUR, academia, the labour market and all other relevant stakeholders. This has hindered the development of a shared vision with respect to the assessment of students' generic learning outcomes promoted by ANVUR with the TECO. This partly explains why a well-defined national project is still lacking and consequently there have been no developments with reference to the regulatory framework. TECO continues to be a project, an initiative characterised by participation on a voluntary basis.

However, recently the Italian government has divided the relevant Ministry, creating an independent Ministry of University and Research. The establishment of a dedicated Ministry has been very positively received by the academic community, who hope that this government reorganisation will provide added-value to the higher education sector and confer greater impact on the specific themes and issues of higher education to the political agenda at the national level.

Even within ANVUR important changes are expected. The political body (Government Board) is redefining the AVA system according to the principles of simplification and greater attention to the evaluation of results. The review of the national accreditation and assessment system is an important opportunity to discuss the role of TECO and more generally the role of the measurement of learning outcomes in enhancing the evaluation of results.

In this period, the agency started drafting the *Report on Italian University and Research system 2021* in which ANVUR captures (supported by longitudinal analysis) the university and research situation in Italy. It proposes critical reflections on strengths and opportunities, and aspects to be improved. Like its predecessors, the 2021 report will have a chapter dedicated to the assessment of learning outcomes and the TECO. This comprehensive report, like the previous, will be published on the website and presented in a dedicated public event to the relevant decision makers and stakeholders.

Finally, it is important to emphasise the importance of the latest developments of the TECO-D. The establishment of the working group of Medicine has focused the academic community's attention on the TECO. Currently, there is a strong debate about the assessment of skills and competences in the health sciences and possible content contamination between the Medicine and Surgery single-cycle master's programme and health professions first-cycle programmes. The 2021 report will show results of the first field trial of students enrolled in Medicine and Surgery.

Regardless of future developments, it is clear that interest in the assessment of generic and disciplinary learning outcomes is growing as shown by the increasing participation in the TECO by universities, students and the establishment of disciplinary working groups. The academic community and ANVUR believe that it is essential to deepen the analysis of teaching and learning results, particularly generic learning outcomes, for the purpose of continuous improvement. Tools like the TECO can certainly help in the analysis.

References

ANVUR (ed.) (2016), "La sperimentazione sulla valutazione delle competenze attraverso il test sulle competenze (TECO – 2013 e 2015)", *Rapporto sullo Stato del Sistema Universitario e della Ricerca 2016*, pp. 259-287. [3]

Bacocco, B. et al. (2020), "Medicina alla prova. La validazione del Progress Test a cura dell'ANVUR (Testing mdeical studies. The validation of the Progress Test by ANVUR)", *Medicina E chirurgia, Journal of Italian Medical Education 85*, pp. 3819-3816, https://doi.org/10.4487/medchir2020-85-6. [10]

Benadusi, L. and M. Stefano (eds.) (2018), *Le competenze: Una mappa per orientarsi (Universale paperbacks Il Mulino Vol. 729)*, Fondazione Agnelli, Bologna: Il Mulino. [4]

Checchi, D. et al. (2019), *Il Problem Solving come competenza trasversale: inquadramento e prospettive nell'ambito del progetto TECO*, Scuola Democratica, https://doi.org/10.12828/93404. [6]

ESG (2015), *Standards and Guidelines for Quality Assurance in the European Higher Education Area*, Brussels, Belgium (ISBN: 978-9-08-168672-3). [1]

Galeoto, G. et al. (2019), *The use of a dedicated platform to evaluate health-professions university courses*, https://doi.org/10.1007/978-3-319-98872-6_33. [9]

Ganzeboom, H. and D. Treiman (1996), "Internationally comparable measures of occupational status for the 1988 International Standard Classification of Occupations", *Social Science Research*, Vol. 25/3, https://doi.org/10.1006/ssre.1996.0010. [8]

Momigliano, S. (ed.) (2018), "La rilevazione delle competenze degli studenti: il progetto TECO", *Rapporto Biennale sullo stato del sistema universitario e della ricerca*, pp. 155-166. [7]

Rumiati, R. et al. (2018), "Key-competences in higher education as a tool for democracy", *Form@re*, Vol. 18, pp. 7-18, https://doi.org/10.13128/formare-24684. [5]

Zahner, D. and A. Ciolfi (2018), "International Comparison of a Performance-Based Assessment in Higher Education", in *Assessment of Learning Outcomes in Higher Education, Methodology of Educational Measurement and Assessment*, Springer International Publishing, Cham, https://doi.org/10.1007/978-3-319-74338-7_11. [2]

Notes

[1] CINECA is a not-for-profit Consortium developing advanced Information Technology applications and services. It is made up of 97 members: the Italian Ministry of Education, the Italian Ministry of Universities and Research, 69 Italian universities and 26 Italian National Institutions (ANVUR included). Today it is the largest Italian computing centre.

[2] Study programmes are: Pedagogy, Nursing, Physiotherapy, Dietetics, Childhood Nursing, Speech therapy, Neuro and Psychomotor Therapy of the Developmental Age, Obstetrics, Biomedical Laboratory Techniques, Occupational Therapy.

12 Assessing the generic skills of undergraduate students in Finland

Jani Ursin, University of Jyväskylä (Finland)

Heidi Hyytinen, University of Helsinki (Finland)

This chapter describes a project on the assessment of Finnish undergraduate students' generic skills. It gives a brief overview of the Finnish higher education system and the policy context that has paved the way for the assessment of generic skills. It describes the aims of the project, and illustrates how it was conducted in Finland. The chapter also presents the key findings on the mastery of generic skills, and the main factors explaining the level of generic skills. Finally, it presents policy recommendations aimed at enhancing the teaching and learning of generic skills within undergraduate studies, and outlines the lessons learnt from the assessment of generic skills in Finland.

This chapter is based on the final report of the KAPPAS! project. For more information, please see Ursin, J., H. Hyytinen and K. Silvennoinen (eds.) (2021[1]), *Assessment of Undergraduates' Generic Skills in Finland – Findings of the Kappas! Project*. Ministry of Education and Culture. Publications of Ministry of Education and Culture 2021:31.

The Finnish higher education system

The Finnish education system can be seen as having two main streams, i.e. a general stream (which provides students with general knowledge, information and skills) and a vocational stream (which provides students with vocational and professional competences). The system is flexible, allowing easy movement between the streams during one's educational career, and few students come to a dead-end. The higher education (HE) system also reflects the two streams, consisting as it does of two complementary sectors: one with 24 professionally-oriented universities of applied sciences (UASs), and the other with 14 research-intensive universities. The UASs train professionals in response to labour market needs and carry out research, innovation and development activities. For their part, the research-intensive universities conduct scientific research, and provide instruction and postgraduate education based on that research. Both types of higher education institutions (HEIs) enjoy autonomy, with freedom to conduct education and research. This freedom is secured in the Finnish Constitution and guaranteed by the laws governing HEIs (Ammattikorkeakoulululaki, 2014[2]; Universities Act, 2009[3]). Nonetheless, as part of the government, the Ministry of Education and Culture (MoEC) allocates core funding to the HEIs and steers the activities of institutions via a process of management by results (Ursin, Hyytinen and Sivennoinen, 2019[4]).

Currently (as of 2021), Finland has 38 HEIs with around 300 000 students (Vipunen – opetushallinnon tilastopalvelu, 2019[5]). Each higher education institution decides on the students to be admitted, and on the criteria for admission. There are three ways of admitting students to the HEIs: entrance examinations, grades in the Matriculation Examination or in vocational upper secondary qualifications, and the Open University route. The first two are the principle forms of student admission. Recently, the admission of higher education students was reformed in such a way as to place more weight on the grades. This means that from 2020 onwards more than half of student places have been filled on the basis of grades, thereby highlighting the importance of success in upper secondary education and especially in the Matriculation Examination. Higher education is free for all students with the exception of those coming from countries that are not members of the European Union or the European Economic Area. Universities offer bachelor's degrees (3-year programmes), master's degrees (2-year programmes) and third-cycle postgraduate degrees (3-year programmes); by contrast, the UASs provide bachelor's degrees (lasting 3-4 years) and master's degrees (lasting 1.5-3 years). In line with the aims of the Bologna process – reflecting the political will of 49 countries to build a European Higher Education Area – a competence-based approach to curriculum development has gained ground in Finnish higher education (Gaebel et al., 2018[6]).

The policy context for the assessment of generic skills

Over the past two decades, there has been active debate on the skills and competences that higher education should promote. In Europe this discussion has touched on ways of improving the quality and transparency of higher education (e.g Ursin (2014[7]))). The European Union has, for its part, emphasised that changes in working life require a broad range of competences from higher education graduates. Taking an intergovernmental perspective, the OECD has stressed the importance of learning outcomes in higher education via a feasibility study on the Assessment of Learning Outcomes in Higher Education (AHELO), conducted in 2010-2013 (Tremblay, Lalancette and Roseveare, 2012[8]). In line with this, generic skills, such as problem solving, communication and co-operation (in addition to professional skills) are considered to be important in working life, continuous learning and digitalisation (e.g. (European Commission, 2013[9])). To take an example, in the era of artificial intelligence, generic skills can be seen as the element that sets humans apart from machines, with technical operations being increasingly left to machines, and with humans focusing on processes that require creativity and originality (European Commission Education and Training, 2019[10]).

In Finland, the government views the competences produced by higher education as crucial for the success of Finland in global education and the labour markets. The government has set as an ideal the objective that Finland should be the most competent country in the world, with higher education producing the best learning and learning environments in the world. Furthermore, the skills generated by higher education are seen as pivotal in Finland in terms of responding to changes in the labour market, and from the point of view of continuous learning. Indeed, for a small country like Finland, higher education is seen as the key to operating and influencing on a global scale (Ministry of Education and Culture, 2017[11]).

Traditionally, higher education policy in Finland has aspired to an equal level of quality across the system (Välimaa, 2004[12]). However, assessments of the quality of teaching and learning in higher education are by no means straightforward. In fact, Finland has up to now lacked information on what students learn during their studies, and on how well the higher education policy – intended to promote equality – actually produces or enhances high quality teaching and learning.

The expertise of undergraduate students can be seen as composed of (1) field-specific knowledge and skills and (2) generic skills. In higher education, the most crucial generic skills are higher-order cognitive skills such as critical thinking, argumentation and analytical reasoning (e.g. Tsaparlis (2020[13]), Arum and Roksa (2011[14]), Lemons and Lemons (2013[15])). Nonetheless, previous studies, both internationally and in Finland, have indicated that undergraduate students face challenges, for example, in argumentation, interpreting and evaluating information, and drawing conclusions (e.g. (Badcock, Pattison and Harris (2010[16]), Arum and Roksa (2011[14]), Evens, Verburgh and Elen (2013[17]), Hyytinen et al. (2015[18])).

Implementation of the CLA+ International in Finland

Project aims and co-ordination

The concerns and political aspirations presented above paved the way for the project entitled Assessment of Undergraduate Students' Learning Outcomes in Finland (Finnish acronym KAPPAS!). Its main aims were (1) to identify the level of Finnish undergraduate students' generic skills, and (2) to determine the factors associated with the level of generic skills. The project was funded by Ministry of Education and Culture (MoEC) and carried out by Jyväskylä University Institute for Educational Research (FIER), together with Helsinki University Centre for University Teaching and Learning (HYPE). The Council for Aid to Education (CAE) participated in the project as an international partner. Altogether, seven (out of 24) Finnish UASs and 11 (out of 14) universities participated in the study.

Translation, adaptation and verification of the CLA+ International

The test instruments, testing platforms, proctor interfaces and test manuals were translated into the two official languages of Finland, i.e. Finnish and (Finnish) Swedish. The translation and adaptation process of the test instruments followed the International Translation Committee guidelines for translating and adapting tests (Bartram et al., 2017[19]); hence it consisted of four phases. In the first phase, the international partners translated the test instruments from English into Finnish and Swedish. Next, two translators (who had knowledge of English-speaking cultures, but whose native language was the primary language of the target culture) in Finland independently checked and confirmed the translations. Thereafter, the national research team reconciled and verified the revisions. After the Finnish translations were checked, the Swedish translations were verified against the Finnish translations, in order to ensure the equivalence of the translations. Finally, the translations were pre-tested in cognitive labs. Each cognitive lab lasted around two hours, and involved think-aloud protocols and interviews among 20 Finnish undergraduate students. The cognitive labs made it possible to check that the translation and adaptation process for both the Finnish and Swedish versions had not altered the meaning or the difficulty of the tasks, and that the instruments tapped into the cognitive processes as expected (Hyytinen et al., 2021[20]; Leighton, 2017[21]). The test instruments and testing platforms were fine-tuned on the basis of the cognitive labs; hence a few consistency issues between the Finnish and Swedish translations were addressed.

Test administration

Data sampling

The target group of the KAPPAS! project consisted of students at the initial and final stages of their undergraduate degree programmes, attending 18 participating Finnish HEIs. The aim of the sampling was to obtain as representative a sample as possible, based on the field of study, and with coverage of the entire country. The starting point of the sampling frame was to select 200 initial- and 200 final-stage students from each participating HEI. Previous experience – including the data collection from the AHELO feasibility study (Tremblay, Lalancette and Roseveare, 2012[8]; Ursin, 2020[22]) – had shown that it is difficult to motivate higher education students to participate in such studies, and that random sampling of individual students has a poor participation rate. For this reason, the research team decided to carry out data sampling via a cluster sampling method. The sampling was carried out within each HEI in such a way that the fields of study were randomly selected. Thereafter, a cluster (such as a tutor or seminar group) within the required fields of study was randomly selected so that the desired number of students was sampled. Overall, the data sampling aimed for the best possible representativeness at the national level rather than at the institution level.

Data collection

A translated and culturally adapted version of the CLA+ International was applied. It included a performance task (PT), a set of 25 selected-response questions (SRQs), and a set of 37 background information questions. It was administered online via a secure testing platform during an assigned testing window (from August 2019 to March 2020). Each test session lasted for 2 hours 15 minutes. Students had 60 minutes to complete the PT, followed by 30 minutes for the SRQs. Thereafter, students filled in a background survey. The PT measured analysis and problem solving, writing effectiveness and writing mechanics. In order to successfully complete the PT, students needed to familiarise themselves with the materials available in an electronic document library and then write an answer to the question, which dealt with the differences in life expectancies in two cities. The SRQs measured critical reading and evaluation, scientific and quantitative reasoning, and critiquing an argument. The SRQs in each section were based on one or more documents. The materials and questions in the sections covered the topics of brain protein, nanotechnology and women in combat.

Each HEI was responsible for (1) inviting students, and (2) administering and proctoring the computer-based tests according to the instructions and manuals provided by the national research team and CAE. The research team also offered training for the contact persons in all the HEIs and support for the proctors. Participation in the KAPPAS! project was voluntary, and informed consent was obtained from the participants. In some institutions, the participating students received small non-monetary incentives such as movie tickets.

Altogether, 2 402 undergraduate students participated in the study. Of these, 1 538 (64%) were initial-stage (first-year) students and 864 (36%) final-stage (third-year) students. The participants consisted of 1 273 (53%) university students and 1 129 (47%) UAS students, comprising in total 1 178 (49%) males and 1 158 (48%) females. The majority of the students took the test in Finnish, with only 156 (6.5%) completing the test in Swedish. The participation rate was 25%. The rate varied between initial-stage and final-stage students, types of HEIs and fields of study. The participation rate was highest among the initial-stage UAS students (39%), and lowest among the final-stage university students (15%).

Data analyses

In order to prepare the data for analysis, each PT response had to be scored by two independent and trained scorers on the basis of the CLA+ scoring rubric. The scoring rubric included three sub-scores relating to analysis and problem solving, writing effectiveness and writing mechanics. Each aspect was scored on a six-point scale with an additional option for responses that could not be scored; for instance, an empty response. In order to secure consistency of scoring, calibration papers were used, and scoring was monitored by a lead scorer.

The approach to the statistical analyses (descriptive statistics, and linear and logistic regression) was design-based, utilising survey weights, and accounting for clustered data. Partly due to the sampling design, and partly due to non-response, there was considerable variation in the inclusion probabilities between student sub-groups (as defined by gender, field of study, institution and study programme). The distortions in the eventual sample data were corrected by using survey weights derived from the Finnish student registers. Because the individuals in a specific study programme tended to be correlated, all variance estimates and resulting confidence intervals and significance tests were computed via methods taking this intra-cluster correlation into account. Furthermore, for all the tasks, a commensurate level of difficulty was determined via item analysis. The midpoint of the PT scale was approximately 990 points, while its range was approximately 510-1 470 points. The midpoint of the scale for the SRQs was approximately 1 090 points and the range around 550-1 630 points. The midpoint of the student's total score scale was 1 040 points and the range 530-1 550 points.

Reports to students and higher education institutions

All students who participated in the study received a report on their test scores plus support material, which allowed them to enhance their generic skills. Each HEI also received a report on their students' test performance. The national research team organised several tailored webinars for HEIs to discuss the KAPPAS! results and consider how generic skills could be better integrated into teaching and learning practices in a given HEI.

Main results

Levels and mastery of generic skills

This section examines Finnish higher education students' mastery of generic skills by the mean scores and level of mastery in the entire dataset, and further by the stage of studies and higher education sector. The CLA+ mean score for the data as a whole was 1 075. The scores in the PT and in the SRQ section were both very close to this figure (Figure 12.1). Nonetheless, there were some variations between student groups. The differences between initial- and final-stage students in total scores and in PT scores were statistically significant; in other words, final-stage students' generic skills were at a higher level than those of initial-stage students. On examining the mean scores of the university and UAS students, it was found that the final-stage university students achieved the highest scores. Their difference from any other student group was especially noticeable in the PT segment in which the final-stage university students scored 45 points higher than the initial-stage university students and as much as 96 points higher than the final-stage UAS students. All these differences were statistically highly significant. Depending on the score under consideration (PT, SRQ or total), the higher education sector explained 5-9% of the variance in the mean scores while the stage of studies explained only around 2% of the variance.

Figure 12.1. CLA+ mean scores of the participants: by stage of studies, type of HEI and overall

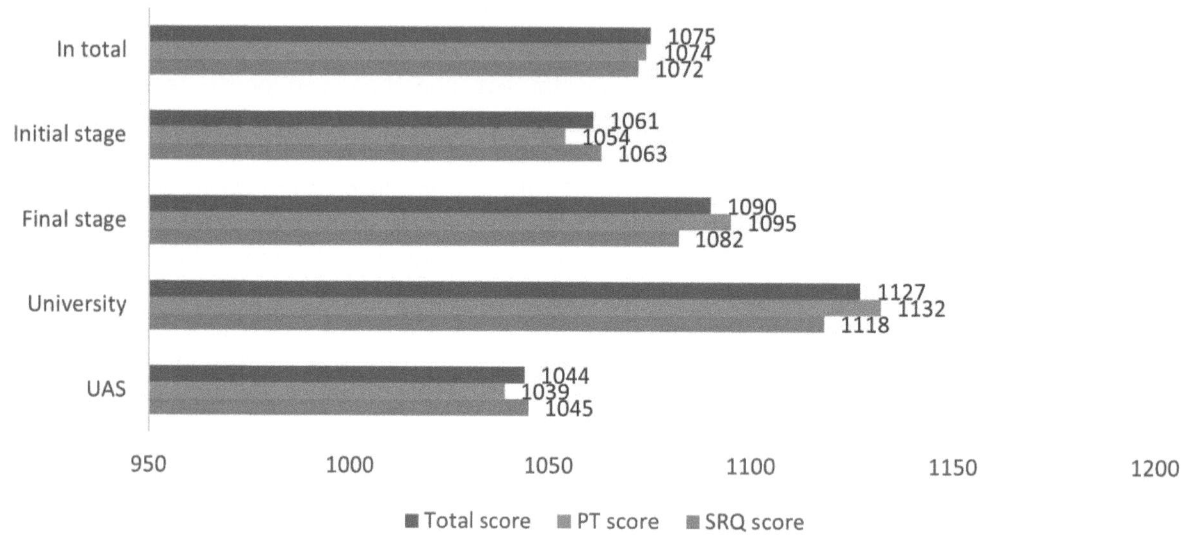

Source: Ursin et al., (2021[1]).

In terms of mastery levels, for almost 60% of the Finnish undergraduate students the generic skills were at a Basic or lower level. For the remainder (about 40%) the skills were at a Proficient or higher level (Table 12.1). Very few students reached the highest (Advanced) mastery level. There was a clear difference between the higher education sectors, with 24% of the UAS students exhibiting the lowest mastery level (Below Basic), whereas among the university students only 7% fell into this category. At the same time 23% of the university students reached the two highest mastery levels, with only 5% of the UAS students achieving these levels. The difference was even more striking when the stage of studies was taken into account. Thus, 29% of the initial-stage UAS students fell below a Basic level of mastery, with only 8% of initial-stage university students falling into this category. Regarding final-stage studies, 28% of the university students reached at least an Accomplished level of mastery, while the corresponding figure for the final stage UAS students was 7%.

Table 12.1. Mastery levels of the participants by stage of studies, type of HEI, and for all participants (%)

	Advanced	Accomplished	Proficient	Basic	Below basic
All participants	0.2	10	31	40	19
Initial-stage students	0.0	7	29	41	23
Final-stage students	0.4	13	32	40	15
University students	0.6	22	39	32	7
UAS students	0	5	27	44	24

Source: Ursin et al., (2021[1]).

Main factors associated with the level of generic skills

The associations with the level of generic skills were investigated with respect to the *field of study, age, gender, educational background, socio-economic background and attitude towards the test*. As age showed no systematic association with the mastery of generic skills, it will not be further discussed in this chapter.

Depending on the mean score observed, *gender* seemed to have a systematic association with the CLA+ mean scores (Figure 12.2). In the PT component the female students scored significantly higher than the males. In the SRQs the result was the opposite, with male students outperforming females. Although the field of study *per se* had no systematic association with the level of generic skills, an association was observed via gender; hence, the best overall PT performance occurred in the fields dominated by women (such as the humanities), while the best SRQ performance occurred in the male-dominated fields (such as engineering). In other words, in the female-dominated fields the skills involving analysis and problem solving, writing effectiveness and writing mechanics were at a higher level than in the male-dominated fields. The male-dominated fields outperformed the female-prevailed fields in the skills measured by the SRQs, i.e. those involving critical reading and evaluation, scientific and quantitative reasoning, and the ability to critique an argument. However, gender only explained around 1% of the variance in the mean scores for the fields analysed.

Figure 12.2. CLA+ mean scores of female and male participants

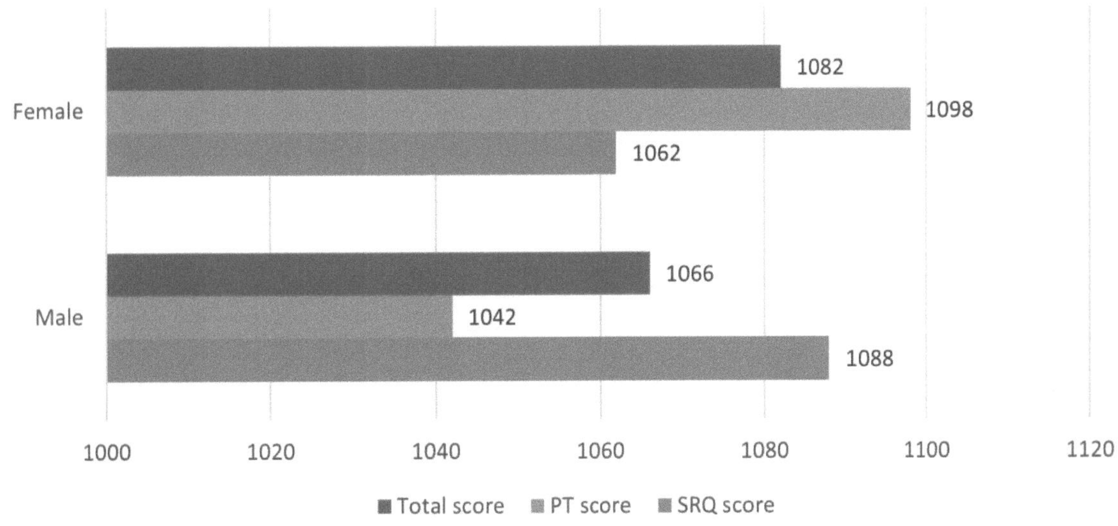

Source: Ursin et al., (2021[1]).

The information on *educational background* consisted of whether or not the participant had taken the Matriculation Examination, how the participant had succeeded in the mother tongue test included with it and whether the participant had a previous degree or qualification. The Finnish Matriculation Examination is a national examination generally taken at the end of the Finnish upper secondary school. The examination consists of a minimum of four tests. One of these, i.e. the test in the candidate's mother tongue, is compulsory for all candidates. The grades in the Matriculation Examination are (from highest to lowest): laudatur (L), eximia cum laude approbatur (E), magna cum laude approbatur (M), cum laude approbatur (C), lubenter approbatur (B), approbatur (A) and improbatur (I, indicating failure in the test).

The proportion of students who had completed the Matriculation Examination in the dataset was 80%. The figure was higher for the university students, with 92% of the university students (as opposed to 66% of the UAS students) having completed the Matriculation Examination. The CLA+ mean scores of students who had completed the Matriculation Examination were on average 84 points higher than for those students who had not done so (Figure 12.3). This difference was statistically highly significant. Indeed, some of the differences between the university and the UAS students can be explained by the larger proportion of persons who had completed the Matriculation Examination among the university students. The Matriculation Examination explained 5-9% of the variance of the mean scores.

Figure 12.3. Matriculation Examination and CLA+ mean scores across the entire data

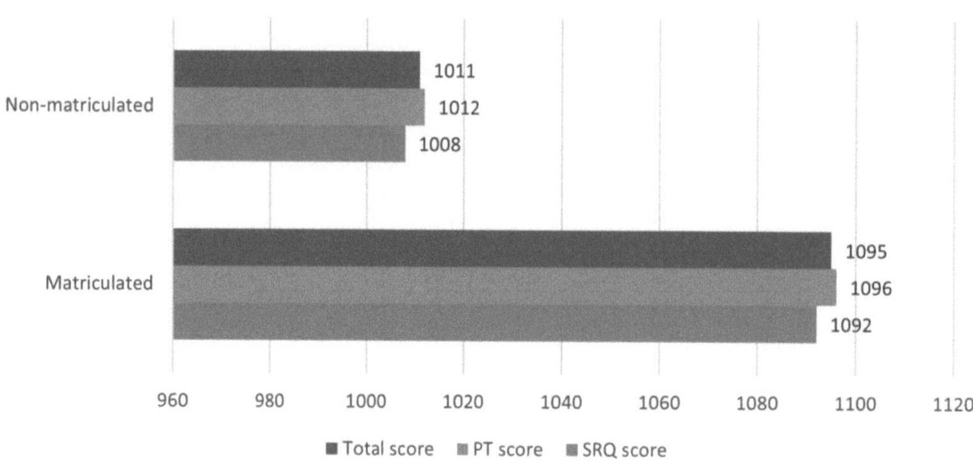

Source: Ursin et al., (2021[1]).

The level of generic skills was strongly associated with the mother tongue skills exhibited in the Matriculation Examination; thus the CLA+ mean scores rose almost linearly with the mother tongue grades, and the differences between the groups were statistically significant (Figure 12.4). Those who failed in the mother tongue test or were non-matriculated showed the lowest level of generic skills, whereas those who had had either of the two highest grades in the mother tongue test had the highest results. The mother tongue grade in the Matriculation Examination was in fact the strongest individual factor explaining the variance in the mean scores (i.e., 11-22% of the variance).

Figure 12.4. Mother tongue grade in the Matriculation Examination and CLA+ mean scores across the entire data

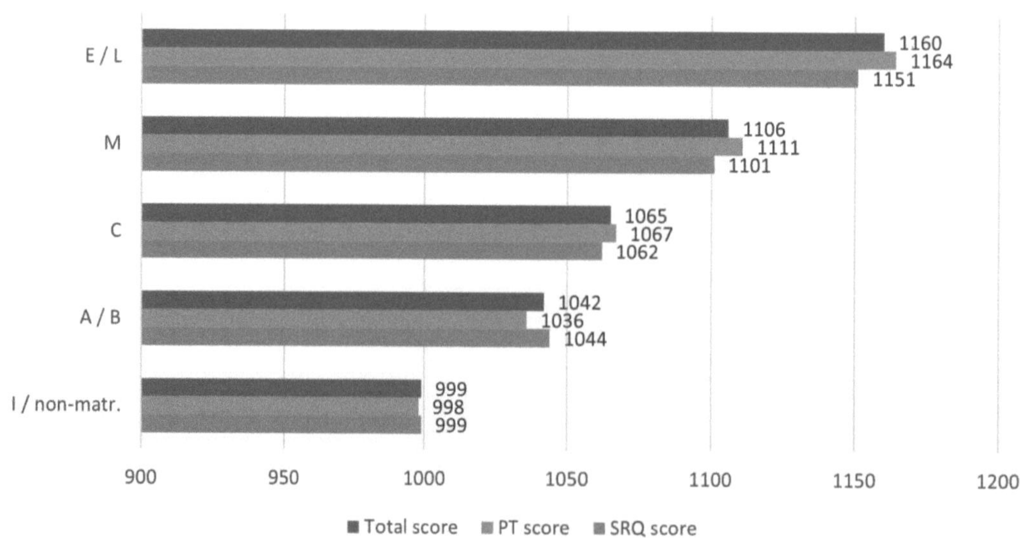

Source: Ursin et al., (2021[1]).

There was a clear difference between university and UAS students in the previous qualifications they had obtained; thus, 76% of the university students and 45% of the UAS students had completed only the Matriculation Examination, whereas for 27% of the UAS students, as opposed to just 2% of the university students, a vocational qualification was the only qualification obtained. Those who had completed both a vocational qualification and the Matriculation Examination accounted for 16% of the UAS students and 7% of the university students. Among the UAS students, 7% already had another higher education degree; the corresponding proportion among the university students was 10%.

The students who had already completed a previous higher education degree performed highest in the CLA+ test; nevertheless, the difference between these students and those who had attained only the Matriculation Examination was not statistically significant (Figure 12.5). Students with only a vocational qualification had the lowest scores.

Figure 12.5. Previous degree or qualification of the student and CLA+ mean scores

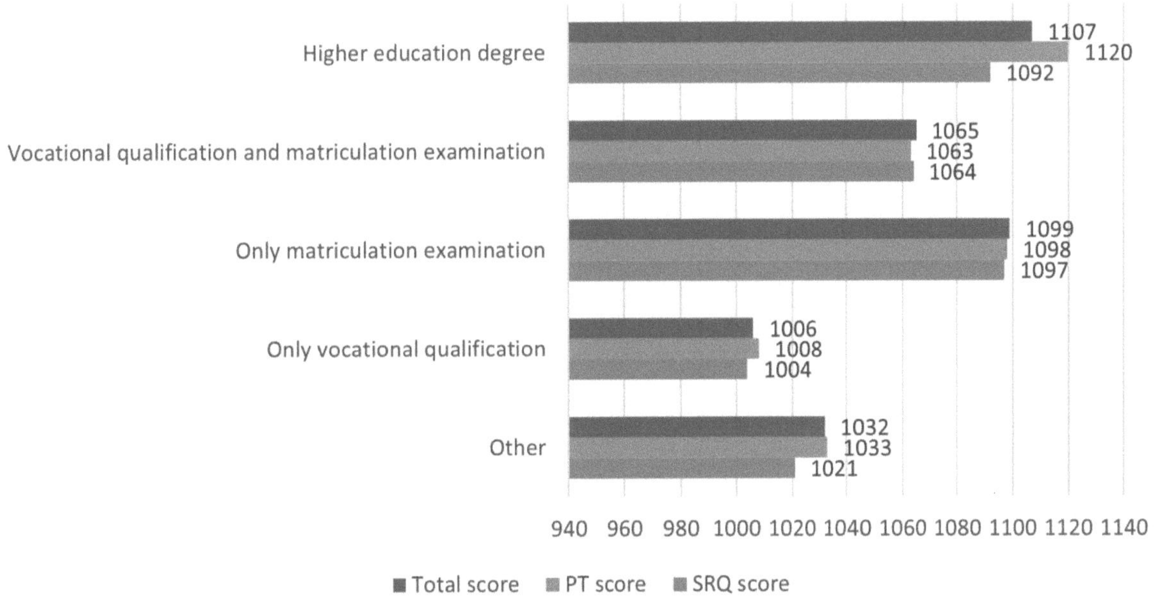

Source: Ursin et al., (2021[11]).

Parental education and the estimated number of books in the student's childhood home were taken to describe the student's socio-economic background. From the data on parental education one can observe that university students' parents are more likely to have a high level of education than the parents of UAS students. In the present dataset, 43% of the university students' parents had at least a master's degree whereas the corresponding proportion for the UAS students was 20%. Conversely, 47% of the UAS students' parents had not gone beyond a secondary level qualification. The corresponding figure among the university students' parents was 27%.

Students whose parents had attained, at most, a basic education showed the clearest distinction from other groups of students, with their mean scores emerging as significantly lower than those of other groups (Figure 12.6). The differences between the other groups were fairly small, with only a few differences in PT or total mean scores showing statistical significance. It was notable that overall the parental education level explained only a small part of the variance (1-4%) in the level of generic skills.

Figure 12.6. Parental education and CLA+ mean scores across the entire data

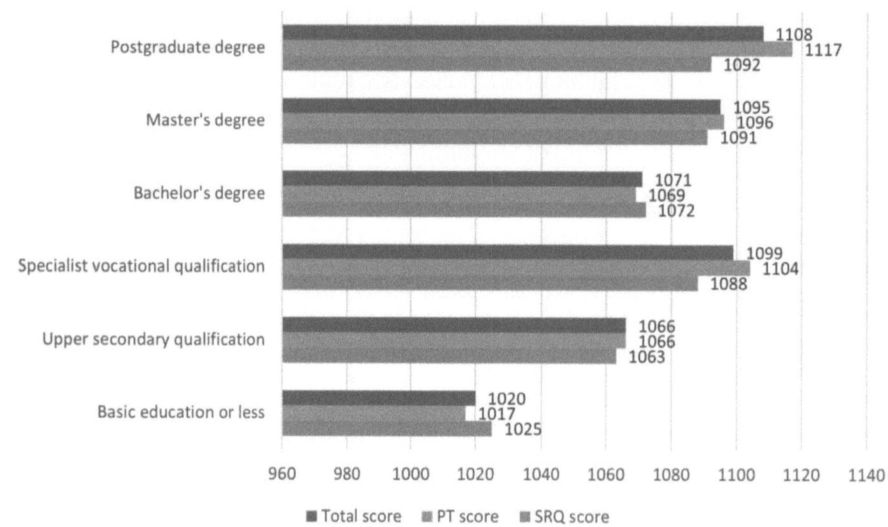

Source: Ursin et al., (2021[1]).

The number of books in the student's childhood home can be used as an indicator of the reading and learning culture associated with the student's home background. The data indicated that university students had on average a higher number of books in their childhood homes than the UAS students. The mean scores in the CLA+ test (in the PT, the SRQ and in total) improved linearly with the increasing number of books in the student's childhood home (Figure 12.7). This positive connection was statistically highly significant for the total scores, the PT scores and the SRQ scores. The number of books in the childhood home explained 5-8% of the variance in the mean scores.

Figure 12.7. Number of books in the childhood home and the CLA+ mean scores across the entire data

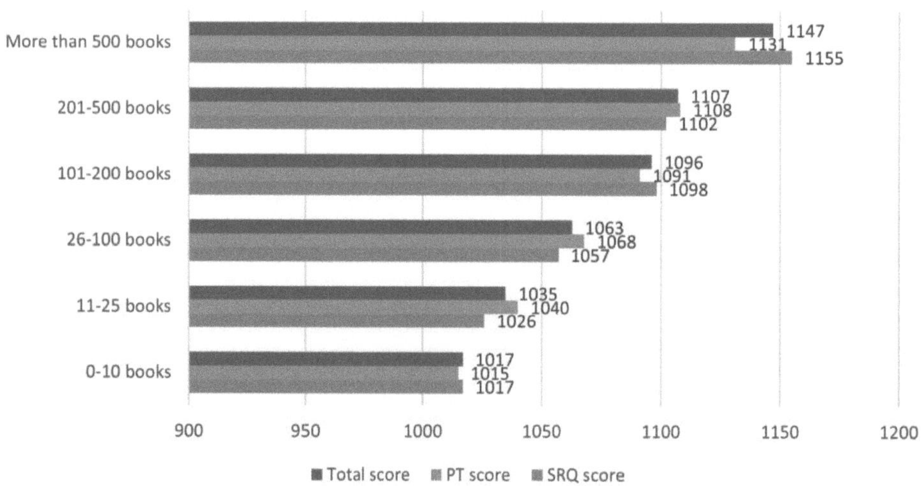

Source: Ursin et al., (2021[1]).

The students' *attitudes* towards the test were explored by asking how engaging they found the tasks included in the test, and how much effort they put into completing the tasks. The distribution of student interest was fairly symmetrical in the data; the majority of students found the test engaging or moderately engaging. University students were more likely to find the test engaging than UAS students. There were no significant differences between initial-stage and final-stage university or UAS students.

Some four out of five students said they had made a lot of effort or applied their best effort in completing the CLA+ International test. One out of three university students reported that they had applied their best effort in the test. Such a major effort was more common among final-stage than initial-stage students, both in the universities and the UASs. Final-stage university students were the most likely to apply their best effort (39%) whereas initial-stage UAS students were the least likely to do so (11%). The proportion of students who said they made little or no effort was only 2% in the data.

Both engagement and effort in the test had a linear and statistically highly significant association with the test results: the more effort a student had applied in completing the test and the more engaged a student found the test, the higher were the results achieved (Figure 12.8 and Figure 12.9). Engagement in the test explained 4-8% of the variance, while effort explained 4-9% of the variance.

Figure 12.8. CLA+ mean scores and students' engagement in the test

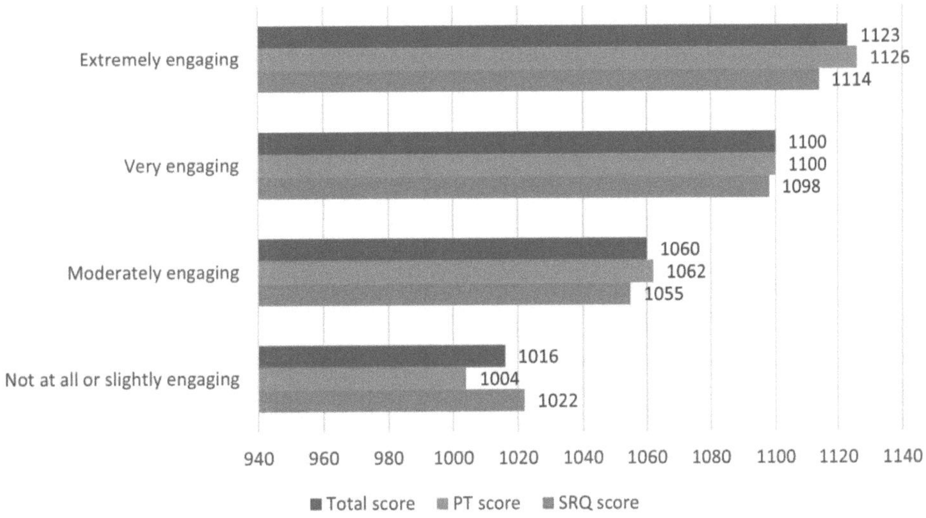

Source: Ursin et al., (2021[1]).

Figure 12.9. CLA+ mean scores and effort applied in completing the test

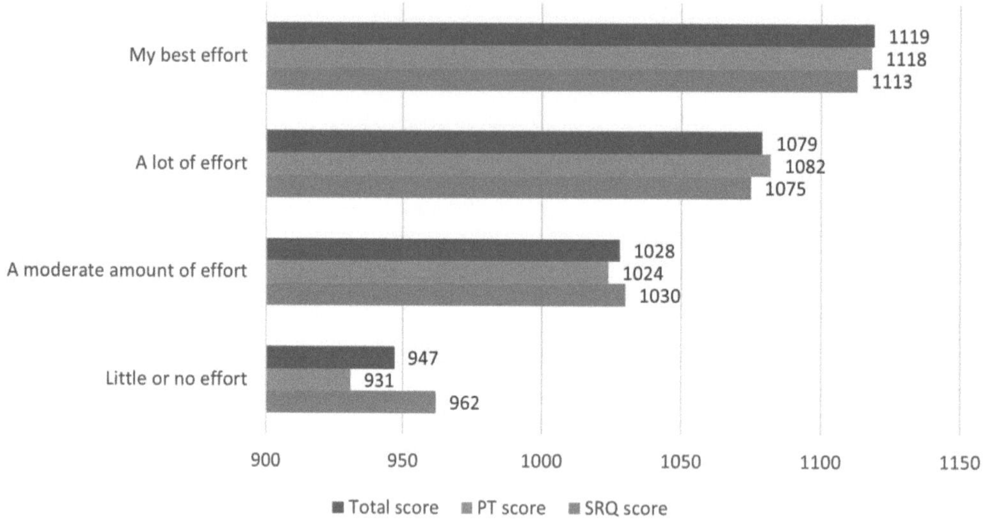

Source: Ursin et al., (2021[1]).

Main factors explaining the level of generic skills among Finnish higher education students

Multiple regression analyses were conducted to examine the relations between the CLA+ scores and background variables. For both university and UAS students, the most significant explanatory variables for all the CLA+ scores were (1) the student's mother tongue grade in the Matriculation Examination, and (2) the amount of effort the student had applied in taking the test (Table 12.2). The number of books in the childhood home explained the variation in CLA+ scores statistically significantly in all but one case (PT for university students), indicating that students who grew up with books at home tended to have a higher level of generic skills. The roles of the other background variables tested varied between the scores. In particular, differences between the fields of study and gender differences often lost their statistical significance when the other background variables were controlled. The regression model coefficients of determination were higher for the PT than for the SRQs, and higher for UAS students than for university students. It was notable that the differences in the UAS students' PT scores could be explained fairly precisely by background factors.

Table 12.2. Statistically significant factors explaining variations in CLA+ test scores within multivariate regression models

	University students			UAS students		
	PT score	SRQ score	Total score	PT score	SRQ score	Total score
n of observations	$n = 1216$	$n = 1175$	$n = 1183$	$n = 1049$	$n = 1024$	$n = 1042$
R-squared	$R^2 = 27\%$	$R^2 = 15\%$	$R^2 = 20\%$	$R^2 = 32\%$	$R^2 = 16\%$	$R^2 = 26\%$
Stage of studies (initial stage/final stage)	***	ns	ns	***	ns	**
Field of study	ns	***	ns	**	ns	ns
Gender (male/female)	ns	***	ns	*	**	ns
Mother tongue grade in Matriculation Examination	***	**	***	***	***	***
Other degree (any) than Matriculation Examination (vocational/HE degree)	**	ns	**	ns	ns	ns
Number of books in childhood home	ns	***	***	**	*	**
Parental education	*	ns	ns	ns	ns	ns
Effort in CLA+ test	***	***	***	***	**	***

Note: *** p<0.001; ** p<0.01; * p<0.05; ns = not significant
Source: Ursin et al., (2021[1]).

Implications and lessons learned

On the basis of the study, four policy recommendations can be made. Firstly, more attention should be paid to the learning of generic skills at the lower educational levels, and also in learning environments outside the school. While the KAPPAS! project focused on undergraduate students' generic skills, the findings show that an important foundation for the development of generic skills is laid in prior education. This finding is in line with previous studies, where it has been found that generic skills are an important predictor of academic achievement and adaptation to higher education (e.g. Arum and Roksa (2011[14]), van der Zanden et al. (2018[23])). Thus, the results indicate a need to emphasise generic skills already at pre-tertiary level (e.g. at secondary level), especially in vocational education and training. Furthermore, the results demonstrate that the scholarly culture of the childhood home is an important predictor of students' generic skills. In this sense, the evidence from this study highlights the importance of reading, and of encouraging reading from a very young age (cf. Leino et al. (2019[24]), Kleemola, Hyytinen and Toom (forthcoming[25])). This could involve paying attention to more than just the scholarly circumstances in the childhood home, and considering how a range of focal learning environments outside the school might be put in place.

Secondly, the role of generic skills in student admission should be explored. In 2020, the admissions procedures in Finnish higher education were reformed; thus, after some political debate, the emphasis in student admission moved away from one-off "high stakes" entrance examinations towards diploma-based admissions involving a focus on National Matriculation Examination grades (Kleemola and Hyytinen, 2019[26]; Kleemola, Hyytinen and Toom, forthcoming[25]). The findings of this project support diploma-based admissions in student selection, insofar as the Matriculation Examination mother tongue grades in particular were a good predictor of the mastery of generic skills. Nevertheless, there are good reasons not to give up entrance examinations entirely. In line with the elementary principle of equal opportunities in Finnish HE, a transition to higher education must be secured for those eligible applicants who have not completed the Matriculation Examination. Entrance examinations of a more generic nature – involving something similar to the CLA+ International – have been proposed as a solution (Talman, 2018[27]). However, before undertaking any comprehensive renewal of the entrance examination, more research on the predictive value of prior generic skills will be needed. To gain more insights into this issue, future research should, for example, focus on testing a wider range of the generic skills that may be relevant in preparedness for higher education (Kleemola, Hyytinen and Toom, forthcoming[25]).

Thirdly, generic skills need to be developed in line with the aims of UAS and university education. The findings of the present study emphasised the differences between university and UAS students' mastery of generic skills, with university students exhibiting more versatile and superior generic skills than UAS students, as measured by CLA+ International. From the HE policy perspective, this observation can be accounted for by the differing missions and student profiles possessed by those HE sectors. In efforts to develop generic skills, it will be important (1) to recognise that the students in UASs and universities display different kinds of critical thinking, argumentation, analytical reasoning and written communication skills, and (2) to consider the consequences of this in terms of ways of supporting students' learning throughout their study path. The skills in question are considered crucial for becoming a genuinely autonomous and participating citizen of the 21st century. Moreover, these skills have been found to be essential for progressing successfully through higher education, and in the transition to working life (Arum and Roksa, 2011[14]; Tuononen, Parpala and Lindblom-Ylänne, 2017[28]; Tuononen, Parpala and Lindblom-Ylänne, 2019[29]).

Finally, the findings indicate that the level of generic skills is surprisingly low, especially for certain groups of students in a country that strives for equality across its HE system. The results in this regard foreground the teaching and learning practices of Finnish HEIs as a matter for debate. There are several means by which HEIs could better promote the teaching and learning of generic skills. For example, in seeking to support the development of generic skills, more attention should be paid to the coherence of the curriculum and to the systematic integration of generic skills throughout students' studies (Hyytinen, Toom and Shavelson, 2019[30]). Generic skills need to be systematically practised in multiple contexts, and within various tasks, combining theory and practice throughout students' higher education studies (Virtanen and Tynjälä, 2018[31]). This means that the learning of generic skills should be expressed within the curriculum and be systematically taken into account in terms of intended learning outcomes, teaching methods, assignments and assessments (Hyytinen, Toom and Shavelson, 2019[30]). Successful integration at the curriculum level involves collaboration between teachers and persons who make decisions on the curriculum. Moreover, higher education teachers need to have a clear understanding of what generic skills actually consist of, and why the skills should be taught. They further need pedagogical competencies that will enable them to integrate the elements of generic skills within their teaching practices.

What, then, were the main lessons from the project? When the participating HEIs in the KAPPAS! project were asked about the usability of the assessment results, many HEIs indicated their intention to use the findings to improve their teaching and learning. The HEIs also found that the project made generic skills more visible in their institutions, thus sparking discussion on the role of generic skills in teaching, and paving the way for the development of more working life-oriented curricula in their study programmes. Hopes were also expressed that the institution-specific findings would be used as part of the teachers' pedagogical training, and ideally also in student guidance, encompassing personal study plans and career guidance. Nonetheless, for the HEIs, the most challenging aspects of the assessment were bound up with the labour-intensive implementation of the test (including the time-consuming student recruitment) and the limitations of the institution-specific findings in cases where the number of participating students remained low. Furthermore, given that in the KAPPAS! project only a handful of the participating students were interviewed on how they could utilise their individual test results, it would be important in future to carry out such enquiry on a larger scale; for example, as part of the actual test.

Although the project team aimed to maintain a high scientific standard in conducting the study, some unavoidable challenges emerged. The difficulties in student recruitment meant that the participation rate remained fairly low although this could to some extent be taken into account in the analyses. Furthermore, there were some reliability issues related to the test instrument, in terms of the limited number of tasks employed. A further point to bear in mind was that the cross-sectional study design did not allow a reliable investigation of the ways in which generic skills actually develop – an issue that is of crucial importance and interest to Finnish HEIs and the Finnish government.

Next steps and prospects

In order to examine the development of generic skills, there is a need for a longitudinal inquiry, within which the same students would be followed from the initial to the final stage of their undergraduate studies. For the HE system as a whole, such follow-up information could indicate whether Finnish higher education is indeed on the way to producing the best learning in the world, as set out by the government in its policy goals. For the HEIs a follow-up study would give students more reliable information on the added-value of their education. In the future, it will also be important to better acknowledge students as cognizant individuals, and to ensure that the assessment actually helps the student to become a better learner. It is therefore important that the assessment of generic skills should provide information that truly supports students in developing their generic skills. Last but not least, given that in Finland standardised testing in education has not been widely adopted, it is crucial that the assessment does not become a "high stakes" once-and-for-all exercise; rather, it should serve the purpose of enhancement-led assessment – a principle that has up to now been paramount in the assessment culture of Finnish higher education. One can anticipate that continued adherence to this principle will promote the assessment of generic skills in Finnish higher education in the years to come.

References

Ammattikorkeakoululaki (2014), *Polytechnic Act (932/2014)*, https://www.finlex.fi/fi/laki/smur/2014/20140932 (accessed on 23 April 2021). [2]

Arum, R. and J. Roksa (2011), *Academically Adrift: Limited Learning on College Campuses*, University of Chicago Press, Chicago. [14]

Badcock, P., P. Pattison and K. Harris (2010), "Developing generic skills through university study: a study of arts, science and engineering in Australia", *Higher Education*, Vol. 60/4, pp. 441-458, https://doi.org/10.1007/s10734-010-9308-8. [16]

Bartram, D. et al. (2017), "ITC Guidelines for Translating and Adapting Tests (Second Edition)", *International Journal of Testing*, Vol. 18/2, pp. 101-134, https://doi.org/10.1080/15305058.2017.1398166. [19]

DeHaan, R. (ed.) (2013), "Questions for Assessing Higher-Order Cognitive Skills: It's Not Just Bloom's", *CBE—Life Sciences Education*, Vol. 12/1, pp. 47-58, https://doi.org/10.1187/cbe.12-03-0024. [15]

European Commission (2013), *High Level Group on the Modernisation of Higher Education*. [9]

European Commission Education and Training (2019), *Key competences for lifelong learning - Publications Office of the EU*, Publications Office of the European Union. [10]

Evens, M., A. Verburgh and J. Elen (2013), "Critical Thinking in College Freshmen: The Impact of Secondary and Higher Education", *International Journal of Higher Education*, Vol. 2/3, https://doi.org/10.5430/ijhe.v2n3p139. [17]

Gaebel, M. et al. (2018), *Trends 2018: Learning and teaching in the European Higher Education Area*. [6]

Hyytinen, H. et al. (2015), "Problematising the equivalence of the test results of performance-based critical thinking tests for undergraduate students", *Studies in Educational Evaluation*, Vol. 44, pp. 1-8, https://doi.org/10.1016/j.stueduc.2014.11.001. [18]

Hyytinen, H., A. Toom and R. Shavelson (2019), "Enhancing Scientific Thinking Through the Development of Critical Thinking in Higher Education", in *Redefining Scientific Thinking for Higher Education*, Springer International Publishing, Cham, https://doi.org/10.1007/978-3-030-24215-2_3. [30]

Hyytinen, H. et al. (2021), "The dynamic relationship between response processes and self-regulation in critical thinking assessments", *Studies in Educational Evaluation*, Vol. 71, p. 101090, https://doi.org/10.1016/j.stueduc.2021.101090. [20]

Kleemola, K. and H. Hyytinen (2019), "Exploring the Relationship between Law Students' Prior Performance and Academic Achievement at University", *Education Sciences*, Vol. 9/3, p. 236, https://doi.org/10.3390/educsci9030236. [26]

Kleemola, K., H. Hyytinen and A. Toom (forthcoming), *Critical thinking and writing in transition to higher education in Finland: does prior academic performance and socioeconomic background matter?*, Submitted for publication. [25]

Kyndt, E. et al. (eds.) (2017), *The transition from university to working life - An exploration of graduates perceptions of their academic competences*, Taylor & Francis, Routledge, http://hdl.handle.net/10138/308628. [28]

Leighton, J. (2017), *Using Think-Aloud Interviews and Cognitive Labs in Educational Research*, Oxford University Press, Oxford, https://doi.org/10.1093/acprof:oso/9780199372904.001.0001. [21]

Leino, K. et al. (2019), *PISA 18 : ensituloksia. Suomi parhaiden joukossa [First results of PISA 18]*, Ministry of Edncation and Culture, ISBN: 978-952-263-678-2, https://julkaisut.valtioneuvosto.fi/handle/10024/161919 (accessed on 1 August 2022). [24]

Ministry of Education and Culture (2017), *Working together for the world's best education. Policies on promoting internationality*, Ministry of Education and Culture. [11]

Talman, K. (2018), *Ammattikorkeakoulujen uuden digitaalisen valintakokeen kehittäminen – määrittelyvaiheen tulokset: Tutkimusraportti. [Development of a New Digital Entrance Examination for Universities of Applied Sciences – Results of the Definition Phase: Research Report*, Metropolia University of Applied Sciences, ISBN:978-952-328-119-6, https://www.theseus.fi/handle/10024/154646 (accessed on 1 August 2022). [27]

Tremblay, K., D. Lalancette and D. Roseveare (2012), "Assessment of Higher Education Learning Outcomes (AHELO) Feasibility Study", *Feasibility study report*, Vol. 1, https://www.oecd.org/education/skills-beyond-school/AHELOFSReportVolume1.pdf (accessed on 1 August 2022). [8]

Tsaparlis, G. (2020), "HIGHER AND LOWER-ORDER THINKING SKILLS: THE CASE OF CHEMISTRY REVISITED", *Journal of Baltic Science Education*, Vol. 19/3, pp. 467-483, https://doi.org/10.33225/jbse/20.19.467. [13]

Tuononen, T., A. Parpala and S. Lindblom-Ylänne (2019), *Graduates' Evaluations of Usefulness of University Education, and Early Career Success – a Longitudinal Study of the Transition to Working Life*, Assessment & Evaluation in Higher Education. [29]

Universities Act (2009), *FINLEX, The Ministry of Justice*, http://www.finlex.fi/en/laki/kaannokset/2009/en20090558 (accessed on 23 April 2021). [3]

Ursin, J. (2020), *Assessment of Higher Education Learning Outcomes Feasibility Study*, SAGE Publications, Inc., 2455 Teller Road, Thousand Oaks, California 91320 , https://doi.org/10.4135/9781529714395.n52. [22]

Ursin, J. (2014), "Learning outcomes in Finnish higher education from the perspective of comprehensive curriculum framework", in Coates, H. (ed.), *Higher Education Learning Outcomes Assessment*, Peter Lang, https://doi.org/10.3726/978-3-653-04632-8/20. [7]

Ursin, J. et al. (eds.) (2021), *Assessment of undergraduate students' generic skills in Finland: Finding of the Kappas! Project (Report No. 2021: 31)*, Finnish Ministry of Education and Culture, http://urn.fi. [1]

Ursin, J., H. Hyytinen and K. Sivennoinen (2019), "Higher Education Reforms in Finland", in Broucker, B. et al. (eds.), *Higher Education System Reform*, BRILL, https://doi.org/10.1163/9789004400115_005. [4]

Välimaa, J. (2004), "Nationalisation, Localisation and Globalisation in Finnish Higher Education", *Higher Education*, Vol. 48/1, pp. 27-54, https://doi.org/10.1023/b:high.0000033769.69765.4a. [12]

van der Zanden, P. et al. (2018), "Patterns of success: first-year student success in multiple domains", *Studies in Higher Education*, Vol. 44/11, pp. 2081-2095, https://doi.org/10.1080/03075079.2018.1493097. [23]

Vipunen – opetushallinnon tilastopalvelu (2019), *Korkeakoulujen opiskelijat. Opetushallinnon ja Tilastokeskuksen tietopalvelusopimuksen aineisto 2.8*, https://vipunen.fi/fi-fi/_layouts/15/xlviewer.aspx?id=/fi-fi/Raportit/Korkeakoulutuksen%20opiskelijat_A1.xlsb. [5]

Virtanen, A. and P. Tynjälä (2018), "Factors explaining the learning of generic skills: a study of university students' experiences", *Teaching in Higher Education*, Vol. 24/7, pp. 880-894, https://doi.org/10.1080/13562517.2018.1515195 (accessed on 23 April 2021). [31]

13 Using CLA+ in a pilot in England for measuring learning gain

J.G. Morris, University of Birmingham (United Kingdom)

S.C. Brand, Birmingham City University (United Kingdom)

Chapter 13 discusses the implementation of the CLA+ in a small set of institutions as part of a pilot study to assess learning gain in the United Kingdom. This case study shows the capacity of the assessment to serve as a diagnostic tool. The chapter also discusses the challenges associated with student recruitment and motivation.

Introduction

Universities in England are described as autonomous, independent organisations which have some government funding but are not owned or managed directly by the government (Eurydice, 2019[1]). There is a diverse range of universities, arising from various changes in the organisation of higher education. Expansion of the sector occurred in the 1960s when the Robbins report established the principle that, based on merit, courses should be much more widely available.

A further very significant change to the English higher education sector happened in 1992. Before this higher education was provided in universities and polytechnics. Universities were autonomous institutions funded by central government for research and teaching; polytechnics, on the other hand, were under local authority control and provided mainly vocational education. Then in 1992, the so-called "binary divide" was abolished and polytechnics became autonomous universities. A feature of this autonomy is the power to award degrees rests with universities rather than the state. This change has provided a diverse range of universities but some distinctions remain: for example, pre-1992 universities tend to be more research-intensive whereas post-1992 universities have a greater focus on vocational courses.

The regulator of the higher education sector in England has been the newly formed Office for Students since January 2018, and it is they who can register new institutions that apply for degree-awarding powers.

The United Kingdom higher education sector comprises about 160 institutions and just over 2.5 million students in 2019-20 (HESA, 2021[2]) of whom 1.89 million were undergraduates and 0.64 million postgraduates. In 2016-17 just under 20% of students were from outside the UK. Of these overseas students about 30% were from within the European Union (EU) and 70% from non-EU countries (Universities UK, 2018[3]). The majority of full-time first-degree courses last for three years.

The Higher Education Initial Participation Rate (HEIPR), an estimate of the likelihood of a young person participating in higher education by the age of 30, grew steadily from 42% in 2006-07 to 49% in 2011-12, but fell sharply in 2012-13 before recovering over the following years. In 2014-15 it rose again to 48%. Indeed the figures for 2011-12 and 2012-13 can now be interpreted as a disturbance to the steady rise over nearly 10 years. After 2013 the increase in HEIPR resumed and rose to just over 50% in 2017-18 (Gov.uk, 2020[4]).

It is interesting that this steady rise in the participation of young people in higher education has occurred in the context of rising tuition fees. These annual fees were introduced in England through the Teaching and Higher Education Act 1998 at the level of GBP 1 000 per year for full-time undergraduate students. The fee level was trebled in the Higher Education Act 2004 with institutions allowed to set fees up to a maximum of GBP 3 000 per year. At this point tuition fees, instead of being paid upfront were mainly covered by tuition fee loans with repayment deferred until graduates reached an income threshold. A further increase in tuition fees followed the Browne Report *Securing a Sustainable Future for Higher Education* (Browne, 2010[5]). From 2012 the government raised the maximum fee to GBP 9 000 per year and also raised the repayment income threshold for graduates to GBP 21 000, (Hubble and Bolton, 2018[6]). Finally, from 2017-18, the maximum fee rose to GBP 9 250. Tuition fees remain manifested for the majority of students as a build-up of debt following the taking up of student loans during their degree course. This is an interesting juxtaposition: before the imposition and subsequent increases in tuition fees the cost of tuition was borne by the state. The current position sees the student as the main bearer of this cost and has perhaps seen a greater tendency for students to see themselves as customers. This in turn has led, particularly over the last decade, to much work in the field of student engagement with the concept of students as active partners rather than mere customers (for example, see (Brand and Millard, 2019[7])).

Policy context for CLA+

The first steps in England that led to our work with CLA+ arose from the government Department for Business, Innovation and Skills (BIS) when the Higher Education Funding Council for England (HEFCE) was asked to consider whether there were better indicators such as measures of student engagement to provide information on what a high quality student experience looked like. This request was put forward in its annual grant letter to HEFCE for 2014-15. The following year's grant letter for 2015-16 set out an expectation that there should be progress towards developing and testing new measures of learning gain.

As a preface to this initiative a report on learning gain was commissioned from RAND Europe, an independent not-for-profit research institute based in Cambridge, UK in 2014. RAND had worked in partnership with BIS, HEFCE and the Higher Education Academy (HEA). In particular RAND was asked to investigate:

1. In what ways and for what purposes are methods and tools for measuring learning gain already in use in English higher education?
2. Analysis of the relative benefits of approaches to measuring generic skills independently of discipline-specific knowledge and measuring generic skills in disciplinary contexts
3. Analysis of the applicability of methods and tools for measuring learning gain for different identified purposes such as to inform improvements to learning and teaching; to provide information to prospective students and their advisers; to investigate the impact of particular learning and teaching interventions and contextual factors; to assist in international comparison; or to form part of the quality assurance of learning and teaching
4. What are the relevant considerations for the use or adaptation of methods or tools for measuring learning gain in an English Higher Education context?
5. What are the relevant considerations for the design and development of robust pilot activities for measuring learning gain that might be drawn from existing practice and literature?
6. What relevant lessons can be drawn from research on value-added undertaken in the UK school sector?

The comprehensive report produced (McGrath et al., 2015[8]) highlighted a number of issues that were key to this work. One such issue was that although 130 out of 147 respondents to a call for information via the Higher Education Academy (HEA) recognised that the "concept of learning gain could be useful", there was also a level of cautiousness as to how such measures might be used for accountability and transparency (McGrath et al., 2015, p. xiii[8])

The RAND report identified 14 possible methods classified in five groups: grades, surveys, standardised tests, mixed methods, and other qualitative methods. Importantly, the report also noted the clear distinction between direct measures of learning gain and proxy measures such as engagement surveys, satisfaction surveys, and graduate employment statistics or graduate salaries. A suggestion emerging in the report was that those who had commissioned it might want to conduct a series of pilots exploring a range of practical, technical, methodological and financial issues when seeking to use some of the methods discussed. Notably the report pointed out that "the concept of learning gain, and its definition, was in its infancy in higher education in England".

Thus, early in 2015, HEFCE invited expressions of interest for "funding for projects that will pilot and evaluate measures of learning gain". There was considerable interest in this call, which eventually led to the award of approximately GBP 4 million across 13 pilot projects involving over 70 higher education institutions. At this stage learning gain was defined by HEFCE as "distance travelled: the improvement in knowledge, skills, work-readiness and personal development demonstrated by students at two points in time". Part of HEFCE's thinking at this time was to seek to demonstrate to the government and to students the value of their investments in higher education. This call made specific reference not only to the five groups listed above but also to the possibility of exploring both longitudinal and cross-sectional approaches.

An interesting feature of the RAND report was the distinction drawn between "Content Knowledge" and "Skills and Competencies". Content knowledge was defined as "a body of information that teachers teach and that students are expected to learn in a given subject or content area," (McGrath et al., 2015, pp. 7-8[8]). The term was taken as referring to facts, concepts, theories and principles that are taught and learned rather than related skills such as reading, writing or researching that students also learn in academic courses. This concept of a generic skills assessment had previously been described in the Assessment of Higher Education Learning Outcomes (AHELO) Feasibility Report in 2012 (AHELO, 2012[9]), which considered a generic skills strand and two subject-specific strands in economics and engineering.

It was in this context that the work, which we led, set out to use the Collegiate Learning Assessment (CLA+). It was one of two funded projects that use a standardised test. We set up an ambitious schedule of testing and our original intention was for a longitudinal study following up to 1 000 students across the four participating universities, all of which were post-1992 institutions. The timing of this work was a critical factor: decisions as to which projects would be funded did not arrive until July 2015 thus leaving only a few weeks to set up the testing activity. Perhaps an even greater challenge was the fact that for all participating students the testing activity would be beyond their curriculum and thus might be perceived by many as a voluntary extra activity.

We refer above to the early cautiousness revealed at a survey carried out by the HEA as to how and for what purpose learning gain information might be used. In the early stages of our project similar concerns were expressed by participating academic staff. The question was posed as to the extent that this work might benefit students both in terms of any potential it might have to lead to enhancements in learning and teaching, and also to assist individual students in their own development of skills.

A further significant development during the time period (2015-18) of our project was the development of the Teaching Excellence Framework (TEF) which had its first full iteration in 2016-17. The TEF was introduced as a provider-level assessment that was delivered to a specification provided by the Department for Education, which was by this time the government ministry responsible for higher education. The TEF concentrated on three "Aspects of Quality": Teaching Quality; Learning Environment; and Student Outcomes and Learning Gain. It seems likely that there was a desire that the funded projects being undertaken might contribute eventually to the choice of some form of standard method for assessment of learning gain to contribute to the TEF as it further developed. The TEF has now been renamed the Teaching Excellence and Student Outcomes Framework. Following an independent review and government response in early 2021, it was proposed that it continue as a periodic review operating every four to five years at institutional rather than subject level (Office for Students, 2021[10]).

Process of implementation CLA+

Project delivery

Our initial target at our institution when implementing the CLA+ was to test students longitudinally from a variety of disciplines through four testing points at various points of their studies. Two of these testing points would occur during the first year of study with the remaining two testing points in autumn of their second and third years. A delay in the confirmation of funding for our project meant that testing was delayed. Our first testing point was moved to the spring of the students' first year and the total number of longitudinal testing points reduced from four to three. As part of our learning gain project, we aimed to recruit up to ~350 students at our institution to test longitudinally and allow for attrition. Much of the recruitment and implementation of the CLA+ was carried out by an institutional lead based in our institution's Centre for Excellence in Learning and Teaching, and the project lead working as a consultant.

It was also important that we worked closely with academic staff within faculty. As we will discuss later on in this chapter, this proved to be one of the integral factors in student recruitment. In addition to our staff leads, we sought to involve students in all of the core aspects of implementing the test. Throughout the three-year delivery period of testing, we employed various student interns who worked closely with us on testing logistics, data analysis and including the student voice in all that we did when interacting with students and disseminating our findings.

Adaption of CLA+ to CLA+ International

In the process of using an American test in a UK context, we worked closely with the Council for Aid to Education (CAE) in adapting the CLA+ to suit the needs and cultural differences of the students taking the test. As Ashford-Rowe et al., (2013[11]) highlight in their work on authentic assessment, the CLA+ aligns with two critical characteristics of effective assessment design: the insurance of knowledge transfer to a single, real-world domain and the role of metacognition. The insurance of knowledge transfer requires "consistency between the assessment and real-world application" (Ashford-Rowe, Herrington and Brown, 2013, p. 208[11]). For example, the Performance Task (PT) based on "building" a baseball stadium was reworked using football (soccer) stadiums based in England. A core feature of the PT asks students to analyse and interpret multiple data sources and perspectives to construct their own argument in the format of a report, a transferable skill to be used in any context. As Zahner and Lehrfeld (2018[12]) highlight, the measurement of such skills have become an important indicator in career placement and workplace success.

Following this, metacognition acknowledges the "importance of critical reflection and self-assessment", a key component encouraged through the test via a self-evaluation survey, and the resulting student reports that indicate their mastery levels (Ashford-Rowe, Herrington and Brown, 2013, pp. 208-209[11]). We also reworked the language to suit UK spelling and grammar in the CLA+, including changing the mastery level terminology to reflect the developmental language used in assessment criteria and grading. One of the notable points of our findings through qualitative and anecdotal feedback was that the structure and topics of the PT were positively received but Selected-Response Questions (SRQs) were received less favourably.

Part of implementing the CLA+ also required staff resources not only in recruiting students and testing logistics, but also for scoring PT submissions. This written response was scored using a bespoke rubric by human scorers on Analysis and Problem Solving, and Writing Effectiveness and Writing Mechanics, all of whom needed to be trained and calibrated prior to testing. CAE and ourselves found this to be a useful opportunity to run scorer training sessions with staff from our institution and our three other partner institutions from the learning gain project. These proved to be fruitful environments that encouraged critical dialogue on the process of scoring, such as different perspectives from individual scorers that may influence overall scores, a feature noted in research by Wyatt-Smith et al., (2010[13]) on marking with rubrics. An interesting aspect of our scoring was that depending on the institutions who were testing in a particular window, the colleagues would not necessarily be scoring students from their respective institution, which was an important consideration for the project team to eliminate any scoring bias.

CLA+ as a diagnostic tool

As noted in our previous section, the contextual factors surrounding the project on measuring learning gain meant that there was a degree of hesitancy from our academic colleagues who were in some cases nominated to aid us with recruitment and testing of students. The prospect of measuring their students longitudinally, and then being compared both institutionally and externally on whether their students had demonstrated development in their critical thinking across their programme evoked some level of anxiety within many of our colleagues. It is also worth noting here that in part, this has been exacerbated by a sector-wide culture of measurement and the increasing view of students as customers, an ideology often perpetuated by the institution as opposed to the students themselves (Woodall, Hiller and Resnick, 2012[14]). It was no surprise then that such resistance occurred. An important feature of our implementation involved persuading colleagues of the value of the CLA+ as not just a platform to measure and track student development but a diagnostic tool as well. In addition, our project team offered their assurance that collected data would not be used as a metaphorical stick to judge the merits/failings of their programmes.

Using such diagnostic data would also align with institutional strategy and wider sectoral research on enhancing student progression and retention (see (Webb et al., 2017[15])). Thus, such work puts student development at the forefront while balancing institutional pressures such as loss of fees from student withdrawals. Many staff, particularly those residing within certain disciplines, instantly saw the value of the test and where possible tried to convince their students of the value of taking the CLA+, including the offer of incentives in certain situations. Despite this, we still experienced a mixture of reactions from colleagues within our institution, ranging from total investment, to apathy and an active effort to dissuade students from completing the test.

Student recruitment and testing

We planned to test students from a variety of disciplines across the university's four faculties. With the TEF subject-level pilots being carried out as the backdrop of our work, we saw a unique opportunity to analyse some of the key differences in student performance in the CLA+, and also how student perceptions of the test would differ depending on their disposition towards the skills it claims to measure. Initially we tested students from English Literature, Social Work, Marketing and Computer Science, but later widened our scope to include a broader range of disciplines, which was mainly influenced by our struggles to recruit students to complete the test. By the end of the project, we had tested students from the following disciplines at our institution:

- Computer Networks and Security
- English Literature
- Engineering
- Graphic and Visual Communication
- Jewellery
- Marketing
- Media and Communication
- Psychology
- Social Work

Testing sessions were all conducted remotely in computer lab spaces, working collaboratively with the university's Information Technology (IT) departments to ensure the CLA+ testing platform could be downloaded without issue prior to the beginning of testing. We would often schedule testing for two hours, despite the test only needing 90 minutes to complete, to allow for the additional time spent setting up and the completion of the demographic questionnaire at the end. The tests were advertised initially as extracurricular activities with incentives such as food, and an eventual shift to gift cards and cash sums to encourage attendance. However, despite these incentives and the benefits reported from participating in such activities, we continued to struggle with student recruitment (Kaufman and Gabler, 2004[16]).

As Stuart et al. (2011[17]) highlight, the problem of student recruitment is no surprise considering the literature that examines student engagement with extracurricular activities. The study provides evidence that students from lower socio-economic backgrounds spend considerably more time working on course material than on extracurricular activities, suggesting the primary motivation for these students is their assessments (Stuart et al., 2011, p. 10[17]). As a widening participation university ourselves, the approaches to learning and circumstances of our students would prove to be an important factor with some of the successful aspects of our project. As we will later discuss, we had particular success with engagement only when embedding the test into the curriculum as a piece of formative, diagnostic assessment.

The student-facing and institutional reports also proved a valuable aspect of this approach and provided programme/module leads and important data on the demographic of their cohorts via performance, language and gender. This would quickly enable us and academic staff to identify struggling students and offer a means to be more inclusive in their approach to student support. The emergence of the CLA+ as a valuable diagnostic tool became the core focus of our project and basis for implementing the test at the institution. Measuring learning gain arguably became a secondary objective.

Main results

In this section we will aim to provide an account of our main findings during our funded project on measuring learning gain. This includes a quantitative narrative on how many students were recruited and tested, how tested students performed on the CLA+ from the institution's datasets, and findings from our longitudinal and cross-sectional studies. In addition to this, we will also include our qualitative findings from student-focus groups.

Testing numbers and student recruitment

In total, our institution tested 774 students over the three years, with 2 090 being tested across all four partner institutions. The large proportion of first-years recruited (87%) to take the test highlighted our struggle to test students longitudinally across multiple years to measure the development of their critical thinking skills over time. The remaining number of second-years from our sample who took the CLA+ tallied to 5.5%, with a slightly larger number of third-years at 7.5% (see Table 13.1 below).

In total, 132 students were tested longitudinally on our project. Although we had initial difficulty with recruitment, we did have some extremely positive case studies involving the use of the CLA+ as a diagnostic tool and piece of formative assessment. This included successfully testing 201 first-year Marketing students with this approach. As we will discuss later, our work with a Marketing degree programme showed the ability of CLA+ also to act as a reflective tool for students' development rather than only performance output. Finally, some of our most impactful findings pertaining to students' perceptions of the test, including factors influencing their motivation to take the CLA+, were revealed in our cross-sectional analysis in 2016-17. This involved students completing the CLA+ followed by a short questionnaire of selected questions from the United Kingdom Engagement Survey (UKES) and a short focus group after to capture reflections. We successfully tested and conducted focus groups with 136 students in total during this study.

Table 13.1. Total number of students tested by year of study and CLA+ scores

	Students tested	Total CLA+ score (Avg.)	Std. dev. of CLA+ score	25th percentile score	75th percentile score	Effect size vs first-years
First-years	1 819	1 089	141	998	1 192	--
Second-years	114	1 098	135	1 007	1 200	.06
Third-years	157	1 162	167	1 042	1 261	.52
All Students	2 090	1 093	143	1 000	1 196	--

Performance data

In the context of overall student performance in the CLA+ as part of our project, analysis was carried out by CAE on students who undertook the CLA+ on the new international platform. It noted a significant difference among years of study when looking at total CLA+ scores. At our institution, students in their third year outperformed both first- and second-year students, with the former having the greatest difference in scores. While this was an output we might have anticipated in our pursuit of measuring learning gain, it is also worth noting that the difference in these overall scores were largely influenced by scores in the PT, with no significant difference between recorded in SRQ scores. In our qualitative data, we consistently noticed that students would highlight the PT as the more enjoyable aspect of the CLA+, noting the freedom offered by its structure as the main reason for this. The link between students' enjoyment or motivation and its correlation with performance was not proven but is an area our project team would have liked to explore further.

Demographic data and CLA+ performance

It is no secret, particularly in UK higher education, that an attainment gap has existed between Black and Minority Ethnic (BME) and their white counterparts in attaining "top degrees", which would typically consist of students achieving either a First-Class Honours or Upper Second-Class Honours (Advance HE, 2017[18]). In their *Equality in Higher Education: Statistical Report* (2017), they noted a 15.6% gap in the attainment of a top degree between BME students (63.2 %) and their white counterparts (78.8%) (Advance HE, 2017[18]). It is with this statistic in mind that students on our project taking the CLA+ also mirrored this issue, adding further evidence to support the work needed to close the gap. In particular, it was among the first-year students that white students on average received higher CLA+ scores than their BME counterparts.

There was also a reported difference in student performance by their primary language. Students whose first language was the same as the language of instruction, in our case, British English, outperformed their peers with different primary languages. This pattern was consistent across all years of study and raises important concerns about assessments centred on measuring constructs such as communication skills, particularly written, potentially disadvantaging these students. In our tested first-year students, we found that students whose primary language was English achieved higher scores than those for whom this was not the case. Noticeably, this difference was more pronounced in the Performance Task, where written communication skills are more important than in the selected-response questions.

Finally, it was also interesting to note that there was a significant difference in students whose parents had received differing levels of education for our first-year students, however this was not found in our second- or third-year student samples. Due to our large sample size of first-years in comparison to second- and third-years, it may be that a robust parental education effect could not be observed due to the lack of statistical power. This difference found in our first-years is elaborated in a study by Vanthournout et al. (2016, p. 53[19]). It notes that the democratisation of higher education has introduced student cohorts with various backgrounds, each with different ways of learning and motivation. Most notably, our first-years whose parents had no more than primary school education were outperformed by all of their peers whose parents had reached higher levels of education. This bears out arguments of social capital and its impact on assessment performance. More importantly, it brings to light the role higher education needs to play in bridging these gaps and the importance of fostering the acquisition of learning strategies for these students.

Using the CLA+ for learning and teaching enhancement

As discussed in previous sections, soon after the beginning of our project it became clear to both our institution and our project partners that a dual approach had emerged. Although our principal aim was to measure learning gain at both institutional and individual levels, the potential value of using the CLA+ as a tool for students to analyse their position in relation to the skills being tested for their ongoing development also became part of our focus. Reflecting on this, it also became clear that the test was more attractive to those studying some disciplines, or indeed key academics running programmes based within these disciplines.

For example, the CLA+ was successfully embedded within our institution's business school as both optional and compulsory elements of curricula. Largely thanks to the programme lead's investment in the CLA+, the test was made compulsory and used as part of a professional development module for first-years. The resulting reports for students acted as a form of evidence that would eventually be submitted in the summative assessment as part of an e-portfolio, with a reflective narrative on how aspects of the portfolio could be fed into areas of ongoing development. This use of the CLA+ and its integration within these portfolios align with the proposal that "authentic assessment design should ensure transfer of knowledge" (Ashford-Rowe, Herrington and Brown, 2013, p. 208[11]) as the knowledge and skills developed through the students' engagement with the CLA+ were transferred beyond this context.

When distributing these reports and to make the link to employability explicit, we encouraged the students to collect the reports shortly after the mid-point of their module during the university's Graduate+ event, a week focussed on development of employability attributes. Naturally, we also considered whether, if at all, there was a difference between students' performance in the CLA+ when analysing those who took the test as optional vs compulsory. To do this, CAE compared and analysed the differences between performance of students from Autumn 2017 (compulsory) and Spring/Autumn (non-compulsory) of 2016 (see Table 13.2 below). As with our main results, there was a "marginal difference" in the total CLA+ scores, with the students taking the CLA+ as a compulsory element of their module slightly outperforming their non-compulsory counterparts. Similarly, the difference appeared to be driven by PT results as there was no reported difference in SRQ scores. Despite these differences, it was also interesting to note that there was no difference in self-reported effort, an area covered in the CLA+ demographic questionnaire, suggesting that assessment did not increase motivation in the case of the compulsory cohort.

Table 13.2. CLA+ total scores by testing requirement and year of study

		M	SD	N
Total CLA+Score	Compulsory	1 105	142	194
	Non-compulsory	1 081	144	396
Performance Task Score	Compulsory	1 183	171	200
	Non-compulsory	1 140	188	400
Selected-Response Score	Compulsory	1 024	160	194
	Non-compulsory	1 017	162	397

Student perceptions of CLA+: Findings from our cross-sectional focus groups

During our time working on the project we naturally sought to have discussions with students about the CLA+ and some of their key motivations for completing it. During our cross-sectional study, 136 students completed the CLA+ and also participated in a bespoke United Kingdom Engagement Survey (UKES) and focus group. The focus groups in particular offered us a space to encourage students to think critically about the core aspects of the CLA+ such as the topic, its ability to test the skills it is designed to, their interest in how results could be used and any key motivators influencing them to take the test.

When asked about the topic of the Performance Task (PT), the majority of students taking the test struggled with engagement due to the lack of relevance to their subject topic. This has been a criticism often fired at the CLA+ in publications such as *Academically Adrift* (Arum and Roksa, 2011[20]), particularly the concern of measuring generic skills over specialised subject skills which students may attend university to learn. However, despite this many also reported back that the process of analysing evidence, formulating a critical argument and adapting this to various real-world situations made the PT more engaging as opposed to the SRQs. Being the latter part of the CLA+, the SRQ section was an area where students consistently cited mental fatigue, having already invested what they perceived as a large amount of time (60 minutes) on the PT task. There were also differences between PT topics, which students highlighted as having an impact on the level of their motivation and engagement. Our small number of students who sat the CLA+ between 2016 and 2017 reported to us that they preferred the second topic as it was more closely related to their discipline, suggesting that content is a key influencer of engagement.

When discussing the skills the CLA+ claims to measure and develop, we found several consistent trends from our students on this, including thoughts on the overall structure, timing and time-tabling for the CLA+. It was mentioned throughout the focus groups that students thought that regardless of their discipline, they should be able to analyse, critically think and problem-solve no matter the context. Despite this, as mentioned previously, there were also concerns that particular disciplines may have an advantage over others in terms of performance when taking the test. For example, students from creative, practical courses felt that students studying programmes that practice writing and analytical skills such as Law would perform better than their Art and Design counterparts. When analysing the performance between disciplines, there was no significant difference between any, suggesting that in fact these core skills are not impacted by subject areas.

Students were also hesitant about whether they would want their CLA+ results to be shared with peers. However, this was also partnered with an interest in how their scores might compare with others who had undertaken the test in an anonymised, aggregated way, a feature that is offered in the individual student result reports. There was also an evident interest in the potential of the results report being valued by employers and top postgraduate programmes.

The option to not have spell-checker or auto-correct was consistently cited as an issue. While this is predominantly thought of as a luxury on our part, it is important to note that spell-checker can be an important feature for inclusivity – a useful and necessary tool for students with dyslexia in particular. We found that CAE was very helpful with other inclusivity concerns such as allowing extra time, with a feature to add this on when pre-registering our cohorts before testing. Not only was time-taken an important factor in engagement but the question of when the CLA+ is taken during an academic year was also discussed. Many highlighted that it would be better to take the test at the start or middle of an academic year due to the latter part of the year having a high assessment load e.g. exams, coursework deadlines. We had encountered some issues with timing so some testing sessions had to be conducted during these busy periods. Unsurprisingly, these were not seen as high priority to students. It was also suggested that these arrangements would have been more readily achieved if the work had been embedded in the curriculum rather than extra-curricular.

Continuing our philosophy of student partnership: Working with student interns

In addition to testing students as part of our learning gain project, we sought to continue our tradition of working in partnership with students in our Centre. This informed everything we did during our research. We employed and worked alongside three students working part-time during their study to help with project delivery and compiling and analysing data. We ensured that both students were regular co-presenters with the project team at conferences to disseminate findings, as well as communicate their own experiences of being project participants. It was an interesting feature of our work with them that they had also taken the

CLA+ as part of our non-compulsory testing cohort. This meant they were able to provide their reflections and experiences of taking the test. These have proved to be invaluable, and we have the following quote from one of the interns:

> *Naturally I was very curious about the test due to the little information given and was very happy to participate. Now that I have taken the test, I found it very challenging but rewarding as it successfully tested my ability to think critically and analytically. – Second-year student, Faculty of Computing, Engineering and the Built Environment*

The employment of our interns extended beyond the initial scope of our project. They were integral to embedding the test in the Business School's curriculum, making the test compulsory. Our interns worked directly with module and programme leads, co-ordinating testing sessions and working with invigilators.

Policy implications and lessons learned

Following delivery of the HEFCE-funded projects an independent evaluation was carried out and presented to the Office for Students (OfS), a non-departmental public body of the Department for Education. This report highlighted a number of important issues. Undoubtedly, the most prominent of these was that of student recruitment to participate in testing. This problem was not peculiar to the two projects that employed CLA+ but was encountered in many other projects that required students to undertake activities they perceived as not a compulsory part of their curriculum. During the course of our project we also discovered that very different recruitment rates for testing were achieved in different subject areas. This appeared to be related to the enthusiasm of the key academic staff with whom the students concerned had strong connections, such as a course leader or year tutor. We conclude that to obtain high levels of recruitment the test would need to be embedded as part of the curriculum. Alternatively, at the very least, a high level of enthusiasm for testing from academic staff would need to be present. Without these levels of recruitment it would be difficult to investigate further the important question of scalability, or to explore potential links with existing university data.

It is also clear from the external evaluation report that there was only limited interest in using learning gain data from senior managers or academic staff in subject areas not involved at this stage in this work. It seems likely that if the use of a standardised test for institutional metrics was required, this position would have to change.

A further key lesson learnt relates to timeliness. As the HEFCE-funded projects had a very short lead in time, it proved impossible to adequately prepare for such necessities as schedules of marking, training of scorers, and results analysis in good time. This in turn meant that it was almost impossible to sustain students' interest in taking the work forward.

A question also arises as to whom the CLA+ testing is for. Our view is that if such activity is perceived as solely relating to measuring institutional performance, then an opportunity would be missed. There is a potential benefit for individual students to see initial CLA+ testing attempt as an important diagnostic function of their generic skills.

Next steps and prospects

The shift in focus from using the CLA+ as a tool for institutional measurement to one that is diagnostic – although a deviation from our initial project aims – opened up several exciting avenues for future work. Due to the success in student recruitment and using the test as part of formative modular assessment, we have continued our work with our institution's Business School. We will continue to embed the test into their Professional Development module and work on embedding the reflection of these results for future development, a core focus of the module. In addition, we will include structuring a session around collecting and making sense of the results to the individual.

One of the key findings from our focus group was the value of CLA+ for employment. Upon completion of the test, the students would receive a report on their performance along with a digital badge confirming their overall mastery level. When asked, students highlighted that they were particularly interested in the idea of digital badging, and the use this would have as part of an evidence portfolio for employers. This suggestion that students would be more likely to take the test if employers and/or other universities valued the results is a useful consideration for programme/modules teams to make when designing and delivering curriculum. This is an aspect of the test we felt we could have communicated more when briefing students on the benefits of taking the test as being confronted with an examination-type assessment with no opportunity to prepare may have been an anxiety-inducing prospect for students.

We are also acutely aware of some of the limitations presented by student recruitment, namely our struggle to test a larger number of students longitudinally (n=132). Due to low sample size, we were unable to provide more useful statistics, meaning we were less able to identify any outliers that could have potentially skewed the data, minimising the margin of error. Even in our cross-sectional study, the number of first-years heavily outweighed the number of second- and third-years tested, meaning that analysing performance via year of study was difficult to achieve. We would like to continue to work on testing more second- and third-year students for both our longitudinal and cross-sectional datasets.

One interesting development we initially discussed at our institution since implementing the CLA+ was the introduction of an assessment centre offering larger scale, personalised assessment testing for students. This stemmed from our refocus on using the test as a diagnostic tool alongside other institutions across the UK higher education sector implementing similar centres. In addition, such a centre would also be integral to addressing some of the challenges around progression, retention and employment of our students. This idea had been adapted from similar practices in the U.S. higher education system where a range of support mechanisms would be linked to similar assessments offered in a single location in one window. Since the close of our project, our institution now has a functional assessment centre on its campus. The centre works with academic colleagues to design and deliver digital developments on their programmes by collaborating with a team of digital assessment designers and technicians. The types of assessment offered are categorised as diagnostic, development and destination, and aid students' understanding of their own abilities in relation to more nuanced skill sets such as academic skills, numeracy, sentence construction and performance in simulated professional examinations.

References

Advance HE (2017), *Equality Challenge Unit. Equality in higher education: statistical report 2017*, Advance HE, UK, https://www.advance-he.ac.uk/knowledge-hub/equality-higher-education-statistical-report-2017 (accessed on 15 July 2021). [18]

AHELO (2012), *AHELO feasibility study interim report*, OECD, Paris. [9]

Arum, R. and J. Roksa (2011), *Academically Adrift: Limited Learning on College Campuses*, University of Chicago Press, Chicago. [20]

Ashford-Rowe, K., J. Herrington and C. Brown (2013), "Establishing the critical elements that determine authentic assessment", *Assessment & Evaluation in Higher Education*, Vol. 39/2, pp. 205-222, https://doi.org/10.1080/02602938.2013.819566. [11]

Brand, S. and L. Millard (2019), *Chapter 4: Student engagement in quality in UK higher education: more than assurance?*, Routledge, London and New York. [7]

Browne, L. (2010), *Securing a Sustainable future for higher education: an independent review of higher education funding & student finance*. [5]

Eurydice (2019), *Autonomous and diverse institutions*, https://eacea.ec.europa.eu/national-policies/eurydice/content/types-higher-education-institutions-94_en (accessed on 3 May 2021). [1]

Gov.uk (2020), *Participation rates in Higher Education: Academic Years 2006/2007 - 2007/2018*, https://www.gov.uk/government/collections/statistics-on-higher-education-initial-participation-rates (accessed on 29 July 2021). [4]

HESA (2021), *How many students are in HE?*, https://www.hesa.ac.uk/news/27-01-21/sb258-higher-education-student-statistics/numbers (accessed on 3 May 2021). [2]

Hubble, S. and P. Bolton (2018), *Higher education tuition fees in England*, The House of Commons Library, https://researchbriefings.files.parliament.uk/documents/CBP-8151/CBP-8151.pdf (accessed on 29 July 2021). [6]

Kaufman, J. and J. Gabler (2004), "Cultural capital and the extracurricular activities of girls and boys in the college attainment process", *Poetics*, Vol. 32/2, pp. 145-68, https://doi.org/10.1016/j.poetic.2004.02.001. [16]

McGrath, C. et al. (2015), *Learning gain in higher education*, RAND Corporation, Santa Monica, California and Cambridge, UK, https://www.rand.org/pubs/research_reports/RR996.html. [8]

Office for Students (2021), *Future of the TEF*, https://www.officeforstudents.org.uk/advice-and-guidance/teaching/future-of-the-tef. [10]

Stuart, M. et al. (2011), "The impact of engagement with extracurricular activities on the student experience and graduate outcomes for widening participation populations", *Active Learning in Higher Education*, Vol. 12/3, pp. 203-215, https://doi.org/10.1177/1469787411415081. [17]

Universities UK (2018), *Patterns and trends*, https://www.universitiesuk.ac.uk/facts-and-stats/data-and-analysis/Pages/Patterns-and-trends-in-UK-higher-education-2018.aspx. [3]

Vanthournout, G. et al. (2016), *Chapter 4: Discovering and Strengthening Learning Strategies and Motivation Using the Lemo-instrument*, Leuven, Lannoo.   [19]

Webb, O. et al. (2017), "Enhancing access, retention, attainment and progression in higher education A review of the literature showing demonstrable impact", *Enhancing access, retention, attainment and progression in higher education A review of the literature showing demonstrable impact*, https://s3.eu-west-2.amazonaws.com/assets.creode.advancehe-document-manager/documents/hea/private/resources/enhancing_access_retention_attainment_and_progression_in_higher_education_1_1568037358.pdf.   [15]

Woodall, T., A. Hiller and S. Resnick (2012), "Making sense of higher education: students as consumers and the value of the university experience", *Studies in Higher Education*, Vol. 39/1, pp. 48-67, https://doi.org/10.1080/03075079.2011.648373.   [14]

Wyatt-Smith, C., V. Klenowski and S. Gunn (2010), "The centrality of teachers' judgement practice in assessment: a study of standards in moderation", *Assessment in Education: Principles, Policy & Practice*, Vol. 17/1, pp. 59-75, https://doi.org/10.1080/09695940903565610.   [13]

Zahner, D. and J. Lehrfeld (2018), *Employers' and advisors' assessments of the importance of critical thinking and written communication skills post-college*, Paper presented at the 2018 Conference of the American Educational Research Association, New York, NY.   [12]

14 Mexico: an innovative focus on evaluation of learning outcomes

Patricia Rosas, University of Guadalajara (Mexico)

Carlos I. Moreno, University of Guadalajara (Mexico)

Rubén Sánchez, University of Guadalajara (Mexico)

Mexico has implemented policies to improve the quality of its higher education for over two decades, spanning four administrations. Evaluation of learning outcomes is one such policy. The institution analysed in this chapter promotes a culture of quality that permits the application of different perspectives and tools to the evaluation process. The results offered here focus on evaluating higher order cognition through performance and constructed response testing. The CLA+ test was applied in programmes currently without exit exams, receiving ample participation across many disciplines and campuses at one public state university. One main result corroborates the existing gap between better-performing students at metropolitan campuses and lower-performing students from socio-economically disadvantaged regional sites. However, certain educational programmes run counter to this disparity, generating better results. Deepening our understanding of the specific contexts producing these different results will enable us to learn from the most effective practices and improve learning outcomes.

Mexican higher education: Socio-economic and cognitive disparities

The higher education system in Mexico is complex, owing to the country's social and regional diversity. Therefore, learning outcomes should be analysed with reference to the national context, the educational system in general, and the variables endogenous to each educational level and subsystem. The worldwide economic recession and COVID-19 have left half of Mexico's population in poverty with predictable increases in educational, digital, cognitive and human inequality. The challenges have become more acute for higher education institutions (HEIs) over a range of issues: governance; the acquisition and fair, transparent distribution of financial resources; quality; and the development of capabilities for consolidating achievements and successfully overcoming new problems.

Mexico is a country of great wealth and diversity. Its gross domestic product (GDP) ranks as the world's 15th highest (World Bank, 2021[1]). Nevertheless, it suffers from enormous inequality: two-thirds of its wealth is concentrated in 10% of the nation's families (ECLAC, 2017[2]), a statistic that ranks it among the top 25% of nations with the highest levels of inequality in the world (Oxfam, 2018[3]). Poverty is an inescapable reality that is responsible for a growing and worrisome chasm of inequality. In the presentation of the 2020 report on Latin America, the director of the Economic Commission for Latin America and the Caribbean (ECLAC) states that, owing to the COVID-19 crisis, Mexico now ranks as the fourth highest country in the region in terms of number of inhabitants living in poverty and extreme poverty (Villanueva, 2021[4]). The report states that from 2019 to 2020, poverty increased 9.1%, affecting 50.6% of the population or 63.8 million Mexicans; extreme poverty grew 7.7% to represent 18.3% of the population, equivalent to 23.2 million people (ECLAC, 2021[5]). According to the World Bank (2020[6]), extreme poverty is defined as having to live on less than USD 1.90 per day.

This economic disparity has repercussions in education. In 2020, 49.3% of the Mexican population above the age of 15 only had a basic level of education (INEGI, 2020a[7]). The rate of illiteracy in Mexico is 4.7%, nearly 6 million people (INEGI, 2020b[8]). The panorama is bleaker still when one takes into account factors such as reading habits and comprehension: of the population that is able to read, only one-fourth fully comprehend what they read (INEGI, 2020c[9]). The results of the Programme for International Student Assessment (PISA) are well known, but although the general results for 2018 in mathematics, reading and sciences are below the mean of member nations in the Organisation for Economic Co-operation and Development (OECD), Mexico has demonstrated a stability in its results since 2003 that could mask trends toward a diminution of disparity in results: "The point level achieved by at least 90% of the students in Mexico improved by 5 points for each three-year period, on average, in each of the three principal areas" (OECD, 2018[10]). Additionally, only 23% of the population between the ages of 25 and 34 has a higher education degree while the average for OECD countries is 44% (OECD, 2019a[11]).

Digital realities exacerbate disparity

Educational disparity amplifies digital disparity and vice versa. Recent results of a study on the impact of COVID-19 on education (INEGI, 2021[12]) reveal a decrease in the level of matriculation for academic year 2020/21 by 5.2 million at all education levels. There are a variety of reasons for this, chiefly including: distaste for online classes; lack of a computer or Internet connectivity; unemployment of one or another of the heads of households; and the need to dedicate oneself to money-earning labour. The pandemic made clear the need to improve digital literacy and methods of active teaching. The United Nations Development Programme (UNDP) calculated a reduction of 15.6% in undergraduate level matriculations for 2020/21, from more than 3.8 million students in 2019/20 to just over 3.2 million projected for 2020/21 (UNDP, 2020[13]). This is a drop of more than half a million students, according to statistics from the Ministry of Public Education (SEP, *Secretaría de Educación Pública*). The digital disparity also impacts education. In Mexico only 56.4% of homes have Internet connectivity (INEGI, 2020d[14]) and only 11.2% of higher education students have a desktop computer, with preference for laptops (55.7%) and smart phones (31.8%).

These educational and digital gaps imply a cognitive disparity. A low level of literacy does not allow information that is easily accessed and viewed on various media to be absorbed, interpreted and skilfully utilised. This has a deleterious effect on the ways thoughts and actions are exercised. As Pozo points out: "… whoever cannot access different cultural forms of symbolic representation (numerical, artistic, scientific, graphic, etc.) is socially, economically and culturally impoverished, as well as overwhelmed, confused and disconcerted by the avalanche of information they cannot translate into knowledge" (Pozo, 2006[15]).

Higher education in Mexico: a complex system

This is the context in which higher education in Mexico has developed. It is a complex system due to its size, regional diversity and 13 subsystems. The subsystems include both state and national public universities; intercultural institutions; technological and polytechnical institution; solidarity-based and private institutions; decentralised federal technical institutes; public research centres; and public and private schools for training elementary school teachers. This complex system generates factors that complicate governance, financing, and institutional capacities.

According to the SEP's General Directorate of Educational Planning, Programming and Statistics (Dirección General de Planeación, Programación y Estadística Educativa [The Mexican Ministry of Public Education's General Directorate of Educational Planning, Programming and Statistics], 2020[16]), total enrolment in higher education for 2019/20 was above 4.9 million students, with 64% in public schools versus 36% in private ones. Among the different subsystems, the combination of public universities and technological institutes represented almost 60% of total enrolment and 92% of the public education subtotal. Enrolment at state universities surpassed 1.25 million or 43% of the entire system of public universities and institutes; that of the federal universities – slightly over half a million students – represents 20% of the total. There are a total of 591 public universities and institutions in Mexico, of which 341 are universities and 250 are technological institutes. These HEIs are crucial to the system and they face tremendous challenges in guaranteeing educational excellence.

Building access to and quality of higher education

For over two decades, national policies have been geared toward increasing access to higher education. These have resulted in a gross coverage rate of 38.4%, which is 10 percentage points below Latin American countries and more than 30 percentage points below the average of OECD member nations (ANUIES, 2018[17]). Although access has been increased, it is important to consider the issue of quality in education, too. The study by Ferreyra et al. (2017[18]) reports that in Latin America the rate of access to higher education for people between the ages of 18 and 24 has increased considerably and estimates that approximately 3 million students – 45% of the total increase in enrolment – come from underprivileged backgrounds and are therefore academically less prepared. Their report points out the existence of an early desertion rate of 35% during the first year, associated with low levels in development of these students' cognitive abilities.

The system also "lacks diversity of fields and levels of study", whether in terms of specific disciplines or interdisciplinary areas. "More than one-third of the students are enrolled in business administration and law." (OECD, 2019a[11]). It needs improvement both in general and specific competencies, as well as in fostering the development of the "soft skills" through active learning methods that are so highly valued by employers.

Over the course of four administrations, Mexico has implemented quality education policies with strong support from the National Association of Universities and Institutions of Higher Education (ANUIES [acronyms are from the Spanish organisational names]). Public state universities have responded positively, not least because they have been able to access extra funding to strengthen institutions and infrastructure; provide student grants for travel and research; and carry out investigation, though many have recently ended. The first step was to introduce design plans for higher education and then to initiate processes of external review. Emblematic institutions are the Inter-institutional Committees for the Evaluation of Higher Education (CIEES); the Council for the Accreditation of Higher Education (COPAES) and its affiliated organisations; the National Centre for the Evaluation of Higher Education (CENEVAL); the now-defunct National Institute for the Evaluation of Education (INEE); and individual state commissions for higher education planning (COEPES), which were set up across the country.

Evaluating learning outcomes

Quality-improvement policies implemented by federal administrations two decades ago created the political context for evaluating learning outcomes by means of the CLA+ test. Processes of evaluation had been introduced in this institution with positive repercussions for admissions and graduation requirements, and evaluation and accreditation of educational offerings. On the other hand, among the international trends in education, the evaluation of learning outcomes appeared as a third-generation indicator for the processes of accreditation of quality. The administrators of this institution became involved in many experiences that offered knowledge about focal points and instruments for evaluation. This contributed to facilitating community participation in new forms of evaluating educational results such as CLA+.

The institution in question is typical of the subsystem of public state universities. Although it enjoys administrative autonomy, its funding comes principally from the state and federal governments. It is a massive institution in terms of enrolment and has campuses both in the state's capital city and various regional locations throughout the state. While carrying out many functions – teaching, research and extension – its particular emphasis is on teaching. Students aspiring to admission must present an aptitude exam, which is considered together with their high school averages. Admission is granted as a function of available space in each educational programme (EP) and points obtained in the selection process.

This institution initiated its processes of external evaluation in 1991, shortly after the creation of the CIEES at a nationwide level. By 2004 it had formalised its policy through the establishment of an institutional fund to defray the costs of the evaluation, accreditation and learning outcome tests. Three years later, it constituted the Committee of Peers for Institutional Self-Evaluation and by 2012 it began its processes of accreditation by means of international organisations.

The institution began evaluating learning outcomes in 2005 as part of its policies for improving quality. It did so initially through the General Graduation Exam for Undergraduate Degrees (EGEL), which is implemented nationwide by the CENEVAL. When the Undersecretary for Higher Education of the SEP later implemented the OECD feasibility study Assessment of Higher Education Learning Outcomes (AHELO) at a nationwide level, this institution participated.

What the AHELO study showed was that though the measurement of general abilities is a good indicator of workplace applicability, it is nevertheless important to combine it, when possible, with an evaluation of specific abilities. Additionally, it was noted that the task of testing awakened enthusiasm in the academic community, which could be parlayed into teaching and future evaluations. One activity resulting from this institution's participation in the AHELO study were the workshops on performance-based tasks offered to teachers by the Council for Aid to Education (CAE), based in the United States. These workshops constituted the basis for the development of a pilot study at four regional campuses with low learning outcome results. The intention was that first-year students would undertake foundation courses that would bring them up to an acceptable level, with lessons concentrated on performance-based tasks to develop their cognitive abilities. The results of these were positive and were published in Rosas and Silva (2019[19]).

In addition, this institution participated in a nationwide project convoked by the SEP's office of the Director General of Higher University Training. The project, which was called Development and Evaluation of Competencies for Learning in Higher Education (DESCAES, in Spanish), measured HEIs' value-added to competencies for managing information, problem solving, communication, metacognition and self-regulation. The tools were designed in 2014 and 2015; they were applied initially in 2016, with a second application in 2019.

The arguments for continuing evaluation of learning outcomes by means of the CLA+ test were:

1. The Graduate Exam for Undergraduate Degrees (EGEL) does not have tests for all of the institution's educational programmes. At the time, 71 of its 214 programmes had no related EGEL.

2. There are 17 undergraduate programmes that are multidisciplinary or interdisciplinary in nature and cannot be properly evaluated by EGEL, which is structured for a single discipline.

3. More than 40% of undergraduate programmes had not been evaluating their outcomes, resulting in two situations:

   a) Comparisons between the institution's departments were not reliable because there are certain campuses where the EGEL test was only applied in one or two programmes while in other centres it was applied in each and every programme.

   b) Some area co-ordinators commented that the level of work was unfairly distributed between programmes subjected to learning outcome evaluations and those that are not.

4. The cost of the CLA+ testing applied across the board would be comparable that of the EGEL. Consequently, adopting the CLA+ model would be a better institutional investment for the evaluation of the totality of undergraduate programmes.

5. The CLA+ offers the possibility of realising value-added studies. The institution would be able to make them available without exorbitant cost if admissions tests were done by the CAE. The cost would be covered by students' paid fees while exit exams would be absorbed by the university's institutional fund.

Implementing the CLA+ testing

Not all of the university's campus centres were willing to participate, especially those where practically all programmes already had EGEL testing. There was also a lack of enthusiasm, even in centres without EGEL testing in most programmes, as they would have to set up structures and logistics to do the CLA+ testing. The agreement, finally, was that programmes without EGEL testing would participate. To this end, a fund was authorised for initiating the new testing model.

Participation varied at each campus where the test was implemented. Three testing sessions per semester were carried out with a total of 8 577 tests, of which 2 176 were administered to graduating students. The rest were administered to newly matriculated first-year students, with the idea of later administering exit exams to evaluate the value-added of their educational programmes. Table 14.1 shows data from the testing.

Table 14.1. Numeric breakdown of CLA+ testing by administration

	2017 2nd Semester	2018 1st Semester	2018 2nd Semester
Campuses	14	13	13
Educational Programmes	55	53	59
Exit Exams	665	717	594
Entry Exams	1 927	1 819	2 655
TOTAL of Tests Applied	2 592	2 536	3 249
Co-ordinators	14	13	13
Test Application Personnel	89	80	77

The implementation process contemplated the following stages:

1. Establishing cognitive laboratories for translating and culturally adapting tests
2. Ensuring a sufficient number of implementation coordinators and test application personnel as well as training for them
3. Administering tests on the CAE platform
4. Receiving test results from the CAE and statistically processing results for the governing board's evaluation and ratification

There were some objections to the CLA+ testing, which had to do with extra workload and limited personnel. This was especially true at regional sites with fewer personnel. There were also concerns over the high cost of evaluating learning outcomes. This would require governmental funding, which can suffer from a lack of continuity when changes in administrations occur.

On the whole, however, the different participants involved gave a generally positive opinion of the CLA+ implementation. For the governing board, this test introduces new forms of evaluation, with the eventual possibility of comparing student performance from other institutions in other countries. It also provides evaluation of programmes that had lacked EGEL testing. Logistical co-ordinators and administering professors felt that this new test awakened enthusiasm among the students who took them.

Finally, students who responded to the brief survey about the CLA+ test were generally positive about it. Nevertheless, some responded that they did not exert themselves to the greatest degree because the tests were not obligatory and were not included in their programme's curriculum. Other stated that the test required a lot of thought and proved stressful for that reason.

Some results: Defiant disparities, once again

Though sampling had not been carried out to guarantee representativity, the number of tests that were applied across a wide variety of campus sites and educational programmes did confirm disparities between metropolitan campus sites and regional ones. While there here has been improvement in access to higher education for a greater number of young people from these underserved regional sectors, their lower levels of cognitive performance jeopardise their ability to remain in school and successfully conclude their studies. The disparity is reflected across the range of educational programmes (EP), too. However, there are results showing that context is not destiny. And, there are also results that push us to reflect on the very design of the educational programmes themselves and the ways in which the material is being taught.

Method of analysis

Our analysis of learning outcomes involved estimates of the probability density function (PDF) and comparison between densities, with a 95% level of confidence. The reason for selecting this analytical option is that, in many cases, the simple comparison of averages is inefficient because it presupposes a normativity that is not always a reality. Or because measurements as a coefficient of variation or degree of effect could be insufficient for determining the estimated average and variation in the readings of interest. It is important to point out that these results only correspond to the exit exams of graduating students and are not representative of the institution's global performance, given that representative samples were not selected at any level.

Thus, we begin our analysis starting with the general results represented in Figure 14.1, in which there can be seen four graphs of probability densities of the scores obtained by participating students for the entire database (upper figure) and, separately (lower figures), for the students who took the CLA+ test during the second semester of 2017 (Figure 14.1, 17B), the first semester of 2018 (Figure 14.1, 18A) and the second semester of 2018 (Figure 14.1, 18B).

Figure 14.1. Probability densities of points, grouped together and separately by academic semester

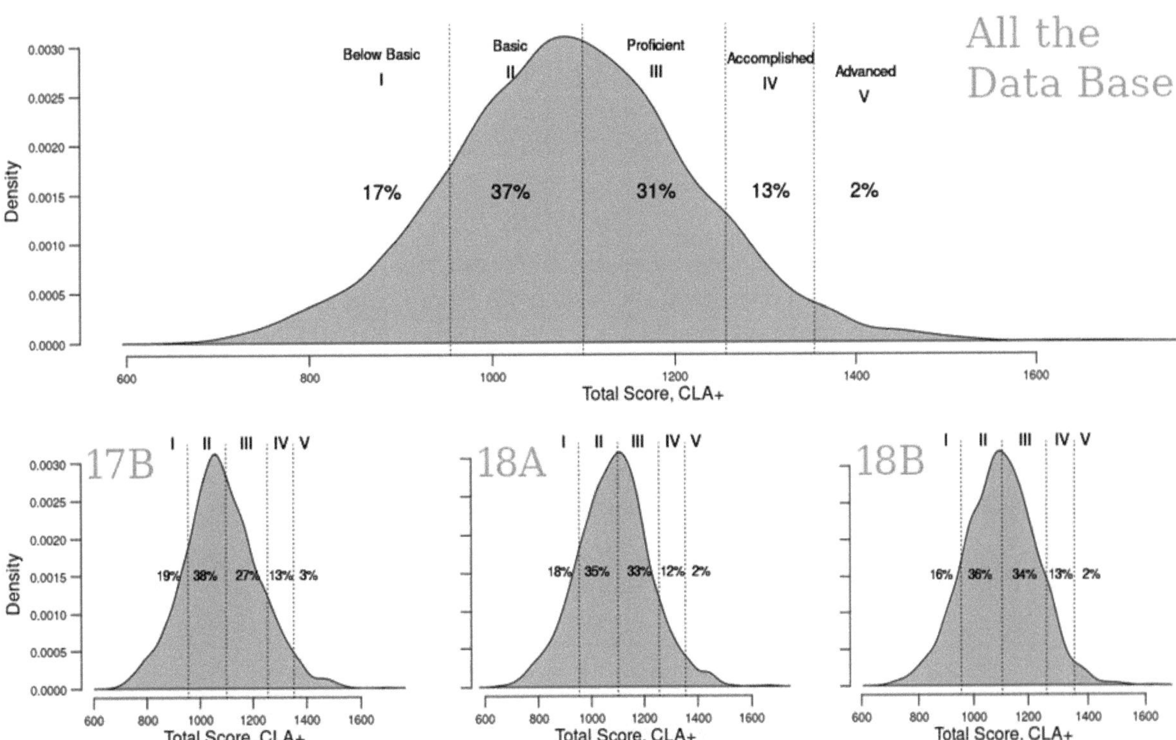

In the same Figure 14.1 there can be seen, from the dotted vertical lines, the skill levels for the abilities evaluated and the percentage of students who reached each of these levels: 2% reached "Advanced" and the levels of greatest probability were "Basic", with 37%, and "Proficient", with 31%. There were no significant differences between the competencies observed across the three academic semesters during which testing was performed.

From results obtained in other tests given by the institution, such as admissions aptitude testing and EGEL exit exams, the performance of students at metropolitan campus sites is generally higher than that of students in the rural, regional centres. Therefore, we proceeded to observe the data broken down by type of campus site. In Figure 14.2 we see that students at metropolitan sites outperformed the regional sites at the levels of "Proficient", "Accomplished" and "Advanced", while students at regional sites had greater probability than those at metropolitan sites to test at the levels of "Basic" and "Below Basic".

This difference can be attributed to various factors, ranging from socio-economic strata to levels of educational supply and demand. Socio-economic factors include the strata of students' families and the availability of highly skilled staff and well-equipped libraries and computer centres at the different campus sites. Regarding supply-and-demand issues, if the number of students who want to go on to higher education does not exceed the number of admissions slots, a given campus site might well admit all comers. But when demand for admission outstrips the supply of available spaces, the possibility of selecting higher ranking students exists, which translates into better academic profiles for the average student at those sites.

Figure 14.2. Contrast of probability densities of scores, grouped by metropolitan and regional dependencies

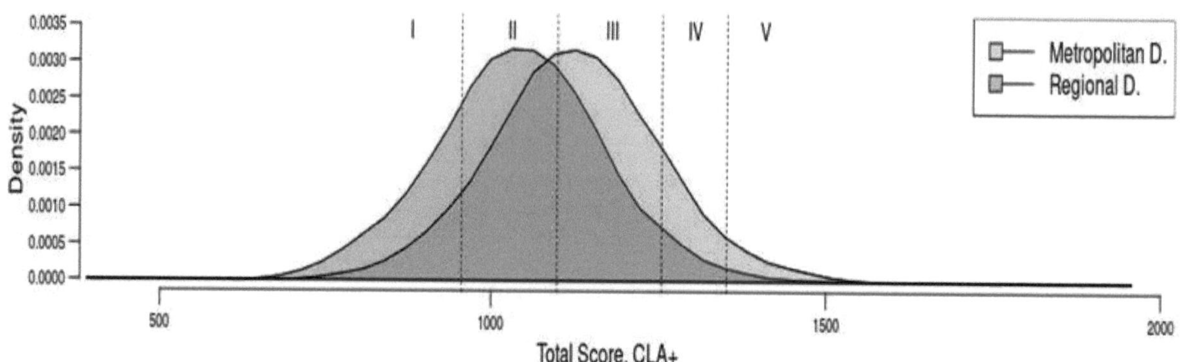

Additionally, to implement a comparative analysis between the 14 institutional dependencies – five metropolitan, eight regional and one virtual site – we order them in descending average performance, where 1 is the highest average score value and 14 is the lowest one. Thus, in Figure 14.3 we observe the performance of students at metropolitan sites. The base taken was the point level of students from site Metro_1 (the institutional dependency with the highest average) and contrasts are provided with students from sites Metro_2 (Figure 14.3A), Metro_3 (Figure 14.3B), Metro_5 (Figure 14.3C) and Metro_10 (Figure 14.3D). Furthermore, to highlight the differences observed in Figure 14.3, in Table 14.2, we show the percentages of students at each mastery level and for each dependency.

Figure 14.3. Contrast of probability densities of scores, grouped by metropolitan dependencies

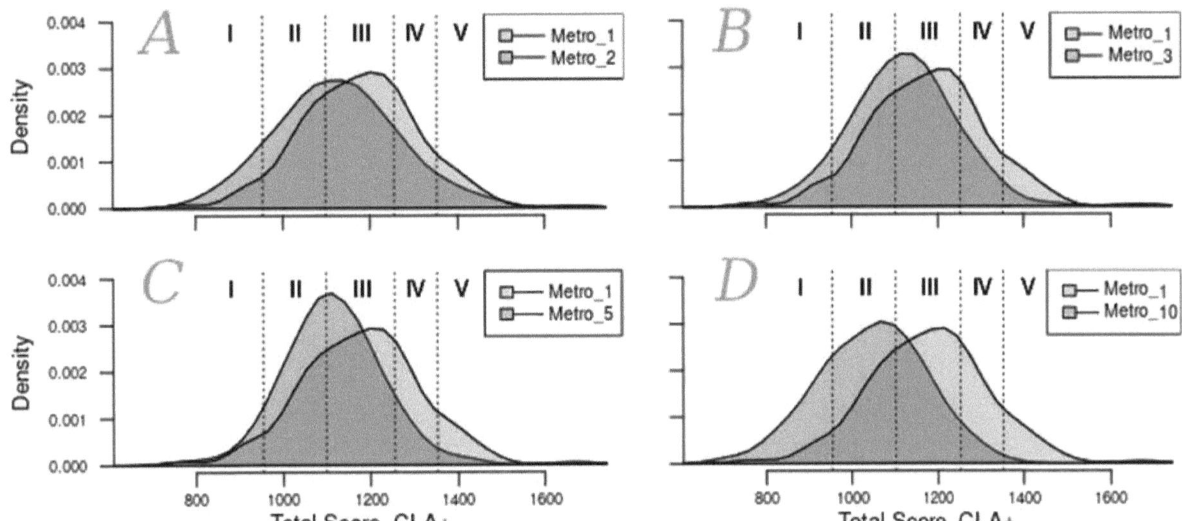

Table 14.2. Percentages of students at each mastery level, by site

Levels	I	II	III	IV	V
Metro_1	4%	23%	35%	29%	9%
Metro_2	13%	31%	33%	18%	5%
Metro_3	9%	33%	39%	17%	2%
Metro_5	7%	37%	41%	13%	2%
Metro_10	26%	38%	29%	6%	1%

Therefore, in Figure 14.3 and Table 14.2, we see that the students at Metro_1 show better performance when compared with the students at Metro_2, Metro_3, Metro_5 and Metro_10, principally in the categories "Accomplished" and "Advanced". In the category "Proficient", Metro_3 and Metro_5 have better results than Metro_1 while Metro_1 and Metro_2 show similar results, and Metro_1 is considerably higher than Metro_10. That D1 has the best performance is consistent with the EGEL test results for the rest of that site's educational programmes, but it is also a site with far greater demand than supply, which accounts for the students admitted to that site having much better developed levels of cognitive abilities. The case of Metro_5 only reflects one of its educational programmes, which does not have a related EGEL test. However, D5 is a site with similar behaviour to Metro_1 in terms of students admitted and their performance as measured on the EGEL test. Metro_3 is the only site at which all its educational programmes applied the CLA+ test because only two of its programmes applied EGEL tests to graduating students. The disciplines offered at this site correspond principally to the field of the arts, but there is also more demand for entry than there is supply of available spaces, which guarantees a selection of students with better profiles. While Metro_10 reflects performance levels similar to those of the regional sites – including, in some cases, below some of them – this site only participated with two of its programmes; the rest of its programmes apply the EGEL tests with better levels of performance than was found in the two programmes measured here. Additionally, because of the type of programmes offered, it routinely admits all aspirants for admission, regardless of their admission-testing performance levels.

Figure 14.4 shows the performance of metropolitan site Metro_1 (with better performance) together with that of Virtual_4 (a virtual site for online learning). At the "Advanced" level, the highest scores were attained by the students of Virtual_4, while the students of Metro_1 exceeded probability at the levels "Proficient" and "Accomplished". At the levels of "Below Basic" and "Basic", students at Virtual_4 exceeded in probability the students at Metro_1. This result could be explained by the fact that the online site admits practically all its applicants, including many who are more mature students with a high degree of self-directedness.

Figure 14.4. Contrast of probability densities of scores obtained by participating students from dependencies Metro_1 and Virtual_4.

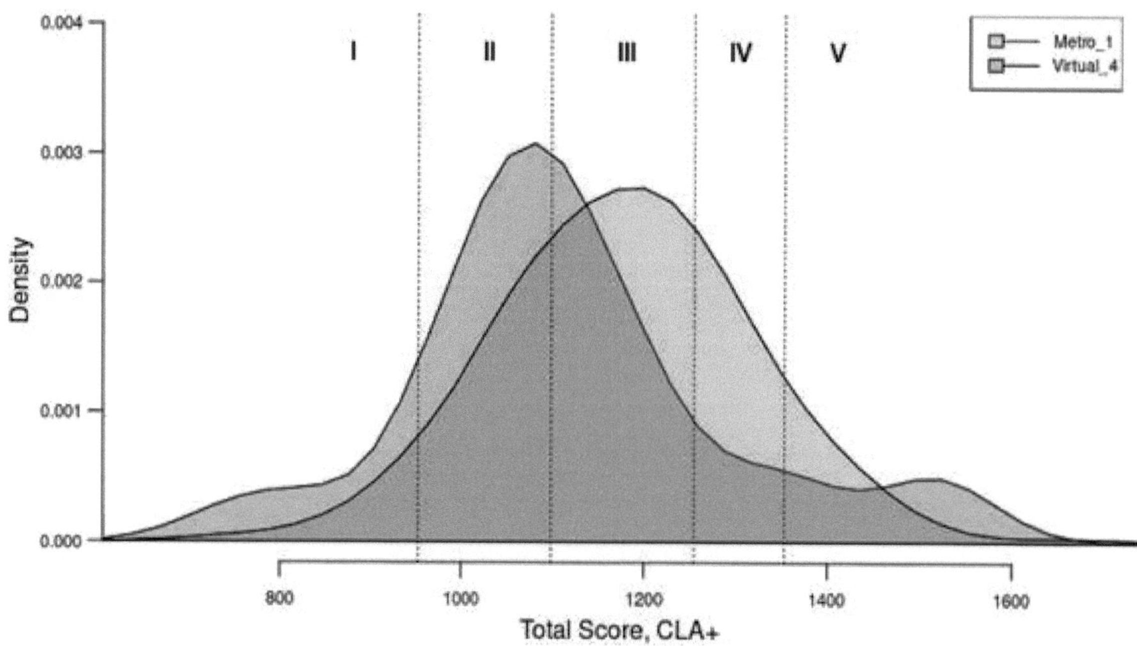

Although performativity among the regional sites is quite similar, Figure 14.5 shows the probability densities of the points obtained by students at the regional sites having the best (Regional_6) and worst (Regional_13 and Regional_14) test results. The greatest number of results in the category "Below Basic" occur at site Regional_14 (Figure 14.5A), with approximately 50% of the students testing at that lowest of the five categories. Both Regional_13 and Regional_14 show similar results (Figure 14.5B), with the greatest proportion of students appearing on the left-hand side of the graph. These sites admit practically all aspirants, regardless of their admissions test scores, especially in the case of the area where the Regional_13 site is located – a region including some municipalities with 30-40% of their population living in conditions of extreme poverty.

Figure 14.5. Contrast of probability densities of scores, grouped by regional campus sites

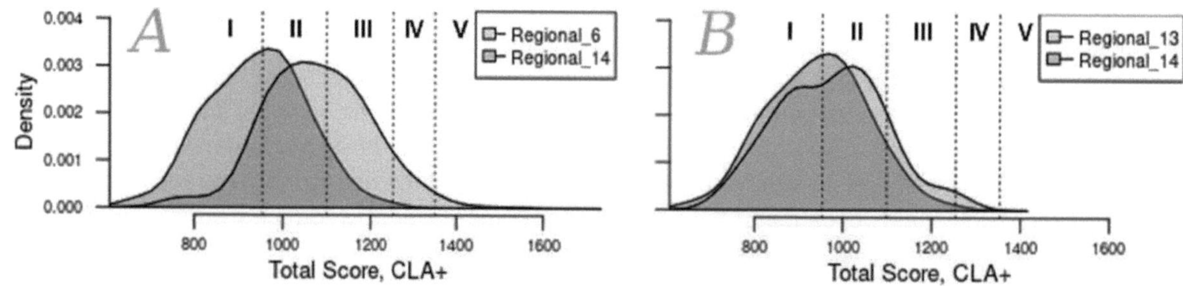

In the combined view of Figure 14.6, we see at a glance the contrasts between students at Metro_1 (the highest average of metropolitan sites), Metro_10 (the lowest average of metropolitan sites), Regional_6 (the highest average of regional sites), and Regional_14 (the lowest average of regional sites). The graph in Figure 14.6C shows the similarity in performance between the lowest metropolitan site (Metro_10) and the highest regional site (Regional_6). This is reinforced by the graph in Figure 14.6A, which shows the disparity between the highest and lowest levels of the metropolitan sites. In Figure 14.6B we can compare the highest averages of the best metropolitan and regional sites; this graph shows comparable behaviour with that shown in Figure 14.6A. The greatest disparity is revealed in Figure 14.6D, in which the highest metropolitan site (Metro_1) is shown against the lowest regional site (Regional_14).

Figure 14.6. Contrast of probability densities of the highest and lowest scores for metropolitan and regional dependencies

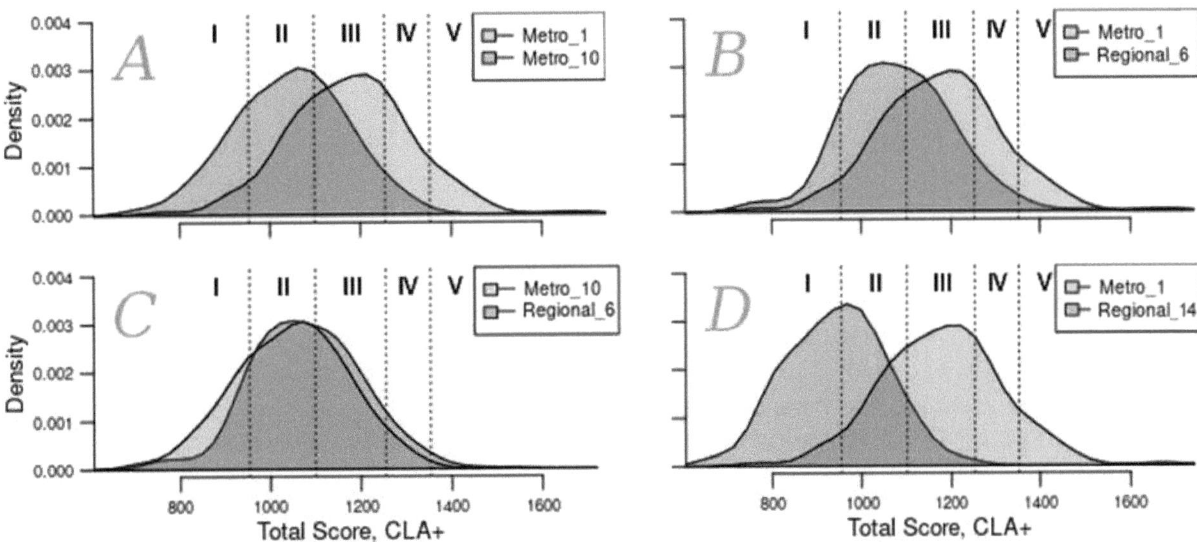

We know that at the micro level particular conditions exist in educational programmes (EP) which may contribute to each site's general performance being either better or worse. In the same way as the sites, we ordered the educational programmes in descending average performance, where EP1 is the highest average score value and EP52 is the lowest. Therefore, we have made comparisons by EP for the metropolitan sites. Figure 14.7 presents a comparison of the data from EP1, EP2, EP10, EP16 and EP46. In Figure 14.7A we see somewhat parallel results. Although the percentage points of students in EP1 exceed those of students in EP2 at the levels "Accomplished" and "Advanced", it is worth noting that both EP are given at the same site (Metro_1) and belong to the same field of knowledge: Science. The graph 14.7B shows the similarity in results in EP10 (Services field) and EP16 (Science field), which are also given at one and the same site (Metro_3). On the other hand, the graph 14.7C shows EP10 (Services field) at site Metro_3 along with EP46 (Science field) at site Metro_2, revealing that EP46 – even though it is offered at a metropolitan site – shows performance similar to the lowest level EPs among the regional sites. Graph 14.7D underscores the enormous difference in results between EP1 and EP46, despite their both being imparted at the metropolitan sites (Metro_1 and Metro_2, respectively) having the highest and second highest overall point averages among all participating sites.

Figure 14.7. Contrast of probability densities of scores by participating students, grouped by educational programme (EP) at metropolitan dependencies

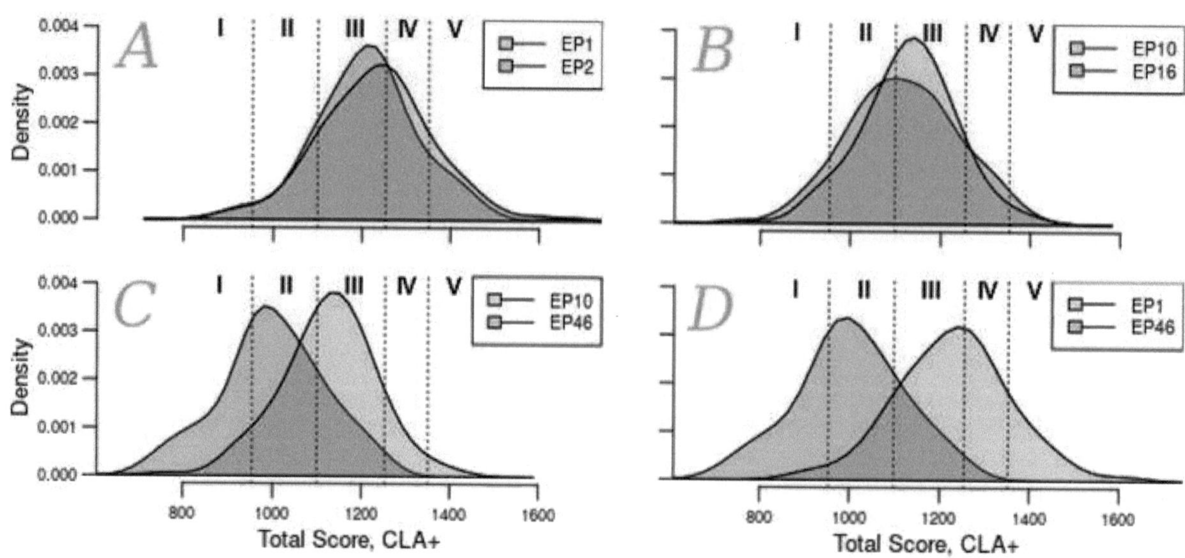

In Figure 14.8 we compare performance by EP in all types of sites for the following programmes: EP1, EP9, EP38, EP46 and EP52. Numerical assignations are based on point averages such that EP1 was the programme with the highest score and EP52 the lowest.

Figure 14.8. Contrast of probability densities of scores by EP in metropolitan and regional dependencies

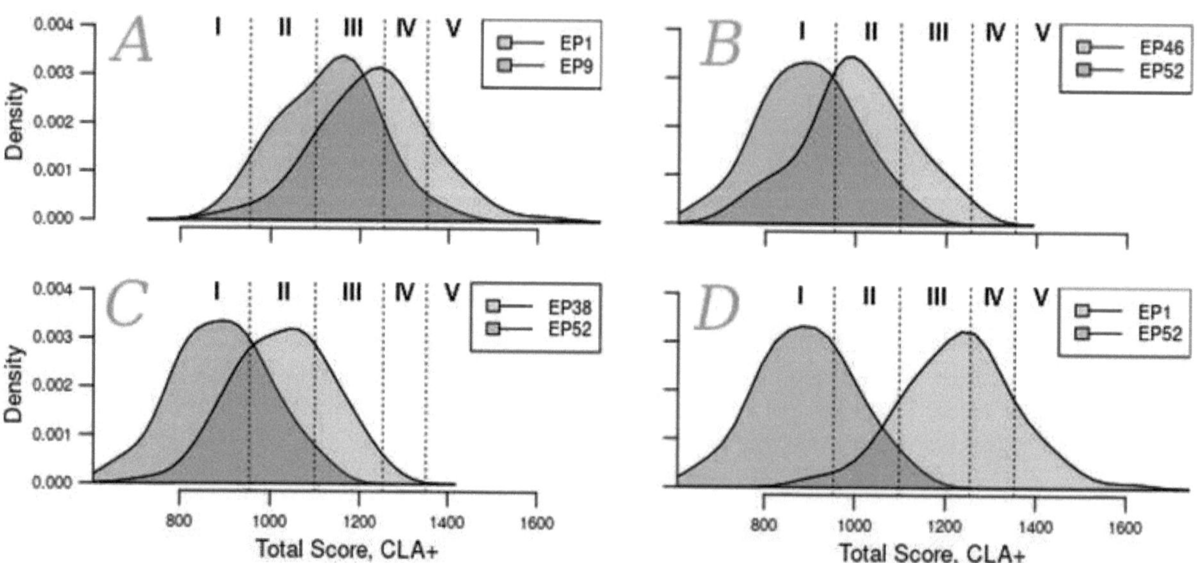

In the graph shown as Figure 14.8D, what stands out is the difference between EP1 (metropolitan site - Science field) and EP52 (regional site – Agriculture field). More than 50% of the EP52 students are concentrated at the lowest level – "Below Basic" – while the inverse is true of EP1 where over 50% of students are within the three highest levels: "Proficient", "Accomplished" and "Advanced". Additionally, Figure 14.8A reveals that in comparing EP1 with EP9 (regional site – Services field), although EP1 shows better performance, the difference is not overwhelming despite the existing disparities between metropolitan and regional sites. In Figure 14.8B there is a comparison between EP46 (metropolitan site –

Science field), which had the lowest average among all EPs given at metropolitan sites, and EP52 (regional site – Agriculture field), which had the lowest average among those given at the regional sites. Here we can see that, despite both being the lowest average of their respective site type, the disparity between geographic locations continues to appear as an important factor. Finally, Figure 14.8C shows a graph enabling us to compare the results of one EP that is offered at both metropolitan and regional sites – Agriculture field. Despite the fact that performance at both locations was low, performance at the metropolitan site was not as low as it was at the regional site.

Main conclusions about these findings

Even though this is not a comparative study, the analysis of students answers to CLA+ test we found important differences in their performance per campuses and among EP. These differences can be attributed to different factors. The first factor is the geographical location that confirms the superposition of the economic gap to the education gap. The disparity in social and economic conditions among regional and metropolitan agencies, in some cases this gap is very evident between high-income and low-income families. The students in regional campuses, where the economic context is more precarious, lower scores are obtained in average, while in the metropolitan campuses, higher scores are obtained. This also happens generally in EP based analysis, the EP attached to the metropolitan sites take the first positions in the ranking, although some of the EP in regional campuses achieve a high rank, but these are exceptions.

A second factor is the offer and demand of these programs. In the metropolitan sites, generally, the demand exceeds the offer; hence, the availability of places in each campus leave an open possibility to select the students with highest access scores. Nevertheless, the results also show, as an exception, that some of the regional PEs had a good performance not as much related to places availability.

Through these responses' analysis we could not respond to some of the concerns such as the differences in the performance of the metropolitan campuses 1 and 10; or between regional and metropolitan PEs. However, through these cues, looking into the future, it could be possible to make comparative studies to explore in depth the causes of these differences; this could constitute an important tool to improve the performance in every EP and all campuses.

What we learned from the CLA+ results

Despite the gap between metropolitan and regional sites, other variables exist that help explain best or worst performances in educational programmes. We consider it indispensable to undertake further, deeper studies in order to fully understand these variables. The variables could be related to the design itself of the educational programmes. This is a provisional conclusion that may be drawn from the testing results of the EP imparted at five different sites, all of which demonstrated poor performance levels, albeit with marginally less dismal results at the metropolitan site. The variables may also include the preparation of faculty, given that we have observed that regional sites geographically closer to the metropolitan area derive some benefit from metropolitan-based faculty members, who generally have no difficulty in commuting an hour or so in order to teach some courses at nearby regional sites. Additionally, analysis is required of the other resources available to the educational programmes for their work in order to understand the degree to which these may have influenced the learning outcomes that resulted. Finally, understanding the results obtained for each ability, in particular, will enable the development of a plan for intervening to improve instruction.

Our position is that all evaluations involve lessons learnt because once we detect aspects that are not working at even a minimum level, it clearly becomes necessary to intervene in order to improve them. Such intervention, however, is not possible without first learning more about their specific contexts. The current evaluation has given us a guideline to begin studies of the value added by higher education. Admissions testing has already been in place and we are at the point where we require the application of exit testing. Although there is uncertainty because of current economic restrictions, we know there is a positive disposition among the institutional directors for continuing with evaluations of learning outcomes. What remains to be done is to assure that the testing continues, that deeper studies are undertaken of the educational programmes analysed here, and that institutional mechanisms are found that guarantee the continuity of evaluations of learning outcomes.

References

ANUIES (2018), *Visión y acción 2030 Propuesta de la ANUIES para renovar la educación superior en México [Vision and Action 2030: Proposal of the National Association of Universities and Institutions of Higher Learning for renovating higher education in Mexico]*, ANUIES, México, http://www.anuies.mx/media/docs/avisos/pdf/VISION_Y_ACCION_2030.pdf. [17]

Dirección General de Planeación, Programación y Estadística Educativa [The Mexican Ministry of Public Education's General Directorate of Educational Planning, Programming and Statistics] (2020), *Principales cifras del sistema educativo nacional" [Principal Statistics of the National Education System]*, https://www.planeacion.sep.gob.mx/Doc/estadistica_e_indicadores/principales_cifras/principales_cifras_2019_2020_bolsillo.pdf. [16]

ECLAC (2021), *Social Panorama of Latin America: 2020*, United Nations Economic Commission for Latin America and the Caribbean, Santiago, http://www.cepal.org/sites/default/files/publication/files/46688/S2100149_en.pdf. [5]

ECLAC (2017), *Social Panorama for Latin America: 2016*, United Nations Economic Commission for Latin America and the Caribbean, Santiago, http://www.cepal.org/sites/default/files/publication/files/41599/S1700566_en.pdf. [2]

Ferreyra, M. et al. (2017), *At a Crossroads: Higher Education in Latin America and the Caribbean*, https://doi.org/10.1596/978-1-4648-1014-5. [18]

INEGI (2021), *Encuesta para la Medición del Impacto COVID-19 en la Educación (ECOVID-ED), Presentación de resultados. Instituto Nacional de Estadística y Geografía [Survey to Measure the Impact of COVID-19 on Education (ECOVID-ED). Outcomes Report. National Institute*, https://www.inegi.org.mx/contenidos/investigacion/ecovided/2020/doc/ecovid_ed_2020_presentacion_resultados.pdf (accessed on 18 March 2021). [12]

INEGI (2020b), *Analfabetismo [Illiteracy]*, http://cuentame.inegi.org.mx/poblacion/analfabeta.aspx?tema=P. [8]

INEGI (2020a), *Características educativas de la población [Educational characteristics of the population]*, https://inegi.org.mx/temas/educacion/. [7]

INEGI (2020d), *"Estadística a propósito del día mundial del internet (17 de mayo) datos nacionales", Comunicado de prensa núm. 216/20*, Vol. 2019, http://www.inegi.org.mx/contenidos/saladeprensa/aproposito/2020/eap_internet20.pdf (accessed on 5 August 2022). [14]

INEGI (2020f), *Población [Population]*, http://www.inegi.org.mx/temas/estructura/. [20]

INEGI (2020c), *press release no. 158/20*, http://www.inegi.org.mx/contenidos/saladeprensa/boletines/2020/EstSociodemo/MOLEC2019_04.pdf. (accessed on 23 April 2020). [9]

OECD (2018), *Panorama de la Educación 2017 [Educational Panorama]*, OECD, Paris, http://www.oecd.org/education/skills-beyond-school/EAG2017CN-Mexico-Spanish.pdf. [10]

OECD (2019a), *Higher Education in Mexico: Labour Market Relevance and Outcomes*, Higher Education, OECD Publishing, Paris, https://doi.org/10.1787/9789264309432-en. [11]

OECD (2019b), *The Future of Mexican Higher Education: Promoting Quality and Equity, Reviews of National Policies for Education*, OECD Publishing, Paris, https://doi.org/10.1787/9789264309371-en. [21]

Oxfam (2018), *México justo: políticas públicas contra la desigualdad*, https://ww.oxfammexico.org/mexico-justo-politicas-publicas-contra-la-desigualdad-0/. [3]

Pozo, J. (2006), *Adquisición de conocimiento, Segunda Edicion [Acquisition of Knowledge, second edition]*, Morata, Madrid, https://download.e-bookshelf.de/download/0003/5619/65/L-G-0003561965-0006870423.pdf. [15]

Rosas, P; Silva, J; (ed.) (2019), *Habilidades cognitivas y desempeño en el pregrado universitario [Cognitive Abilities and Performance in Undergraduate University Studies]*, ANUIES, Mexico City. [19]

UNDP (2020), *Desarrollo Humano y COVID-19 en México: Desafíos para una recuperación sostenible [Human Development and Covid-19 in Mexico: Challenges for a sustainable recovery]*, UNDP, http://www.mx.undp.org/content/mexico/es/home/library/poverty/desarrollo-humano-y-covid-19-en-mexico-.html. [13]

Villanueva, D. (2021), *México, entre los países de AL con más pobres por pandemia: Cepal [Mexico among the Latin American countries with the most poverty because of the pandemic: ECLAC]*, http://www.jornada.com.mx/notas/2021/03/04/economia/mexico-entre-los-paises-de-al-con-mas-pobres-por-pandemia-cepal/. [4]

World Bank (2021), *Banco de datos: Indicadores del desarrollo mundial (DataBank: World Development Indicators [database])*, https://databank.bancomundial.org/reports.aspx?source=2&series=NY.GDP.MKTP.CD&country=# (accessed on 18 March 2021). [1]

World Bank (2020), *COVID-19 to Add as Many as 150 Million Extreme Poor by 2021*, press release no. 2021/024/DEC-GPV, http://www.bancomundial.org/es/news/press-release/2020/10/07/covid-19-to-add-as-many-as-150-million-extreme-poor-by-2021 (accessed on 18 March 2021). [6]

15 CLA+ in Latin America: application and results

J. Enrique Froemel, Pontifical Catholic University of Valparaíso (Chile)

Although the chapter's title refers to the region, CLA+ was implemented only in Chile. Nevertheless, higher education in Latin America will be briefly described because reactions to the wider outreach effort are still pending in various countries. In Ibero-America (Latin America plus Portugal and Spain) the annual higher education average enrolment rate increased by 3.5% between 2010 and 2016, totalling almost 30 million students (OEI, 2018[1]). According to Trow's (Trow, 2008[2]) classification, Argentina, Chile, Spain, and Uruguay are already at the universalisation stage with gross higher education enrolment rates over 50% (OEI, 2018[1]). The remaining countries are at the expansion stage with rates going from 15 to 50%.

Figure 15.1. Higher education student percentage by country in Latin America (2018)

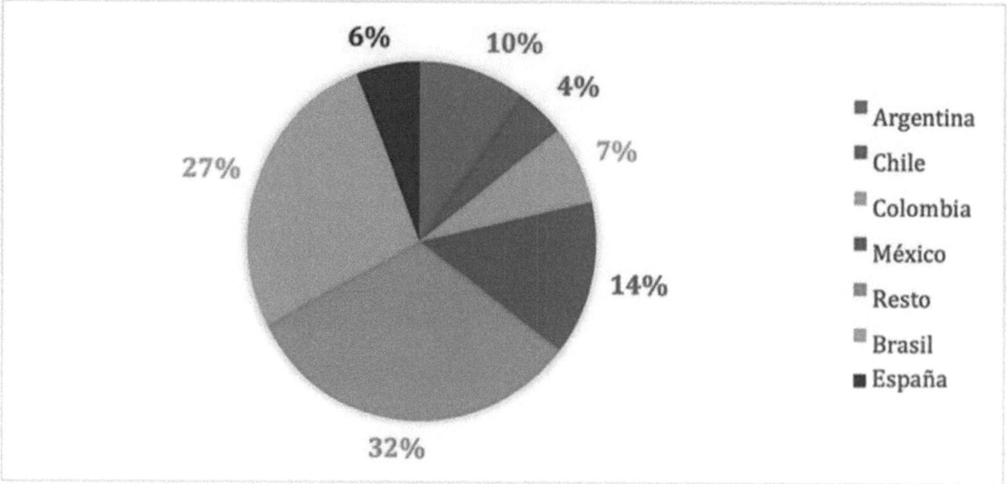

Source: OEI-Observatorio CTS (2021[3]), *Papeles del Observatorio N° 20, Abril 2021: Panorama de la educación superior en Iberoamerica a través de los indicadores de la Red Indices.* http://www.redindices.org/novedades/139-papeles-del-observatorio-n-20-panorama-de-la-educacion-superior-en-iberoamerica-a-traves-de-los-indicadores-de-la-red-indices (accessed on 26 April 2021).

Chile

Chile's higher education structure dates from 1981 when a radical, deep, and somewhat controversial restructuring of the segment took place. It has been maintained since then with some changes. Three types of higher education institutions presently exist: universities, professional institutes, and technical training centres. Among those, only universities are entitled to grant all types of higher education credentials: academic, professional, and technical degrees, requiring five-year programmes for reaching the degree of "Licenciado". They also teach one-year post-graduate diploma programmes; master's degrees, doctoral degrees, and other advanced certificates (e.g. medicine and dentistry) (OECD/The World Bank, 2009[4]). Professional institutes can only grant four-year professional degrees below the bachelor's degree level. (OECD/The World Bank, 2009[4]). Technical training centres can solely offer technical degrees in 2 to 2 1/2 year-programmes (OECD/The World Bank, 2009[4]).

Regarding the system's size, 150 higher education institutions were operating in the country in March of 2020 (59 universities, 39 professional institutes, and 52 technical training centres) (Servicio de Información de Educación Superior SIES, 2020[5]).

Table 15.1. Number of higher education institutions by type, in 2013

Higher education institution type	Institutions (2013)
Public state, CRUCH members	16
Private, not for profit, with public orientation, CRUCH members	9
Private, not for profit, non CRUCH members	35
Universities subtotal	60
Professional institutes	43
Technical training centres	54
Subtotal of non-university institutions	97
Total	157

Source: OECD (2017[6]), *Education in Chile, Reviews of National Policies for Education,* OECD Publishing, Paris, https://doi.org/10.1787/9789264284425-en (accessed on 28 April 2021).

Three groups of autonomous higher education institutions have existed in Chile since 1981 as shown in Table 15.1. One, gathered under the Council of Rectors of Chilean Universities (CRUCH), created in 1954, includes all public-state universities and a group of private, not-for-profit public-oriented institutions. These private universities (9) existed before 1981 or were campuses of private institutions already operating at that time and later evolved into independent entities. All the CRUCH member institutions, public or private, have historically received direct state funding. Recently, two new public universities were created and joined the CRUCH with full status. Also, recently, three private universities, established after 1981, were admitted to the CRUCH, although they are not granted direct state funding, as opposed to all other CRUCH institutions.

A second group includes only private universities created after 1981 and constitutes the bulk of the existing university segment in the country (35). None of them can operate on a for-profit basis since Chilean law does not allow the existence of that type of educational institution.

The third group includes all existing professional institutes and technical training centres (43 and 54, respectively). All these institutions are private although the government is in the process of creating and establishing 15 new public technical training centres, distributed in some regions of the country (OECD, 2017[6]).

Over the past 40 years, higher education in Chile underwent explosive and uncontrolled growth, jumping from fewer than 20 institutions in 1981 to over 150. This growth meant an increase in higher education study opportunities for students of all social conditions since they were complemented by state financing programmes. Notwithstanding, higher education quality deteriorated, triggering the enforcement of more stringent accreditation norms and rules for creating new higher education entities. This has resulted in a serious overall quality drive at most institutions.

Student enrolment grew accordingly with the creation of higher education entities, reaching gross growth rates of over 50% in 2016, as reported earlier (OEI, 2018[1]). In 2020, however, a reduction in the upward trend of the number of applications to higher education institutions occurred, as shown in Table 15.2.

Table 15.2. Total enrolment variation by degree level 2016-2020

Degree level	2016	2017	2018	2019	2020	Percent variation 2016-2020	Percent variation 2019-2020	Enrolment distribution 2020
Undergraduate	1 178 480	1 177 177	1 187 873	1 194 310	1 151 727	-2.3%	-3.6%	94.3%
Graduate	47 584	48 698	46 875	48 391	45 483	-4.4%	-6.0%	3.7%
Diploma	21 114	22 418	27 588	25 803	23 807	-12.8%	-7.7%	1.9%
Total	**1 247 178**	**1 248 293**	**1 262 336**	**1 268 504**	**1 221 017**	**-2.1%**	**-3.7%**	**100.0%**

Source: SIES (2020[5]), *Informe 2020 Matrícula en Educación Superior*, SiES, Santiago, https://www.mifuturo.cl/wp-content/uploads/2020/07/Informe-matricula_2020_SIES.pdf (accessed on 18 March 2021).

The enrolment percentage differentials between female and male participation by field of speciality is a remarkable characteristic of the Chilean higher education system. Table 15.3 displays that in all areas except in two (Science and Technology), when female enrolment percentages have positive values, they are higher than males and when negative, those of males are higher. This is particularly evident in Health, Education, and Social Science. What is even more striking is that in those areas where females show higher enrolment differentials, there is also an upward trend for the considered years.

Table 15.3. Undergraduate enrolment percentage differential between female and male, by field of speciality, between 2005 and 2020

Field of speciality	2005	2011	2016	2017	2018	2019	2020
Administration, business, and commerce	-1.96	5.94	10.25	10.04	11.41	11.95	12.65
Agriculture, forestry, fisheries, and veterinary medicine	-12.21	-5.02	1.5	2.23	4.22	6.41	10.57
Art and architecture	-7.45	-2.30	0.04	1.85	2.51	3.35	4.70
Science	0.04	-1.26	-7.39	-7.21	-7.74	-8.42	-9.99
Social science	38.28	38.24	40.35	38.86	41.29	41.89	42.46
Law	1.84	3.64	6.59	8.54	8.93	10.01	11.64
Education	39.78	37.02	45.43	47.92	50.76	50.38	50.95
Humanities	17.01	11.52	10.71	11.83	9.77	9.19	10.32
Health	39.22	47.17	52.26	52.23	52.08	52.34	52.31
Technology	-63.91	-59.63	-56.22	-56.78	-58.77	-59.87	-59.63

Source: CNED (2020[7]), *Informe Tendencias de Estadísticas de Educación Superior por Sexo*, CNED, Santiago. https://www.cned.cl/sites/default/files/2020_informe_matricula_por_sexo_0.pdf (accessed on 18 March 2021).

CLA+ outreach process in Latin America and Spain

The Council for Aid to Education (CAE), through its Fellow in Latin America, based in Santiago de Chile, deployed an outreach effort in the region between 2017 and 2021. Selected higher education entities, including universities and institutes as well as ministries, university associations, and supporting agencies were contacted. Approach and information activities took considerable time and consisted of an iterative process including information provision and discussion as well as question-formulating and answering between the Fellow and each of the institutions.

Latin America is understood here as composed only of countries in South America, Central America, and the Caribbean since Mexico's participation in CLA+ was initially handled separately. Nevertheless, after 2020 Mexican institutions were also included, as depicted below.

Duration and difficulty of the outreach process could be attributed to two sources, namely: a widespread but incipient development of the General Studies curriculum where Critical Thinking constitutes a key set of competencies; and a generalised misunderstanding of characteristics and a pervasive distrust of standardised testing.

Considering the high value attributed to university autonomy in Latin America, most contacts with universities and institutes were individual. Ministries were only reached for them to be informed about the existence of the CLA+ Study in the region. Nevertheless, collaboration from university independent supporting entities active in the region such as the Centro Interuniversitario de Desarrrollo (CINDA) and the Consejo de Educación Superior, in Paraguay, were sought and enlisted.

Up to 2020, only four universities, all from Chile, participated in CLA+, although several other promising contacts were already pending at the end of the outreach process and could not be finalised.

Table 15.4. CLA+ outreach in the region and Spain

Higher education associations and supporting entities	**04**
Ministries of Education	**03**
Higher education institutions (universities and others)	**64**
Bolivia	01
Chile	28
Colombia	13
Dominican Republic	03
Ecuador	01
Mexico	36
Nicaragua	01
Paraguay	08
Peru	09
Spain	01
TOTAL	**71**

Policy context for CLA+

Agreements signed between CAE and CLA+ participating institutions prescribe that institutional-level data are not to be disclosed together with entity identification. Consequently, the report anonymises individual institutions' results, although for contextualisation some of their characteristics are shown and the four institutions are labelled with capital letters (W, X, Y, and Z).

The CLA+ participating universities in the region were all located in Chile. Though the approach to universities in Chile was carried out on an individual basis, direct contact was made concurrently with the Undersecretary of Education who later became Minister of Education. Later, the new Office of the Undersecretary of Higher Education was created, and contacts followed with the person appointed to that post. The purpose of that approach was exclusively to inform governmental authorities about CLA+, its characteristics, and the intended recruitment of institutions in the country to join the study.

Both authorities were extremely positive about the potential implementation of CLA+ in Chile due to two main reasons. The first one dealt with the already growing relevance of Critical Thinking as part of General Studies in higher education both globally and in Chile. The second stemmed from the CLA+'s high quality and objectivity vis-à-vis internal university assessment tools, designed and administered as it is by an external entity.

All four Chilean participating universities are private, though one has a public orientation and belongs to the Council of Rectors (CRUCH) while the other three do not belong to CRUCH.

University W

University W, which is outside CRUCH, was founded over 30 years ago and operates in various regions of the Chilean territory. It offers undergraduate and graduate programmes in most fields of speciality, organised into seven *facultades* (groups of schools) and operating research centres. This institution, with over 25 000 students, has successfully passed all prescribed cycles of institutional accreditation by the National Accreditation Commission (CNA-Chile) and has a growing research component. It started preparing for participation in the CLA+ in autumn 2017 (southern hemisphere).

This was the first university in the region and the country to enrol in the study. The main motivation of its president stemmed from the need to assess the outcomes of a new educational model being implemented at the time. Such a competency-based type model, applied for the first time in this university, introduced strong General Studies curricula effective in all programmes, including cognitive, affective, and performance elements. CLA+ was very timely as it could fulfil the university's hard-data results requirements about student achievement in the cognitive component of the General Studies curricula model.

University X

University X belongs to the same group as W, and was founded in the early 1990s. It now enrols 7 000 students and includes most undergraduate programmes. It has also been successfully accredited by CNA in all cases. It operates six *facultades* and 12 research centres, with significant growth of the graduate segment in the past decade. It participated in CLA+ in 2020 over a timespan that, due to the pandemic, covered autumn and winter (southern hemisphere).

This institution has implemented significant curricular changes and a strong learning achievement assessment component. It grants high relevance to General Studies as well, establishing its own department. Consequently, CLA+ represented a timely and useful tool for standardised evaluation of Critical Thinking student achievement. Its approach was to apply CLA+ to gauge student achievement as the curriculum transformations were implemented and affected subsequent classes.

University Y

University Y is part of the same group as W and X, has over 30 years of existence, and is located in major urban locations. It has over ten *facultades* and several research centres. Presently, it enrols over 40 000 students in undergraduate and graduate programmes. It has successfully passed all the National Accreditation Commission's mandatory institutional accreditation processes and has also obtained institutional accreditation abroad. Its first participation in CLA+ started in the summer of 2020 (southern hemisphere) and is still underway because of the pandemic, into the first semester of 2021.

As mentioned, University Y is institutionally accredited in the United States and although the Chilean system does not yet require institutions to provide evidence on General Studies student achievement, the U.S. regional agencies do. After exploring alternatives for fulfilling this need, University Y joined CLA+ in 2020 motivated by the need for formal provision of evidence as an institutional accreditation requirement. Nevertheless, the university also uses CLA+ data for diagnosing entering students' mastery of Critical Thinking competencies; for gauging further learning of those same skills during university studies by testing the graduating class; and for obtaining an indication of value-added learning in those competencies as the differential between both classes.

University Z

University Z is a mature full member of the Council of Rectors with over 90 years of academic life and a history of very high-level institutional accreditation accomplishments. Its enrolment exceeds 15 000 students in undergraduate and graduate programmes (doctoral, master's, and diploma). It has nine *facultades* and several research entities, and operates several campuses in a focused location in Chile. The initial CLA+ participation of University Z, due to the constraints posed by the COVID-19 pandemic, has been extended for almost two years, having started in 2019.

This institution recently updated its undergraduate and graduate education model. Such a change, on the one hand, implies adopting a competency-based curricular structure. On the other hand, it improves the definition of its education coverage into three broad areas of study: disciplinary, professional, and fundamental competencies (General Studies). A particular new emphasis is placed on General Studies, thus including eight different components, one of them being the Scientific Competency Area. This area requires students to develop scientific capacity including analytic, abstract, and critical thinking for problem solving, knowledge generation and self-learning skills. CLA+ was adopted as a valid and high-quality standardised assessment tool for evaluating the Scientific Competency Area.

In addition, this institution developed a special project for improving teacher-education programmes, funded by the state. This government grant support requires that all participating students be tested for achievement in those constructs included in Critical Thinking. Once again, CLA+ came in handy for assessing the entire 2020 entering class and its follow-up over the first three years of study.

Despite the small number of participant institutions in the region, the CLA+ application's design versatility must be highlighted in the case of Chile. Although the actual application designs for each university will be described further on, it is relevant to point out here that in the four considered institutions where policy contexts and needs were different, the battery was able to adapt to those contexts and fulfil those different demands. In one case the purpose was summative assessment; in another it was diagnosis and obtention of learning gains (effect-size); in yet another, it was certification purposes evaluation; and in the last one, it combined cross-sectional learning achievement assessment in some programmes and longitudinal gains follow-up for a complete teacher education cohort over several years.

Process of implementation of the CLA+

As mentioned before, the outreach effort aimed at Chilean universities took place on an individual basis through direct contacts with each university. Initial contacts in Chile started in 2017 and were the first to begin in the region.

The battery test forms, originally in English, were already translated into Spanish, adapted to the language usage of South America, and were provided by CAE to the participating universities through an interactive Internet platform.

University W

The administration process at University W included three phases. A team from the Academic Vice-President's Office took charge of the process, information exchange with CAE took place, and regular meetings were held. The preparation phase, among the university, the Fellow in Latin America, and the New York-based CAE team, began in April 2018.

Issues addressed included the appointment of counterparts and task definitions on each side; mutual exchange of requirements; technical aspects definition; agreement on the structure of the application design; decisions on the sample design, selection, and approval; relevant dates definition; training of university application teams; and solving of emerging problems. A deliberate, campus-stratified sample and a cross-sectional effect-size analysis design were agreed upon, including the 2018 entering and graduation classes.

The four-week implementation phase comprised the sample selection, identification and contacting of subjects, and testing platform trials. The sample was selected, and its database was uploaded to the CAE platform, and subject identities verified at the access to the testing facilities. Testing was part of the regular teaching activities and participation was consequently mandatory. Notwithstanding, according to Chilean law, every participating student signed an affidavit *Consentimiento Informado* (Informed Agreement), authorising the university to use his/her results for research and evaluation purposes. If the person did not sign the document, he/she would be deleted from the sample with no consequences whatsoever and replaced by another who would be willing to participate. In University W, no student rejections occurred and a low absentee rate was observed.

The administration phase was simultaneously executed in one week and students were tested in groups of approximately 30 subjects on-site at the university computer facilities and using institutional equipment. The administration was uneventful with a high completion rate of the sample. A total of 562 students belonging to the 2018 entering and graduation classes from the *facultades* of Administration and Business;

Architecture and Construction; Education; Health Sciences; Law; and Social Sciences and Humanities in all four campuses were tested, as shown in Table 15.5.

Table 15.5. Subjects sample distribution at University W, by class and campus

Class	Campus				
	Campus I	Campus II	Campus III	Campus IV	Students
Entering 2018	86	75	65	62	288
Graduating 2018	57	49	92	76	274
Total	**143**	**124**	**157**	**138**	**562**

University X

University X was the second institution to join CLA+, in early 2019, and few meetings between the University authorities and the CAE Fellow for Latin America were deemed necessary. The decision was fast, and the process ended with the actual assessment considering the same customary three phases. The preparation phase included two video conferences with the CAE New York team for sample and application design discussion. The University's General Studies Department head and some members oversaw the process and a swift information exchange process with CAE took place with regular communications and two video meetings. The issues addressed were the same as those covered in the previous case. The CAE Fellow proposed University X to receive feedback from Universidad W's experience with CLA+. Contact was established, and interactions took place between both teams.

A deliberate, field-of-study programme-stratified sample, and a cross-sectional effect size analysis design, were planned. In this case, the comparison included three cohorts since student achievement on General Studies curriculum effects was to be explored over three subsequent classes.

The original implementation plan was altered by the effects of social unrest in the country and the COVID-19 pandemic. Consequently, only students belonging to the 2019 entering class could be tested on-site at university facilities, using institutional computers in October and November of that year. Those belonging to the 2017 and 2015 cohorts who could not take the test in the first place were scheduled for the online proctored mode application in 2020. The 2017 entering class was tested between November and December of 2020 as well as a small segment of the 2015 entering class, thus the planned three-class comparison was accomplished by only two. Since University X wants to build a follow-up of its General Studies curriculum application results over time, another application was agreed with CAE for 2021, including, this time, three entering classes: 2017, 2019, and 2021.

A similar process to that of University W was applied in X and participating students were selected, the database uploaded to the CAE platform and subject identities verified upon access to the testing facilities for the 2019 entering class. For the bulk of the 2017 entering class sample, proctored online testing protocol was used, and student identity was verified by the proctors before subjects accessed the testing platform. In this case, 5 groups of approximately 25 students and 1 proctor each were organised. Each student used his/her computing device (computer or tablet).

For X University students, the application was voluntary. This mode required a deeper and longer effort on the part of the university team to convince and follow up on subjects. This was expected to affect results since students voluntarily chose to participate. Initial absenteeism was higher than in the case of W and despite follow-up efforts implemented by the university team, final figures ran short of expectations. As legally prescribed by law, students also signed an agreement affidavit.

A total sample of 308 students belonging to the 2019 and 2017 entering classes was tested belonging to the *facultades* of Education; Engineering; Health Sciences; Medical Sciences; Science and Technology; and Social Science, as shown in Table 15.6.

Table 15.6. Subjects sample distribution at University X, by class

Entering class	Students
2019	220
2017	108
Total	**328**

University Y

Although it was an early contact in Chile, it took time and several meetings for University Y to join CLA+. The first video conference was held as early as January 2019 with the CAE Fellow and the New York CAE team before the decision and signature of the agreement. The Director of the Humanities Department was appointed to be in charge of the CLA+ application. During the preparation phase, one video conference was held in September 2019 and several contacts took place with the CAE Fellow. Frequent e-mail correspondence was exchanged with the CAE New York team as well for discussing the design and the sample. Issues addressed were coincident with those covered by universities W and X. The CAE Fellow proposed University Y to receive feedback from Universities W and Z experience in the application of CLA+ and interactions occurred between Z and Y. Since the faculty official in charge of CLA+ at this university had a good user-level knowledge of assessment issues, preparation and application phases were swiftly organised and management was autonomous. From the start, University Y decided its participation in CLA+ would be cyclical in the sense that the battery would be applied on a biennial basis to serially gauge their learning achievement in General Studies.

A deliberate, field-of-study programme-stratified sample, and a cross-sectional effect size analysis design, were planned for the 2020 and 2017 entering classes. Both sample and design were submitted by the university and approved by the scientists at the CAE New York team. Results of this application were considered among the evidence required by a U.S. regional agency for accreditation validation in 2021 in addition to providing feedback on these classes' General Studies curriculum learning results.

As in the case of University X, the implementation plan was negatively affected by the 2019 period of social unrest in the country and the COVID-19 pandemic. This delayed administration until late 2020 and required use of an online proctored protocol instead of the on-site procedure originally planned. In addition to the delay, the sample could not be entirely tested during this period and the remainder underwent further testing in the first semester of 2021 to complete the graduating class component. In keeping with the university's intention of a longitudinal series of CLA+, a potential new testing process is expected for 2023.

The mechanics of the process at University Y were like those at W and X. Students in the sample were chosen, the database uploaded to the CAE platform and subject identities verified by proctors before accessing the online testing platform. The administering of the test to both cohorts, which was supervised by externally hired proctors trained by the university, took place between September and December of 2020. Testing of the remaining 2017 entering class is still pending and should be completed during the first half of 2021. Each proctor oversaw approximately 100 students. Each student used his/her computing device (computer or tablet). Test-taking for students was voluntary. And as was the case for Universities W and X, students signed affidavits.

A total of 882 students belonging to the 2020 and 2017 entering classes were tested out of 11 *facultades*. The sample shown in Table 15.7 focused on Economics and Business; Education; Humanities and Social Sciences; Engineering; Law; Medicine; and Nursing. The other two groups tested, although on a lesser scale, were Exact Sciences and Life Sciences.

Table 15.7. Subjects sample distribution at University Y, by class year

Entering class	Students
2020	662
2017	220
Total	882

University Z

This institution was the second in the country to agree to participate in CLA+, in January 2019. The CAE Fellow started consultations with its top officials in July 2018. A video conference attended by the Academic Vice-President and his staff, the CAE New York team and the Fellow in Latin America was held in August of that year to finalise the decision.

A team led by the Student Development Director, which included three other officials, was appointed to be in charge of the CLA+ application. Before actual applications started, the team held three remote meetings with the CAE Fellow and the New York team over similar issues as those covered in the other three Chilean participating universities. In this case, it was helpful that a multidimensional team (including administration, computer, and statistics professionals) was in charge as sample and design structures posed multiple, diverse, and complex challenges.

University Z's CLA+ participation was different from the rest due to testing being performed over several years and over two different cohorts. The cohorts consisted of students from the Engineering and the Teacher Education programmes. For Engineering, deliberate samples of each year's entering and graduating classes were defined. For Education, the entering class was tested on a census basis. Different comparison designs were applied for each of the cohorts. In the case of Engineering, a yearly cross-sectional, effect size comparison of entering and graduating classes was included. In the case of Education, two comparisons were planned: one was a yearly, cross-sectional, effect size, class, census comparison; and the other was a longitudinal census comparison of entering classes over three years, starting in 2019. Both sample/census structures and comparison designs were submitted, discussed, and approved through contacts between the university and the scientists of the CAE New York team. All subjects were to be tested on-site at the university computer facilities, using institutional equipment.

As in the X and Y universities' cases, the 2019 period of social unrest in Chile and the COVID-19 pandemic caused serious drawbacks in University Z's testing implementation plan that year. The original application for 2019 was expected to finish in December of 2019, and it did with only partial coverage of the 2019 entering classes for both cohorts and no subjects from the graduating classes at all. Consequently, those from the 2019 entering class subjects who had not been tested were tested over several sessions from August to December 2020. This required the use of an online proctored protocol instead of the on-site mode originally planned. Adding to the delay, the 2019 graduating class subjects could not be tested at all so no cross-sectional effect size analyses could be performed for the 2019 data as only one-shot testing had occurred. As University Z planned a longitudinal series of applications of CLA+ between August and December of 2020, a testing process parallel to that for remaining 2019 subjects was implemented using online proctoring for the corresponding populations and classes belonging to that year.

The test-taking process at University Z had only minor differences from those of W, X, and Y. Students in the sample were chosen by the university and the database was uploaded to the CAE platform. In 2019, supervisors verified subject identities before entering the testing facilities. In the 2020 online administering of the test, proctors checked test-takers' identifies before they accessed the testing platform. University supervisors and proctors were trained by the university and groups of approximately 50 students were organised in both modes. In the online mode, five proctors oversaw 10 students each and each student used his/her computing device (computer or tablet). As planned, new applications should be performed in 2021 although only cross-sectional effect size analyses will be calculated, thus discontinuing the planned longitudinal trend. Test-taking at University Z was voluntary and took place during regular teaching hours. This option required students to be followed individually to ensure attendance at testing sessions. Consent was verbally provided via telephone contact. Only students who formally agreed to be tested were provided with the test platform link.

As shown in Table 15.8, 1 341 students, belonging to the 2019 and 2020 cohorts were tested, from the Engineering and Teacher Education programmes. Students from five of the *facultades* participated: Agronomic and Food Sciences; Economics and Business; Engineering; Philosophy and Education; Sea Sciences and Geography; and Science.

Table 15.8. Subjects sample distribution at University Z, by class

Class	Students
Entering 2019	567
Entering 2020	623
Graduating 2020	151
Total	**1 341**

Main results

University W

In this institution's design, which included comparing entering and graduating classes samples for 2018, the mean total score is higher for the graduating class than for the entering class. Standard deviations (SD) are very close in value, indicating a similar spread of scores in both classes. The effect size (ES) value shows that, as expected, the graduating class performed better than the entering group.

In the Performance Task (PT) scores, both the entering and graduating classes mean scores are higher than their total scores. The graduating class mean PT score is higher than that of the entering class and their SD values are identical. There is a positive ES, very close to that of the total score, and a reduced effect of the university curriculum in this type of Critical Thinking skill may be concluded. For the Structured Response (SR) scores, the graduating class has a higher mean score than mean scores in both the total and the Performance Task and the SD is lower than that of the entering class. The ES in this case is lower than that of the total. The mean performance level of both classes is Basic.

Table 15.9. Scores in CLA+ at University W, by class

Class 2018	N	Mean Score	Standard Deviation	25th Percentile Score	75th Percentile Score	Percentile Rank Mean Score	Effect size
Entering PT	288	1 100	174	1 001	1 226	76	
Entering SR	288	1 049	170	921	1 172	54	
Entering Total	**288**	**1 074**	**136**	**982**	**1 176**	**68**	
Graduating PT	274	1 121	174	1 046	1 226	51	0.12
Graduating SR	274	1 055	164	930	1 711	10	0.04
Graduating Total	**274**	**1 092**	**135**	**991**	**1 187**	**26**	**0.13**

Performance levels percentages of the entering class show a right skew and a more normal distribution appears for the graduating class with bimodal values. Furthermore, only for the graduating class do a few Advanced level cases exist, thus indicating a more scattered general performance.

Figure 15.2. Performance levels percentages at University W, entering class

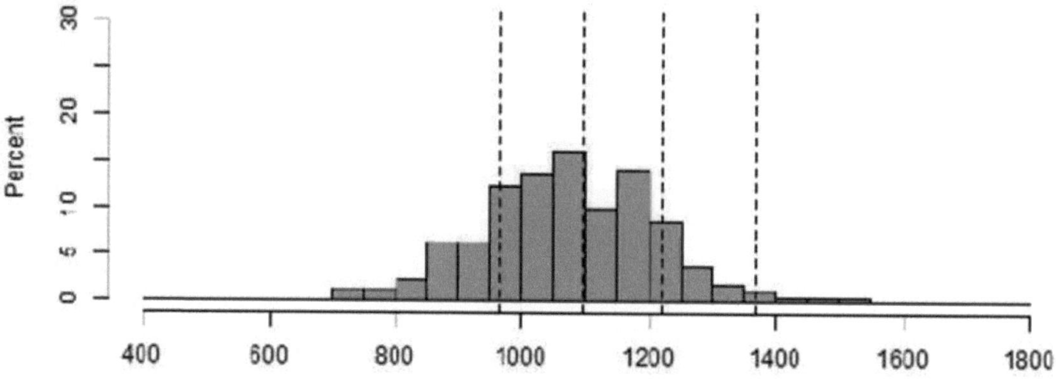

Figure 15.3. Performance levels percentages at University W, graduating class

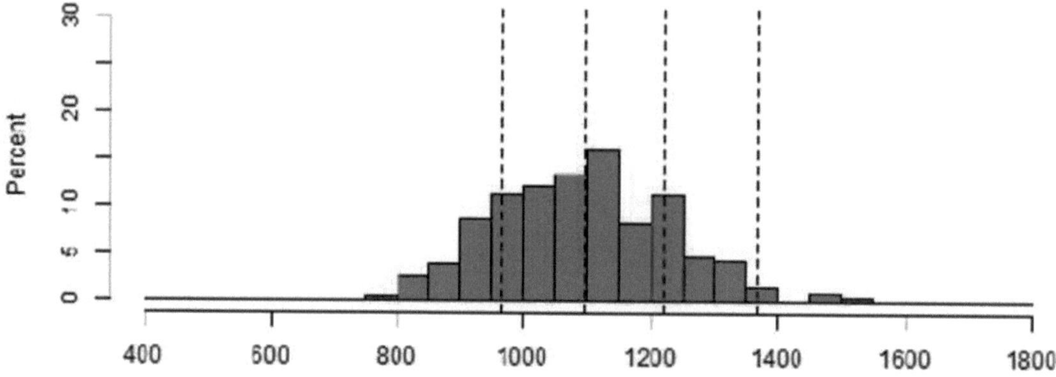

University X

This institution, in 2019, did not complete testing of the graduating class and only completed that of the entering and the third-year classes.

Consequently, smaller differences between classes and values of ES should be expected. Mean total scores in both classes are almost identical and SDs are close. The total score effect size (ES) value is small and negative, thus suggesting a small effect of the new General Studies curriculum. Performance Task (PT) mean scores are higher for the entering class and SDs of both classes are close. ES is negative and half a standard deviation in value. The reason for this absence of learning effect of the new General Studies curriculum could stem from several sources, among those the General Studies' insufficient achievement effect on the third-year class or a high initial skill level of the entering class. Results for the Structured Response (SR) section look more as expected since the third-year class mean score is higher than that of the entering class. SDs are different and the entering class shows a more heterogeneous performance. The ES is positive and close to 0.4 SD.

Table 15.10. Scores in CLA+ at University X, by class

Class	N	Mean Score	Standard Deviation	25th Percentile Score	75th Percentile Score	Percentile Rank Mean Score	Effect size
Entering 2019 PT	220	1 165	116	1 091	1 286	93	
Entering 2019 SR	220	1 040	153	919	1 137	53	
Entering 2019 Total	**220**	**1 104**	**101**	**1 033**	**1 170**	**78**	
Third Year 2019 PT	108	1 105	110	1 012	1 181	38	-0.52
Third Year 2019 SR	**108**	**1 099**	**140**	**993**	**1 201**	**26**	**0.39**

The mean performance level for both classes in this institution is Proficient. The performance level percentage distribution for both the entering and third-year classes show a right skew. The third-year class distribution is bimodal and both classes have close mode values, the entering class distribution having a few Advanced level outliers.

Figure 15.4. Performance levels percentages at University X, entering class

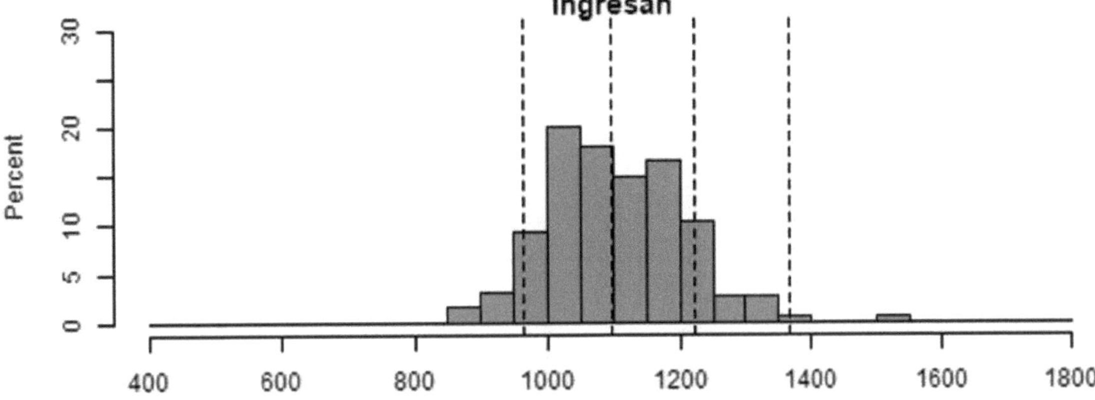

Figure 15.5. Performance levels percentages at University X, third-year class

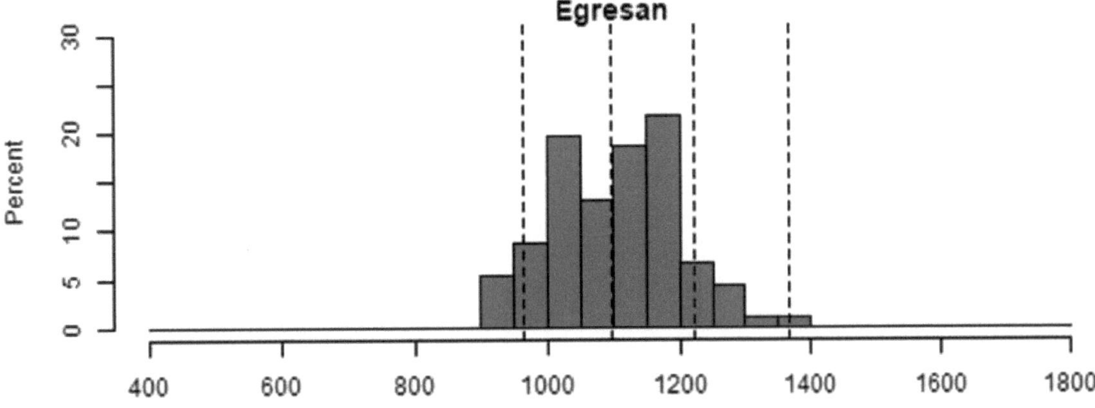

University Y

At University Y, both 2020 entering and graduating classes were tested online. As Table 15.11 shows, total mean scores have a substantial difference in favour of the graduating group with over a 1.0 standard deviation ES, thus suggesting higher and more homogeneous performance in the General Studies achievement of the graduating class. For both classes, the SD value and the spread are close.

As for the total score, a positive difference in favour of the graduating class is shown in Table 15.11 for the Performance Task (PT) results as well as over a 1 SD effect size value. In this case, the spread for both groups is also fairly close. All this may be explained by the acquisition of higher-level competencies by the graduating class subjects during their education at University Y. For the Structured Response (SR) scores, a positive, although lower, difference in favour of the graduating class is found as compared to the total and Performance Task scores as well as a positive and lesser value of ES, somewhat over 0.6 SD, is observed. These results can be interpreted as confirming conclusions derived from the previously analysed scores. Spread remains very similar for both classes.

Table 15.11. Scores in CLA+ at University Y, by class

Class	N	Mean Score	Standard Deviation	25th Percentile Score	75th Percentile Score	Percentile Rank Mean Score	Effect size
Entering 2020 PT	662	1 004	131	911	1 091	37	
Entering 2020 SR	662	1 060	168	935	1 171	58	
Entering **2020 Total**	**662**	**1 033**	**121**	**942**	**1 114**	**49**	
Graduating 2020 PT	220	1 144	135	1 046	1 226	65	1.07
Graduating 2020 SR	**220**	**1 165**	**163**	**1 046**	**1 288**	**64**	**0.63**

At University Y the general performance level for the entering class is Basic and Proficient for the graduating group. For the performance levels percentage distribution of the entering class, a right skew, a higher mode value, and a few Advanced Level cases as well, are observed. For the graduating class, the distribution shape is closer to normalcy with a lower mode and more abundant Advanced level percentage cases. All these features concur with earlier comments about University Y results.

Figure 15.6. Performance levels percentages at University Y, entering class

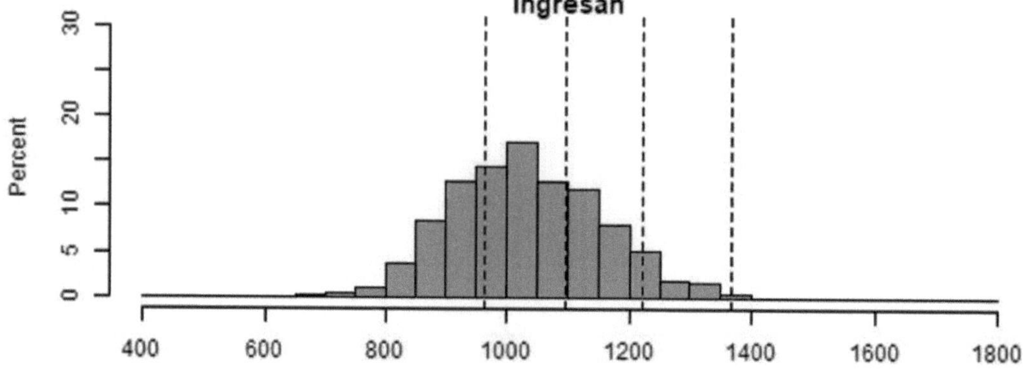

Figure 15.7. Performance levels percentages at University Y, graduating class

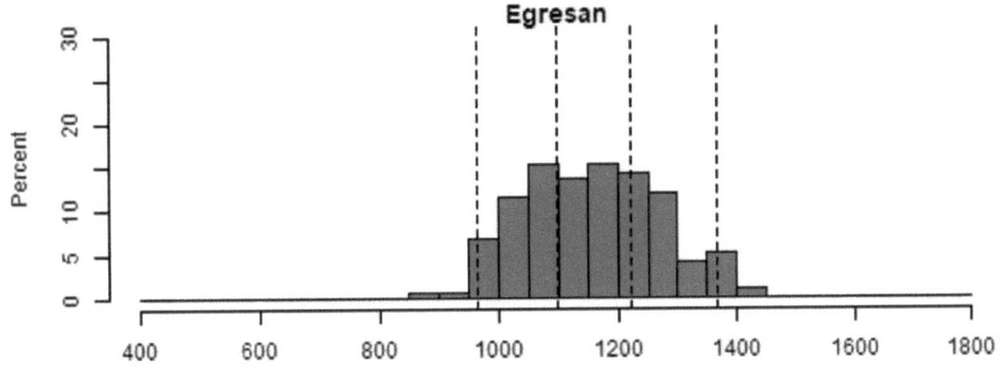

University Z

University Z held testing in two windows. The first one was between August and December 2019, using the on-site mode and university computers, and the second from August to December 2020 using an online proctored protocol and students' equipment due to pandemic constraints. Since the 2019 graduating class could not be tested due to social unrest in the country, available results for that year correspond only to the entering class. In 2020, both classes were examined and ES was calculated. In 2019 the mean score of the Performance Task is higher than the total and the Selected Response scores, thus suggesting that the entering class had a better initial status in the connected higher mental processes with that task.

Table 15.12. Scores in CLA+ at University Z, entering class 2019

Scores	N	Mean	Standard Deviation	25th Percentile	75th Percentile
Performance Task	567	1 171	145	1 091	1 271
Selected Response	567	1 122	178	983	1 245
Total	**567**	**1 145**	**124**	**1 065**	**1 237**

The performance level counts show a right skew with a median close to 1 110 score points and very few cases in the Advanced level (beyond 1 400 score points) area.

Figure 15.8. Performance levels subject count at University Z, entering class 2019

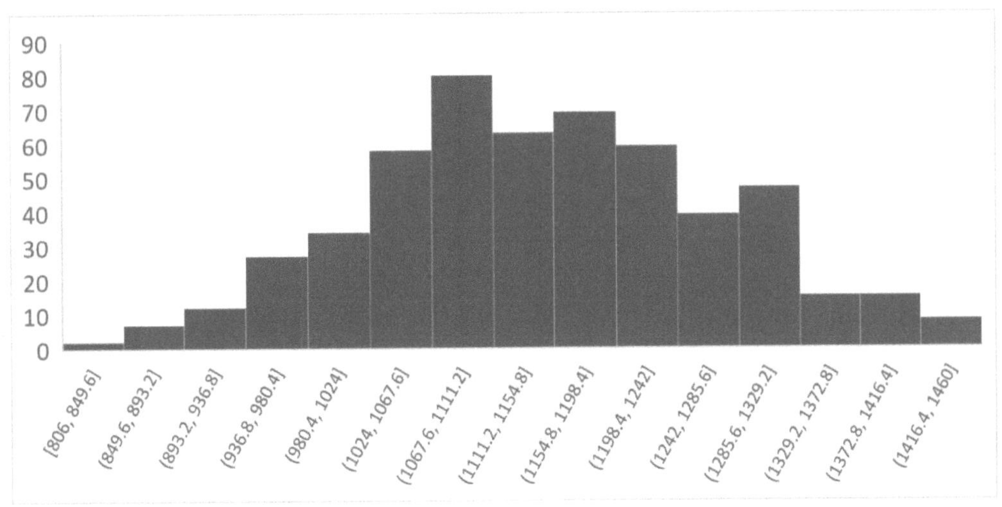

In 2020 total scores show a higher mean value for the graduating class and close variance values. A small positive ES also appears, thus indicating a somewhat stronger Critical Thinking entering class. The Performance Task mean scores show even a smaller difference between classes than the total mean scores as well as a very low ES, thus suggesting a slightly better performing entering class in the tested construct. The Selected Response mean score shows higher figures although similar low differences as the previous mean scores and the ES as well.

Table 15.13. Scores in CLA+ at University Z, by class

Class	N	Mean Score	Standard Deviation	25th Percentile Score	75th Percentile Score	Percentile Rank Mean Score	Effect size
Entering PT	623	1 094	107	1 046	1 136	75	
Entering SR	623	1 154	171	1 041	1 273	92	
Entering Total	**623**	**1 127**	**111**	**1 053**	**1 206**	**86**	
Graduating PT	151	1 103	121	1 046	1 181	38	0.08
Graduating SR	151	1 178	171	1 061	1 302	73	0.14
Graduating Total	**151**	**1 146**	**109**	**1 076**	**1 221**	**57**	**0.17**

For this university, the general performance level is Proficient for both classes. Both performance levels percentage distributions approach normalcy, with few extreme cases at both ends and the graduating class is bimodal.

Figure 15.9. Performance levels percentages at University Z, 2020, entering class

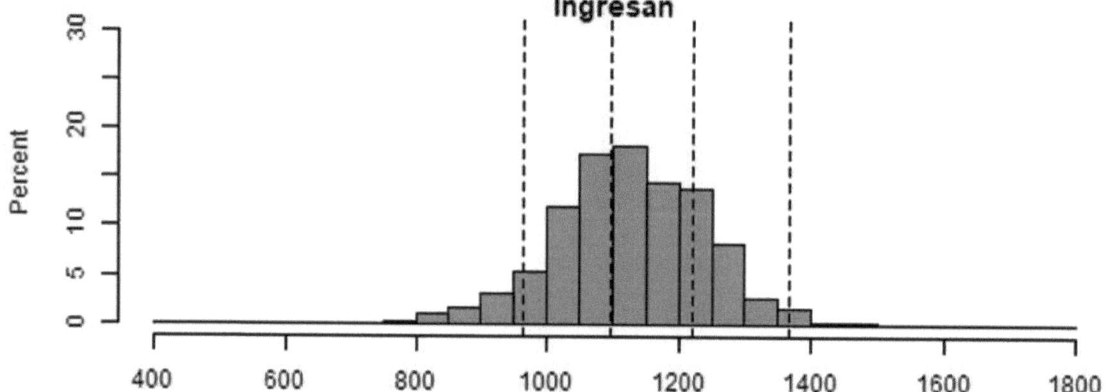

Figure 15.10. Performance levels percentages at University Z, 2020, graduating class

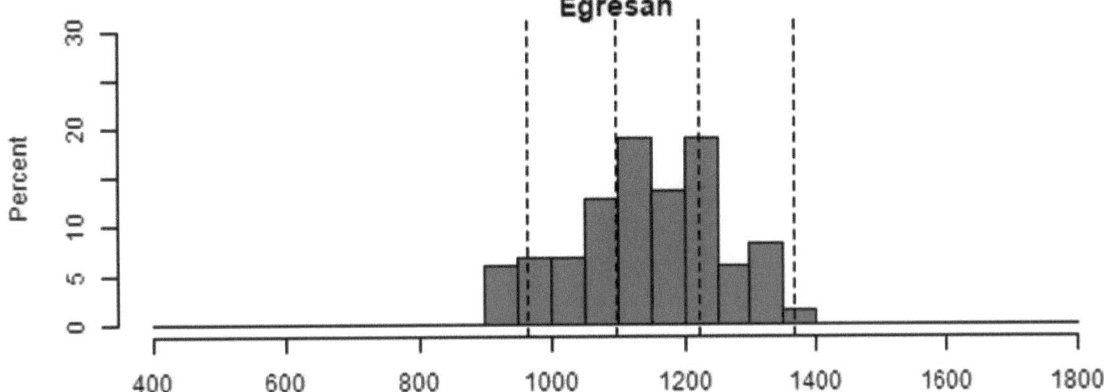

Policy implications and lessons learnt

Despite the case-study origin of the available evidence, a prudent and general implication is the increasing importance assigned to Critical Thinking as part of the General Studies curriculum in Chilean higher education. Among the four institutions reviewed, two of them, Y and Z, included results for General Studies student achievement data as evidence to be submitted to foreign (U.S.) and Chilean institutional accreditation bodies as one of the policy reasons for participating in the study.

A related aspect is that all Chilean universities involved consider General Studies as part of the curricular changes they recently implemented. In two of the cases, this affects their educational model and required hard evidence of student performance for ongoing adjustments of those new policies.

A third policy issue is a greater awareness in the country of the need for integrating assessment actions into higher education. In three of the Chilean institutions, W, X, and Z, diagnostic information was sought from the study results, and in all four of them, the study data was used for formative purposes, either at the student or system level.

Lastly, acquaintance with and a drive to use assessment instruments of high technical quality are becoming the rule in Chilean higher education institutions. In this sense, standardised testing is recovering its prestige mainly by using performance tasks and improved selected response items such as in CLA+ that allow for valid, reliable, and comparable assessments of higher mental processes.

Some of the lessons learnt deal with the outreach process. The direct outreach approach proved to be valid as governmental authorities acknowledged that they could not validly approach universities on academic issues. As well, participating universities reacted positively to being contacted directly. It is, however, worth considering contacting higher academic education organisations as they can contribute to assessment credibility and allow for a more efficient and collective outreach to universities and other higher education institutions.

Another aspect is the length of the decision process in joining the study

Participating in a joint assessment venture requires careful thought not only financially but in terms of institutional image as well. Nevertheless, this makes the whole process long and sometimes cumbersome. Consequently, the assessment provider must use experience and provide clear-cut and timely information.

Due to the absence of in-house technical assessment capacity in most universities in the region, sample structure and comparison design are two issues demanding close and expert support from the provider. Scientific-based help in these matters is essential.

As this is an international study, thus involving different countries, languages, and cultures, the participation of a locally positioned member of the study staff is very important. Although language is a primary concern, in most cases there is also a need to familiarise institutions with the ways and means of up-to-date assessment and to adapt the relationship to local procedures.

Verification of technical computer and communication issues by the provider using permanent support and supervision and trial runs is very important, particularly under prevailing pandemic conditions requiring the use of secure platforms and proctoring. In this same respect, the online mode confronts students with technological demands that some of them are not able to comply with. The rise in the number of young people from lower-income echelons having access to higher education in Chile and the region has meant that many students cannot cope with online proctored application requirements because they lack access to adequate equipment, software or connections.

Next steps and prospects

Contacts established with institutions in Chile and the rest of the region reveal a generalised awareness of the General Studies component in higher education curricula critically affecting graduates' ability to perform in an information society. This triggers the need to ensure that those competencies are attained by students, and that reliable and credible evidence about it is generated for certification purposes for graduates, employers, and institutional and governmental authorities.

There is also a growing tendency for higher education accrediting entities to demand hard evidence from academic institutions about the added value they contribute to their students, particularly on the so-called "fundamental competencies" included in the Critical Thinking construct assessed by CLA+.

Consequently, the initial assessment trend developed for some Chilean universities with CLA+ requires expansion to the rest of the region's higher education institutions. Three out of the four Chilean institutions whose participation was analysed here have already planned and subscribed agreements with CAE for subsequent participation. Unfortunately, hurdles – some, hopefully, transitory – are presently hampering this extension to other entities.

Notwithstanding, even if elements such as the pandemic are, we hope, transitory, some of its effects are here to stay, such as the growth of remote teaching, learning modes and, foremost, assessment modes. Most likely, education will never be the same as before COVID-19 and assessment systems such as CLA+ will have to consider relying substantially on fully remote modes of application.

Another hurdle affecting regional expansion in Latin America is the lack of funding. Although CLA+ has a comparatively moderate cost, several institutions are willing to participate but cannot pay for its application. Consequently, there is a need for motivating national, regional and global funding entities to contribute resources either to CAE to generate programmes in Latin America or directly to higher education institutions in the region so that they can take advantage of this unique assessment opportunity.

In the psychometrics aspect, the CLA+ diversity of item types could be supplemented with other forms of questions. At present, this is the single available battery able to validly assess competencies that include higher mental processes. Another aspect to improve stems from the very essence of the competency approach which considers three components: cognitive, performative, and affective. Today's CLA+ battery includes the first two Critical Thinking competencies. The third, which is the affective realm, is still to be developed and included in the battery. This realm should consider testing some of the soft skills related to the main Critical Thinking construct.

References

CNED (2020), *Informe Tendencias de Estadísticas de Educación Superior por Sexo*, CNED, Santiago, https://www.cned.cl/sites/default/files/2020_informe_matricula_por_sexo_0.pdf (accessed on 18 March 2021). [7]

OECD (2017), *Education in Chile*, Reviews of National Policies for Education, OECD Publishing, Paris, https://doi.org/10.1787/9789264284425-en. [6]

OECD/The World Bank (2009), *Reviews of National Policies for Education: Tertiary Education in Chile 2009*, Reviews of National Policies for Education, OECD Publishing, Paris, https://doi.org/10.1787/9789264051386-en. [4]

OEI (2018), *Panorama de la Educación Superior en Iberoamérica a través de los indicadores de la Red Indices*, OEI, Buenos Aires, https://oei.org.uy/uploads/files/news/Oei/191/panorama-de-la-educacion-superior-iberoamericana-version-octubre-2018.pdf (accessed on 18 March 2021). [1]

OEI-Observatorio CTS (2021), *Papeles del Observatorio Nº 20, Abril 2021: Panorama de la Educación Superior en Iberoamerica a través de los indicadores de la Red Indices*, OEI, Buenos Aires, http://www.redindices.org/novedades/139-papeles-del-observatorio-n-20-panorama-de-la-educacion-superior-en-iberoamerica-a-traves-de-los-indicadores-de-la-red-indices (accessed on 28 April 2021). [3]

Servicio de Información de Educación Superior SIES (2020), "Informe matrícula 2020 en educación superior en Chile", *Servicio de Información de Educación Superior*. [5]

Trow, M. (2008), "Reflections on the Transition from Elite to Mass to Universal Access: Forms and Phases of Higher Education in Modern Societies since WWII", in *International Handbook of Higher Education*, https://doi.org/10.1007/978-1-4020-4012-2_13. [2]

16 Assessing students' generic learning outcomes in Australia and New Zealand

Mark Keough, Council for Aid to Education (Australia)

This chapter deals with the outlooks for implementing the CLA+ assessment in professional and vocational colleges across Australia and New Zealand.

Introduction

Post-secondary education operates in two primary systems. The higher education sector incorporates universities and private not-for-profit and for-profit providers. This system is standardised and governed by the federal government where qualifications are defined by a national structure, the Australian Qualifications Framework.

Most professional education in the traditional professions is delivered in collaboration between universities and professional colleges with a university and industry accreditation system for professional practice. A national system of accredited qualifications governs technical and vocational education and training.

There are 39 public universities and approximately 130 private higher education providers (for-profit and not-for-profit) across the seven states and territories. According to the Australian Skills Quality Authority (ASQA), close to 4 000 registered training organisations address the technology and vocational education and training (TVET) market for domestic and international students.

Universities are clustered around research interests and profile. For example, a cluster known as the Group of Eight (G8) Universities focuses on the traditional professions (for example law and medicine) and formal research studies while the Australian Technology Network clusters five universities focussed on technology. Some universities offer dual-sector provision of both higher degrees and vocational education and training. Dual-sector provision is particularly prevalent in one state of Australia, Victoria.

Since 1985, the federal government has allowed universities to charge overseas students for enrolments. The post-secondary sector has grown to become the most extensive service-based export industry in Australia, contributing AUD 37.6 billion to the total Australian GDP of AUD 1 397 billion in 2019. The ratio of domestic to international students is close to 70:30.

The Australian system is regulated by the Tertiary Education Quality and Standards Agency (TEQSA) for higher degrees and the Australian Skills Quality Agency (ASQA) for vocational levels qualifications. The overarching framework is a structure of nationally regulated qualifications under the Australian Qualifications Framework (AQF). There are 10 levels of the framework, with a standardised nomenclature for qualifications. The TVET sector is represented by Levels 1 to 6 and uses a national qualifications framework that specifies detailed competency outcomes. The competency 'warehouse' is known as the Australian Quality Training Framework (AQTF).

Table 16.1. Australian Qualification Names

Level 1	Certificate 1
Level 2	Certificate 2
Level 3	Certificate 3
Level 4	Certificate 4
Level 5	Diploma
Level 6	Advanced Diploma/Associate Degree
Level 7	Bachelor's Degree
Level 8	Bachelor's Honours, Graduate Certificate, Graduate Diploma
Level 9	Master's Degree
Level 10	Doctoral Degree

In New Zealand, there are eight public universities[1], 16 public polytechnic institutes and a similar profile of domestic and international students. Connections to the extended Association of Southeast Asian Network (ASEAN; 16 countries) co-operation group includes many Indo-Pacific nations[2]. While there are many detailed differences between the Australian and New Zealand systems, the New Zealand post-secondary system operates in a very similar manner to the Australian system. It is governed by the New Zealand Qualifications Authority (NZQA).

Policy context

Critical Thinking and Problem Solving are among the ecto-curricula[3] skills identified by each sector as contributing to employability, a key focus for the domestic education component of all education providers.

Employability influences the international student sector, where support for career mobility and options is vital in choosing education pathways. One of the key themes in the region defined as the greater ASEAN region, or what is increasingly identified as the Indo-Pacific, is the prevalence of student mobility. Students in this region actively seek education experiences from countries with a Western education tradition, such as Malaysia and Singapore, Australia and New Zealand.

A few authors and research bodies contribute to this field of study in Australia and New Zealand. Deakin University's Centre for Research in Assessment and Digital Learning in Education (CRADLE) is a dedicated research body with a peak interest in the field. Emeritus Professor Beverly Oliver is among the eminent writers on employability and graduate attributes, especially in the higher education sector. Australian vocational education focuses on employability and ecto-curricula learning outcomes on what are known as foundation skills. Sources of research include the National Council for Vocational Education Research and the National Skills Commission. In New Zealand, interest in this field is concentrated at the research institute, AKI Aotearoa[4].

There is currently a significant suite of reform processes underway in Australia for the TVET sector. There is wide-ranging discussion among practitioners, academics and public policy makers about micro-credentials. Like any over-arching or jargon term, though, the question may well be raised about whether the word is itself a panacea for a deeper problem. It may be offering a convenient label for a set of ideas when more profound examination and insight is needed of what immediate and small credentials may provide in terms of skills development and enhancement.

Whether one considers the micro-credential discussion a trend or a fad, small amounts of learning will always need evaluation to ensure that learning utility is achieved. Education does not require a specifically tangible employment outcome context to be relevant. No matter how small, a learning outcome may find its context in ecto-curricula analysis, successful skills for career entry and/or career transition or progression. This kind of context suits such skills as critical thinking, creative thinking, critical analysis, comprehension, synthesis, and communication.

Technical and vocational education and training sector initiatives

In this light we can observe the public discourse in Australia and New Zealand on vocational training, where employability as a trend has been part of the general commentary for many years.

The Employability Skills Framework developed by the Australian Chamber of Commerce and Industry and the Business Council of Australia in 2002 remains in current use. The eight skills identified within that framework are: communication, teamwork, problem solving, initiative and enterprise, planning and organising, self-management, learning, and technology.

Building on this earlier industry research-based initiative, the Core Skills for Work Developmental Framework was created in consultation with employers in 2013. The aim was to assist training providers, employment services and any other organisations providing services to groups seeking to help people become work-ready. These core skills have also found expression as 10 core work-ready behaviours: manage career and work-life; work with roles; rights and protocols; communicate for work; connect and work with others; plan and organise; make decisions; identify and solve problems; create and innovate; recognise and utilise diverse perspectives, and work in a digital world.

In 2016, while seeking to address the employability needs of young people, the Australian Federal Department of Education, Skills and Employment drew on this overall body of work to identify core skills for employability. The Business Council of Australia released the publication *Being Work Ready: A Guide to What Employers Want*, (Business Council of Australia, 2016[1]) which groups skills and attributes desired by employers into three categories: values, behaviours and skills. Being Work Ready is designed to show the minimum standard of skills employers expect from job applicants soon after they have started the job.

Table 16.2. Summary of skills adapted from Business Council of Australia publication

Being Work Ready

Values	Behaviours	Skills
Accountability	Adaptable	Business literacy
Honesty	Business-minded	Data analysis Literacy
Respect	Customer-focused	Problem-solving
Work ethic	Globally aware	Critical analysis
	Authentic	Digital technology
	Collaborative	Numeracy
	Flexible	Technical skills
	Self-aware	
	Resilient	

Note: Copyright Business Council of Australia (2016[1]).

As part of a significant set of reforms for the vocational education sector, the Australian federal government in July 2020 created a National Skills Commission.

In 2020, this new statutory authority established a data science-driven approach to skills to develop job and training matching services. Project JEDI (Job and Education Data Infrastructure) seeks to create a common language for skills; link jobs to appropriate training; forecast future needs based on analytics; and use a single data engine to support many outcomes and services in the Australian context. The Commission classifies core competencies, including employability skills, soft skills, foundational skills and transferable skills.

There has been a strong emphasis on definitions, stakeholder input and the establishment of overarching strategy. Unfortunately, this has led to many different meanings, confusing public dialogue. We can observe substantial inputs but limited outcomes or clarity.

Some describe scholarly work in employability research in Australia as under-developed, lacking, and nascent (McArthur et al., 2017[2]). This perspective likely arises because the published work has often focussed on descriptive analysis rather than an inquiry about economic impacts and social perspectives.

There is no doubt this is an emerging area of interest as the regional population becomes more transient in their job and career experience. New initiatives such as Project JEDI will take some time to find their feet. There is hope that there will be interest among academics to investigate the effectiveness of these initiatives in terms of economic and social outcomes.

In the New Zealand context these skills are defined through the careers promotion context. The site offers guidance through self-assessment resources including the "skill matcher" tool.[5]

Higher education sector policy initiatives

TEQSA has defined graduate attributes in this way: "Generic learning outcomes refer to transferable, non-discipline-specific skills that a graduate may achieve through learning that have application in the study, work and life contexts." Graduate employability and citizenship are critical outcomes attributed to the development of university graduate attributes in the Australian context (Oliver and Jorre de St Jorre, 2018[3]). In 2000, Bowden et al. (2000[4]) acknowledged that graduate attributes were distinguished from the technical or domain knowledge and skills in a curriculum by their capacity to prepare graduates as agents of social good in an unknown future.

Oliver et al. suggest three pivotal questions regarding graduate preparation from Australian universities for 2020 and beyond:

1. Which graduate attributes should be emphasised given the massive changes occurring in society?
2. Beyond embedding, how are attribute outcomes assured?
3. Which attributes equip for employability?

Measurable outcomes are not guaranteed. Where measurement occurs, it is likely based on generic, opinion-based surveys rather than empirical and objective data. The core reasons why universities promote graduate attributes are perhaps open to question. Oliver rightly considers whether it is more about marketing potential outcomes to potential students than a steadfast commitment to extrinsic and measurable results after graduation.

There has been considerable work undertaken in the interest of teaching and learning standards funded by the Australian Teaching and Learning Council. These are standards of delivery but not yet a measure of outcomes. Oliver and Jorre de St Jorre continue to find that graduate attributes are consistent in their emphasis in broad terms. If more explicit definitions can be achieved, a more significant analysis of objective outcomes may be possible. There seems to be an emerging place in the Australian and New Zealand context for the empirical and longitudinal study of effects rather than the current emphasis on inputs and satisfaction surveys.

Follow-up work in 2015 indicated that while most universities published graduate attributes, fewer than half of Australian non-university higher education providers followed suit. Universality and consistent definition remain a challenge in terms of measurement.

Currently, despite emphasising employability skills and graduate qualities in public policy and policy-associated rhetoric, the outcomes for students are not clear. Graduate outcomes supporting employability skills are largely unmeasured.

Indicators from Oliver's work suggest that much has been done to understand the types of assessment that engage students. The consistent application of those principles to graduate attributes may be ahead of us still, rather than in everyday practice (Oliver and Jorre de St Jorre, 2018[3]).

Qualification relevance to employability under question

Micro-credentialling is a trend as industry representatives seek to address immediacy and job relevance in accredited training and education options. The benefit of just-in-time learning related to current or prospective job needs has significant appeal to employers and potential job candidates. It is also relevant for retraining existing employees. Agility in enterprise for both employers and potential employees is key to success as technology enhancements increasingly accelerate the pace of change.

It is difficult to find direct evidence of benefit for micro-credentialling as a trend or clear benefits of the emphasis on employability skills, however. Progress on the development and implementation of 21st-century skills has been reported by the Brookings Institution in October 2020 (Taylor et al., 2020[5]).

Their Center for Curriculum Redesign (CCR) has defined 12 competencies and are monitoring their progressive inclusion in curriculum on a jurisdictional basis. The 12 competencies are defined under the CCR framework.[6] The report concludes that institutions are trending toward including these competencies in curriculum, moving beyond pure academic pursuits and focussing on the needs of the 21st-century learner. The report (p9) indicates that Australia is a leader in the comprehensive consideration of all 12 competencies in the framework.

Quality Indicators of Learning and Teaching (QUILT) is a group of Australian surveys supported by the government which seeks to measure student experience, graduate outcomes, longitudinal graduate outcomes and employer satisfaction. The data sets from these surveys underpin the CompareED website. (www.compared.edu.au). This website provides comparison data against national averages based on the survey outcomes. Oliver identifies that the challenge with the QUILT surveys is that they are national and generic across whole institutions rather than specific to particular areas. The self-reported outcomes of students and employers are reported rather than objective views based on data-driven measures. Nonetheless, they do provide some useful comparisons of satisfaction and a basis of institutional comparison in the higher education sector. The QUILT surveys are an opt-in measure and not compulsory.

What about secondary school curriculum?

Employability skills are also the focus in the late secondary years. Problem solving and critical thinking have been identified as essential in the transition from secondary education into workplaces for further study. The Australian curriculum for secondary schools describes these skills as "General Capabilities". Dr Paul Weldon of the Australian Council of Education Research (ACER), writing in April 2020[7], laments that there is a lack of agreement about the fundamentals of the construct of general capabilities. He further emphasises that job automation is a driver of change away from domain-specific skills and knowledge, and towards such critical capabilities as critical thinking and problem solving (Weldon, 2020[6]). The emphasis from the OECD Learning Framework 2030[8] favours "the mobilisation of knowledge, skills, attitudes and values through a process of reflection, anticipation and action, to develop the inter-related competencies needed to engage with the world".

COVID-19 impacts on policy

International student numbers have been decimated by COVID-19 as the Australian border has remained closed since the first quarter of 2021 despite (mostly) an absence of community spread of COVID-19 cases in Australia and New Zealand. The policy emphasis in a post-COVID-19 world seems to be on investment in skills and training for employment. Student mobility will likely be de-emphasised for some time, perhaps several years. The emphasis on employment perhaps comes as an unfortunate focus when employability is a subtly different motive or outcome. Employability is a state of being whereby societal contribution focuses on productivity in a broader social sense than simply an employment outcome. Successful employment is a direct outcome of employability.

The discourse about skills and know-how has moved to focus on the domestic employment market in response to the pandemic. Staying job-ready for those challenged by employment opportunity in this new era seems a common motif in governmental response. Some authors see some risks and perhaps unsupported assumptions that maintaining skills rests entirely with the learner, student or the unemployed. There appears to be an emphasis on responding solely to the continuing automation of work and developing skills for labour markets as a simple supply and demand arrangement. Increasing amounts of work will become task-oriented rather than career-oriented (O'Keeffe and Papadopoulos, 2021[7]).

Indications are that this contracting economy, often called the gig economy, will grow significantly in the next five years. Casualisation and gig- or bid-based work are factors leading to the importance of transferable skills for participants. Just how important and how quickly the sector is growing is often in the realm of market forecasters such as Deloitte, Gartner, and Forbes rather than academic research so it is often highly speculative. From these sources, indications suggest we might consider growth from 25% of the adult workforce in Western developed economies in 2020 and 2021 to 40% in 2025. Research commissioned by the Institute of Actuaries of Australia show that the gig economy grew ninefold in 2015-2019.[9] For many workers, employment can consist of more than one contract (or gig) at a time, perhaps even using entirely unrelated skills. Developing and curating a lifelong warehouse of skills is critical to employment success.

Gig workers also need these skills to be transferrable between roles and, preferably, measurable. To win contract roles, a gig worker relies on referrals from previous clients and projects. Embedded in those referrals is an acknowledgement of a worker's employability skills or transferrable skills. But, unfortunately, there is little objective measurement of those skills. As it stands, subjective views on a worker's skills is such that good client or customer reviews can bring work while negative ones deny employment.

Taking an ASEAN and Indo-Pacific view, we revisit the question of mobility. Aspirational economies in these regions thrive on encouraging their students to pursue an academic career overseas. While many repatriate to their country of origin, others find new homes as citizens of the countries they chose to study in. The notion that citizenship is as essential as employability is a clear finding by Oliver (Oliver and Jorre de St Jorre, 2018[3]). In this manner the CLA+ assessment provides a value-added benefit to students who may seek to use 21st-century skills in seeking to work, or even settle, outside of their home country.

Next steps and prospects

The employability of vocationally focussed lifelong learners and university graduates is the policy driver for the focus on foundation skills in Australian and New Zealand vocational post-secondary learning. But there appears to be a significant gap in implementation and measurement of both learning and learning outcomes. The policy is deep in desire but not intense in terms of the methodology or measurement of learning and learning outcomes.

The CLA+ and its derivative analysis tools offer a ray of light in empirical analysis and detailed benchmarking for skills measurement in foundation or employability skills. Through potential pilot programmes in a range of industry settings, there is a likely benefit in introducing the CLA+. Under consideration are skills transition projects in military veterans moving from service into civilian employment, healthcare management, and the late secondary years when students transition to either work, vocational education, or higher education. In this setting, the CLA+ offers insights regarding employability for younger people.

The Council for Aid to Education (CAE) has established a Memorandum of Understanding with the Australian National Council for Vocational Education Research. Under this arrangement there are plans in the latter half of 2021 to undertake a pilot project with a regional public vocational education provider (Goulburn and Ovens Valley TAFE) in Victoria. This project will afford students an empirical measure of their foundation skills. It will provide validated insight into their relative strength and weaknesses in those skills. We look forward to understanding the impact of this approach.

The secondary graduation examinations and learning pathways are currently under review with several research projects underway. Unlike national regulation of post-secondary education, secondary education in Australia is overseen by state authorities.

Currently, QUILT surveys serve the university sector. The challenge with these surveys is that they are used to target potential students in the market for a university rather than providing empirical evidence on student learning. Many universities are autonomous in their scope and automated in terms of quality, and so working with university partnerships is highly desirable. The CLA+ would offer an established data set to allow immediate benchmarking.

Given employability is a key theme, connecting graduate attributes and foundation skills with indicators of employment success would seem a valid connection to pursue in the Australia and New Zealand context.

Conclusion

Transferability of ecto-curricula skills is crucial in the post-pandemic economies of the Indo-Pacific region, encompassing a gig economy, plural careers, transferability and regional mobility. As Australia and New Zealand re-establish their role as providers of post-secondary and pre-employment education for the region, measurement and assurance of outcomes for cohorts of students is of increasing importance. As individual students take more responsibility for curating their skills throughout their career, data-based measures of relative learning progression such as the CLA+ are likely to increase in importance.

References

Bowden, J. et al. (2000), *Generic capabilities of ATN university graduates*, Australian Government Department of Education, Training and Youth, Canberra. [4]

Business Council of Australia (2016), *Being Work Ready: a guide to what employers want*, https://www.bca.com.au/being_work_ready_a_guide_to_what_employers_want. [1]

McArthur, E. et al. (2017), "The Employers' View of "Work-Ready" Graduates: A Study of Advertisements for Marketing Jobs in Australia", *Journal of Marketing Education*, Vol. 39/2, pp. 82-93, https://doi.org/10.1177/0273475317712766. [2]

O'Keeffe, P. and A. Papadopoulos (2021), "The Australian Government's business-friendly employment response to COVID-19: A critical discourse analysis", *Economic and Labour Relations Review*, Vol. 32/3, https://doi.org/10.1177/1035304621997891. [7]

Oliver, B. and T. Jorre de St Jorre (2018), "Graduate attributes for 2020 and beyond: recommendations for Australian higher education providers", *Higher Education Research and Development*, Vol. 37/4, pp. 821-836, https://doi.org/10.1080/07294360.2018.1446415. [3]

Taylor, R. et al. (2020), *Competencies for the 21st Century*, Center for Curriculum Redesign, and Brookings Institution, Boston, MA. [5]

Weldon, P. (2020), *Defining Skills for the furure: What's in a name?*, https://www.acer.org/au/discover/article/defining-skills-for-the-future-whats-in-a-name (accessed on 21 October 2021). [6]

Notes

1 https://www.universitiesnz.ac.nz/about-university-sector/key-facts

2 www.lowyinstitute.org/the-interpreter/indo-pacific-new-asia

3 Ecto-curricula skills are skills that are gained through the process of learning, or participation in a programme of learning. They are, however, not a direct part of the curriculum or learning objectives. These skills may be colloquially known by a number of terms in common use such as soft skills, foundation skills, employability skills or 21st-century skills.

4 https://ako.ac.nz/knowledge-centre/graduate-outcomes/

5 https://www.careers.govt.nz/plan-your-career/get-ideas-for-your-career/skills-employers-are-looking-for/

6 https://curriculumredesign.org/framework/

7 www.acer.org/au/discover/article/defining-skills-for-the-future-whats-in-a-name

8 www.oecd.org/education/2030-project/teaching-and-learning/learning/

9 https://actuaries.asn.au/Library/Opinion/2020/GPGIGECONOMYWEBtest.pdf

17 Conclusions and prospects

Dirk Van Damme, OECD (France)

This final chapter summarises the main conclusions of the report and lessons learnt from the country experiences presented in the individual country chapters.

Introduction

This volume brings together assessment data and analyses of academic skills such as critical thinking from institutions in six different higher education systems, using the Council for Aid to Education's (CAE) CLA+ assessment instrument and its international variants. This is the first internationally comparative endeavour to assess generic, 21st-century academic skills across institutions and systems. The OECD's AHELO Feasibility Study (2008-13) proved that such comparative assessment is feasible but did not publish the assessment data from the study and failed to transform into a Main Study. Over the past 10 years since the end of the AHELO Feasibility Study, the assessment of higher education learning outcomes has become an important ambition for policy makers, researchers and higher education leaders. Various projects have seen the light of day, often at national level and using very different approaches and assessment instruments. This is not necessarily a bad thing, but rather a sign of the collective learning going on in higher education systems.

There is great demand for valid and reliable internationally comparative assessments of skills that matter for the 21st-century workplace. The global market place clearly values generic skills such as critical thinking and problem solving. Global employers no longer automatically trust that higher education degrees and qualifications reliably signal these skills and have increasingly turned to their own assessment practices (see Chapter 1 in this volume). The almost complete lack of reliable comparative metrics of what students learn in higher education institutions could, potentially, become a major systemic risk for the sector. International rankings of higher education institutions are used as a proxy for the quality of institutions and the credentials they deliver but contain little measure of the quality of teaching and learning. Yet, in the absence of any better metric, the heavy usage of such rankings indicates the clear need for reliable data on the skills graduates need to compete in the labour market.

No one has yet developed reliable comparative metrics of learning and skills development in higher education. But the present volume shows that we are making progress. In this closing chapter of the book, we will summarise the main results of our collaborative enterprise, reflect on the lessons learnt and indicate some prospects.

Feasibility of critical-thinking skill assessment in higher education

Perhaps the first conclusion is the most important one: An international, comparative assessment of one of the most relevant learning outcomes of higher education is feasible. The chapters in the first part of this volume discuss in detail the construct validity, reliability and cross-cultural validity issues associated with an international assessment of higher education learning outcomes in the domain of generic skills. Their conclusion is clear: the CLA+ International instrument has potential as a valid and reliable assessment instrument. Of course, it is not the only assessment tool available on the market, and it only covers a specific segment of relevant learning outcomes and skills, but it has shown to function well in different contexts, across different systems and for various groups of students.

Moreover, as shown in Chapter 7, the CLA+ assessment has empirically confirmed predictive validity on career and labour market outcomes later in life. Analysis of the US assessment data linked to surveys administered to employers and career advisors demonstrate that the critical thinking skills assessed by the CLA+ instrument are predictive of future educational success, career development and labour market outcomes. Assessments of relevant employability skills such as critical thinking provide more powerful indicators of human capital than measures of foundation skills such as literacy and numeracy.

That an international assessment is feasible was already the conclusion of the AHELO Feasibility Study, completed in 2013. But the CLA+ has further improved by learning from its implementation, analytical research on the data gathered, and the international collaboration of which this report is the result (see Chapter 3 in this volume). Significant progress has been made on, among others, item development and, more recently, computer-based testing and computer-assisted scoring. This has greatly contributed to the useability and cost-efficiency of the assessment instrument, the processing of the data and the reporting of the analysis.

The experiences in the systems reported on in Part III of this volume and the methodological robustness of the instrument provide convincing proof that a wider implementation of the assessment in more institutions and systems is possible. A closer look into the substantive findings from the assessment in six systems in the next section will suggest that it is also worth doing.

Do students learn to think critically at university?

Part II of this report analyses the data of the assessment of over 120 000 students included in the aggregated database across institutions and systems. Of these, close to 100 000 were students in the United States. These students, almost equally split between those entering and exiting a first-degree programme, were assessed with equivalent versions of the CLA+ instrument over the period between 2015 and 2020. With the exception of Italy, all systems carried out multiple administrations of the assessment.

Across the sample, students entering a higher education programme on average performed at 'developing' mastery level of the test. Exiting students on average performed at 'proficient' mastery level. The shift is relatively small (d = .10) but significant. The total distribution remains more or less the same across both subsamples, suggesting that the entire distribution moved to a higher score. The distribution is quite large, with on average 21% of students (average of country averages) performing at the lowest 'emerging' performance level. Thus, across countries, 20% of students performed at the lowest mastery level while 15% of students performed at 'accomplished' and 'advanced' mastery levels.

These general results across the six systems can be interpreted in different ways. Overall, it is encouraging to see that during their time in a higher education programme, students improved their critical thinking skills. However, given the importance that most higher education programmes attach to promoting critical thinking skills, the learning gain is smaller than could be expected. If universities really want to foster 21st-century skills such as critical thinking, they need to upscale their efforts. While universities produce graduates who can be considered, on average, as proficient in critical thinking, the distribution of achievement is quite wide, with one-fifth of students performing at the lowest level. With half of exiting students performing at the two lowest levels, it is difficult to claim that a university qualification reliably signals a level of critical thinking skills expected by the global market place.

The analysis cannot positively confirm that the learning gain is caused by the teaching and learning experience within university programmes. It is possible that, for example, selection effects (selective drop-out), general maturing of the student population or effects of learning outside university contribute to the average learning gain. However, the fact that the distribution in achievement remains more or less the same from entering to exiting students shows that the entire student population moves upwards, suggesting that the learning gain is caused by a common, shared learning experience.

Do background variables influence critical thinking skill development?

International large-scale assessments of learning outcomes such as PISA, PIAAC, Trends in International Mathematics and Science Study (TIMSS) and others show that variations in learning outcomes are quite heavily influenced by students' background such as gender, language, family background, migration status and other. It is interesting to examine whether this also is the case for the assessment of critical thinking learning outcomes at university.

The impact of language (whether students' primary language is different from the instruction/test language or not) shows to be statistically significant but rather small. Both entering and exiting students with a different mother tongue than the language of instruction perform slightly lower than other students except for the US sample of entering students. But, given the importance of linguistic proficiency for completing the test, these results are actually quite positive. Language barriers do not meaningfully hinder critical thinking.

This analytical finding from the entire database conceals contradictory findings in individual countries. With regard to language, it is interesting to note that in the United States sample, entering students with a different native language than the language of instruction performed better than students whose native language was the same as the language of instruction but that this advantage was reversed when they left the institution (see Chapter 6). In the England sample, both entering and exiting students whose native language was English outperformed students with a different native language (see Chapter 13). There are also interesting differences in the impact of language on the two different components of the test, the Performance Test (PT) and the Selected Response Questions (SRQ), which mobilise different language proficiency skills.

Gender does not seem to have a huge impact. There are some minor, statistically significant but, overall, small, differences between male and female students but no clear general pattern. However, as the country chapters in Part III illustrate, at a national level, gender can play a role. This is the case for Finland, where gendered patterns in scores by field of study can be identified (see Chapter 12).

The impact of family background has been examined through the parents' educational attainment variable. In contrast to language and gender, parents' educational attainment did show to have an impact on students' critical thinking performance, both among entering and exiting students and for both the international and the US sample. This points to a persistent effect of students' social-economic-cultural status on their educational achievement, even at this stage of their educational trajectory. Students from more disadvantaged backgrounds are more disadvantaged in critical thinking.

The question of whether parents' education also influences the learning gain between entering and exiting a university programme could not be answered in a conclusive way. The data suggest that students with higher parental educational status achieved a slightly higher learning gain than students with lower parental educational status. However, the relative impact of selection/attrition versus education remains unclear. More sophisticated research designs, preferably longitudinal, would be needed to answer that question.

Some of the country chapters in Part III explore other relevant background variables and their relationship with CLA+ assessment data. For example, in Mexico (Chapter 14) large differences were noted between students in campuses in metropolitan areas and students in campuses in remote, rural areas. In a country like Mexico, geography plays an important role through its association with economic development, social prosperity and levels of poverty and exclusion.

Do students demonstrate different levels of critical thinking by field of study and type of instruction?

Analyses reported in Chapter 8 show that there are significant differences in assessment of critical thinking skills between non-US students in programmes in different fields of study. On average across countries with relevant data, students in business and agriculture were found to have relatively low scores while students in the humanities, sciences and social sciences were found to have relatively high scores. This pattern holds for both entering and exiting students, suggesting a combination or interaction between selection and education effects. However, the highest learning gain achieved between entering and exiting university was found with students in health and welfare.

A more or less similar pattern was found for US students but with a slightly different ranking. Students in science and engineering were found to have the highest scores, both when entering and exiting, followed by social sciences and humanities.

Chapter 8 also reports on an interesting analysis of differences in CLA+ scores for different instructional formats for exiting non-US students. Although differences are relatively small, seminars, lectures and science laboratories are associated with the highest scores (with averages in the 'proficient' mastery level) whereas service learning and field work is associated with low scores. The positive result for lectures and negative result for service learning and field work contradict popular opinions on higher education pedagogy, which favour activating instructional formats. Critical thinking seems to flourish in instruction that requires deep engagement with content, as is the case for lectures, laboratories and seminars.

Differences between countries

Although the present study is not based on representative sampling within countries (except for Finland, which administered a system-wide assessment but with some institutions opting out), it is interesting to see whether there are meaningful differences in CLA+ results between countries. Chapter 9 analyses country-level differences in CLA+ scores for samples in five countries: the United States, the United Kingdom, Finland, Chile and Mexico. In the reporting of the results, countries were anonymised, as agreed with the country project managers in the study. Given limitations in the sampling, the impossibility of considering national data as reliable measures at the country level, and the agreement with participating institutions that they have full ownership of the assessment data, it was not possible nor desirable to rank countries. Still, some very interesting observations can be made. The comparison between countries is useful in exploring the importance of the national level as a relevant variable.

The data reported in Chapter 9 show clear variations in mastery levels between the five countries. Already, when students enter university, they exhibit very different proficiency levels in critical thinking. In countries A and D, half or more of the entering students scored at 'proficient', 'accomplished' and 'advanced' levels whereas in other countries half or more of entering students scored at the two lowest mastery levels. Large variation was also shown for exiting students. In country D, 70% of exiting students scored at the 'proficient' level or higher whereas in country C only 45% of exiting students scored at those levels. The average learning gain achieved while students were in university was unrelated to their mastery level when they started. Students in country C gained very little in proficiency even if they had started at a low level. Students in country D started at a much higher level but advanced a great deal before exiting while students in country E started at a much lower level but gained nearly as much. The results in country C are clearly disappointing. Other systems show greater levels of progress but country D makes clear that even with already high levels of critical thinking among entering students there is much opportunity to make significant progress during university.

The variability of CLA+ scores across country samples suggests that there are indeed significant differences between countries in the capacity of their education systems prior to and within higher education to develop critical thinking skills. As shown in the country-specific chapters in Part III of this volume, education systems differ in the policies, educational objectives and cultures within institutions. Still, in an increasingly global context for higher education institutions and, especially, for the employability and social participation of graduates, higher education systems that are better equipped to foster critical thinking skills will find themselves in a better place in the 21st-century environment. Given the changes in skill demand that are impacting all countries, though this varies depending on where countries sit in the global value chain, all countries should enable higher education institutions to perform better in fostering critical thinking.

That said, the variability in the country-level data is not high. International rankings have created the perception that quality differences between higher education systems are huge but the country-level data in this report contradict this. There are interesting country-level differences in the assessment of generic 21st-century skills but they are small and certainly do not mirror the steep hierarchical perception suggested by international rankings. In any case, with the exception of the United States and Finland, larger and more representative samples are needed for other countries before anything meaningful can be concluded about performance differences between countries.

Experiences in individual countries

The chapters on individual countries or systems participating in this project in Part III clearly indicate the wide variability in decision-making processes, implementation of the assessment, its outcomes and their policy relevance. Nonetheless, despite different trajectories, all these systems want to better understand the role of generic, 21st-century skills development in higher education programmes.

The CLA+ assessment instrument was developed in the United States, where it has been implemented in a wide range of institutions and has become part of the assessment infrastructure for higher education (Chapter 10). It constitutes a response to the demand of the Spellings Commission (2006) for more evidence-based accountability of institutions through the assessment of students' generic skills. Implementation of the assessment over the past 15 years has generated a wealth of data, fuelling interesting analyses and inspiring policy debates within institutions and at state and federal levels.

Italy was the first country to implement the CLA+ outside the United States. It was carried out as part of an initiative by the national evaluation agency, ANVUR, to assess student learning in Italian universities following the country's participation in the OECD AHELO Feasibility Study (Chapter 11). In 2013, the CLA+ assessment was administered to samples of students from 12 Italian universities followed by a second administration in 2015 in another 26 universities. The implementation in Italy was not without difficulties, especially with regard to student selectivity and motivation, and scoring. However, the experiences with the Italian implementation were very instructive for other systems in the following years. After 2016, ANVUR turned away from the assessment of generic, 21st-century skills to more discipline-focused testing.

Finland was the most recent country to implement the CLA+ instrument (Chapter 12). Like Italy, Finland was a participant in the AHELO Feasibility Study and had been looking for opportunities to develop its own implementation. Finland was the first country to implement the CLA+ at a system-wide scale with representative sampling of students in participating institutions. The Finnish experience thus provides the richest experience outside the United States in terms of the administration of the CLA+, analysis of data and relevance for policy development. To date, the Finnish project provides the most extensive data of CLA+ implementation outside the United States.

In England, the government asked the Higher Education Funding Council for England (HEFCE) (2015) to assess learning gain in higher education institutions. It would be an opportunity to start a research initiative in two newer or post-1992 universities to assess the development of generic 21st-century skills using the CLA+ instrument (Chapter 13). The Teaching Excellence Framework (TEF) (2016-17) provided space and funding for work on learning gain. Interestingly, the experiment in England included a longitudinal design, which proved ambitious. The project in England also demonstrated the potential of the assessment as a diagnostic tool for institutional improvement as well as accountability-focused measure.

Like Italy and Finland, Mexico was an enthusiastic supporter of the OECD's AHELO Feasibility Study. There, a large public university pioneered the CLA+ instrument in response to governmental initiatives to improve the quality of university teaching and learning (Chapter 14). Performance-based testing was seen as a powerful tool to assess the generic skills needed for workplace success. In 2017-18 three testing sessions were administered for over 8 500 students. The project not only generated very interesting data and analyses but stimulated the institutional drive towards improving teaching and learning, and tackling huge disparities within student performance.

Outreach activities in Latin America, starting in 2017, provided the necessary groundwork for the implementation of CLA+ in some countries on the continent (Chapter 15). Up to 2020, four private universities in Chile started a project to use the CLA+ with support from the government. The case studies not only provided very interesting data but an important institutional learning opportunity. The implementation of the assessment also stimulated the interest in critical thinking as a learning objective in the curriculum.

Finally, while no actual testing has taken place in Australia and New Zealand (Chapter 16), policy developments have taken place that could eventually lead to the implementation of the CLA+ assessment. It is notable that interest is mainly coming from the vocational post-secondary sector rather than from universities. The chapter describes the growing interest in generic, 21st-century skills such as critical thinking for employability and citizenship, and how this is driving policy debates on the implementation of CLA+ as a measurement tool.

Over the past years, discussions with many more countries than the ones this book reports have taken place. Many systems see the relevance of assessing generic skills like critical thinking. But many face barriers. Resistance from institutions, faculties and staff; implementation; and funding problems are just some of the issues that must be confronted to take the necessary steps forward.

Lessons learnt in participating countries

The experiences in individual countries illustrate that a shared interest in the importance of generic, 21st-century skills for employability and citizenship drives decisions to implement the CLA+ assessment. In all countries, strong political interest, often triggered by external stakeholders such as the business community, has been a necessary condition for moving ahead. When there is clear political consensus in favour of generic skills and a supportive political context for institutions, things start to move.

A second lesson learnt is the power of assessment to drive the reform agenda in higher education. The saying that only what is assessed matters, is true. Without assessment, debates on the importance of generic skills risk becoming partisan and divisive. With a credible evidence base, even if imperfect, the debate is fuelled with data and becomes realistic.

A third lesson is about the importance of an inclusive approach. The institutional context in higher education is extremely important, implying that no government – let alone an international organisation – can impose an assessment on institutions. In all countries, institutional consent has proven to be a critically important condition for success. The failure of the AHELO project to move to a Main Study was probably due to the fact that conventional decision making at governmental level, without duly organised processes of discussion and negotiation with institutions, is doomed to fail in a higher education environment. Several country reports in Part III of this volume also point to the importance of motivating staff to positively support the assessment.

The fourth lesson learnt is about students. In a higher education environment, it is nearly impossible to force students to sit a test if they don't see the added-value for themselves. Several chapters in this volume explore the topic of student motivation and engagement. Suboptimal student motivation not only negatively affects participation rates but the quality of the assessment results too. Students are willing to sit the test and do their best if they view it as a reliable tool for their own interests. From this perspective, it is interesting to see the development of the CLA+ assessment towards rewarding successful students with digital badges and credentials. Prospective employers can access these to get an idea of the person's generic skills. This is a very promising development.

Prospects

It would be premature to call the present volume and the experiences in the participating countries a sufficient basis for moving to a large-scale assessment of generic, 21st-century skills in higher education. However, this volume illustrates the power of assessment to drive the policy debate on the importance of generic skills such as critical thinking. An important opportunity is opening for governments and institutions to develop initiatives to assess critical thinking, using the CLA+ instrument or others. Such initiatives will be powerful collective learning opportunities from which the entire global higher education community can benefit.

Printed by Libri Plureos GmbH in Hamburg,
Germany